Social Discredit
Anti-Semitism, Social Credit, and the Jewish Response

In *Social Discredit* Janine Stingel exposes a crucial, yet previously neglected, part of Social Credit history – the virulent, anti-Jewish campaign it undertook before, during, and after the Second World War. While most Canadians acknowledged the perils of race hatred in the wake of the Holocaust, Social Credit intensified its anti-Semitic campaign.

By examining Social Credit's anti-Semitic propaganda and the reaction of the Canadian Jewish Congress, Stingel details their mutual antagonism and explores why Congress was unable to stop Social Credit's blatant defamation. She argues that Congress's ineffective response was part of a broader problem in which passivity and a belief in "quiet diplomacy" undermined many of its efforts to combat intolerance.

Stingel shows that both Social Credit and Congress changed considerably in the post-war period, as Social Credit abandoned its anti-Semitic trappings and Congress gradually adopted an assertive and pugnacious public relations philosophy that made it a champion of human rights in Canada. *Social Discredit* offers a fresh perspective on both the Social Credit movement and the Canadian Jewish Congress, substantively revising Social Credit historiography and providing a valuable addition to Canadian Jewish studies.

JANINE STINGEL is a research consultant in Ottawa.

McGill-Queen's Studies in Ethnic History
Series One: Donald Harman Akenson, Editor

1 Irish Migrants in the Canadas
A New Approach
Bruce S. Elliott

2 Critical Years in Immigration
Canada and Australia Compared
Freda Hawkins
(Second edition, 1991)

3 Italians in Toronto
Development of a National
Identity, 1875–1935
John E. Zucchi

4 Linguistics and Poetics of Latvian
Folk Songs
Essays in Honour of the Sesquicen-
tennial of the Birth of Kr. Barons
Vaira Vikis-Freibergs

5 Johan Schrøder's Travels in
Canada, 1863
Orm Øverland

6 Class, Ethnicity, and Social
Inequality
Christopher McAll

7 The Victorian Interpretation of
Racial Conflict
The Maori, the British, and the
New Zealand Wars
James Belich

8 White Canada Forever
Popular Attitudes and Public
Policy towards Orientals in
British Columbia
W. Peter Ward
(Second edition, 1990)

9 The People of Glengarry
Highlanders in Transition,
1745–1820
Marianne McLean

10 Vancouver's Chinatown
Racial Discourse in Canada,
1875–1980
Kay J. Anderson

11 Best Left as Indians
Native-White Relations in the
Yukon Territories, 1840–1973
Ken Coates

12 Such Hardworking People
Italian Immigrants in Postwar
Toronto
Franca Iacovetta

13 The Little Slaves of the Harp
Italian Child Street Musicians
in Nineteenth-Century Paris,
London, and New York
John E. Zucchi

14 The Light of Nature and the
Law of God
Antislavery in Ontario,
1833–1877
Allen P. Stouffer

15 Drum Songs
Glimpses of Dene History
Kerry Abel

16 Louis Rosenberg
Canada's Jews
Edited by Morton Weinfeld

17 A New Lease on Life
Landlords, Tenants, and Immi-
grants in Ireland and Canada
Catharine Anne Wilson

18 In Search of Paradise
The Odyssey of an Italian Family
Susan Gabori

19 Ethnicity in the Mainstream
Three Studies of English
Canadian Culture in Ontario
Pauline Greenhill

20 Patriots and Proletarians
The Politicization of Hungarian
Immigrants in Canada, 1923–1939
Carmela Patrias

21 The Four Quarters of the Night
The Life-Journey of an
Emigrant Sikh
*Tara Singh Bains and
Hugh Johnston*

22 Resistance and Pluralism
A Cultural History of Guyana,
1838–1900
Brian L. Moore

23 Search Out the Land
The Jews and the Growth of
Equality in British Colonial
America, 1740–1867
*Sheldon J. Godfrey and
Judith C. Godfrey*

24 The Development of Elites in
Acadian New Brunswick,
1861–1881
Sheila M. Andrew

25 Journey to Vaja
Reconstructing the World of a
Hungarian-Jewish Family
Elaine Kalman Naves

McGill-Queen's Studies in Ethnic History
Series Two: John Zucchi, Editor

Inside Ethnic Families
Three Generations of Portuguese-
Canadians
Edite Noivo

A House of Words
Jewish Writing, Identity, and
Memory
Norman Ravvin

Oatmeal and the Catechism
Scottish Gaelic Settlers in Quebec
Margaret Bennett

With Scarcely a Ripple
Anglo-Canadian Migration into
the United States and Western
Canada, 1880–1920
Randy William Widdis

Creating Societies
Immigrant Lives in Canada
Dirk Hoerder

Social Discredit

Anti-Semitism, Social Credit, and the Jewish Response

JANINE STINGEL

McGill-Queen's University Press
Montreal & Kingston · London · Ithaca

© McGill-Queen's University Press 2000
ISBN 0-7735-2010-4

Legal deposit first quarter 2000
Bibliothèque nationale du Québec

Printed in Canada on acid-free paper

This book has been published with the help of
a grant from the Humanities and Social Sciences
Federation of Canada, using funds provided by
the Social Sciences and Humanities Research Council
of Canada.

McGill-Queen's University Press acknowledges the
financial support of the Government of Canada
through the Book Publishing Industry Development
Program (BPIDP) for its publishing activities. We also
acknowledge the support of the Canada Council
for the Arts for our publishing program.

Canadian Cataloguing in Publication Data

Stingel, Janine, 1966–
 Social discredit : anti-semitism, Social Credit, and the
 Jewish response
 (McGill-Queen's studies in ethnic history)
 Includes bibliographical references and index.
 ISBN 0-7735-2010-4
 1. Antisemitism – Alberta – History – 20th century.
 2. Alberta Social Credit League. 3. Canadian Jewish
 Congress – History. 4. Jews – Alberta – Politics and
 government. 1. Title. II. Series.
 JL339.A57S75 2000   C99-900853-6
            305.8'92'40712309043

Typeset in Sabon 10/12
by Caractéra inc., Quebec City

For Keegstra's "children," whose trust was betrayed

"I never really knew much about Jews until this year. In other grades, all I was told was that the Jews are a RACE that are discriminated against. They had never had a fair chance. But not one of the teachers ever stopped to tell me of their TRUE origin. This year I learned of their origin and their wicked plans, and I am very scared that the world is going to fall to them. I only hope that we Christians will be strong enough to fight off their Satanic hate."

Student essay, Eckville High School, quoted in "Keegstra's Children," by Robert Mason Lee, *Saturday Night*, May 1985

Contents

Tables xi
Preface and Acknowledgments xiii
Abbreviations xvii
Map xviii
Illustrations between pages 78–84

1 Introduction 3

2 Social Credit and the Canadian Jewish Congress 8

3 Early Confrontations 32

4 Denials and Duplicity 56

5 A Worsening Climate 85

6 "Hamlet without the Ghost" 122

7 A Period of Watchful Waiting 152

8 Conclusion 187

APPENDICES

A Social Credit Career Sketches 193

B Canadian Jewish Congress Career Sketches 203

Notes 211
Bibliography 251
Index 271

Tables

1   Alberta provincial election, 22 August 1935 / 15

2   Alberta provincial election, 21 March 1940 / 16

3   Alberta provincial election, 8 August 1944 / 22

4   Alberta provincial election, 17 August 1948 / 127

Tables

Preface and Acknowledgments

During the 1983–84 school year, Robert David, school superintendent for the Lacombe County Board of Education in Alberta, visited the Mirror-Alix-Clive Central High School, otherwise known as MACC High. The school is located in Alix, a small village in central Alberta about thirty miles east of Red Deer. David quietly entered the grade twelve social studies classroom and sat in the back. The teacher continued to give the lesson, seemingly unaware of David's presence. However, the dozen or so students in the class could not stop staring behind them. In a high school of eighty-five students in grades ten through twelve, any new face was justification for immense curiosity. At the time, none of the students knew why they had a visitor.

I was in that classroom the day Robert David came by. Only later did I discover that a teacher named Jim Keegstra from Eckville High School had been teaching students "bad things" about Jews. The school superintendent was visiting other rural high schools in Lacombe County to ensure that similar material was not being taught elsewhere. It was later still before I understood the implications of the Keegstra affair – of a man who taught rural Alberta teenagers that the Holocaust was a hoax and that there was an international Zionist conspiracy to take over the world.

The Keegstra affair was the beginning of my interest in the Social Credit movement. At the time of his dismissal from Eckville High School in 1983, Keegstra was second Alberta vice-president of the national Social Credit party. In 1988, when I began taking courses at Red Deer College towards a Bachelor of Arts degree, three years after

Keegstra had been convicted of wilfully promoting hatred against Jews, I wrote a history paper on Keegstra, Malcolm Ross, and Ernst Zundel. My history instructor, Dr David Elliott, was an expert on the Social Credit movement and co-author of *Bible Bill: A Biography of William Aberhart*. His work, and especially an article he wrote on Keegstra and the Social Credit movement, sparked my interest in the anti-Semitism within Social Credit in the 1930s and 1940s. From there I began reading more about Social Credit's anti-Semitic ideology and learned the craft of research and writing. The rest, as the saying goes, is history.

I wrote this book because I was motivated to analyse my province's history as well as my own past. Racism and religion are powerful determinants of ideas and opinions, and I have tried to understand how they affected Alberta's history and my own. The Social Credit years were much before my time, but my experience as an Alberta high school student in the early 1980s at the height of the Keegstra affair launched me into an exploration of the Social Credit crusade. That discovery has led me here, and to those people who assisted in my endeavours, I extend my deepest thanks.

Although I never had the opportunity to meet him, I would like to thank the late Louis Rosenberg of the Canadian Jewish Congress, whose exhaustive work on Social Credit enabled me to write this book. John Zucchi of McGill University, who supervised my doctoral dissertation, on which this book is based, was well aware of my abilities and limitations and gave me free rein to explore both. Jerome Black, Gershon Hundert, Leonard Moore, Suzanne Morton, and Brian Young at McGill University also provided helpful comments on my work. Other scholars who provided advice, support, and constructive criticism and who deserve special thanks include Irving Abella, Alvin Finkel, Jack Granatstein, Ira Robinson, Harold Troper, and Gerald Tulchinsky.

I would like to thank the History Department staff at McGill University and the library staffs at McGill University, Concordia University, and the Jewish Public Library of Montreal for their courteous assistance in obtaining documents. I would especially like to thank Janice Rosen, director of the Canadian Jewish Congress National Archives in Montreal, for her good will and professionalism. I am grateful to the Archives nationales du Québec in Montreal; the National Archives of Canada, the National Library of Canada, and the Library of Parliament in Ottawa; the Ontario Jewish Archives and B'nai Brith Canada in Toronto; the Provincial Archives of Manitoba and the Jewish Historical Society of Western Canada in Winnipeg; the Saskatchewan Archives Board in Regina; the City of Lethbridge Archives; the Glenbow-Alberta Institute in Calgary; the Alberta Legislature Library and the Provincial

Archives of Alberta in Edmonton; and the Vegreville Public Library for their helpful assistance with archival sources and photographs. Mike Bechthold deserves warm thanks for his cartographical skills. Ben Kayfetz and David Kirshenblatt were kind enough to read earlier drafts of this manuscript and provide me with valuable first-hand responses.

I deeply appreciate the institutions and organizations, including the Alberta Heritage Scholarship Fund, Red Deer College, University of Victoria, McGill University, and the Social Sciences and Humanities Research Council of Canada, that have made an investment in my academic career. I would like to extend very special thanks to Donald Akenson, Susan Kent Davidson, Roger Martin, and Joan McGilvray of McGill-Queen's University Press, and to the two anonymous readers for the Press and the Aid to Scholarly Publications Programme who urged me to strive for excellence. Errors and omissions remain my own responsibility.

Finally, I wish to acknowledge those who travelled with me on my own crusade. Thank you, Danny Frank, for our many conversations about Alberta, both past and present. Thank you, Béatrice Ste-Marie, for your role as mother and friend. Most of all, thank you Serge Durflinger, for being you – historian, companion, commiserator – and, by the way, for the title.

Abbreviations

ADL	Anti-Defamation League of B'nai Brith
AJC	American Jewish Committee
CCCJ	Canadian Conference of Christians and Jews
CCF	Co-operative Commonwealth Federation
CJC	Canadian Jewish Congress
CJCNA	Canadian Jewish Congress National Archives
DSCC	Douglas Social Credit Council
Glenbow	Glenbow-Alberta Institute
JHSWC	Jewish Historical Society of Western Canada
JPRC	Joint Public Relations Committee of the Canadian Jewish Congress
LSE	London School of Economics
NA	National Archives of Canada
OJA	Ontario Jewish Archives
PAA	Provincial Archives of Alberta
PAM	Provincial Archives of Manitoba
PEP	Political and Economic Planning
SC	Social Credit
SCAC	Social Credit Association of Canada
UFA	United Farmers of Alberta
UJPO	United Jewish People's Order
UN	United Nations Organization
UNRRA	United Nations Relief and Rehabilitation Administration

Map of Alberta

Social Discredit

1 Introduction

In 1935 William "Bible Bill" Aberhart and his religious-political crusade swept the Alberta provincial election, winning fifty-six out of sixty-three seats. Nearly two generations later, the Social Credit era came to an end with the ascension of Peter Lougheed and the Conservatives in 1971, but it had by then formed a large part of Alberta's history and greatly influenced the province's political and economic development. The party's thirty-six-year rule both reflected and created a special political culture in Alberta based on individualism, free enterprise, relative abundance, and a commitment to "good government." While Aberhart lifted the hopes of desperate Albertans during the Great Depression, Ernest Manning, Aberhart's successor after 1943, helped to set the province on a firm footing through an artful combination of conservative politics and successful venture capitalism. In retrospect, the Manning years were the halcyon days of Alberta, when the oil flowed and post-war prosperity made Alberta one of the richest provinces in Canada.[1] Albertans took (and take) great pride in their province's transformation from a "have-not" province to a relatively powerful force on the Canadian economic and political scene. In many ways the Social Credit regime, in keeping with the province's tradition of third-party prairie protest, helped to build Alberta into the economically independent and politically populist province that it is today.

There is a part of Social Credit history, however, that is less admirable: the pervasive anti-Semitism manifest in party and government propaganda during the Second World War and the early post-war period. Social Credit's anti-Semitism was based on a conspiracy theory that blamed the "international Jewish financier" for the world's, Canada's, and Alberta's economic and political ills. According to the theory, the international Jewish conspiracy was extremely far-reaching and included organizations from the Bank of England to the American Federal Reserve Board to the Bank of Canada. Moreover, the Jewish Holocaust and Zionist efforts to establish the state of Israel were also ostensibly part of the international Jewish plot for world control. Social Credit was the only democratically elected party in Canada whose political and economic philosophies were based on anti-Semitism and whose propaganda organs competed easily with contemporary right-wing anti-Semitic publications in Europe and the United States.

Yet Social Credit's anti-Semitism was strictly rhetorical and ideological. At no time was the movement anti-Semitic in the Third Reichian sense of officially adopting and transforming that ideology into a policy of discrimination, then executing the policy by a system of aggression. Nor were Premiers Aberhart or Manning overt anti-Semites. There is little evidence that the electors of Alberta, at either the provincial or federal levels, voted for the party solely because of its anti-Semitism. The evidence suggests, however, that Social Credit promoted anti-Semitism in a manner that far surpassed the efforts typical of a fringe movement, and core sections of the Alberta government and federal and provincial Social Credit parties disseminated it. Premiers Aberhart and Manning, as leaders of the provincial party and heads of the government, were responsible for their organization's actions. Both publicly repudiated anti-Semitism but did little to prevent its dissemination. In late 1947 Manning began a purge of the anti-Semites from the movement and conducted an ideological house-cleaning. Yet his actions were based on economic and political pragmatism, not humanitarianism, and were conducted with little thought of their positive impact on the Canadian Jewish community.

During this period the Jewish community was in desperate need of a helping hand. With the emergence of fascist groups in Canada in the early 1930s and the federal government's blatant refusal to allow the admission of Jewish refugees, the Canadian Jewish Congress, the national representative organization for Canadian Jewry, whose operations since 1919 had languished, was rejuvenated in 1934 in an attempt to confront these difficulties. Congress quickly added Social Credit's anti-Semitic propaganda to its list of problems. From the party's ascension in 1935 to Manning's purge of the anti-Semites in 1947, Congress viewed Social Credit's anti-Semitic propaganda with increasing alarm. Given the virulence of the party's rhetoric and the experience of European Jewry during this period, it was not unreasonable for Congress to be extremely uneasy and to decide that such propaganda must be eliminated. Indeed, Congress's actions were part of a broader attempt to address and dispel anti-Jewish prejudice and discrimination throughout the country, for in an era of relative rampant anti-Semitism, Social Credit was merely one of Congress's public relations problems. Yet Congress viewed this problem as the most serious and ubiquitous because, as a political party and provincial government, Social Credit was an entrenched and legitimate part of the Canadian political landscape. That it was promoting anti-Semitism with impunity lent an urgency to Congress's endeavours.

Notwithstanding several years of effort, Congress was unsuccessful in stopping Social Credit's anti-Semitism. Throughout the war it attempted various counteractive measures such as educational, Jewish-centred anti-defamation work, but these proved utterly ineffective. By the end of the war Congress's leadership and rank and file considered Social Credit to be their most serious public relations problem. The organization tried to adopt a more pro-active and forthright public relations approach, not only because of the near-complete destruction of European Jewry but also because Social Credit had intensified its anti-Semitic campaign. This too had little impact. Social Credit's anti-Semitism was not dissipating; in fact, while the rest of Canadian society gradually acknowledged the perils of race hatred in the wake of the Holocaust, Social Credit seemed to be marching to the tune of a previous drummer. As Congress became increasingly frustrated, it also became more determined, and its lack of success compelled it to consider a more aggressive public relations philosophy. Yet Social Credit was also beginning a period of change over which Congress ultimately had little control.

Beginning in early 1947 Social Credit experienced a backlash from its own anti-Semitism, which eventually resulted in a split in party ranks. Later that year Manning began purging the anti-Semites within his movement, but Congress was sceptical that his actions were much more than cosmetic and driven by political expediency. Congress realized that despite its efforts it had exerted little influence over Social Credit, and now Congress leaders could only hope that Manning's actions would accomplish what they had not. Indeed, for a time it seemed that Manning's purge was destroying the movement, as splinter groups emerged and threatened to discredit the Alberta government. Yet in the end his repudiation of anti-Semitism prevailed, and Social Credit's anti-Semitic philosophy was seemingly sanitized.

It was only after Manning's purge that Congress began executing a more aggressive public relations approach, which, significantly, had been initiated by Alberta Congress officers and agents. They realized the extent to which Congress's philosophy of "quiet diplomacy" had impeded the organization's ability to confront Social Credit, and continued to impede its chances to capitalize on recent gains. Even before Manning's purge they believed Congress needed a national public relations policy that would promote and protect Jewish rights, irrespective of Social Credit's stance on anti-Semitism. No longer should Social Credit be appealed to to end its Jew hatred; Congress must ensure that the government and party simply be stopped. Yet before the Alberta branch could assemble the necessary political weaponry, the Social Credit threat had dissolved from within. This was not a sweet victory; it appeared to be more a failure in Congress's public relations work. The organization realized too late that it was much easier to adopt a coherent public relations philosophy than it was to execute a workable policy.

Yet Congress's failure is what makes its response worthy of investigation. Although it was not successful in halting Social Credit's anti-Semitism itself, Congress experienced a certain success in defeat. Its travails with Social Credit, together with the wartime context in which the organization fought against entrenched, systemic governmental anti-Semitism,[2] compelled it to adopt a strong, effective public relations approach against all forms of prejudice. Indeed, from Congress's reorganization in 1934 until the early post-war period, its public relations philosophy evolved and matured in three discernible but not mutually exclusive stages. Its initial public relations philosophy focused on educational, good-will, anti-defamation work with a concomitant assumption that anti-Semitism could be combated by altering the attitudes of non-Jews. The next phase of its philosophy focused on broadly based social appeals emphasizing the universality of race hatred and the perils posed to society by all prejudice, not just anti-Semitism. The final phase emphasized a rights-oriented, legislative-directed approach to Jewish protection, abandoning the assumption that non-Jewish attitudes towards Jews could be altered and instead ensuring that prejudice was not translated into discrimination. Over the years Congress attempted to implement all three philosophies in its battle against Social Credit, with little success. However, even though Congress could not take credit for Social Credit's purge of anti-Semitism, it eventually won its own war against intolerance. By the post-war period Congress had adopted an aggressive and pugnacious public relations philosophy that made it the champion not only of Jewish rights but of all minority rights in Canada.

Examining Congress's response to Social Credit's anti-Semitism reveals new aspects of both organizations. The perspective of organized Canadian Jewry is a key aspect of Social Credit history that has not been examined before. Although several scholars have discussed Social Credit's anti-Semitic philosophy,[3] none has examined the effects of its philosophy and propaganda on that group most directly affected and potentially threatened. Scholars of Canadian Jewry have not addressed this facet of Canadian Jewish history either. While there are some excellent monographs on the history of Canada's Jews,[4] and Congress itself has published several works,[5] there are few studies that discuss the impact of Canadian politics on organized Jewry and none that examines the impact of Social Credit on Congress.

The sources upon which this book relies also separate it from other works on Social Credit and Canadian Jewry. They come predominantly from the Canadian Jewish Congress National Archives in Montreal, which contain previously unexamined material on both organizations during the tumultuous war years. These sources exist thanks to the meticulous work of Louis Rosenberg, Congress's national research director from 1945 until 1968. In 1966 Rosenberg presented his collection of over three hundred books, numerous manuscripts, and files to Congress's national library and archives. One of the most comprehensive sections dealt with the anti-Semitic propaganda of the Social Credit party in Alberta and Canada.

Thus, this book fills a lacuna in Social Credit and Canadian Jewish historiography. It examines Social Credit through the perspective of Congress, thereby revealing the nature of both the stimulus and the response. While the history of Social Credit is not solely about anti-Semitism, the party's record on that score is a crucial part of its story that has heretofore been inadequately addressed. At the same time, examining Congress's response contributes to Canadian Jewish historiography. By focusing on organized Jewry as the *subjective* interpreter of Social Credit rather than as the *object* of Social Credit's prejudice, its objectified status is eliminated and it becomes the "subject of its own discourse."[6] Such an analysis deliberately rejects the dehumanization of Jews caused by Social Credit's conspiratorial projections and assesses Congress as a minority ethnic organization attempting to confront those projections. This is a necessary departure from most studies of Canadian racism, discrimination, and ethnic hierarchy,[7] which rarely discuss intolerance from the perspective of the objectified party – that is, the group under attack.[8] In sum, giving a voice to Congress at a time when it lacked one clarifies its position as a minority organization operating and evolving within a dominant majority culture. Congress's response to Social Credit becomes more than a case-study of anti-Semitism; it speaks directly to the issues of Canada's political culture of intolerance and the development of ethnic organization and strength within that culture.

2 Social Credit and the Canadian Jewish Congress

Although Social Credit's rise to power is well known among students of the movement, its anti-Semitic origins are less well understood. Some scholars view Social Credit's history as a success story – how the teacher-preacher-premier and his disciple-protégé led Alberta into the most prosperous years it had ever experienced. Others see it as a story of third-party protest, Depression-era conflict, and radical economic theories. Yet very few have assessed it as a story of intolerance, provincialism, and duplicity – of a government and party that promoted anti-Semitism with impunity. It is this facet of Social Credit history that has been neglected, and while it is important to remember that Aberhart and Manning ultimately served their electorate well, it is Social Credit's "scalier side"[1] that is under scrutiny.

Social Credit's anti-Semitism arose out of the same economic and political constraints that enabled the party to come to power. The Great Depression wrought great economic hardship throughout the world, but few places suffered so sharp a decline in income or required so much government assistance to survive as the Canadian prairie provinces. From 1928 to 1932 Canada's agricultural economy declined 68 per cent, while the Prairies' declined 92 per cent. In Alberta the average per capita income in 1928–29 was $548; in 1933 it decreased by 61 per cent to $212. The Canadian average per capita decrease during the same period was 48 per cent.[2] But economic indices do not tell the story of the chaos and bewilderment that the Depression wreaked. Alberta's farmers could not understand an economic system in which they received nothing for their crops while shops in towns and cities were filled with goods that no one could purchase. That granaries were full and farmers were getting nothing for their labour eluded logic; but during the Depression, it has been said, nothing seemed logical. Semi-starvation was not uncommon, and in some areas of Alberta the need for food forced people to pickle gophers.[3] In 1935 Aberhart spoke of Albertans who had nothing to eat for days, and of people in the dry belt who were living on gopher stew: "There are children in Alberta who have not tasted butter or milk in the last three years although they live on farms. Their fathers have to sell all the milk the cows produce to live ... Children are crying for food out in Alberta tonight. The boys and girls are hungry." Sociologist Jean Burnet, who studied the effects of the Depression on the farming community of Hanna, Alberta, commented that Aberhart's statements produced great indignation, "but at most he exaggerated conditions which needed no exaggeration to be shocking. A diet of potatoes and milk has become legendary in the Hanna area ... Probably the effects of malnutrition in the thirties will be evident for many years."[4]

Low prices for farm produce led to overwhelming farm debts. Even in good economic times a farmer's need for credit was great. The equipment for mechanized farming by the 1930s was expensive; the year's income fluctuated wildly and was received only after the harvest went to market; and agriculture was a specialized cash-crop business rendering subsistence agriculture nearly impossible. During periods of economic prosperity the farmer was urged to expand his use of bank credit, but during the Depression he suddenly found himself caught in an economic vise. The debt burden became crushing; to pay taxes or to pay the interest on old debts was nearly impossible. Interest became "the crop that never fails," while foreclosure became a terrifying possibility.[5]

Thus farmers' need for credit began a cycle of dependence that fostered great resentment, and the money and banking system (and specifically financiers and bankers) became the focus of criticism. The farmers were correct in pointing to the economic system to explain the Depression; indeed, there was an insufficient distribution of purchasing power among the populace, compounded by an economy that could not provide markets for the immense agricultural production. However, these were intangible factors related to the production and distribution of wealth in a capitalist economy.[6] For most Albertans suffering from economic privation, the tangible representation of these factors was money, and its alarming scarcity could easily be blamed on a conspiratorial dictatorship of bankers and financiers who had consigned Albertans to "poverty in the midst of plenty."

Albertans' economic straits combined with long-standing political grievances against "the east," and specifically against the federal government in Ottawa. In geographic terms Albertans were far removed from the centres of power and decision-making in Canada, but they were also distanced politically and economically. In addition to their weak political representation in the House of Commons, Albertans were subjected to Crown control of their natural resources until 1930. Thus there was a widely held perception that their province's political and economic subordination were inseparable. To many Albertans, Canada was the Ottawa-Montreal-Toronto triangle that lived off the hinterland, with the federal government remarkably insensitive to western interests and influence. They saw their economic exploitation as part of eastern financial domination and old-party hegemony. Correspondingly, they connected financiers to the distant power centres and plutocrats who caused western economic and political powerlessness. It was financiers who puppeteered the federal government and shamelessly manipulated western agrarians for their own business-oriented urban interests.[7]

For these Albertans, feelings of economic and political powerlessness also reinforced a long-standing tradition of political alienation and negative bias against the old-party system. Although members of an "old" party themselves, the Liberals had been in power from the province's inception in 1905 until 1921. Their success rested on maintaining the territorial tradition of keeping provincial and federal politics separate, and in the beginning at least they adapted to the agrarian interests of Alberta. However, the province's distrust of old-line politicians was established early because of the Liberals' scandalous contractual dealings in the construction of the Alberta and Great Waterways Railway, whose exposure nearly defeated the government.[8] Alberta farmers already appreciated their political isolation and economic weakness and concluded that neither the Liberals nor the Conservatives would protect or promote their interests. They joined organizations like the Non-Partisan League, the Canadian Council of Agriculture, and the United Farmers of Alberta to circumvent the power of the old parties, which they believed were controlled by the same eastern financial interests that ensured economic discrimination in western grain marketing and CPR freight rates. In their view it mattered little which of the old parties was in power; both pandered to the interests that kept farmers in a condition of "feudal dependence."[9]

It was not surprising then that in 1921, as part of that broader prairie farmer protest that elected the National Progressive party to the House of Commons, Albertans elected a government of the United Farmers of Alberta (UFA).[10] In both ideology and organization the UFA shared many characteristics with the nineteenth-century American Populists, whose ideas greatly influenced Alberta's agrarian leaders. The Populists embraced a conspiratorial view of history, emphasized egalitarianism, and opposed the "money powers." As Richard Hofstadter has noted, the five basic characteristics of the Populists were the idea of a golden age, the concept of natural harmonies (in which harmony would reign among the producers once the exploiters were removed), a dualistic vision of social struggle, a conspiracy theory of history, and the doctrine of the primacy of money.[11] Henry Wise Wood (an American Populist who had immigrated to Alberta) along with other UFA leaders used traditional Populist slogans about the "eastern capitalists," "vested interests," and "financiers" to focus Alberta farmers' discontent on Ottawa. Through the UFA they instilled in Albertans a near-instinctual repugnance to the party system and party machinery.[12] It should be noted, however, that the UFA did not import Populism's darker side. It would be Social Crediters, not the United Farmers, who would adopt the Populists' conspiratorial view of history and preponderant focus on monetary powers to make "international Jewish finance" an object of vilification.[13]

Eventually, the UFA undermined itself by abandoning its third-party characteristics while simultaneously creating a political environment conducive to them. As the UFA transformed itself from a farmers' party to an orthodox government attempting to balance various economic interests and forging links with labour via the Co-operative Commonwealth Federation (CCF),[14] Alberta farmers looked increasingly to the theories of Social Credit, which used a similar rhetoric of political alienation and economic powerlessness but proposed a new program for economic and political reform. Social Credit also offered the farmers an acceptable, identifiable enemy against whom to wage war.

Social Credit was a British import, created by Major C.H. Douglas, a Scottish electrical engineer. He established it as a movement in Liverpool in the early 1920s, and in 1933 created the Social Credit Secretariat,[15] a voluntary, non-party, non-class organization whose main function was the "organisation and supervision of the study of Social Credit by those who desire to undertake it seriously." In 1938 Douglas founded a weekly journal called the *Social Crediter*, whose mandate was to express and support the policy of the Secretariat. As other Social Credit organizations were created in Commonwealth countries, they began to publish their own publications, such as the *Australian Social Crediter*, the *New Times* (Melbourne), the *New Era* (Sydney), the *New Zealand Social Crediter*, and in Canada, *Today and Tomorrow* (renamed the *Canadian Social Crediter*) and *Vers Demain* (Quebec). These organizations had close connections with the Secretariat, and their publications quoted extensively from the *Social Crediter*.[16]

While the program for economic and political reform that Douglas advocated through the Social Credit movement has received extensive scholarly examination, one of the earliest analyses of that program remains the most succinct. John Irving summarized the three basic doctrines of Social Credit philosophy thus: "a monetary theory which both 'explains' the inner workings of the capitalistic financial system and offers a remedy for its unsatisfactory functioning in periods of depression and inflation, a political theory which redefines the role of the individual in the democratic state, and an interpretation of history in terms of a long-existing Judaic plot or conspiracy to secure control of and dominate the world."[17] Douglas believed that the economic system could be reformed by implementation of the famous "A + B" theorem, and the political system reformed so that control of the general will was held by the people but executed by selected experts. Both reforms were necessary to oppose the machinations of the international financial Jewish conspiracy.

The essence of the A + B theorem was that, "since 'all payments made to individuals (wages, salaries, and dividends)' (A) and 'all payments made to other organizations (raw materials, bank charges, and other external costs)' (B) 'go into prices, the rate of flow of prices cannot be less than A plus B.' But 'the rate of flow of purchasing-power to individuals is represented by A' only, and obviously, 'A will not purchase A plus B.' Hence the necessity to create money to distribute as social credit dividends to consumers to cover B, or as subsidies to producers to permit them to fix prices at A." Maurice Pinard notes that the theorem "rested on a basic fallacy stemming from the ambiguous statement that total money incomes were not sufficient to buy all that was produced."[18] Indeed, several scholars have shown that the A + B theorem was unsound and based on a blind blaming of the banking system. As one critic stated in 1937, "those who have sincerely studied the writings of Major Douglas will agree that it is an exasperating task. His mind evidently functions according to the advice of a famous cynic: 'If you would make your doctrine immortal, make it incomprehensible, for then no one can prove that it is wrong.'"[19] Yet others considered the A + B theorem avant-garde, and even economist John Maynard Keynes agreed that Douglas's criticisms of the banking and credit system had merit.[20]

Douglas's program for political reform advocated an attenuated form of democracy since, in his view, the present political system was the apparatus of a coercive power placed at the disposal of the real power-holders. No matter how democratic its constitution, the government was merely a tool of the international financiers who had as their willing or unconscious helpers politicians of all parties.[21] Thus, Douglas advocated a "union of electors" that would elect government representatives to carry out its wishes and not be bound by party discipline or other trappings of the party system. He also advocated abolition of the secret ballot, arguing that it led to electoral irresponsibility and was a "Jewish" technique first used by the murderers of Christ to ensure that the robber Barabbas was freed and Christ was crucified.[22] As will be detailed ahead, Douglas's economic and political doctrines were wholly dependent on an anti-Semitic conspiracy theory.

As an economic doctrine, Social Credit had been advanced in Alberta as early as the 1920s, most notably by UFA members William Irvine and Henry Spencer.[23] But it took Aberhart's ingenious combination of media manipulation, religious symbolism, and organizational acumen to translate Douglas's theories into a viable economic and political reform program. Significantly, he did this with little understanding of them.[24] There is the well-worn story of Aberhart's asking John Hargrave, a Social Credit expert from England: "If I issue a dividend, how do I get it back?" During the 1935 election campaign Aberhart often used the example of electricity to explain Social Credit theories: "You don't have to know all about Social Credit before you vote for it. You don't have to understand electricity to make use of it, for you know that experts have put the system in and all you have to do about Social Credit is to cast your ballot for it, and we'll get experts to put the system in."[25]

But Albertans had faith in Aberhart, with good reason. Already well known in Alberta in the 1920s as a radio evangelist and founder of the Calgary Prophetic Bible Institute, by 1935 Aberhart and his religious broadcasts had become "a provincial institution, as popular as radio itself and an intrinsic part of it." It has been reported that, "at its peak in 1935, Aberhart's religious radio audience was computed at 300,000, the Bible Institute listed 1,275 supporters, [Aberhart's] Calgary church had over 500 adult members, [and] the radio Sunday school with its printed lesson material reached 8,000 families."[26] When he incorporated Social Credit theories into his radio sermons and led a grass-roots campaign to organize hundreds of Social Credit study groups, he used his position as the province's leading radio evangelist not only to educate Albertans about Social Credit but to create a religious-political crusade for it.

Between 1933 and 1935 Aberhart's techniques of resource mobilization created a "movement culture"[27] that completely usurped UFA power and influence. He deliberately modelled Social Credit study groups on existing UFA locals and held lectures by invitation at UFA locals across southern Alberta. In 1933 UFA Premier John Brownlee agreed to an inquiry on Social Credit because of its widespread appeal as an economic solution. He invited Douglas and Aberhart to speak in the legislature, more in the hope that they would be discredited and pressure would be taken off the government.[28] But the result was increased support for Social Credit, and Aberhart used his exceptional organizational talents to form more study groups, "monster" rallies, and Sunday picnics that not only overshadowed any earlier UFA attempts but effectively infiltrated its organizational apparatus.[29]

Thus, by building on a political infrastructure already in place, the Social Credit movement fit in easily with the UFA style of popular-democratic government.[30] When the Brownlee government proved to be paralysed by the Depression, politically orthodox yet socialist-leaning, and also prone to scandal,[31] Aberhart's explanation of Social Credit, which offered similar populist ideas about the "vested inter-ests," held resonance for an electorate facing economic devastation, political powerlessness, and imminent starvation. For many Albertans the Social Credit crusade offered a way out of their desperate circum-stances. Farmers saw a new movement that would ameliorate their economic problems through radical monetary reform, which the UFA had refused to implement. Others saw Social Credit as an alternative to the socialist CCF. Some saw it as a return to popular democracy, led not by an old-line politician but by a preacher. Thus, through the medium of a religious-economic crusade, Social Credit became a polit-ical party. Given Albertans' antipathy to traditional parties, this was crucial. By portraying itself as a non-political movement, Social Credit not only evaded political scrutiny until it had permeated the existing political framework, but it also offered Albertans a new message of religious hope and the promise of economic and political redemption.[32]

Aberhart's organizational efforts likely would have elected Social Credit to power. However, his promise of twenty-five dollars a month to every adult Albertan ensured it. He promised them increased pur-chasing power through the distribution of monthly dividends, or "social credit," which was extremely enticing, given their dire circum-stances. As John Barr notes, "at a time when eggs sold for a nickel a dozen and good roasts for seventy-five cents, good dwellings rented for nine dollars a month, and the standard, made-to-measure suit in the catalogue of Tip-Top Tailors sold for $24.50 (vest included), the prospect of a second income of at least twenty-five dollars a month was irresistible."[33] Indeed, it has been speculated that much of Social Credit's 1935 electoral success was due to Albertans' hope of receiving their monthly twenty-five dollars. An oft-told but perhaps apocryphal story concerns areas with substantial immigrant populations, where the most frequent question on election day supposedly was "Vich vun twenty-five-dollar man?"[34] The day after the election, people lined up outside Social Credit headquarters in Calgary and phoned the legisla-tive buildings in Edmonton to collect their dividends.[35]

Table 1
Alberta provincial election, 22 August 1935

Political party	Votes received	% of vote	Candidates nominated	Candidates elected
Conservative	19,358	6,41	39	2
Communist	5,771	1.91	9	0
Economic Recon.	192	0.06	1	0
Independent	2,740	0.90	7	0
Ind. Conservative	258	0.08	1	0
Ind. Labour	224	0.07	1	0
Ind. Liberal	955	0.31	1	0
Labour	5,086	1.68	11	0
Liberal	69,845	23.14	61	5
Social Credit	163,700	54.25	63	56
UFA	33,063	11.00	45	0
United Front	560	0.19	1	0
TOTALS	301,752	100.00	240	63

Source: Statistics are from Alberta, A Report on Alberta Elections.

But Aberhart had made a promise he did not know how to keep. When Social Credit landed fifty-six farmers, workers, teachers, and small businessmen[36] in the Alberta legislature, facing only five Liberals and two Conservatives (see Table 1), some very inexperienced, surprised, and rather frightened Social Credit MLAs argued that what was important was not a detailed and intricate explanation of Douglas's theories and how they could be implemented but a strong faith that such theories would produce the necessary results. As is well known, the twenty-five-dollar dividend never materialized. However, during his tenure as premier from 1935 to 1943 Aberhart attempted nearly everything else. He refused to pay interest on maturing government bonds, defaulted on the province's bond payments, issued government scrip called "prosperity certificates," and attempted to cancel farm debts, prevent farm foreclosures, and muzzle the Alberta press.[37] Nearly all his legislation was declared *ultra vires* and disallowed by the federal government.

Yet Aberhart maintained power, although with a reduced majority in his second term (see Table 2). Until his death in 1943 he tried to serve his province well and promoted provincial rights at a time when the federal government (notwithstanding its 1937 conference on Dominion-provincial relations) had little interest in them. He attempted to grant Albertans much-needed debt-reduction and debt-adjustment legislation and ensured that the province's health and education systems

Table 2
Alberta provincial election, 21 March 1940

Political party	Votes received	% of vote	Candidates nominated	Candidates elected
CCF	34,316	11.11	36	0
Communist	1,067	0.35	1	0
Independent	131,172	42.47	59	19
Ind. Farmer	314	0.10	2	0
Ind. Labour	251	0.08	1	0
Ind. Liberal	1,136	0.37	1	0
Ind. Progressive	1,726	0.56	4	0
Ind. Social Credit	362	0.12	1	0
Labour	3,258	1.05	2	1
Liberal	2,755	0.89	2	1
Social Credit	132,507	42.90	56	36
TOTALS	308,864*	100.00	165	57

* First vote count used.
Source: Statistics are from Alberta, *A Report on Alberta Elections*.

were expanded and revamped.[38] Aberhart may have been authoritarian; he may have sullied political discourse by his lax appreciation of the separation of religion and politics; and he may have made as many enemies as friends; but his concern for his province's welfare was beyond reproach.

None the less, there was that darker side to Social Credit's program, springing from Douglas's paranoid conviction that a group of international Jewish financiers manipulated the world's economic and political systems in its bid for world domination. Douglas's conspiratorial mentality suggests that he suffered from paranoia; indeed, near the end of his life he was hospitalized and diagnosed as certifiably insane. Long before, however, critics accused him of harbouring a "highly developed persecution complex" that caused him to see "a 'financier' with a false beard watching him behind every bush and conspiracies hatched by statesmen and bank governors (who probably do not even know his name) to encompass his destruction."[39] Bob Hesketh argues that Douglas's economic and political theories can be understood only within the context of his conspiratorial beliefs, which he absorbed from reading the *Protocols of the Learned Elders of Zion*.[40]

The *Protocols* purported to be a report of twenty-four (in some versions, twenty-seven) meetings held in Basle, Switzerland, in 1897 by the First Zionist Congress under the presidency of Theodore Herzl, the "father of modern Zionism." Ostensibly, the purpose of these meetings was to draft plans to subvert Christianity and gain world control. The *Protocols* were first published in Russia in 1905 under the title *Secrets of the Wise Men of Zion* by Sergei Nilus, a tsarist civil servant. In 1920 the *Protocols* were translated into English and published by Eyre and Spottiswoode of London under the title *The Jewish Peril*. They were translated into several European languages and became a staple of anti-Semitic propagandists. In 1920 Henry Ford's *Dearborn Independent* reprinted the *Protocols* in a series of articles that were then published as *The International Jew*, five hundred thousand copies of which were circulated in the United States. The book was eventually translated into sixteen languages. As Norman Cohn writes: "*The International Jew* probably did more than any other work to make the *Protocols* world-famous." Significantly, the notorious American anti-Semite Gerald L.K. Smith (of whom more will be said later) prepared and abridged the articles for book publication.[41]

The spurious nature of the *Protocols* was first revealed in 1921 by *The Times* of London, which demonstrated their obvious resemblance to a book published in Brussels in 1864 entitled *Dialogue aux Enfers entre Machiavel et Montesquieu, ou la Politique de Machiavel au XIX Siècle, par un Contemporain*. The author, Maurice Joly, a Parisian lawyer and publicist, intended to satirize Napoleon III but soon found himself arrested by Napoleon's police and sentenced to eighteen months' imprisonment. Later investigations revealed that the *Protocols* were a forgery prepared by the Russian Black Hundred, the secret police of tsarist Russia under General Rachowsky, to support the Tsar's pogroms against Jews. The Russian forgers had lifted no fewer than 1,040 lines directly from Joly's book. In 1934 the Union of Jewish Communities in Switzerland sued the leaders of the Swiss National Socialist party for publishing the *Protocols*. On 14 May 1935 a Swiss court determined at the famous "Berne trial" that the *Protocols* were a forgery, terming them "ridiculous nonsense." However, in 1937 a Berne appeal court overturned the guilt of the accused on the grounds that "as the *Protocols* were not salacious, the law concerning indecent literature could not be applied to them." Accordingly, the sentence was quashed. Notwithstanding its verdict, the appeal court maintained that the question of the authenticity of the *Protocols* was entirely irrelevant to its decision, and ruled that "this scurrilous work contains unheard-of and unjustified attacks against the Jews and must without reservation be judged to be immoral literature."[42]

The ideas expressed in the *Protocols* were offensively anti-Semitic, and significantly, Douglas relied heavily on them in his writings. His

most popular work was *Social Credit*, the basic and official handbook
of the movement. In it Douglas accused Judaism of being the foundation upon which "monopoly capitalism" was based, and argued that
pre-war Germany and post-war Russia were under the direct influence
of Jews who were the protagonists of "collectivism," which included
socialism, communism, and big business. In his opinion the solution
to Jewish collectivism was the breaking up of Jewish group activity.
He expressed belief in the *Protocols* and considered their questionable
authenticity to be of little importance.[43]

The Big Idea was a collection of Douglas's articles in the *Social
Crediter* from January to May 1942. He argued that the Second World
War had been caused by Jews and their non-Jewish friends; that Jews,
Freemasons, the Old Testament, and the anti-Christ were working in
tandem against the forces of the New Testament and Christianity; that
German Jewish bankers, the Federal Reserve Bank of the United States,
the London School of Economics, the Bank of England, B'nai Brith,
and Freemasons were part of the "conspiracy of international Jewish
bankers"; and that Hitler was a grandson of an illegitimate daughter
of Baron Rothschild. Douglas concluded that "the Jew" was "the most
undesirable Oriental the world has produced."[44]

The Land for the (Chosen) People Racket appeared serially in the
Social Crediter between December 1942 and March 1943. In this series
Douglas did not discuss Social Credit theories but focused on the
nationalization of farmland in England, which he argued was a Jewish
plot as proven in the *Protocols*. He blamed land nationalization on
several eminent British and American Jews and argued that the British
government's attempts to combat foot-and-mouth disease by slaugh-
tering all cattle suspected of being infected was a Jewish-socialist plot
against English cattle owners.[45]

Programme for the Third World War was a compilation of articles
appearing in the *Social Crediter* between April and August 1943.
Douglas argued that a third world war was imminent and, like the
second, would be deliberately planned by a secret group of international Jewish conspirators hoping to dominate the world through the
banking system, the Communist party, and socialist parties of various
countries. Among several allegations, he declared that German Jewish
bankers conducted the political and economic policies of Germany,
Great Britain, and the United States; Jewish bankers had been instru-
mental in the rise of Japanese power; Freemasonry was part of the
international Jewish conspiracy for world control; Hitler was a Jew
and a member of the Rothschild family and his anti-Semitism was not
genuine; and Jews were fabricating their persecution so they could
infiltrate Great Britain as German spies. In one instance, he remarked:

If the Germans are to be credited with elementary intelligence, they must see that nothing could ensure the safety of the Jews so effectively in a European War as a ferocious display of anti-Semitism ... It immediately establishes the "persecuted" as non-combatants; it provides a mass of "refugees," many of whom are perfect spies and propagandists ... I am completely agnostic as to the extent of genuine barbarity by Germans to Jews. Some of the atrocity stories, such as the use of Jewish babies as footballs, are merely idiotic. But even if I were convinced that it is considerable in extent, my comment would be that it is not a tithe of the suffering endured by the fighting troops, and is an example of using an army, not without loss, but with a minimum of loss, and the minimum of risk of final defeat. I am convinced that the Jewish High Command desires the ultimate victory of Germany, and will fight tooth-and-nail, *not to end the war*, but to see that Germany is not defeated in the peace.[46]

The Brief for the Prosecution was an amalgam of articles printed in the *Social Crediter* between May and September 1944. It reflected Douglas's anxieties about the post-war world in which the United Nations Organization (UN) would hold seemingly extraordinary powers. In this widely advertised book he claimed he had uncovered evidence of an international Jewish financial conspiracy that planned to impose an "alien culture" on the world by first destroying the British Empire and then creating a totalitarian government in every state. The conspirators planned to impose an "international financial authority" and "international police force" on Britain in their bid for world control. They would use their manipulation of the Communist party in England, the London School of Economics, the British Political and Economic Planning Organization, the Bank of England, and the American Federal Reserve Board to help implement their alien policy. Douglas dismissed rumours of a German policy of Jewish persecution during the war as "patently absurd" since "there is abundant evidence that Hitler received exactly the same kind of support from powerful Jews as did the Kaiser."[47]

Even this cursory description of Douglas's writings reveals he was an overt anti-Semite. Yet in the harsh circumstances of 1930s Alberta his economic and political theories became highly appealing. They offered a ready explanation for Albertans' economic and political woes and an acceptable and traditional enemy – bankers and financiers – against whom to wage war. When Aberhart began studying Douglas's theories in 1932, he absorbed, in varying degrees, their economic and political aspects along with the concept of a Jewish world plot. Partly because of his inadequate understanding of Douglas's theories but mostly because of his propensity for independent action, Aberhart created his own brand of Social Credit, whose purpose was to liberate the people "from the yoke of the present financial system" and foster "the universally recognized principles of Christianity in human relationships."[48] By mixing his fundamentalist religious beliefs with Douglas's conspiracy theories, Aberhart was able to conclude that "the principles of the old-line politicians and their henchmen are like those of the man who betrayed the Christ. Gold was his god and millions have suffered because of it. The moneychangers upheld his right and crucified the Christ and they have been crucifying everyone since who follows in the steps of the Saviour." For Aberhart it was a short step from discussing Judas, money-changers, and Christ-killers to embracing Douglas's theory of an international financial Jewish conspiracy.[49]

Yet Aberhart's views about the conspiracy were not as explicit as Douglas's. Most scholars accept that Aberhart believed in the international financial conspiracy but did not accept that it was Jewish-controlled.[50] Certainly, he expressed contradictory views about Jews and Judaism. At various times he stated that Social Credit not only opposed anti-Semitism but condemned it in the strongest possible terms. In 1935 he publicly denounced the *Protocols* as a forgery. When the Alberta Jewish community solicited his greetings for various Jewish holidays, he gave them freely.[51] When the Western Division of the Canadian Jewish Congress asked him to speak at its conference in Calgary in 1939, he attended and expressed sympathy with the plight of European Jews, stating: "There will never be more than a temporary solution to the problems facing the Jewish race until you find a place to seek your destiny in freedom."[52] In an interview for the *Jewish Post* in the autumn of 1939, when asked about the possibilities of permitting and assisting Jewish refugees to settle in Alberta, Aberhart responded that if Ottawa permitted it and if they were supported independently, "so as not to become a burden on the government," then "we would gladly open the doors to Jewish sufferers ... As to refugees with any capital of their own, they are certainly welcome."[53]

These statements have led David Elliott to conclude that, "while he was Premier, Aberhart was perceived by the Jewish community in Alberta and western Canada as a friend." Yet Elliott emphasizes that Aberhart's positive statements about Jews were balanced by equally negative statements. During a lecture at the Calgary Prophetic Bible Conference in 1922, Aberhart explicitly opposed Zionism and argued that because Jews had not accepted Christ they would never succeed in regaining the Promised Land of Zion: "The JEWISH RACE must yet acknowledge that the CHRIST who was crucified to the CROSS of Calvary was the SON of GOD, their MESSIAH. Until they will acknowledge that they must expect the curses of the world and can not expect the Blessings of GOD." In other sermons Aberhart criticized the Jewish nation for its sinfulness, including the sins of selfishness, hypocrisy, usury, violence, injustice, and discontent with wages. He viewed Christianity as a war against the Antichrist and suggested that when Armageddon came, most Jews would be duped by the Antichrist, believing him to be their Messiah.[54]

Moreover, Aberhart fully embraced Douglas's conspiracy theory about international financiers, even if he demurred on their ethnicity. In a vitriolic condemnation of the "bankers" in 1943, Aberhart declared: "Do you not realize that unless we make definite plans for dealing with this slimy octopus which is wrapping its clammy blood-sucking tentacles around every man, woman and child in this Canada of ours, we shall find ourselves bound in abject slavery to the lords of finance who, by this iniquitous swindle have gained such power that they are virtually super-dictators to whom democratically elected governments have to go cringingly, cap-in-hand, to obtain permission to carry on?"[55] On another occasion, he repeated Douglas's claim that in Germany there existed a Jewish group of financiers who were responsible for the persecution of Jews in that country while they themselves remained unscathed and prospered economically.[56]

In short, Aberhart's stance on Jews and their relationship to an international financial conspiracy was ambiguous, and it is possible that he embraced positive feelings towards Jews while still accepting that part of Douglas's theories that blamed the shadowy "international Jewish financier" for the world's economic and political ills. After examining Aberhart's contradictory statements within the context of his Christian fundamentalism, Howard Palmer concludes that "Aberhart's beliefs about Jews were so ambivalent and complex that they are difficult to characterize; one might even argue that his attitudes were not simply ambivalent but were, on this question as in many other cases, simply a bundle of contradictions."[57] Elliott astutely recognizes that Aberhart's acceptance of the international financial Jewish conspiracy was tempered by his "humanitarianism, his compartmentalized thinking, and his leadership ambitions," which resulted in an "antithetical relationship between his theology and his political ideology."[58] Palmer similarly notes that, "although Aberhart's fundamentalism and Social Credit beliefs gave his opinions about Jews a particular cast ... [h]is belief in prophecy and his view of the religious significance of Jews were too strong, his sense of justice too highly developed, and his personal animosity for Major Douglas too intense for him to become deeply involved in the theories and rhetoric of anti-Semitism."[59] Significantly, however, as leader of Alberta Social Credit and interpreter of Douglas's theories, Aberhart expressed views ambivalent enough to allow the founder's anti-Semitic ideology to permeate

Table 3
Alberta provincial election, 8 August 1944

Political party	Votes received	% of vote	Candidates nominated	Candidates elected
CCF	70,307	24.92	57	2
Farmer's Labour	390	0.14	1	0
Independent	47,239	16.75	36	3
Labour Progressive	12,003	4.26	30	0
Labour United	1,788	0,63	1	0
Single Tax	480	0.17	1	0
Social Credit	146,367	51.88	57	51
Veterans & Active Force	480	0.17	1	0
TOTALS	282,106	100.00	184	57

Source: Statistics are from Alberta, A Report on Alberta Elections.

his movement. Although scholars emphasize that Aberhart repeatedly denied that he or Social Credit was anti-Semitic,[60] they are less willing to acknowledge that he allowed anti-Semitism to form a significant part of the movement's philosophy and propaganda.

When Ernest Manning took over the premiership after Aberhart's death in May 1943, the former student-disciple-protégé appears to have deviated little from his master's principles. Like Aberhart, Manning's fundamentalist religious beliefs prevented him from embracing overt anti-Semitism, and he never included the word "Jewish" in his denunciations of the international financial conspiracy. After winning the 1944 provincial election (see Table 3), Manning declared that "the task [of the] Social Credit Government is nothing less than establishing ... a properly functioning democracy, in which ... social justice will sweep away the evils of our present finance dominated economic system. Powerful forces consistently have barred the way to that goal – anti-democratic and anti-Christian forces that seek to establish a ruthless and pagan dictatorship over the lives of men."[61] In a Canada-wide radio broadcast in late 1943 he discussed the anti-Christian character of the international financiers, whose philosophy of life was: "If men must have life they shall have it less abundantly, and we shall do everything possible to make them as miserable as we can." In his view, the financiers "who control and manipulate our financial system" were part of an anti-Christian conspiracy that Social Credit must fight: "What we are up against is a system which has been organized ... in methodical opposition to every fundamental principle of our Christian faith ... somewhere behind the scenes there is a deliberate conspiracy to prevent the principles of Christianity ... [from] being put into operation and made the basis of our social life ... we have to deal not merely with an un-Christian system, but a positive anti-Christian conspiracy, seeking to destroy everything which can be identified with the true Christian way of life."[62]

In this instance as in all others, Manning never stated that the conspiracy was Jewish-controlled. However, shortly after the above-noted speech, the Social Credit party organ, *Today and Tomorrow*, used his "courageous broadcast" to show that the battle against anti-Christian forces was in fact against Jews: "The issue is identical with that which arose in Palestine nearly two thousand years ago to become the pre-eminent event in history ... just as the criminals, who remained in the background manipulating the popular clamour for Our Lord's crucifixion, were forced to reveal themselves as the perpetrators of the crime, so the arch-enemies of Christianity today will be forced more and more into the open until they, too, stand revealed before the world."[63] Thus, *Today and Tomorrow* used Manning's broadcast to launch its own diatribe against Jews as Christ-killers. This was possible because Manning's rhetoric was consistent with Social Credit's theory of an international financial Jewish conspiracy. He simply refrained from stating that it was Jewish. As Hesketh notes: "Although Aberhart and Manning found anti-Semitism distasteful and worked to eliminate it within Social Credit, it took hold because they were saying virtually the same things as the party's anti-Semites. The only real difference was the absence of anti-Semitic slurs in Aberhart's and Manning's rhetoric about the anti-Christian conspiracy they believed was trying to take over the world, but anti-Semites were accustomed to employing insinuation and innuendo to make their case and could reasonably claim approval. This similarity in beliefs provided the anti-Semites with a veil of respectability."[64]

Yet Manning's regime was different from his mentor's. During his tenure as premier, Manning presided over three significant changes within Social Credit. The first was the extension of Social Credit to the federal arena in 1944 with the creation of the national Social Credit party. Social Credit MPs had been elected as early as the 1935 federal election, but in 1939 they organized under the banner of the New Democracy Movement and in 1941 under the Democratic Monetary Reform Organization of Canada. In 1944 the Social Credit group was formally organized into the national Social Credit party, which operated under the jurisdiction of the Social Credit Association of Canada (SCAC). All provincial Social Credit organizations were brought under the jurisdiction of the SCAC, including the Social Credit Association of Canada in British Columbia, the Alberta Social Credit League, the Saskatchewan Social Credit League, the Manitoba Social Credit

League, the Ontario Social Credit League, and the Institut d'Action Politique (later superseded by the Union des Electeurs). The SCAC was composed of a national executive and a national council, the latter of which included members from the national executive and the heads of each provincial organization. Only Manning did not hold a seat on the national council. Yet he exercised much influence over the policies of the SCAC.[65]

The other two changes under Manning were his abandonment of Social Credit theories and attempts to implement them, and his repudiation of anti-Semitism and purge of the Social Credit purists, or Douglasites. These changes were closely connected: when Manning attempted to abandon Douglas's economic and political theories, he was also forced to abandon their concomitant anti-Semitism. This necessarily brought him into conflict with those national and provincial party members who embraced Douglas's economic, political, and anti-Semitic theories. Indeed, Douglas's theories were so rooted in the idea of an international Jewish financial conspiracy that when Manning discarded Social Credit principles, he was also compelled to purge the principle of anti-Semitism. This tore the national and the provincial movements apart, for anti-Semitism was too much a part of Social Credit for its extraction to be conducted painlessly. Yet because Manning was responsible for this purge, scholars have since idealized him as a leader who refused to tolerate anti-Semitism, and exempted him from any responsibility for the anti-Semitism promoted during his premiership. Yet such interpretations overlook Manning's own ambivalent views on the "international Jewish financial conspiracy" and obscure the complex economic and political motives that caused him to repudiate Social Credit's anti-Semitism when he did.

Although Hesketh claims that Social Credit was no more anti-Semitic than most contemporary organizations or groups,[66] examining the response of those Canadians most directly affected and potentially threatened suggests otherwise. The response of Canadian Jewry and, specifically, the Canadian Jewish Congress reveals that it was extremely distressed by Social Credit's anti-Semitism and perceived it to be a serious threat to its welfare. Congress, the watchdog of the Canadian Jewish community, worked tirelessly to end Social Credit's anti-Semitism, yet its years of efforts were long, frustrating, and mostly unsuccessful. Examining Congress's perspective is crucial to understanding in more human, subjective terms that ideological, abstract battle that pitted Social Credit against the shadowy "international Jewish financier." Social Credit's anti-Semitism may not have made Albertans into Jew-haters, but it placed the Albertan and Canadian Jewish communities in a very precarious, uneasy, defensive position at a time when they were numerically and politically weak and occupied with the plight of European Jewry.

Canadian Jewry in 1941 numbered approximately 170,000, or 1.5 per cent of the population. There were 70,000 Jews in Ontario, 66,000 in Quebec, 19,000 in Manitoba, 4,000 in Saskatchewan and Alberta each, 3,400 in British Columbia, and 3,500 in the Maritimes. Nearly 77 per cent of Jews lived in Montreal and Toronto, yet proportionately their numbers were extremely small. Only Ontario, Quebec, and Manitoba had Jewish populations of around 2 per cent of their populations. The remaining provinces had less than 0.5 per cent.[67] In Alberta in 1941 Jews were present in the following numbers: Calgary, 1,794 (2 per cent of the city's population); Edmonton, 1,449 (1.5 per cent); Lethbridge, 153 (1.1 per cent); Medicine Hat, 93 (0.9 per cent); Drumheller, 29 (1.1 per cent). In each of sixty-four other communities throughout the province fewer than twenty Jews resided, never forming more than 2 per cent of the population.[68] The notable exception was Rumsey, a tiny farming community that had previously been the site of an attempted Jewish farming settlement. In 1941 the three resident Jews formed 3.3 per cent of the total population.[69]

Politically, the Jewish community was relatively powerless during this period. The Canadian Jewish Congress had been organized in 1919 in response to problems arising from the First World War, specifically the oppression of Jews overseas, immigration of Jewish refugees, and the renewed hopes for a Jewish homeland in Palestine that were raised by the 1917 Balfour Declaration. But the broader purpose of Congress was to act as the representative body of the Canadian Jewish community and as broker for Jewish interests in the broader Canadian polity.[70] Although its creation was considered a watershed in the community's history, its permanence was not guaranteed. After 1919 interest and enthusiasm quickly waned among Canadian Jewry; Congress's activities faltered, and in a few years the organization was virtually defunct. It then disappeared as a force in Canadian Jewish life, not to be revived until 1933. The reasons for Congress's "enforced hibernation" were lack of leadership, lack of funding, and apathy towards its agenda. Outside its three regional offices of Montreal, Toronto, and Winnipeg, it failed to set up any mechanism to maintain enthusiasm and continuity between its proposed annual conferences. Consequently, few delegates appeared at the plenary sessions of 1920 and 1921, and by the following year Congress dispensed with national meetings altogether.[71]

This lapse was a serious setback for Canadian Jewry, which was now "without its parliament, without its forum of opinions from across the intellectual spectrum, and without a voice for its collective concerns."[72] Although the 1920s were a relatively peaceful interlude for Canadian Jewry, anti-Semitism in Canada was well entrenched and required only more volatile economic and political conditions to flourish. These conditions arose during the Depression and the increased political extremism of the 1930s. By 1929 the Montreal schools question, a thorny problem spanning nearly four decades, had reached crisis level.[73] The Jewish community found itself at the mercy of the Protestant community, which would not grant Jewish parents a seat in the administration of the schools their children attended. That same year in Quebec, Adrien Arcand established the Parti National Social Chrétien and began his anti-Semitic campaign in the pages of *Le Goglu*, *Le Miroir*, and *Le Chameau*.[74] Within the province's political and religious hierarchy there was little support for the Jews under attack. Although the Montreal schools question appeared to be resolved in 1930 with the passage of a provincial bill providing for a separate Jewish school commission equal in power to the Catholic and Protestant school boards, the Quebec Catholic Church was vehemently opposed, and the act was subsequently repealed.[75]

In 1933 the election of Adolf Hitler as chancellor of Germany created further anxiety for Canadian Jewry. Political and religious officials in Quebec, as in the rest of Canada, were unwilling to open Canada's doors to German Jewish refugees.[76] The *achat chez nous* movement, a campaign of economic nationalism directed mostly against Jewish businessmen, also reached its apogee in the early 1930s. In many ways an anti-Semitic boycott, *achat chez nous* portrayed itself as a patriotic project to strengthen the economy and the morale of the francophone Catholic population. However, the effect of the movement was that Jewish businessmen were injured in their commerce and some of them driven from their stores.[77] In 1934, "one of the most bizarre strikes in Canadian history" occurred at the Notre Dame Hospital in Montreal, where fourteen resident doctors walked off the job rather than work with Samuel Rabinovich, a Jew.[78] Although scholars have argued that anti-Semitic agitation in Quebec in the interwar period was more virulent than in the rest of Canada,[79] Quebec was not the only province to experience heightened anti-Semitism. Indeed, the only recorded incident of physical violence against Jews occurred in Ontario, during the Christie Pits riots in Toronto in 1933.[80] The *Deutsche Bund* was active in nearly all German and Ukrainian communities in Saskatchewan in the 1930s, while the fascistic Canadian Nationalist party, created in Winnipeg in 1933, found adherents among many Canadians, not solely those of German origin. Later in the decade Social Credit embarked on a widespread anti-Semitic propaganda campaign that lasted several years. On the national level,

Prime Minister Mackenzie King visited Hitler in Germany in 1937 and, despite his knowledge of Hitler's persecution of Jews, found himself favourably disposed towards the chancellor.[81]

Further, it was not uncommon in the late 1930s for Jews to be barred from hotels, public beaches, golf courses, and parks of communities and summer resorts throughout Canada. In the late 1930s there was a startling increase in the number of individuals and companies who refused to rent living quarters to Jews, adopted policies of not employing Jews, and attempted to involve Jews in disturbances and acts of violence. But as H.M. Caiserman, general secretary of the Canadian Jewish Congress, noted, "the most frightening development in Canada during the 1930s was the transition from sporadic and unorganized types of anti-Semitism to organized activities sponsored by national organizations directed by professional agents of Nazi Germany." For Canada's Jews, the increase in anti-Semitic agitation confirmed not only that their country was anti-Semitic but that they needed a strong and active organization to protect themselves. In short, much of the impetus for the reactivation of Congress in 1934 came from the need to counter the increasingly virulent anti-Semitism in Quebec and Canada. As Caiserman wrote: "Canadian Jewry, for the first time, was faced with an organised violent anti-Jewish propaganda ... [In Quebec] neither the French-Canadian religious, political or cultural leaders, nor the General Press of the Province (French and English alike) uttered a single word of disapproval or condemnation of the most irresponsible and libellous accusations levelled against the Jewish population. This was a sad realisation and was therefore the deciding factor in the re-convening of the Canadian Jewish Congress at its second general session."[82]

In May 1933 Jewish societies in Winnipeg formed the Western Canadian Jewish Congress Committee and invited delegates from across the west to attend an emergency meeting. Hundreds of delegates unanimously agreed to re-establish Congress in order to deal with the problems of Canadian anti-Semitism and the plight of European Jewry. The next month the Western Canadian Jewish Congress Committee, the League for the Defence of Jewish Rights of Toronto, and the Pro-Congress Committee of Montreal sponsored a conference in Toronto to protest Nazi atrocities and re-establish Congress. A provisional national executive committee was organized, which conducted a Canada-wide fund-raising campaign to provide relief for Jewish refugees, combat anti-Semitic agitation, and boycott goods from Nazi Germany. Delegates then were elected in each Jewish community across Canada, and met at Congress's second plenary session in Toronto from 27 to 29 January 1934. There Congress was reborn. It comprised forty-one executive officers, including most of the founders of the 1919 Congress; Samuel Jacobs was elected its new president.[83] The organization was also restructured as a union of three semi-autonomous regions – Eastern Division, Central Division, and Western Division – whose headquarters were in Montreal, Toronto, and Winnipeg respectively.[84] The National Dominion Council and the National Executive Committee, both headquartered in Montreal, were responsible for overseeing various new departments and committees, including the United Jewish Relief Agency and the overseas relief department, the immigration of refugees department, the public relations department, and various educational and cultural departments.[85]

The constitution and resolutions passed at Congress's second plenary session reflected its renewed commitment to Canadian and world Jewry. Congress's constitutional mandate was to safeguard the civil, political, economic, and religious rights of Jews and to combat anti-Semitism; to study problems relating to the cultural, economic, and social life of Jews and to seek a solution to such problems; to assist the United Jewish Relief Agency in its program of work for Palestine; and to co-operate with world Jewry. General resolutions were passed concerning anti-defamation work, a Jewish home in Palestine, the World Jewish Congress, immigration of German Jewish refugees, Canadian Jewish economic problems, Kehilla (community) matters, boycott of German goods, relief of stricken Jewry, Jewish education, a Canadian Jewish archives, and public welfare. Specific resolutions included maintaining Congress as a permanent organization, participating in the World Jewish Congress, calling upon the British government to remove restrictions against Jewish immigration to Palestine, and assisting the United Jewish Relief Agency in supporting the development of a Jewish national home in Palestine.[86]

In the years following its reorganization one of Congress's central priorities was to co-operate with other Jewish organizations in solving the problems of world Jewry. After 1934 Congress worked closely with the World Jewish Congress, providing support and attending its various deliberations. During the Second World War it assisted in the relief of war-stricken Jewry by working with the American Jewish Joint Distribution Committee. At war's end Congress representatives were present at the United Nations Relief and Rehabilitation Administration (UNRRA) conferences, peace conferences, United Nations sessions, and other international meetings of importance to world Jewry. Congress continually worked (albeit with limited success) to enlist the support of the Canadian government in defence of Jewish needs and rights. It initiated the organization of the United Jewish Refugee and War Relief Agencies, which worked to persuade the Canadian government to lift its immigration restrictions on European Jewish refugees.[87] Thanks in large part to the efforts of Samuel Bronfman, Congress president from 1938 to 1962, and his "right-hand man," Saul Hayes, Congress's national executive director from 1940 to 1959, the United Jewish Refugee and War Relief Agencies became one of the most effective Canadian Jewish bodies, ranking with any humanitarian institution in the country. By 1948, in the wake of the horrors of the destruction of European Jewry but with the promise of a Jewish homeland in Palestine, Congress could look back on nearly fifteen years of hard work and hard-won achievements. By the post-war period it had truly become the "parliament of Canadian Jewry," nationally representative and unchallenged in its authority.[88]

At the domestic level Congress focused much of its efforts on anti-defamation work and creating an administrative framework to execute it. At its 1934 plenary session Congress resolved to call upon "all just and fair-minded citizens of this Dominion, of every race and creed," to join it in denouncing the "individuals and groups who disseminate false and libellous anti-Semitic propaganda aimed to undermine the standing and reputation of the Jewish citizens of this Dominion." Congress pointed to the *Protocols* and their "widespread and methodical dissemination by ill-disposed persons" and resolved that "immediate steps be taken for the proper refutation of the statements therein contained by an authority, and that the same be given widespread distribution, and that a special committee be appointed by this Congress to carry out this resolution."[89] It also resolved that legislation should be sought to make defamation of any religious or racial group actionable, and it invited the co-operation of the various Canadian B'nai Brith lodges,[90] which had long been devoted to service, charity, community work, anti-defamation, and human rights, to assist Congress in its public relations work. This overture eventually led to a joint organization of Congress and B'nai Brith in 1938 under the national Joint Public Relations Committee (JPRC).[91]

Congress's anti-defamation work became more organized, coherent, and administratively streamlined with the creation of the JPRC, which also ended a jurisdictional dispute between Congress and B'nai Brith going back to the former's reorganization in 1934. Now the two organizations operating under the umbrella of Congress could work together "to obviate any friction or duplication of effort in the fight against our common enemy."[92] Through its national and regional branches the JPRC drafted Congress's policies on public relations and anti-defamation work and acted as troubleshooter for anti-Semitic propaganda. The JPRC also collaborated with other organizations, specifically the Committee on Jewish-Gentile Relationships, established in 1934 and renamed the Canadian Conference of Christians and Jews (CCCJ) in 1940. The mandate of the CCCJ was to create a better understanding between Jews and non-Jews through various educational programs, including distribution of literature, publication of its bulletin, *Fellowship*, public addresses, and co-operation with organizations and religious bodies committed to combating prejudice against minority groups.[93] Thus the CCCJ acted as a sister agency upon which the JPRC could rely in its public relations work.

In terms of its day-to-day functioning, the JPRC maintained regular contact with its regional committees in the Eastern, Western, and Central divisions, the Maritimes and British Columbia, and in some individual communities. When cases of anti-Semitism came to the attention of the regional JPRCs, their staffs responded promptly and often on an emergency basis. Similarly, inner executives of the regional JPRCs made immediate decisions if necessary, but their actions were ultimately subject to ratification by the national JPRC. On a non-emergency basis, the national and regional JPRCs formulated policy and gave general directions to JPRC staff. Congress's national executive director and regional directors also submitted reports of their public relations activities to the national JPRC. The national executive director then sent out fortnightly confidential reports to all officers of the JPRCs.[94] In sum, the mandate of the JPRC was to conduct public relations and anti-defamation work under the jurisdiction of Congress. This work was not executed in a haphazard manner, although some cases of anti-Semitism were responded to quickly without resort to Congress's organizational infrastructure. For the most part, however, the JPRC attempted to formulate a coherent public relations philosophy to deal with both positive and negative aspects of Jewish-Gentile relations.

Social Credit's anti-Semitic propaganda campaign soon occupied a significant part of the negative aspect of Congress's public relations work. Indeed, Congress was severely tested when it attempted to eliminate Social Credit's anti-Semitism. It employed numerous tactics against Social Credit – from educational public relations work to broad-based social appeals to proposals for legal action – but nearly all its attempts met with limited success or negative repercussions. Congress quickly discovered that, although it was important to create a coherent and intelligent public relations philosophy, converting philosophy into policy and policy into action was more complicated. Social Credit formed a provincial government and later a national party, and was an accepted part of the Canadian political landscape. Given the federal government's stance towards Jewish refugees and the nature of political and public discourse in which anti-Semitism was *de rigueur,* Social Credit's anti-Semitic propaganda received implicit sanction from the surrounding political environment and was allowed to become an entrenched part of the movement. In such a climate of intolerance, Social Credit would not easily be convinced to dispense with its anti-Semitic attacks, especially not by appeals from delegates of the "enemy." What Congress did not immediately understand was that Social Credit was in a battle against the international financial Jewish conspiracy until the end. Only after years of unsuccessful attempts would Congress begin to appreciate the extreme difficulty, if not impossibility, of solving its most serious public relations problem.

3 Early Confrontations

When the Social Credit movement was established in 1935, the Canadian Jewish Congress was a newly reorganized entity concerned more with the plight of European Jewish refugees and the activities of domestic fascists like Adrien Arcand[1] than with a somewhat curious prairie protest movement. But when Social Credit began holding up the "international Jewish financier" as an object of vilification, Congress justifiably felt compelled to respond. Although it perceived Social Credit as a major irritant, its negative reaction was moderated by a public relations approach that emphasized political considerations and public niceties. By the beginning of the Second World War, however, Congress considered Social Credit's anti-Semitism to be a serious problem and tried to implement a more effective policy to stop it. But its continued passivity prevented more assertive measures, and, not surprisingly, Congress experienced little success. Moreover, the slippery, insinuating nature of Social Credit's anti-Semitism and the duplicitous stance of Social Credit politicians made more assertive actions difficult, if not counterproductive. Examining Congress's early responses to Social Credit's anti-Semitism reveals the challenges of, and the differences between, formulating a coherent philosophy and executing an effective policy.

In the beginning Congress assumed that the purpose of public relations was to influence non-Jewish opinion about Jews positively. Like its American sister organizations – the American Jewish Congress (AJC), the American Jewish Committee, and the Anti-Defamation League of B'nai Brith (ADL) – which were facing similar problems of increased anti-Semitism and domestic fascist agitation in the interwar period,[2] Congress assumed that if non-Jews could become favourably disposed towards Jews, they would help to combat anti-Semitism and protect the Jewish community from discrimination. Thus, Congress embraced the somewhat naïve hope that if non-Jews could be rid of their biases, Jews would be protected and anti-Semitism would cease.[3]

This perception was evident in Congress's early public relations activities. After its reconstitution in 1934, Congress began researching Canadian Jewish social and economic life in response to standard accusations about the supposed wealth and power of Jews. Based on the findings of the Dominion Bureau of Statistics and independent research, Congress replied to these accusations through the press and published pamphlets. It also co-operated closely with various religious denominations in Canada, although its efforts were undermined by the increase in Nazi propaganda throughout Canada in the late 1930s.[4] Thus, although Congress conducted anti-defamation activities against fascist and anti-Semitic groups, many of which were successful,[5] behind nearly all its efforts lay the assumption that education and moral suasion were the most effective tools in ending anti-Semitism.

Congress's officers and agents actively promoted this early philosophy. In 1935 Rabbi Maurice N. Eisendrath commented on Congress's exemplary anti-defamation work in the past year. He discussed activities such as the compilation of strategic mailing lists of "wholesome Jewish materials" to universities, churches, and the press, the "checking and aborting" of anti-Semitic propaganda, and numerous educational and research projects. He noted enthusiastically that "with amazing swiftness an effective machinery has been established. All that it needs now is the driving power to be derived from a decent measure of personal effort and some dignified financial support."[6] In 1935 Rabbi Harry Joshua Stern similarly reported that Congress had been doing "phenomenal work" in its battle against the rising tide of anti-Semitism in Canada. However, he emphasized the secretiveness of its work: "Anti-defamation is of such a nature that it cannot be publicized. Hence the failure of the Congress executive to record in the general press its accomplishments in that important direction."[7] Covert activity was an important aspect of Congress's early work, and it would discover the costs of both retaining and abandoning this approach when it tried to confront Social Credit's anti-Semitism.

A similar orientation was evident at Congress's Western Division conference in Calgary in August 1939, where Western vice-president Louis Rosenberg discussed the educational and preventative methods taken to combat anti-Semitism. He stated that anti-Semitism was not yet a factor in Canada and that "the Jewish problem" was basically one of educating other groups, largely minority groups like itself, to an understanding and acceptance of the Jewish people. He suggested various ways to promote understanding among non-Jews, such as spreading the "gentle reminder" that British and Jewish culture stemmed from the same origin, showing free films about Jewish achievements in Palestine, holding educational exhibits at exhibitions and fairs in towns and cities throughout Canada, and setting "a fine personal example" in everyday life. He also emphasized the need to conduct "positive" rather than "negative" or defensive public relations, arguing that the way to combat anti-Semitism was not to retaliate against it but to use congenial, preventative measures against defamatory propaganda. "Let us be constructive ... Let us think in terms of mutual understanding, of education work, of public relations of all the various groups in this country. We can act as the link, because of our love of democracy."[8] Rosenberg's opinions were apparently shared by other Congress officials, for when the national Joint Public Relations Committee (JPRC) was reorganized after 1941, it too decided that its approach should become more positive and constructive rather than negative and defensive.[9]

In many ways the early phase of Congress's public relations work emphasized education of the non-Jewish public about the true social and economic situation of Jews in Canada.[10] Most Congress officers and agents had great faith in the power of education, yet even Rosenberg, one of its greatest proponents, did not believe that education alone would convert the anti-Semite: "I do not for a moment hold out the hope that people already suffering from a chronic or acute case of anti-semitism can be cured by nicely phrased speeches, scientific facts or accurate statistics. Nevertheless it is worth while to know the real truth about the economic situation of the Jews in Canada."[11] Rosenberg would eventually publish his famous *Canada's Jews*, which is still the most comprehensive study of the socio-economic status of Canadian Jewry. Congress's initial approach was best summarized by its general secretary, H.M. Caiserman: "The Canadian Jewish Congress, in the interests of Canadian Jewry and in the interest of the Dominion as a whole, observes vigilantly the plans and activities of our enemies. It exposes their plans by educational methods, publishes correct facts in reply to misrepresentations directed against us, and promotes good will, understanding and co-operation with all religious groups in Canada."[12]

During the Second World War, Congress began to question the efficacy of its public relations work because, notwithstanding its efforts, anti-Semitism in Canada was increasing. Indeed, despite popular notions that anti-Semitism decreased as the extent of Hitler's annihilation of European Jewry became known, Congress found itself increasingly burdened with anti-defamation work. In 1940 the Central Division's JPRC reported that, "contrary to expectations that a spirit of brotherhood would sweep this country in the face of the thrust of a common enemy, anti-Semitism apparently increased."[13] In 1942 the Western Division's JPRC similarly noted that anti-Semitic prejudice and discrimination had increased rather than decreased since the war's outbreak. While Congress officers continued to emphasize a traditionally positive and constructive approach rather than a negative and defensive one,[14] such public relations methods were increasingly suspect. Congress's focus on "congenial" anti-defamation work was inadequate to solve the systemic anti-Semitism in the Canadian political, economic, and social milieux. Nowhere were the limitations of Congress's approach clearer than in its attempts to confront what it called (in an ironic reversal of the term "the Jewish problem") "the Social Credit problem."

From Social Credit's inception, Congress had monitored its anti-Semitism. Rosenberg had documented the anti-Semitism in Douglas's writings since at least 1935, and in 1936 concluded that Social Credit's founder was a raving anti-Semite. In his view Douglas was "the high priest of the Social Crediters" who "mumbles mysteriously about the long discredited *Protocols of the Elders of Zion* and spices his stew of 'a + b theorems' and 'social dividend' with a little anti-semitic paprika to taste, reaching the pinnacle of nonsense by turning the fair-haired teutonic Lombards into Jews in order to suit his theories concerning the wicked 'collectivist Communist Jewish bankers.'"[15] Rosenberg knew that Douglas's attitudes were permeating the Alberta movement, and he brought it to the attention of Congress leadership in the late 1930s. However, no action was taken.[16]

Congress's failure to respond was mainly owing to more pressing concerns about European Jewry and domestic fascists, but it was also a result of the geographic and cultural distance between its national headquarters in Montreal and the Jewish community in Alberta. The bulk of Canadian Jewry resided in Montreal and Toronto, and it was there that the Canadian Jewish community, small as it was, flourished. Alberta's Jews were too few in number to be of pressing significance to the larger Jewish community. Thus geography and demography ensured that their concerns were not paramount at Congress's national headquarters. Not surprisingly, Congress found it very difficult to form a coherent, unified, national response to Social Credit's anti-Semitism.

However, this situation was mitigated in 1940 when Rosenberg, now executive director of Congress's Western Division and secretary of the Winnipeg JPRC, began to examine Social Credit's anti-Semitism closely.

From his western perspective he assessed the impact and threat of Social Credit to Alberta *and* Canadian Jewry. His exhaustive analyses of Social Credit's propaganda became invaluable to Congress, and his persistent relaying of information to national headquarters prodded awareness there that Social Credit was a threat to the entire Jewish community. Yet Rosenberg's analyses did not completely bridge the gap between centre and periphery. Communication between national headquarters and the Alberta branch was not always continuous or bilateral, and for several years Congress's public relations policy lacked direction and leadership. Often it consisted of simply observing and detailing Social Credit's anti-Semitic propaganda.

By the early 1940s, however, it was obvious that Social Credit's anti-Semitism was a chronic characteristic and that Congress must respond. In 1941 Rosenberg told national headquarters that the movement's anti-Semitism was more than the fulminations of a radical fringe and represented official Social Credit policy. By this time he had examined all of Douglas's writings and concluded that Social Credit's founder subscribed to and actively promoted views expounded in the *Protocols of the Learned Elders of Zion*.[17] Even more seriously, Social Credit politicians in Canada were espousing similar views. Consequently, he announced his intention to confront Social Credit. The catalyst for his decision was a published letter by one of Social Credit's most notorious anti-Semites, Norman Jaques, member of parliament for Wetaskiwin, Alberta.

Jaques was a firm believer in Douglas's theories of an international financial Jewish conspiracy and was well known for abusing his parliamentary privilege by attacking Jews and attempting to read excerpts of the *Protocols* into *Hansard*.[18] One of Jaques's – and Social Credit's – favourite bogeymen was the American-based Union Now Movement. Also known as Federal Union, Union Now was headquartered in New York City and run by Clarence K. Streit, author of *Union Now* and *Union Now with Britain*. It was created as a "non-profit membership association" in the early 1930s in response to the autocratic ambitions of Hitler and Mussolini. With chapters in the United States, Great Britain, and most British dominions, Union Now advocated a union of the Western democracies in which a central world government would preside over a union citizenship, union defence force, union customs-free economy, union money, and a union postal and communications system. Its mandate was to create a "democracy composed of democracies" in which all participating countries would share in the responsibilities of maintaining an equitable and peaceful world order – economically, socially, politically, and militarily.[19] Social Credit, in keeping with its paranoid philosophy, was vehemently opposed to

Union Now. An international order in which nations shared government power for a greater purpose certainly meant surrendering complete national sovereignty to a totalitarian international power. For Social Credit, it was obvious that Union Now was part of the international conspiracy to achieve world control.[20]

MP Jaques actively promoted this view, and on 30 January 1941 the Saskatoon-based *Western Producer* published a letter by him stating that Union Now was attempting to achieve "the surrender of our national sovereignty to international control ... there is only one thing that ... functions as a 'power' on an international basis and that is International Finance. And who controls International Finance? A gang of German-Jewish 'international' bankers ... Not only German military totalitarianism, but its evil twin, German-Jewish financial totalitarianism, must be destroyed." Jaques added that although little was known about the origins or authenticity of the *Protocols*, "the fact remains that all of the moves predicted therein are a precise replica of contemporary history ... they project the International government, which is depicted by the American Wall St. Jew – Clarence Streit in his 'Union Now.'"[21]

Rosenberg decided to respond to Jaques's letter as a private citizen and not on behalf of Congress, although he had the support of its national executive. He wrote a letter to the *Western Producer* providing evidence that world finance was not, in fact, controlled by "German Jewish International Bankers." He cited statistics showing that German Jews had never formed more than 3 per cent of the world Jewish population; that in 1925 only 3.3 per cent of all persons in Germany who engaged in banking and stockbroking were Jewish; that there was not a single Jew on the board of directors of the Bank of England; that there were only 3 Jews among the 150 directors of the "Big Five" banks in Great Britain, and not one Jew on the directorates of all the other clearing-houses in England; that of the 420 directors of the nineteen member banks of the New York Clearing House, only 30 were Jews, and half of these were connected with two of the comparatively smaller banks; that there were no Jewish directors on the boards of any of the larger banks such as the National City Bank, First National Bank, or Chase National Bank; that the Morgans of the banking house of J.P. Morgan and Company were Episcopalians of Welsh origin; and finally, that there was not a single Jew on the board of directors of any chartered bank, trust company, mortgage company, or railway company in Canada.[22]

Rosenberg also assailed Jaques: "Such a hodge-podge of ignorance and malice as displayed in [Jaques's] letter would not merit reply under normal circumstances. The results of Hitler's propaganda technique however, have shown that no propaganda, no matter how false or ridiculous, can be ignored if it can secure publication … What does concern me is that there sits in the House of Commons, at a time when we are engaged in a life-and-death struggle with Hitlerism and all it stands for, a man who does not scruple to warm up and offer to the readers of the *Western Producer* a rehash of all the venomous propaganda with which Hitler's publicity machine has been flooding the world since 1933." Rosenberg admonished the *Western Producer* for "spoil[ing] good newsprint by printing second-hand versions of Deutsche Bunde propaganda" at a time when Canadians were being asked to prevent waste and salvage paper.[23]

Rosenberg also met with the paper's editor, with whom he was personally acquainted. The editor informed him that readers of all opinions had the right to have their letters published in the paper. "He seems to have the curious idea," Rosenberg remarked, "that to refuse to publish such letters as those of Mr. Jaques would be transgressing the freedom of the press." Rosenberg surmised that the editor, a Social Credit supporter, was "not inclined to criticize anything which a Social Credit member may have written."[24] Not surprisingly, the editor did not publish Rosenberg's letter. When questioned on his decision, he merely stated that he did publish some letters on the subject but was unsure whether Rosenberg's was among them: "As is our rule, we try to make the best [choice?] we can to cover any particular subject under discussion and according to the space we have to spare – It is not necessarily the letter with the most merit that is published but such as we think have covered the subject from various angles."[25]

From this earliest encounter, Rosenberg realized that confronting Social Credit's anti-Semitism would not be easy. Yet part of the problem rested with Congress. It had not publicly protested against Jaques's allegations and only tacitly supported Rosenberg's decision to write the letter. Even then, Rosenberg used a pseudonym, W.H. McCollum.[26] These were not the tactics of an aggressive organization. Rosenberg was fully aware of the limitations of Congress's approach, for in a letter to Oscar Cohen, executive secretary of Congress's Central Division in Toronto, he expressed his frustration: "I have long felt that the Anti-Semitic tendencies among Social Credit propagandists should be exposed, but there happens to be a Social Credit government in office in … Alberta and some Congress workers in that province are rather doubtful concerning the advisability of making any public statements on this subject at the present time … Aberhart['s] … relationship with the Jewish communities in Alberta has always been cordial, and he has been a prominent speaker at Jewish goodwill gatherings. However it will be nothing strange if Mr. Aberhart himself was unaware of these tendencies in Social Credit propaganda, as he is unaware of quite a few things in connection with Social Credit."[27] Clearly, workable minority-majority group relations were important to Western Canadian Jewry. What was less obvious was the inherent tension between attempting to formulate policy at the national level and implementing it at the grass-roots level. At this juncture, neither Congress's national headquarters nor its Western Division realized the importance of the latter's participation and leadership in creating an effective response.

For his part, Rosenberg was determined that Social Credit's anti-Semitism be stopped, and refuting Jaques's published allegations was the first step. He contacted Morris Fine of the American Jewish Committee and asked him to obtain a declaration from Union Now that its director, Clarence Streit, was not, as Jaques had alleged, a "Wall Street Jewish banker." E.W. Balduf of Union Now acknowledged to Rosenberg that "Mr. Streit is not a banker and has never had any connection with any banking house or any other business house. Mr. Streit also is not Jewish."[28] Rosenberg asked Balduf if he would write to the editor of the *Western Producer* and insist upon publication of these facts. "It would not be necessary," Rosenberg added, "to mention that the statements had been brought to your attention by the American Jewish Committee and by myself, as this would be used to confirm the impression of Mr. Streit's 'Jewishness.'"[29] Yet there is no evidence that Balduf wrote to the *Western Producer*. In the end, the paper did nothing to counter Jaques's anti-Semitic statements and in fact continued to publish similar letters in its columns.[30] Yet Rosenberg's failure to silence Jaques was not for lack of trying, for he employed various tactics to refute the MP's allegations. Without the public backing of Congress, however, Rosenberg was simply one person – and given his pseudonym, a non-Jew at that – who opposed one Social Crediter. But Congress was not ready to take more confrontational measures.

Several months later Congress received another opportunity to confront Social Credit, and specifically its party organ, *Today and Tomorrow*, which was the movement's largest disseminator of anti-Semitism. Its history dated to 1935, when, a few months after the party's electoral victory, it was established as Social Credit's semi-official paper, replacing the earlier *Social Credit Chronicle*. It was originally owned and edited by MLA Lucien Maynard, but in 1943 it was taken over by the Alberta Social Credit League and became the party's official organ.[31] When the national Social Credit party was formed in 1944, *Today and Tomorrow* became the official national party organ and was renamed the *Canadian Social Crediter*. Although precise circulation figures are unavailable, *Today and Tomorrow*'s readership ostensibly numbered over ten thousand.[32]

One of the main purposes of *Today and Tomorrow* was to inform readers about the international financial Jewish conspiracy. It argued that international finance was composed of a small group of men, mostly of Jewish origin, that operated behind the scenes to manipulate the world money system in order to establish a world slave state under its control. The conspiracy was responsible for any adverse international event, including the world-wide economic depression of the 1930s, the totalitarianism of Germany and Russia, the Second World War, and the socialism within European and North American democracies. The paper's most common strategy was to declare openly that the conspiracy was international and financial but imply or only occasionally state that it was Jewish. Although scholars have referred to the anti-Semitic propaganda in the party organ, few have systematically analysed it. Some examples from *Today and Tomorrow* will reveal the nature and extent of its anti-Semitic propaganda.

Today and Tomorrow regularly argued that the economic and political ills of the 1930s were caused by international financiers: "The last war was fought and won by the Allied powers, but the so-called peace which followed was won by International Finance – a gang of arch-criminals whose treachery, slimy intrigue, brutality and lust for power has all but reduced civilization to a shambles."[33] In the paper's view, the same international financial conspirators who caused the Depression and allowed Nazism to come to Germany were also responsible for the rise of European socialism: "Since the last war most of the European countries have been 'socialized' and the people collectivized into 'masses,' armed to the teeth, and all control centralized in ruthless dictators. This 'New Order' was lavishly subsidized by international finance ... Those countries remaining democratic became the victims of ... financial crises and depressions ... imposed by International Finance ... Every Allied leader declares we are fighting to preserve our democratic freedoms ... At the same time there is a promise, or a threat of a 'New Order,' a transformation from National Democracy to International Socialism. And who is to be the controller of the new order? A Hitler or a Shylock? Gangster or Racketeer?"[34]

The party organ also implied that because the international financial conspirators were Jews they posed a direct threat to Christianity: "When we come to the Christian attitude to the usurious money system we find that Christ condemned it outright ... The word for usurer in Hebrew, was the same as the word for viper, and the figure of speech is not too strong, for the taking of usury is a poisonous snake that kills. It is significant that International Finance has chosen the snake as its symbol."[35] In another instance the paper more explicitly stated: "Christianity condemned interest, not profit, and for good reasons. From the earliest times, interest was known to result in unpayable debt and the destruction of civilized society. In modern times, Shakespeare pierced its heart when he asked the Jew, 'Does your money breed like ewes and rams?'"[36]

On more than one occasion *Today and Tomorrow* published a series of fictionalized letters alleging to be secret correspondence dated 1863 between the Rothschild brothers in England and a banking house in the United States in order to imply that international finance was headed by Jews conspiring for world financial domination.[37] Significantly, the name Rothschild usually headed the list of conspirators. In subsequent years the paper repeated the statement allegedly made by Meyer Amschel Rothschild in 1790: "Permit me to issue and control the money of a nation and I care not who makes its laws."[38]

Today and Tomorrow described how contemporary organizations and institutions were part of the international financial Jewish conspiracy. It argued that the Bank of England was a major player because it had been under the control of the Rothschilds and other conspirators since its inception. The bank was also culpable for the Depression: "There is no record in all history of such universal monetary chaos, stagnation of trade, unemployment and human suffering as under the regime of ... Montagu Norman, Governor of the Bank of England ... As a result of [his] policy two and a half million people committed suicide ... men and women [were] suffering from illness and insanity brought on by the feverish fight for a living ... men and women were imprisoned, not because they were wicked but because they were poor."[39]

Today and Tomorrow also accused England of housing international financial conspirators in the London School of Economics (LSE). It claimed that the LSE had been "founded by Fabian Socialists 'to train the bureaucracy of the future world Socialist State,' and endowed, for that purpose, with a million sterling by the late Ernest Cassel – of the same Germanic racial origin as most other international financiers." Several prominent figures were allegedly part of the conspiracy because of their connection with the LSE, including William Beveridge,[40] "formerly head of the London School of Economics"; Leonard Marsh,[41] "entrusted with the adaption of the Beveridge Plan to Canada"; and Dr Cyril James, principal of McGill University, whom the "Federal Government [has] placed at the head of the Reconstruction Council."[42] The party organ implied that the LSE was a front for socialist and international financial plotters, most of whom were Jewish. Any Jew who was a graduate or member of the staff at the LSE was absolute proof of the conspiracy. Non-Jewish graduates of the school such as Beveridge, Marsh, and James simply pointed to the conspiracy's far-reaching nature.[43]

Focusing its attention southward, *Today and Tomorrow* attacked the Federal Reserve Board, the central banking authority of the United States. It described the board as a totalitarian, international financial institution controlled by German Jews, specifically the Warburgs, a German Jewish family whose members were eminent in banking, philanthropy, and scholarship in Europe and America.[44] Three members of this family were particularly subject to attack: Paul Warburg, chairman of the Federal Reserve Board and member of the American bank Kuhn, Loeb and Company; Paul's brother Max, head of the German banking firm Warburg and Company and financial adviser to the German delegation to the Paris Peace Conference of 1919; and Paul's son James, banker, economist, and member of Franklin Roosevelt's original "brain trust." *Today and Tomorrow* called the Warburgs "ruthless ... international bankers" whose firm, Kuhn, Loeb, was "the headquarters of international finance." Paul Warburg was working towards the same aims in the United States as his brother Max in Germany – both were international financiers bent on world control – and their American and German connections were simply proof of "the extent to which this international money power had its tentacles spread."[45]

The conspiracy did not end there. According to *Today and Tomorrow*, a close accomplice of the Warburgs and the Federal Reserve Board was the Union Now Movement. In 1940 James Warburg wrote a book entitled *Peace in Our Time?* which offered proposals for world peace similar to those in Clarence Streit's *Union Now*. The paper described both books as "scheme[s] for the World Slave State" and concluded that Streit and Union Now were under the control of Paul Warburg and Kuhn, Loeb and Company, which also controlled the *New York Times*. *Today and Tomorrow* wondered if it was "curious coincidence" that the international financiers who "financed Von Papen, Germany's No. 1 Saboteur, and also Hitler's rise to power – should be sponsoring World Federal Union?"[46]

To corroborate its argument, *Today and Tomorrow* published statements by Premier Ernest Manning in which he also connected the Federal Reserve Board with the "totalitarian schemes" proposed by Union Now. In his discussion of *Peace in Our Time?* Manning described James Warburg as "the son of the founder of the American Federal Reserve Banking System [Paul Warburg] and ... closely associated with the same group of International financiers. There can be no doubt about the source from which these schemes originated." He noted that Union Now, and specifically Clarence Streit, "was connected with a New York paper [the *New York Times*], which, on the evidence of Sir Cecil Spring-Rice, British Ambassador to Washington during the last war, was controlled by a banking house [Kuhn, Loeb and Company] that is an integral part of International Finance." Manning vowed that Social Credit would declare war against the international financial conspirators who were attempting "to use the conditions created by the war to put [their scheme] over, so that when the war was won by the democratic nations the fruits of victory would be their complete enslavement to a supreme international dictatorship – the very thing our boys are dying to prevent."[47]

The party organ's antagonism to the Federal Reserve Board and Union Now was similarly applied to the British organization Political and Economic Planning (PEP), a non-partisan research agency created in 1933 to help deal with Britain's social and economic problems. PEP issued a series of influential reports dealing with industry, economic development, and issues of social concern, and contributed to the state planning and nationalization of industry that reached its apex under Chamberlain in the late 1930s.[48] According to *Today and Tomorrow*, PEP and its publication of the same name were the vehicles of international Jewish finance. Having publicized the fact that PEP was headed by a Jew, Israel Moses Sieff,[49] the paper implicated him with other alleged conspirators: "New York sources associate Mr. Sieff with the group of Jews which includes Mr. Felix Frankfurter and Mr. Bernard Baruch, both of Mr. Roosevelt's 'Brains Trust,' and has included the late Justice Louis Brandeis, and the late Mr. Jacob Schiff, of Kuhn Loeb and Company, who were interested, financially and otherwise, in the establishment of ... the Soviet State in Russia." The party organ also blamed Max, Paul, and James Warburg "and others of the same breed" for helping to create PEP. It was they who had "plunged the democratic nations into poverty, unemployment and economic stress, built up the dictatorships, propagated revolution and socialism in this fertile soil, set up the machinery for the coming tyranny – as for example ... PEP ... – and entrenched a vast network of cartels dominated by Nazi Germany, and set the stage for the present war."[50] Thus, according to *Today and Tomorrow*, PEP was one more example of the far-reaching nature of the international financial Jewish conspiracy.

This conspiracy-theorizing extended to domestic affairs as well. *Today and Tomorrow* warned that the Canadian government's wartime planning was a further example of the ubiquitous international conspiracy. Specifically, it accused the Rowell-Sirois Commission, which suggested centralization of industry and introduction of price controls, of being connected to Union Now and hence the international conspirators.[51] It also blamed Bernard Baruch, American financier, presidential adviser, and Jew, for Canada's adoption of wage and price controls. The paper surmised that Baruch, who had become "virtually dictator of the U.S.A.," had imposed his proposals for "rigid price ceilings" on Canada. Consequently, implementation of the Baruch proposals was creating a similar dictatorship north of the border, making Baruch "one of the most sinister figures in the orbit of International Finance."[52]

For *Today and Tomorrow*, any attempts at wartime centralization were proof of the international financial conspiracy. When the Allied powers began to discuss a world bank based on the gold standard, the party organ became very alarmed. It vehemently criticized attempts to restore the "obsolete, outworn gold standard" and impose it on the Western democracies. In the paper's opinion "this diabolical gold standard which a few men control and use for the enslavement of humanity" was the epitome of evil, and it exhorted Canadians to "refuse to bow before this false worship of mammon or else future civilization will be far worse than mankind has ever experienced."[53] The paper also predicted that the term "dollar" would be abandoned when the new international currency was introduced, and in its place "both saints and cynics claim 'shekel' will be used." In another issue *Today and Tomorrow* vowed that schemes advocating international organizations like Union Now or "World Federal Union" meant a return to the gold standard, "and it means BACK – DOWN – AND OUT: It means a world of beggars!"[54]

Clearly, the agenda of *Today and Tomorrow* was to prove, implicitly and at times explicitly, the existence of an international financial, Jewish conspiracy. This was certainly the conclusion of Richard Needham, columnist for the *Calgary Herald*. On 2 February 1942 he wrote an editorial exposing the pervasive anti-Semitism in *Today and Tomorrow* and connecting Social Credit's anti-Semitic philosophy with those of Nazi and fascist leaders. Citing numerous examples to show how the party organ "rarely loses an opportunity to throw an oblique punch at the Jews," he wondered why Premier Aberhart allowed such anti-Semitism: "It seems strange for it to have the official sanction – however indirect – of a democratic government. English-speaking governments should not need to descend to this kind of vulgarity."

Upon reading Needham's article, two Alberta lawyers and local Congress officers, L.M. Fradkin of Calgary and H.A. Friedman of Edmonton, agreed that the anti-Semitism in *Today and Tomorrow*, if allowed to go unchecked, "may develop into something serious to the

Jewish people of Alberta and Canada."[55] They decided to approach Aberhart directly, confront him with the fact that his party organ contained anti-Semitism, and if possible persuade him to bring *Today and Tomorrow* into line. Friedman made plans to meet Aberhart in Edmonton but was not optimistic about this meeting. As he stated to Fradkin, "I am sure [Aberhart] will disclaim any Anti-Semitism so far as he personally is concerned and also in respect to his party in this Province, but this in itself is of little value to us." In Friedman's opinion, getting *Today and Tomorrow* to quit publishing anti-Semitic statements "is about all we can hope to accomplish."[56]

However, plans were rearranged so that Rabbi Solomon Frank, executive director of the Winnipeg JPRC, would meet with Aberhart, who had gone to Winnipeg to attend a Social Credit conference. It was now incumbent upon the rabbi to confront the premier. Although they apparently had a candid discussion, one might conjecture that this meeting would have gone differently had Friedman, a lawyer, confronted Aberhart on their home turf. Yet Frank later told a fellow Congress officer that he found Aberhart "most cordial, convincing and sincere in his reactions" to the issues he raised, namely the anti-Semitic statements of Social Credit politicians and specifically those of MP Jaques, whose letter in the *Western Producer* had greatly distressed Congress. In the course of their discussion, stated Frank, Aberhart gave him the following assurances:

1 That anti-semitism and racial hatred of any kind are entirely foreign to [Aberhart's] own philosophy of life.
2 That [Aberhart] deprecated most strongly any anti-Semitic tendencies on the part of members of his party. Furthermore that he had taken it upon himself … to express himself in accordance with this thought to those of his party who were guilty of anti-semitic statements. Though he would want his party to be clear from any racial or religious biases of any kind, he of course could not be held responsible for isolated utterances, particularly when these ran counter to his way of thinking.
3 That if, in spite of [Aberhart's] repeated warnings to the contrary, these anti-semitic utterances on the part of his membership were to continue, he would take whatever steps he possibly could in order to definitely squelch any anti-semitic tendency.

Frank added that Aberhart "seemed sincerely upset by the actions of those within his party that would seek to connect him with anything of an anti-semitic character." Although Aberhart did not ask that their conversation be kept confidential, Frank felt that any statement made by a man in public office must be treated with a certain degree of confidence. Accordingly, he insisted that Aberhart's statements not be publicized.[57]

Two aspects of this exchange are noteworthy. The first is that Aberhart did not dispute the fact that certain Social Crediters were spouting anti-Semitism. Rather, he adopted a tone of apology and even personal injury on hearing that members of his movement were engaging in such destructive actions. This stance is significant because it would not be continued after Aberhart's death. After 1943 Social Credit's anti-Semitism would become more daring and more vocal, and Social Credit leaders like Solon Low and even Premier Manning would deny that their party was anti-Semitic. The second noteworthy aspect is that the exchange between Frank and Aberhart was congenial and genuine. Aberhart told Frank at the end of their conversation that he would be happy to listen to any representation the rabbi cared to make to him at any time.[58] In a similar show of respect, Frank asked Alberta Congress officers not to publicize their meeting.[59] However, such conventions of etiquette did little to solve the real problem, which was the promotion of anti-Semitism by certain Social Crediters and the party organ. Aberhart's assurances aside, little was done to silence Jaques or *Today and Tomorrow*. Consequently, an opportunity for Congress to publicize the dangers of Social Credit's anti-Semitism and, even more importantly, to publicize Aberhart's acknowledgment of the problem had been relinquished.

Yet Congress continued to scrutinize Social Credit's anti-Semitism in the following months.[60] In spring 1943 Congress's national executive director, Saul Hayes, wrote to Rosenberg indicating that something needed to be done about Jaques, and inquired whether any Congress agents near Wetaskiwin knew the MP.[61] Rosenberg told Hayes he had been watching Jaques's antics for some years, subscribing to *Today and Tomorrow*, and scrutinizing Jaques's articles and Aberhart's transcribed broadcasts. He remarked that Jaques was like the great majority of Social Credit "fanatics" who had swallowed all the propaganda regarding the *Protocols* and international Jewish bankers, and noted that the MP never missed an opportunity to inject anti-Semitic remarks into his speeches and articles. Rosenberg also noted that in recent months the main theme of Aberhart's broadcasts had been the link between an international financial conspiracy led by plotting capitalists and socialists and the LSE, where the conspirators made their headquarters. According to Aberhart, this conspiracy was also behind Union Now, whose object was to enslave Canada and Great Britain to the United States. In Rosenberg's view, Aberhart was no less culpable than his more overtly anti-Semitic colleagues: "The only difference between Wm. Aberhart and Norman Jaques is that Mr. Jaques repeatedly inserts the word 'Jewish' between 'international financiers,' whereas Aberhart omits the word 'Jewish' leaving you to guess."[62]

Consequently, Rosenberg believed that Social Credit's anti-Semitism was increasingly serious. "I have long felt that this is no longer a question of ignoring a crank [Jaques], but it is a question of countering the activities of a group of men as crazy as the [William Dudley] Pelleys and [Father Charles] Coughlins in the United States and equally as dangerous." He told Hayes he had discussed the problem of Jaques with the Winnipeg JPRC and some Alberta Congress agents. However, "the tendencies in the past among some of our friends in Alberta has been to urge us to leave the matter alone, since the Social Crediters [form] the Provincial Government in that province, and since Norman Jaques is supposed to be a very sick man with an incurable disease who will soon bother us no longer. Personally, I am inclined to take the matter more seriously, and believe that the activities of the Social Credit Party and its speakers ... from Wm. Aberhart ... downwards, are sufficiently dangerous to merit active opposition."[63] Hayes was impressed with Rosenberg's assessment and agreed Jaques needed to be taken more seriously.[64] Yet in the following months Congress took no concrete action against Jaques or Social Credit. According to Rosenberg, Congress's inaction was a result of the Alberta branch's unwillingness to create unnecessary problems by confronting the provincial government, and national headquarters' inability to lead any concerted action four provinces away. Although he may have been correct about some Alberta officers and agents, in fact there were others just as determined as he to confront Social Credit. The impetus for their actions was exposure of the anti-Semitism within the Alberta Social Credit Board.

The Alberta Social Credit Board had been created in 1937 to quash an imminent party revolt by insurgent backbenchers who believed Aberhart had no intention of implementing Douglas's Social Credit theories. They wanted to obtain either Douglas or one of his top aides to serve as the "expert" who would finally bring Social Credit to Alberta. In June 1937 Douglas sent two emissaries, G.F. Powell and L.D. Byrne, to mend the rift between the Douglasites and the government. The board was organized as part of the Alberta civil service and was composed of a commission of five experts who were expected to administer Social Credit theory and make recommendations for Social Credit legislation.[65] Although Powell was soon jailed for libellous activities,[66] Byrne carried on as the board's technical adviser. Others who served on the board through its ten-year existence included MLAs A.J. Hooke, Norman B. James, R.E. Ansley, Floyd M. Baker, William Tomyn, and A.V. Bourcier. After 1938–39, when the board's Social

Credit legislation was declared *ultra vires*, it abandoned its original mandate and became the propaganda arm of the Alberta government.[67] Its main task was now the stocking, advertising, and distribution of Social Credit literature. Significantly, the vast majority of this literature was blatantly anti-Semitic, and a substantial proportion did not even refer to Social Credit theories. The board advertised many of Douglas's books, such as *The Big Idea, The Brief for the Prosecution, The Land for the (Chosen) People Racket, Programme for the Third World War,* and *Social Credit.*

The Social Credit Board also advertised the works of Nesta Webster, a notorious anti-Semite from England who had a strong influence on Douglas and whose conspiracy theories rivalled his own. Webster, a member of the British Fascists, was an arch conspiracy-hunter who headed crusades against various esoteric movements. In her works she specifically attacked Jews and Judaism because they ostensibly formed part of the web of secret societies that desired world domination. Some of her anti-Semitic treatises (which were used by extreme right-wing groups in the United States and Canada) included *Secret Societies and Subversive Movements, The Surrender of an Empire, Socialist Network,* and *World Revolution.*[68] As Rosenberg noted, none of these works dealt with Social Credit theories, but all focused on anti-Jewish propaganda.[69] Significantly, the Social Credit Board disseminated Webster's and Douglas's literature through its office in the Alberta legislative buildings, through *Today and Tomorrow,* and at Social Credit meetings. In addition, it published its own pamphlets, many written by Social Credit politicians, which included anti-Semitic references.[70] The board also submitted to the legislature annual reports that, as C.B. Macpherson notes, "came to contain practically nothing about the work for which it had been established, on which indeed there was nothing to report, but more than made up for this, at length, by elaborate restatements of the world plot thesis."[71]

For example, the board's 1942 annual report stated: "The evidence is overwhelming that the objective of International Finance in the present struggle centred in the war is the destruction for all practical purposes, of the British Commonwealth of Nations as the bulwark of democracy." The report attacked Union Now as "poisonous propaganda," "the voice of finance," and "an evil plot," while dismissing Britain's 1942 Beveridge Report as a "deceptive document" and "parsimonious scheme" leading to "ultimate disaster." Technical adviser Byrne was a leading proponent of the board's anti-Semitism. At a meeting before the Rocky Mountain House Board of Trade in May 1943, he explained how the "deplorable pre-war conditions" of the

1930s were the result of an international financial conspiracy that had wreaked havoc in all democratic countries. He postulated that the conspirators had "a deliberate world plan to establish totalitarianism and the enslavement of the individual" through German Nazism and Russian socialism, and that both were linked to Karl Marx and Friedrich Engels, who were "of the same racial origin and philosophy." Significantly, Byrne's speech was reprinted in *Today and Tomorrow*, and the board published it as a pamphlet entitled *Battle for Freedom*.[72]

A few weeks after Byrne's speech in Rocky Mountain House, James A. MacPherson, leader of the Labour-Progressive party in Alberta, wrote a scathing article in the *Canadian Tribune* condemning Byrne's and the board's anti-Semitism. He pointed out that the Alberta legislature financed the board, which then used these public funds to "disseminate ... the most violent anti-Jewish material." While the board conducted a "deliberate campaign to destroy the United Nations alliance and to obstruct Canada's war effort against Hitlerism," *Today and Tomorrow* disseminated "pro-fascist propaganda" and "anti-Jewish material." MacPherson quoted from two pamphlets distributed by the board: the first, entitled *True Prosperity*, claimed that "the American and French revolutions were utilized by the Jews to gain control of world finance" and that "in 1932 President Roosevelt promised to drive the money changers from the temple, but to date has been unsuccessful ... Perhaps if he got rid of B.M. Baruch, the Jew, and all his associates he might be successful." The other pamphlet, entitled *Rending of the Veil*, stated that "there was an agreement between Karl Marx and the Jewish bankers ... The Jewish bankers entered into an agreement with the Marxists as to the necessity of starting the conquest of Russia." MacPherson quoted Byrne's recent anti-Semitic speech and added that Premier Aberhart "brands all opposition and criticism, and all post-war proposals such as the Beveridge and Marsh reports, as schemes of 'sinister international money sharks, revolutionary financiers, Marxists, Socialists, Communists, totalitarians, internationalists and money bags.'" In short, MacPherson provided a sweeping indictment of Social Credit's anti-Semitism. He revealed a provincial government that condemned wartime measures such as rental control, price control, national selective service, and labour-management councils as the first steps towards national socialism in Canada, and that deemed the Beveridge and Marsh reports as well as the United Nations itself to be schemes conjured up by international communistic financiers. According to MacPherson, leading Social Credit politicians believed that communism, fascism, and Nazism were one and the same, and that Jews were involved in all three "conspiracies."[73] No one reading this article could ignore the serious allegations against Social Credit, and it certainly did not go unnoticed among Alberta Congress officials.

Although there were several reactions among Congress officials to the article, it was Fradkin of Calgary who took the lead. Aberhart had died on 23 May 1943, and there was hope within the Alberta branch that, regarding the promise to eliminate anti-Semitism, Manning would do what Aberhart had not. Accordingly, after seeking Rosenberg's advice, Fradkin decided to try to end the anti-Semitism in *Today and Tomorrow* by confronting the new premier.[74] He recalled that the previous winter Alberta Congress officers had planned to interview Aberhart over the same issue, but no meeting had transpired. Now, in light of MacPherson's article, Fradkin was unwilling to let matters slide any longer. In a letter to Moe Lieberman, an Edmonton Congress officer, Fradkin stated: "We are greatly perturbed over this matter, and it is absolutely essential that some action be taken forthwith. My [Calgary] Committee is prepared to co-operate with your [Edmonton] Committee in every way and, if necessary, to assist you in the proposed interview [of Manning] ... we consider this matter of the utmost importance."[75] Yet Lieberman replied that someone in fact had spoken to Aberhart in February 1942 regarding the anti-Semitism in *Today and Tomorrow* and "since that [meeting] no articles appeared in *Today and Tomorrow* which were objectionable." He noted that Edmonton Congress officers were still subscribing to *Today and Tomorrow* and were perusing the paper carefully.[76]

Lieberman's response is very peculiar. First, there is no evidence of a meeting between Edmonton Congress officers and Aberhart in February 1942, although it cannot be assumed that it did not occur. But it is curious that there was no correspondence on the matter. Moreover, it is quite incredible that any Congress officer perusing *Today and Tomorrow* would state that since February 1942 no articles had been "objectionable" – that is, anti-Semitic. An examination of the paper during these months reveals a consistent infusion of anti-Semitism. It seems there was poor communication between the Edmonton and Calgary committees. Lieberman admitted to Fradkin: "There is no question ... that the statements made by members of the Social Credit Board and their attacks in particular against international financiers are anti-semitic. This problem has for some time been receiving our careful consideration and attention."[77] Yet despite these declarations of vigilance, Lieberman and the Edmonton committee were unwilling to take advantage of the *Tribune's* exposé. Eventually the issue blew over, and nothing was done. It is possible the Edmonton officers were

determined not to create problems for themselves by openly confronting Social Credit, or there may have been jurisdictional in-fighting
between the Edmonton and Calgary committees. It is plausible that
the Edmonton officers saw Social Credit as their concern since the
government was in their city, and wanted to deal with Manning as
they deemed fit. Perhaps traditional jealousies between the two cities
were being played out within the Alberta branch of Congress. Whatever conjectures may be offered, the result was that Alberta Congress
officers did not confront Manning in 1943.

Throughout that summer Rosenberg continued to scrutinize Social
Credit's anti-Semitism from his office in Winnipeg. By this time he
harboured no illusions about the late premier's promises to quell anti-
Semitism in his movement. In a letter to Harry Olyan, a Congress
agent in Vegreville, Alberta, Rosenberg stated: "There can be no
possible doubt that the whole ... Social Credit ideology and propaganda is honey-combed with anti-semitism ... The late Mr. William
Aberhart, although he claimed to be well disposed towards Jews, and
denied being anti-semitic, nevertheless did nothing whatsoever to prevent prominent members of his Party from repeating anti-semitic statements. In fact he made similar charges about International Bankers
and International Conspiracies. The only difference was that he was
careful to omit the word Jewish in any of his public statements."
Rosenberg was determined that something must be done, and others
shared his conviction. Vegreville Congress agents were planning to
confront Solon Low, provincial treasurer of the Alberta government.
The national JPRC was also assessing the situation, and Rosenberg
inferred its position was that, "unless the Social Credit Party in Alberta
and throughout Canada can be induced to repudiate the anti-semitic
remarks of Mr. Blackmore, Mr. Jaques and Mr. Hlynka, and to expel
them from the Party, if they refuse to cease making anti-semitic statements, then we shall have to face them as an open enemy of the Jewish
people."[78] In Rosenberg's mind the JPRC was planning to take a strong
stand and was even willing to oppose the Alberta government openly.
However, it is unlikely that Congress had such a dramatic plan in
mind; in fact, the JPRC did not execute *any* action that summer.

Yet the summer of 1943 was not without incident. Shortly after
Aberhart's death a letter sent by Jaques to one O. Reidell in Swift
Current, Saskatchewan, eventually landed on the desk of Congress's
general secretary, H.M. Caiserman. Reidell, a concerned private citizen,
had corresponded with Jaques and engaged in debate over the latter's
employment of the *Protocols* in the House of Commons and the press.
Reidell was clearly antagonistic towards the MP's anti-Semitism, and

when Jaques sent him a letter explaining his views, Reidell forwarded it to Congress. Jaques's letter, written on House of Commons stationery, reveals a man who was blatantly anti-Semitic:

All History proves that no nation can tolerate control by the Jews ... I have never said that the *Protocols* are genuine. I do say that what they predict is now coming to pass ... The attempt to destroy the *Protocols*, and to threaten, and intimidate those who mention them is a good indication of what we may expect if these people have their way. You have to remember the Jews control all means of gathering news and of propaganda, so that we hear one side of the case ... Before the war millions of Russians died of starvation, or were done to death ... But all we hear about is Jewish suffering and persecution. The Jews['] religion is that they are the chosen people and that the gentiles are cattle (goyim) and that it is no crime to exploit them, which is the reason for their persecution in reprisal ... I am against surrender of any sovereign power to international control – the Jew[s] being the only people, and money the only thing which is international. Hence I defend the Crown against the "3 brass balls" of Shylock, Ricardo and Marx.[79]

Caiserman handed the letter to Rosenberg, who wrote Reidell thanking him for informing Congress. "It is indeed regrettable," stated Rosenberg, "that at this time when unity and mutual understanding among all citizens of Canada is so necessary, that Mr. Jaques, a member of the House of Commons should abuse his privileges by spreading the same antisemitic propaganda which is peddled by Goebbels and the Nazis."[80] Rosenberg circulated copies of Jaques's letter to Congress's Central and Western Divisions and to the Edmonton and Calgary JPRCS. He also sent a copy to M.J. Coldwell, national leader of the CCF. Coldwell had tangled with Jaques several times in the House of Commons over Jaques's attempts to read excerpts of the *Protocols* into *Hansard*. Rosenberg told Coldwell he could use the letter to expose Jaques when he pled innocence to charges of anti-Semitism. He added that Jaques's accusation that "'Jews control all means of gathering news and of propaganda' is a choice one, particularly since there is not a single general daily newspaper printed in Canada owned or controlled in any way by a Jew. The source of Mr. Jaques' inspiration and information is revealed when he translates the Hebrew word 'goyim' in his letter as cattle. This false translation was given in the Nazi propaganda spread throughout Canada before the war. The true translation of the word 'goyim' as any Hebrew scholar will tell you is 'nations.' The Greek word is 'gentile.'"[81]

Shortly thereafter Rosenberg wrote an extensive memorandum describing Jaques's employment of the *Protocols* and sent it to

Congress officers in Montreal, Toronto, Winnipeg, Edmonton, and Calgary. He summarized Social Credit's anti-Semitic theories, which included the bogeys of the gold standard, the banking system, the *Protocols*, the Bank of England, the LSE, the Federal Reserve Bank, and Union Now. He discussed Jaques's anti-Semitism as well as that of Anthony Hlynka, MP for Vegreville, and John Blackmore, MP for Lethbridge and leader of the New Democracy (Social Credit) party. Rosenberg re-emphasized that the late Aberhart, although denying that he had ever mentioned the word "Jewish" in his attacks on "International Bankers," none the less made the same charges as Jaques but merely omitted the word "Jewish" from his diatribes. Through Aberhart's radio addresses, *Today and Tomorrow*, and Jaques's antics, a wide audience received Social Credit's anti-Semitism. Moreover, stated Rosenberg,

in the past the tendency has been to ignore Mr. Jaques as being an old and sick man who is not taken seriously by anybody. Because of the position which he holds, and the privileges which he abuses in the House of Commons, I do not believe it will be wise to ignore his activities, and the antisemitic activities of Social Credit members of Parliament in general any longer. While it may be advisable to approach Mr. Blackmore, the Leader of the Social Credit or New Democracy Party in the House of Commons, and Mr. Manning the Premier of Alberta, and endeavour to secure from them a repudiation of the antisemitic remarks of Mr. Jaques and other Social Credit members, nevertheless I believe little [if] any value can be accomplished by doing so. References to the *Protocols of the Elders of Zion*, to international Bankers and any other antisemitic remarks have become too much an integral party of the Propaganda and policy of the Social Credit Party in Canada to be repudiated by its leaders.[82]

Rosenberg had provided a hard-hitting assessment of Social Credit's anti-Semitism, and he exhorted Congress to create an effective public relations policy to eradicate it. He recommended that the entire matter be brought before the next meeting of the national JPRC so that a formal plan could be adopted to deal with Jaques, Social Credit, and their use of the *Protocols*. He further advised that this policy be adopted in conjunction with JPRC officers from Alberta. One wonders whether Rosenberg was frustrated with Congress's inability or unwillingness to adopt a more aggressive approach. This was not the first time he had outlined the Social Credit threat and recommended that Congress adopt more assertive measures. Yet there is no evidence that the JPRC considered his suggestion, even though it soon obtained further evidence corroborating Jaques's anti-Semitism.

A few weeks after Congress received the documentation from Reidell, another private citizen relayed similar information. He was William Steiner, a Jew from Vancouver who had written to Jaques in an attempt to persuade him to end his anti-Semitic attacks. Jaques again responded on House of Commons stationery, which Steiner forwarded to Congress. Jaques stated: "Your people complain of the way they are regarded – and treated by others, but do they not regard themselves as different – set apart from all other races and creeds? Are they not the 'Chosen people?'" Jaques told Steiner that the percentage of Jews among communists was much higher than the percentage of Jews among the entire population, and although he was not "complaining" about this fact, he wondered: "Why did the Communists violently oppose any armed resistance to Hitler until he invaded Russia in 1941? Are we to suppose that Hitler was neither a Jew-baiter, nor a 'Fascist,' until that time? Or was it that the 'Communists' thought it more worthwhile to destroy the capitalists than to rescue the Jews of Europe? Why do the Jews and the Communists continue to support one another after this callous treatment?" He then referred to the millions of Russian peasants who had been liquidated in bloody purges since the Russian Revolution, and asked: "Why is there *no propaganda* on *their* behalf? Is it because these unfortunate people are non Jewish, and because Jews engineered the revolution and have since controlled the communist party in Russia[?] To whom are Jews loyal? To Canada or to Jewry?" Finally, he expressed scepticism about the existence of European Jewish refugees: "If Jews are under the control of Hitler, how can they be free to leave Europe? If they are so free how can they be persecuted?"[83]

Congress received Steiner's letter and duly noted Jaques's blatant anti-Semitism, but made no attempt to publicize his Jew hatred. It was a telling commentary on the effectiveness of Congress that concerned private citizens, Jews and non-Jews alike, were more willing than Congress to confront Social Credit's leading anti-Semite. In fairness, during this period Congress was fighting fires of more immediate danger. By this time the extent of Nazi destruction of European Jewry was well known among the Allied nations; yet, despite Congress's extensive efforts, the Canadian government refused to open its doors to Jewish refugees. On this issue as well Congress's officers and agents – at the national, regional, and local level – questioned their organization's effectiveness and criticized its passive "cap-in-hand" approach.[84] It appeared that Congress needed a more aggressive public relations policy on a variety of fronts, both foreign and domestic.

It cannot be presumed that Congress was not attempting to solve its public relations problems. Late in 1943, in response to a request from general secretary Caiserman, Rosenberg (now the Western Division's executive director) listed "three outstanding cases of Public Relations work accomplished this year in the Western Division." First, the western JPRC had exposed the anti-Semitic activities of MPs Hlynka and Jaques. Second, it had traced the frequent attacks on Jews by Social Credit MPs and in *Today and Tomorrow* to anti-Semitic sources in the United States and to Nazi propaganda, and was keeping political leaders and the non-Jewish press informed of such connections. Third, the western JPRC had challenged Jaques's allegations that Streit, founder of Union Now, was a German Jew and that Union Now was instigated by "German-Jewish bankers" in order to subordinate Canada and Great Britain to the United States. In rebuttal, the JPRC had obtained information from Streit himself that he was not Jewish but a Christian of remote German origin, and that charges concerning proposed Anglo-Canadian domination were entirely false. Lastly, in response to Blackmore's and Jaques's charges that the Bank of England was controlled by "international German-Jewish bankers," the JPRC obtained evidence that there was not a single Jewish director of any kind on the Bank of England and that there had not been for several years.[85]

These were not insignificant accomplishments. During this early phase, educational anti-defamation work was the basis of Congress's public relations work, and both the national and regional JPRCs worked dedicatedly to refute allegations against Jews. Certainly, the Western Division and especially Rosenberg were keeping a watchful eye on Social Credit. But adopting more assertive measures towards Social Credit would not be accomplished easily, mostly because Congress still believed that educational work, moral suasion, and amicability would convince Social Credit to abandon its anti-Semitism. Even worse, while others openly confronted Social Credit in the press, Congress's national headquarters and the Alberta branch deliberated on methods. To Rosenberg's dismay, only Rabbi Frank had met with Aberhart, and little had been accomplished. Meanwhile, the party organ and anti-Semites like Jaques spewed their conspiratorial rhetoric at will. Although Congress was extremely displeased with the situation, at this stage it did not possess the public relations tools to achieve anything further.

4 Denials and Duplicity

By the time Ernest Manning took over the premiership of Alberta in the spring of 1943, the Canadian Jewish Congress was convinced that Social Credit's anti-Semitism was an entrenched part of the movement and would not be eradicated easily. As the war progressed, so too did Social Credit's denunciations of Allied co-operation and plans to create an international peacekeeping association for the post-war period, which it viewed as part of the international financial Jewish conspiracy. Even more disturbing for Congress was Social Credit's propaganda opposing the acceptance of Jewish refugees and accusing them of fabricating the extent of their persecution to further the aims of the Jewish world plotters. In spite of the increasingly offensive nature of Social Credit's propaganda, Congress's public relations philosophy remained predominantly passive. Yet some Congress officers and agents, especially those in the eye of the storm, believed that more direct action was necessary and that educational anti-defamation work and moral suasion were insufficient.

In early 1944 the Alberta branch adopted a more confrontational approach to Social Credit when Harry Olyan of Vegreville met with Solon Low, now minister of education and provincial treasurer. Olyan gave Low copies of letters written by MP Jaques (whose letters to Reidell and Steiner were likely among them), as well as copies of Jaques's anti-Semitic statements in the House of Commons. After speaking with Low about the injurious nature of Social Credit's anti-Semitism, Olyan "obtained the promise of Mr. Solon Low, who is originally a Mormon – a very sympathetic and liberal person – to do

his very best to stop Mr. Jaques' anti-semitic utterances and activities."
Low told Olyan that he had already talked to Jaques and hoped there
would be no reason for further complaints.[1] Olyan seemed appeased
by Low's assurances and did not pursue the matter further.

Upon hearing of Olyan's encounter with Low, Louis Rosenberg
wrote to H.M. Caiserman, Congress's general secretary, expressing his
opinion that such a meeting was futile. He emphasized that Jaques's
anti-Semitic remarks were only the most overt manifestation of a much
deeper problem, one that would not be solved by Low's quick assurances. The problem was Social Credit's conspiratorial philosophy,
which was promoted by Douglas and embraced to varying degrees by
Manning, Jaques, Blackmore, Low, and others. This philosophy, stated
Rosenberg, was that "'an international German (Jewish) financial
conspiracy,' led by communists, socialists and international bankers
keeps Canada in slavery, and wishes to bring about an amalgamation
of Canada with Great Britain and the United States under the control
of American and London Jewish bankers, and that the Social Credit
Party in Canada wishes to save Canada from this awful fate." The
only difference between Jaques and the others, Rosenberg asserted,
was that Jaques spoke openly about "international Jewish bankers"
and had no qualms about listing various Jewish names, whereas Manning, Blackmore, and Low used the same propaganda and quoted from
the same list of names, but merely omitted the word "Jewish." Therefore, he concluded, "I am strongly of the opinion that nothing can or
will be accomplished by approaching individual members such as Mr.
Solon Low, and accepting their assurances of friendship."[2] In Rosenberg's view, the idea of an international Jewish financial conspiracy
was too deeply ingrained in Social Credit philosophy for individual
expressions of friendship to mean much. As later events would show,
he was correct about Low, who revealed himself to be as avid an
adherent of Social Credit's anti-Semitic philosophy as Douglas himself.

Another development in early 1944 showed that, despite its lagging
public relations approach, Congress was still willing to confront the
Social Credit problem. General secretary Caiserman and L.D. Morosnick, a Congress agent and lawyer in Winnipeg, discussed plans to force
Today and Tomorrow to cease publication. Caiserman advocated legal
action in the form of personal affidavits by various Jews protesting the
anti-Semitic propaganda in *Today and Tomorrow*.[3] Morosnick, believing that affidavits would not be of much use, argued that the real goal
was to determine whether the party organ was a menace and whether
it was doing grave injustice to the Jewish people and to Canada. If this
were the case, Congress must ensure that the party organ was suppressed and put out of business. In Morosnick's opinion, too much

attention was being devoted to not offending the "interests" of certain "friends" – that is, those Social Credit politicians who were on good terms with Jews in Alberta and elsewhere. If Congress were to achieve any success in stopping Social Credit's anti-Semitism, he argued, it would have to take a much harder line: "The sooner your committee grapples with that problem realistically the better for all concerned including the very publication which we desire to suppress."[4]

Caiserman appreciated Morosnick's strong stance but emphasized to him that "we live in a free country, where all kinds of racketeers operate within or outside of the law ... Congress is not a better business bureau, and cannot determine which act is an act of racketeering and is to be suppressed, since we should not compete with the Police. Under these circumstances Congress, truthfully speaking, cannot handle the problem, unless Jewish public opinion would be so organized and Congress be given such authority – which as yet it does not possess – to deal with a problem of this nature when it presents itself. The most important Public Relation item possible is one which prevents anti-semitism, and we are doing enough work in this respect to please even such a discriminating person as you." Thus, with regard to preventative anti-defamation work Caiserman believed that the JPRC was doing a "really good and fine job," but in counteracting existing anti-Semitism, it could not deal successfully with all such manifestations. As for attempts to combat Social Credit's anti-Semitism specifically, "I am of the sincere and honest opinion that neither Congress, nor B'Nai B'Rith, nor any group of individuals who are responsible, can do a real job on the matter under discussion."[5]

This was an accurate portrayal of Congress's current public relations philosophy, but it was not what Morosnick wanted to hear, and he minced no words. It was "trite," he chastised Caiserman, to say that Congress was not a better-business bureau and could not determine acts of racketeering. Whether Congress was accomplishing other goals or whether its activities pleased "such a discriminating person as myself" was not the issue. If there was a racketeering, anti-Semitic publication it was the duty of Congress and "all right-thinking Jews" to suppress such an evil, regardless of whether some "of their best friends" were involved in that practice. Further, stated Morosnick, "I am familiar with the very good work that the Congress, the B'nai B'rith and Canadian Public Relations Committees are doing but is there a limit to even the personal accomplishments of your Congress and these Committees[?] Do you ever arrive at a saturation point in Jewish life? Can you afford to sit back and say that we have done enough or that there is no more work to be done[?] If you want to be realistic and are honest this is one of the most important things which should occupy the attention of the Congress in its local activities."[6]

Morosnick had incisively assessed the limitations of Congress's public relations philosophy. It is significant that the most serious criticisms came from Congress's Western Division, which was clearly more *au courant* with Social Credit's impact than national headquarters. While western Jewry considered Social Credit to be a greater threat than did national headquarters, the discrepancy in perception between periphery and centre was only one aspect of the problem. The larger issue was national headquarters' response – that is, its reticence in creating a coherent, effective, national public relations policy that western Jewry could implement. Caiserman agreed with Morosnick that "Congress can certainly not afford the luxury of sinking back and saying that we have done enough," and he emphasized to him that national headquarters was not indifferent to any manifestation of anti-Semitism, including Social Credit's. "On the contrary, we are mobilizing all our ingenuity, intelligence and energies to meet each problem." However, he qualified, "to say that we always succeed would be an empty pretense."[7] Thus, the central question remained: would national headquarters be able to adopt a more assertive public relations approach to end Social Credit's anti-Semitism? The matter was in no way settled. Yet Caiserman seemed to understand the necessity of involving the west in creating a solution and agreed to hand the whole problem over to John Dower, a "hard-boiled businessman" and Edmonton Congress agent, to see if he could achieve some results.[8]

While Morosnick and Caiserman were debating Congress's public relations philosophy, Social Credit was confronting the issue of anti-Semitism in its own ranks. Since Manning had taken over the helm, he had been confronted with an entrenched faction of Social Credit purists who promoted Douglas's economic and political theories and their concomitant anti-Semitism. Although Manning embraced many of Douglas's Social Credit theories and wholeheartedly attacked the international financial conspiracy,[9] he was less comfortable with the Douglasites' anti-Semitism. Faced with an upcoming summer election and barraged by charges of Nazism by Alberta CCF leader Elmer Roper, Manning decided to wipe the pre-election slate clean. On 2 March 1944 he broadcast a statement in which he "unequivocally" repudiated anti-Semitism within Alberta Social Credit. However, his statement was remarkable for its equivocation:

It has been brought to my attention that an erroneous impression has been created in certain quarters that the Social Credit movement is anti-Semitic. Nothing could be further from the truth ... Social Credit is not opposed to any religion or race, as such. It is only when the adherents to any religion, or the people of any race take collective action as a group to attack the principles of Christianity and democracy which are fundamental to Social Credit that conflict arises ... In exposing and opposing the conspiracy of individuals and corporations seeking to impose a state of financial and economic dictatorship upon all nations the advocates of Social Credit consider it most important that the facts of the case be placed before the people irrespective of the color, race or creed of the conspirators.

Manning apparently believed it was both politically safe and morally correct to deny anti-Semitism but still expose the enemy of Christianity and democracy since its "color, race or creed" was irrelevant. But his repudiation of anti-Semitism rang hollow and became even more suspect when he compared Social Credit's battle against the international financial conspiracy with the party's fight against Nazism. He argued that because Nazi Germany attacked Christianity and democracy, this necessarily brought it in to conflict with Social Credit, which upheld these principles. "However," declared Manning, "we were not attacking Germans as Germans." He made no further comment, but the insinuation had been made: the fight against Nazism necessitated war against Germans, but no one doing so was anti-German *per se*. Likewise, the fight against the international financial conspiracy necessitated war against Jews, but no one doing so was anti-Semitic. Manning concluded by calling for "tolerance and co-operation," proclaiming that "in a properly functioning democracy we have to overcome the divisions of party politics, religion and racial origin which have been deliberately fostered by those who seek to enslave the people. In this crusade for human liberation there is no place for anti-Christianity, anti-Semitism, anti-Catholicism or anti-anything else."[10]

Rosenberg was not impressed by Manning's so-called repudiation. In correspondence with other Congress officers, Rosenberg remarked: "Evidently the leader of the Social Credit Party in Alberta does not like to be called an anti-semite, although he has done nothing to repudiate the repeated anti-semitic remarks which appear regularly in his official paper *Today and Tomorrow* and the anti-semitic statements made by the Social Credit members in the House of Commons." Moreover, "Premier Manning's repudiation is all very well, but is of little use as long as the party, its official paper; Mr. Blackmore, its official leader in the House of Commons and many of its prominent members continue to express their belief in the *Protocols of the Elders of Zion* and to attack persons merely because of their Jewish names." In other correspondence Rosenberg noted that notorious Jew-baiters like Jaques and Hlynka, instead of being reprimanded and their statements repudiated, were supported by the party's leaders. Again, Rosenberg emphasized that the only difference between blatant anti-Semites like Jaques and Hlynka and "more circumspect and careful men" like

Manning and the late Aberhart was that the former invoked the word "Jewish" in their fulminations about the international financial conspiracy whereas the latter "use the same arguments and the same phraseology but omit the word Jewish, leaving their true meaning to be understood." In short, Rosenberg's assessment of Manning's repudiation was sceptical at best: "Mr. Manning's repudiation is good insofar as it goes, but personally, I am far from convinced and I believe that the Social Credit party and its propaganda will bear careful watching insofar as its attitude towards Jews is concerned."[11] Rosenberg had good reason to be sceptical. This would not be the first time Manning would repudiate anti-Semitism within his movement while his colleagues continued to flaunt it.

It did not take long for Rosenberg's scepticism to be confirmed. Near the end of April 1944 an article in *Today and Tomorrow* revealed that Social Credit's anti-Semitism had not diminished. The article discussed the international financial conspirators who had schemed and plotted at the end of the First World War in order to achieve "world tyranny" and were plotting for the same goals during the present war. Names and corporations associated with the conspiracy included Max, Paul, and James Warburg, Kuhn, Loeb & Company, Dr Carl Melchior, Israel Moses Sieff, Sir Felix Schuster, Baron Schroeder, Otto Kahn, Kleinworth & Company, "and others of the same breed." Streit and Union Now, the Federal Reserve Bank, Britain's Political and Economic Planning organization, and compulsory state insurance schemes were evidence of the sinister character of the "New Order" that international finance was foisting on the Allies as the war neared its end.[12] The article contained the standard accusations and the standard bogeys. In a memorandum to Hayes, Rosenberg called it a "re-hash" and compared it to the writings of the Silver Shirts, an American right-wing extremist organization led by William Dudley Pelley: "In history, in sympathies, in propaganda and its attitude towards Jews, the Social Credit Party in Canada has shown itself closely allied with the isolationist, fundamentalist, fringe of cranks in the middle western United States, which were originally looked upon with amusement and contempt, but which have proved themselves so dangerous since the outbreak of the war."[13]

A few days later Rosenberg read two more disturbing articles in *Today and Tomorrow* that dealt with the Ontario government's recent anti-discrimination legislation and also an anti-discrimination bill introduced in the House of Commons by Angus MacInnis, CCF MP for Vancouver East.[14] The party organ called both pieces of legislation "muzzling bills." One article remarked that the Ontario legislation would now make it "illegal for a citizen of Ontario to attack any group for preaching atheism, to expose the activities of any racial groups engaged in disruptive activities or to denounce the mischievous and treacherous intrigues of the group of international gangsters who seek to destroy the British Commonwealth and democracy." Moreover, "both these measures are the thin edge of the wedge on enactments in all dictatorship countries having for their purpose the suppression of criticism against the ruling regime under savage penalties." The other article noted the "hidden power" and "sinister plan" behind such legislation: "Both measures obviously [intend] to suppress freedom of speech and protect its originators from exposure of something they are doing. Who is this hidden power? And what are they afraid of having exposed? ... Surely this evidence of an open attack on the constitutional liberties of Canadians should arouse them to action. Only a flood of protests ... is likely to thwart this further advance towards the Slave State."[15]

In response to these articles Rosenberg sent a memorandum to Hayes and other Congress officers. Noting that *Today and Tomorrow* had attacked both pieces of anti-discrimination legislation, he surmised that "the official organ of the Social Credit Party in Alberta counts the privilege of making defamatory statements against racial or religious groups an important weapon in its arsenal, and is strongly opposed to any legislation which would curb such attacks."[16] After reading Rosenberg's memorandum, Caiserman thanked him for the work he was doing and made a very telling remark: "I wish to express my appreciation for the trouble you are taking to document the activities of the Social Credit Party, chiefly because their actions are not taken seriously in Eastern Canada."[17] If Caiserman's statement is accepted *prima facie*, Congress's passive stance was in fact due to the indifference of national headquarters, notwithstanding his earlier assurances to Morosnick. It appears that Congress's inability to adopt an effective response *was* the result of its unwillingness to see Social Credit as a national problem. If this was the case – that national headquarters viewed Social Credit as a western concern of small import to the majority of Canadian Jewry – then little could be accomplished. Yet for his part national executive director Hayes very much wanted the issue of Social Credit's anti-Semitism to receive national attention, and he placed it on the agenda of the next national JPRC meeting so that appropriate action could be taken.[18]

That was the spring of 1944. Matters followed their regular course: Congress discussed, debated, and deliberated, and ultimately adopted no official policy to deal with Social Credit's anti-Semitism. Meanwhile, *Today and Tomorrow* continued to spout its conspiracy theories, especially about Allied plans for the post-war world. It pointed out that the "experts" at Bretton Woods and Dumbarton Oaks[19] had been trained at the London School of Economics (LSE), and dismissed both conferences as part of the international financial Jewish conspiracy. It viewed the creation of the United Nations Organization (UN) as the most dangerous of the post-war plans and announced that it too was driven by the conspirators. The paper's columnist, MLA Norman James, berated the federal government for its willingness to sacrifice Canadian democracy and sovereignty at the feet of the conspirators. Recalling the 1939 British royal visit to Canada, James remembered how "the whole country went wild with delight, at having [the King and Queen] with us ... Some of the higher ups even toured the country with them basking in reflected glory." Now, however, "these same people are suggesting ... that we no longer need our King and Queen, our Crown, our Constitution and the British Empire, and that we should transfer our loyalty to a mysterious, nondescript INTERNATIONAL POWER, composed of some off-colour individuals of no particular country, and who are incapable of loyalty except to Gold or its equivalent." In James's opinion, "if these saboteurs have their way," Germany's national socialism would develop into an "International Socialism with a gang of INTERNATIONAL FINANCIERS on top."[20]

The party organ also used Premier Manning's statements to bolster its stance against the UN. Like his more anti-Semitic colleagues, Manning publicly declared that the international conspirators had plotted the creation of the UN. Specifically, he argued that plans had been laid as early as 1939: "Ever since the first gun was fired in the war, a carefully laid conspiracy has been at work using the conditions created by the war in an effort to rob nations of their national sovereignty, to eliminate true democracy, to undermine the British Empire ... and to set up a World Dictatorship under a supreme international authority which would be able to dominate the economic life of every nation by controlling its money system, and its armed forces."[21] However, in keeping with his religious beliefs, Manning refrained from stating that the international conspiracy was Jewish.

For its part, *Today and Tomorrow* questioned the extent of Jewish persecution during the war and opposed attempts to assist "fraudulent" Jewish refugees. In one instance it described "the carefully organized campaign which is in full swing to win support for bringing tens of thousands of refugees to this country," noting that "those who are most vocal in demanding a haven for the refugees are persons known to hold communist or extreme socialist views." It also wondered how these "refugees" were able to escape: "If the refugees for which this plea is being made are the victims of Nazi persecution, how can they get away? Are the Nazis permitting them to leave? ... If the Nazis are allowing them to leave, then can they be described as victims of persecution? Unless it served the purpose of the Nazis, would they permit these refugees to leave? Is it probable that in the main these refugees are active communists whom the Nazis are only too glad to export in order that they may attack us from within? Can they be the spearhead of the Red Revolution?" The paper concluded that the Canadian economy was in a greater state of emergency than were the Jews of Europe: "Why this compassion and concern about the victims of Nazi persecution in Europe, and the callous indifference to the tens of thousands of Canadians who are the victims of financial persecution right here in our own country?" Indeed, many Canadians were worse off than the European refugees, because "they cannot escape anywhere." Accordingly, the paper judged, "charity should begin at home."[22]

Jaques's views on Jewish refugees were also covered in the party organ. In one issue he criticized Anna Louise Strong, contributor to *Maclean's* magazine, for her article describing the horrors of Nazi persecution of European Jews. Jaques called her a "Communist" and implied that she was working with other communists to spread propaganda "the purpose of which is so to harrow our sympathies that Canada will open her gates to an invasion army of Communist party workers." He announced that Jewish refugees were not "refugees" at all, and questioned why there was such a "determination" to bring them to Canada: "Why not compensate these victims by sending them to the Communist Paradise – Soviet Russia?" Jaques also wondered whether Jews were "the only, or even the chief, victims of Nazi persecution ... Is it not a fact that the Nazis persecute all their opponents? Do not the Jews form but a small percentage of these victims?"[23]

Congress was deeply concerned about Social Credit's forays into what would become known as Holocaust denial. Despite his earlier reticence about directly confronting Social Credit, Caiserman took its anti-Semitic propaganda very seriously. During the summer of 1944 he referred to Social Credit's conspiracy theorizing as one of the most blatant examples of race hatred in Canada at the time, and emphasized how important it was for the national, regional, and local JPRCs to "watch, explain and defend" against such attacks. He also made a broader statement regarding anti-Semitism in Canada: "Our neighbours must be convinced of the truth that anti-semitism is as much their problem as it is ours and that we must together extirpate it. The press, the elementary, secondary and higher educational institutions of the Dominion, the literature of the country, the political parties and organized labour must be reached and convinced that race-hatred is the common danger of a united Canada."[24] Caiserman's comments provide the first hint of Congress's changing public relations philosophy, which acknowledged that anti-defamation work focusing solely on Jewish issues was not entirely effective. As the war continued and as Social Credit's anti-Semitism progressed, Congress realized that refutation of anti-Semitic allegations achieved few results, and more forthright measures must be considered. In the shadow of mass anti-Semitic hysteria in Europe, Congress would begin to apply the bitter lessons of the war to its own situation by showing that race hatred damaged all society. And for some officers and agents of Congress, Social Credit was viewed as the worst threat to Canadian Jewry *and* Canadian society.

Notwithstanding Caiserman's insight and direction, it was not until the autumn of 1944 that another glaring example of Social Credit's anti-Semitism caused Congress to refocus its attention on creating a more effective response. This confrontation was between Jaques and Reverend C.E. Silcox, director of the Canadian Conference of Christians and Jews (CCCJ). In May 1944 Silcox, as editor of the CCCJ's monthly bulletin, *Fellowship*, published an address recently delivered by Rabbi Abraham Feinberg of Holy Blossom Temple in Toronto. Feinberg spoke about the crucifixion of Christ and how various interpretations of the crucifixion story contributed to anti-Semitism:

A surprisingly large group of scholars regards the stigma on Jews as the alleged murderers of Jesus to be the underlying cause of anti-Semitism. Taught in Sunday Schools, it becomes an integral part of the sub-conscious mental inheritance and intrudes on every judgment ... In recognition of this danger, as an obligation to truth, and because of the need to establish a ground-work for mutual fellowship in youth first of all, a group of 155 Protestant ministers in the United States last year agreed to revise the text-books now used in Christian Sunday-Schools, in order to expunge hatred-inciting, unauthentic and prejudiced accounts of the Jewish role in the crucifixion. A commission to change these books is now at work. God prosper its labors!

Feinberg reconstructed the story of the trial and crucifixion of Christ and noted that "the documentary basis for the charge that the Jews caused the death of Jesus can be found in only one of the four Gospels ... the Gospel of St. John, which students universally consider the least reliable of all and the one written after the longest interval."[25]

Feinberg's address appeared in the May 1944 edition of *Fellowship* without much notice. A few months later Jaques wrote a letter to the *Edmonton Bulletin* claiming that Silcox, the CCCJ, and *Fellowship* were all prominent Canadian "Leftists" and "Internationalists" who had "interlocking control." He misquoted Rabbi Feinberg as stating: "We must agree to expunge from our Sunday schools hatred-inciting, unauthentic, and prejudiced accounts of the Crucifixion. This account is to be found only in the Gospel of St. John which students universally consider the least reliable of all the Gospels." Jaques attributed to Silcox the demand that "we must look to the Old, not to the New Testament for our inspiration since ... the Gospels are unauthentic and anti-semitic." To these misrepresentations, Jaques ranted: "So the Christian Gospels now are labelled 'unreliable and unauthentic' – untrue, while St. John is named as an anti-semite." However, he proclaimed, "Ours still is a Christian nation, guided and inspired by Christian ideals."[26]

Jaques also raised the issue of wartime anti-Semitism, alleging that because nearly all Jews were communists, their attempts to raise the "bogey" of anti-Semitism was really a "communist smokescreen." In his mind, "anyone who publicly denounces the surrender of our national loyalties to international control is accused of 'anti-semitism'; (pro-fascism, anti-communism and anti-semitism – these terms mean the same to the communists.)" Moreover, it was only when Germany invaded Russia in 1941 that the "Commu-Socialists" regarded the Nazis as their enemies. Before 1941, although Jews "presumably ... suffered with the Gentiles ... oddly enough, the Jews then were of no concern to those who today are so alarmed about anti-semitism."[27] Jaques's strange logic was thus: since all Communists were Jews and they did not oppose Hitler until after 1941, Hitler must not have been persecuting them before this date. However, even if he had been, the Jew-communists were more concerned with supporting Russia than protecting their fellow Jews.

Jaques's rantings did not go unnoticed, by either Silcox or Congress. Silcox responded with his own letter in the *Edmonton Bulletin*. Regarding Feinberg's address, Silcox emphasized that "the learned rabbi was pleading for a revision of the attitude of many Christians towards the responsibility of the Jewish people for the crucifixion of Jesus ... when Mr. Jaques puts in quotes certain parts of the article, he should at least be fair enough to quote with accuracy." Silcox also traced the discrepancy between Feinberg's address and Jaques's rendition: "I leave it to the unprejudiced reader to judge how Mr. Jaques perverts a simple statement into a vague demand. It is not primarily a question of the authenticity of the gospels at all!" He also denied Jaques's charge that he was a "Commu-Socialist" and remarked that such a term was clearly "a kind of pink elephant haunting [Jaques's] fevered brain." Silcox concluded that "Mr. Jaques is doing exactly what he blames other people for doing. He accuses them of calling every anti-Semitic a fascist, and he simply reverses the procedure and calls everybody who seems to be defending the Jews a 'communist' or a commu-socialist, to use his own beautiful and original phrasing. He ought to brush the cobwebs out of his own mind, if he can locate it."[28]

Congress observed the public exchange between Jaques and Silcox, but, although Rosenberg and others corresponded on the matter, no one suggested further action. Silcox had defended himself and Feinberg effectively, and Congress clearly felt that his response was sufficient to meet Jaques's attack. Yet it is significant that other groups like the CCCJ were engaging in public disputes with Social Credit while Congress hovered in the background. Making allegations about Jews and communism and undermining the extent of Jewish persecution were the stock-in-trade of wartime anti-Semites – especially Social Crediters – and Canadian Jewry needed an organization that would protect and defend it from such attacks. It was questionable whether Congress was fulfilling this mandate. In fairness, Congress intended to discuss the matter of Jaques and Silcox, as it was on the agenda of the upcoming national JPRC meeting in Montreal. Unfortunately, Rosenberg, now accepted as Congress's Social Credit expert, was unable to attend. Thus, the issue was discussed only cursorily and then set aside until he could be present.[29]

Meanwhile, Social Credit's own rank and file were expressing dissatisfaction with their party's anti-Semitism. In November 1944 a Social Credit supporter from Bowden, Alberta, wrote to the party organ (now renamed the *Canadian Social Crediter*) to complain about the "ugly sarcasm ... mudslinging and calling of names" in which the paper engaged: "Your paper is the official organ of the Social Credit Association of Canada and must therefore be sanctioned by members of the Social Credit Party in Alberta, the elected representatives of the people of this Province, of whom I am one." Yet the reader felt ashamed of his provincial government and unable to show the *Canadian Social Crediter* to his friends, although he wanted them to learn about the party's principles: "Many of you like to call yourselves Christian gentlemen and your party a Christian party ... Yet it seems you are noting a splinter in your brother's eye and overlooking that you may have a plank in your own." The *Canadian Social Crediter* published this letter, albeit only to vindicate itself: "Sometimes – often, in fact – we do use sarcastic language. More often, we use strong, destructive language. Here's why. When men go into battle they do not play checkers with the enemy. We're in a battle – how great, many people do not realize. Right now the issue is our way of life, the free, Christian way – as opposed to the godless, regimented way ... and we're fighting against groups of international financiers who would blow us to atoms if they dared ... If we sound rough, remember we're fighting. And if a cause isn't worth fighting for – Well, it's a poor cause."[30] For the party organ, the battle-lines had been clearly drawn. Yet the fact that Social Credit's own supporters were vocalizing opposition to its anti-Semitism suggests that not everyone was on side.

Meanwhile, Congress remained unable or unwilling to confront Social Credit in any organized, public manner. Although it was beginning to explore more confrontational measures, implementing any kind of coherent, assertive policy was still in the future.

The Alberta branch, which naturally felt most vulnerable to Social Credit's anti-Semitism, was becoming impatient with Congress's passivity and began making plans to mobilize independently. In late 1944 a confrontation erupted between Alberta Congress officers and Solon Low, now leader of the newly created national Social Credit party. Yet this encounter, like previous encounters, was initiated by individuals outside Congress. In December the *Canadian Tribune* published an editorial entitled "Social Credit Mask for Nazi Propaganda." It harshly criticized Social Credit for its transparent attack on Jews and its "double-talk" about international finance and the "hidden hand of Satan."[31] In response, the *Canadian Social Crediter* argued that the *Tribune*'s attempt to label "the Social Credit attack on so-called Communism and other totalitarian doctrines as ... anti-Semitic" was a ploy to protect the real conspirators – the "gang of German Jews" that backed Hitler: "Hitler would never have gained power unless he had been well-financed. Who was able to finance him? And is it an accident that Hitler, reputed to be an illegitimate grandson of a Rothschild, should have been chosen? ... Is it an accident that his '*Mein Kampf*' was inspired ... by the notorious *Protocols of Zion*? Is it an accident that as a result of his persecution of Jews, any enemy alien refugees from Germany and occupied Europe gained key positions at the expense of nationals in Great Britain, the U.S.A. and elsewhere during the war?" A.V. Bourcier, MLA for Lac Ste Anne and chairman of the Social Credit Board, also denied the *Tribune*'s charges. At a Social Credit meeting in Edmonton, Bourcier proclaimed: "I have never at any time attacked the Jewish people. I have no hatred for any race or any religion." He assured his audience that "I have always attacked the group of men whom we call International Finance – and I will continue to attack them, whether their names be Finklestein or MacGregor!" With that remark, Bourcier's audience broke into cheers.[32]

After witnessing the exchange between the *Tribune* and the party organ and Bourcier, Alberta Congress officers and agents decided to act. However, the result was not as positive as they had hoped, and raised serious questions about the efficacy of direct confrontation. On 30 December 1944 H.A. Friedman and John Dower met with Low at the legislative buildings in Edmonton. They talked with him for nearly two hours about Social Credit's attitude on the "Jewish question" and showed him several issues from the *Canadian Social Crediter* that were anti-Semitic. On the surface, the meeting went well. Low was conciliatory, assuring both Friedman and Dower that he was strongly opposed to anti-Semitism and that it definitely was not part of Social Credit policy. He gave them "his personal assurance that he would no longer tolerate the type of articles that we brought to his attention in the party's paper ... that he would disavow any member of the party who indulged in Anti-Semitic statements ... that he would ... make a public statement to the press on the question of Anti-Semitism, which he assured us we would find fully satisfactory." Friedman told Low that while such a public declaration could serve a very useful purpose, it could also do more harm than good if the national leader "hedged his statement too much and did not come out openly and convincingly on the question." Low promised him that "there would be no hedging and that [his] statement would be frank, open and forceful." Friedman was hopeful but not elated, remarking to Hayes privately: "About all I can say is that we will have to wait and see."[33]

Soon after their meeting Low informed Friedman of an upcoming public meeting in which he intended to address Social Credit's stance on anti-Semitism: "I hope that [the address] will have the desired effect of removing any misunderstanding and will put an end to these repeated accusations of anti-Semitism which have been directed against us besides bringing our own speakers and writers into line."[34] True to his word, on 9 January 1945, at a public meeting in Lethbridge, Low made a public statement on the subject. Unfortunately for Congress, Low's statement was blatantly anti-Semitic. He began his speech by stating: "Some Jewish friends of our movement have told me that we are being identified with anti-Semitism because of our persistent and outspoken exposures of a group of international financiers and world plotters who are engaged in a criminal conspiracy to destroy democracy and Christianity and to enslave mankind to their rule." By construing his meeting with Friedman and Dower in these terms, Low simultaneously refuted and reaffirmed Social Credit's anti-Semitism: "Some of these men happen to be of Jewish racial origin, and to be more specific, of German-Jewish origin." Yet they were not *exclusively* Jewish, he qualified, and although many were, this was no reason to condemn the Jewish people as a whole. Accordingly, it was important to clarify for everyone, including Canada's Jews, Social Credit's stance on anti-Semitism:

We very definitely are not anti-Semitic or anti any race or religion ... The only times when the Canadian Social Credit movement can possibly be brought into conflict with any racial or religious group would be if those comprising such a group conspired together as a group in an organized attack on democracy and Christianity. I am sure that our fellow Canadians of Jewish origin recognize that a truly democratic and Christian society ... alone will give them the social objectives they seek as individuals in common with all Canadians ... it is fantastic for anybody to suggest that as Social Crediters we are anti-Semitic. I will go further and point out to our fellow Canadians of Jewish origin that actually the Social Credit movement is the most powerful influence in the country working for their emancipation.

Low also explained why anti-Semitism was "sweeping" England, Australia, New Zealand, and the United States as well as Canada. (Germany, interestingly, was not mentioned.) His explanation served only to publicly reinforce Social Credit's anti-Semitism: "Our Jewish friends should recognize that the cause of the growing anti-Semitism ... is not due to propaganda alone ... anti-Semitism is spreading, because people cannot fail to observe that a disproportionate number of Jews occupy positions of control in international finance, in revolutionary activities, and in some propaganda institutions, the common policy of which is the centralization of power and the perversion of religious and cultural ideals. This gives people the impression that therefore there must be a Jewish conspiracy to gain world control." Low then invoked the "good Jew–bad Jew" argument. He declared there was only one way in which Jews could put an end to anti-Semitism, which was by "denouncing the arch-criminals who are engaged in the world conspiracy against human freedom, be they Gentile or Jew, and, through their powerful organization, join in the growing battle against international finance, and the world plotters." He promised he would ensure that other Social Crediters and the *Canadian Social Crediter* faithfully reflected the views he had just expressed, and that "they do not say or print anything which can properly be interpreted as an attack on the Jewish people." Low concluded that Social Credit's alleged anti-Semitism was now a dead issue: "Now that I have made our stand clear on this question, I hope that we shall hear no more nonsense about Social Crediters being anti-Semitic. This is, of course, too much to expect from our vociferous communists who are always ready to denounce anybody opposed to their totalitarian doctrine as being fascists, and anybody opposed to their allies, international finance, as being anti-Semitic. But this deliberate mongering in blatant falsehoods does not deceive anybody."[35]

Low's speech had made a mockery of his meeting with Friedman and Dower and was the absolute antithesis of what they had hoped for. One wonders what the two men thought when they read Low's address. Undoubtedly it was a great disappointment. Although they might have assumed that Low had not dealt with them in good faith and responded maliciously to their meeting, a closer examination of his statements offers a more complex interpretation. It seems that Low responded to Friedman and Dower as "good Jews" while never abandoning his ideas about the "bad Jews" who made up international finance and the group of world plotters. It is noteworthy that Low was a Mormon and believed in the fulfilment of biblical prophecy in which Jews would be returned to Palestine; in fact, earlier that year he had become a member of the Canadian Palestine Committee, which operated in conjunction with the Zionist Organization of Canada.[36] Thus, it is probable that Low's religious beliefs enabled him to relate positively to "good Jews" on a personal level while his belief in Social Credit's conspiracy theories caused him to demand that "good Jews" denounce the "bad Jews" who were international financial plotters. Of course, this raises the fanciful question of what Low's response would have been if an actual international Jewish financier had met him at the legislative buildings.

In any case, Western Division Congress officers were extremely dismayed by Low's address. "There is no retraction there," stated S. Hart Green of Winnipeg to a fellow Congress officer in Lethbridge, "and it is a fine example of our objections causing re-iteration and further publicity." Moreover, Green remarked, since Social Credit's philosophy was based on anti-Semitism and the world Jewish financial conspiracy, "to do away with these doctrines you have to do away with the Social Credit Party."[37] In Edmonton, Lieberman also expressed how "terribly disappointed" he was upon reading Low's statement and commented to Fradkin in Calgary that "a leopard does not change his spots easily."[38] Fradkin himself told Rosenberg that he too was "terribly disappointed" by Low's statement. Interestingly, Fradkin implied to Rosenberg that an earlier meeting of the Western Division's JPRC had decided against such openly confrontational methods and that Friedman and Dower had approached Low without their colleagues' approval. Clearly, Fradkin wanted to distance himself from Friedman's and Dower's actions: "I want to emphasise that I had nothing at all to do with this interview and same took place without my knowledge or consent." Yet, he added hastily, "I do not think it is necessary at the present time to reprimand or take this matter up with the Edmonton [Joint Public Relations] Committee, but I shall be glad to have your reaction and hear from you."[39] Fradkin's comments clearly indicate that the Western Division was divided over its public relations methods. In addition, Rosenberg's input, if not approval, seemed to be a prerequisite for action. Most importantly, there was obviously no coherent, unanimous, national public relations policy, and Alberta officers had tired of waiting for one. However, in the wake of their unilateral action and Low's deliberate anti-Semitic statements under the guise of pro-Semitism, Congress officers and agents across the country became wary of a more confrontational approach.

Shortly thereafter, Rosenberg wrote a confidential memorandum stating that Social Credit's anti-Semitism was not merely the opinions of irresponsible individual politicians but formed "an integral part of the basic 'philosophy?' and policy of the Social Credit movement." He conceded that Social Credit was not the only political party containing anti-Semites and that other parties in Great Britain, Canada, and the United States had their share. However, while other party leaders either repudiated, censured, or ignored their irresponsible members, Social Credit was in a league of its own. The *leaders* of the party were the anti-Semites; therefore, "the anti-semitic propaganda of the Social Credit Party in Canada can no longer be considered as the mouthing of a 'lunatic fringe.'" Rosenberg thus concluded:

For the first time in the history of any English speaking country, we have a provincial government in power in a British Dominion, which lends its prestige and facilities to the distribution of anti-semitic literature similar to that previously distributed by the Fichte Bunde in Nazi Germany and the Gerald K. Smiths, Winrods, [and] Coughlins in the United States. The official statement issued by Mr. Solon Low and published in the *Canadian Social Crediter*, the official organ of the Social Credit movement in Canada, reveals the policy and tactics of the Social Credit movement in their true light. It pretends to be a repudiation of anti-semitism. In fact it dots the *i*'s and crosses the *t*'s of much of the anti-semitic propaganda distributed by Nazi propaganda agencies, and gives this propaganda the official backing and prestige of a political Party in power in a Canadian province.[40]

Once again Rosenberg had provided an accurate and incisive assessment of the Social Credit problem. In his opinion, it was time to take the matter more seriously. Yet again there was no agreement on a national public relations policy. Indeed, when Caiserman received Rosenberg's memorandum, he fully agreed with it: "It shows without a doubt the verification of your thesis that the Social Credit Movement is anti-Semitic." However, "it will be interesting to learn the opinion of the Joint Public Relations Committee as to what measures should be taken *if any* [italics added]."[41] In fact, the national JPRC raised the issue at its meeting in Toronto in January 1945 and again at its meeting in Montreal in March, and the Dominion Council's Eastern Division meeting in February also discussed the "problem of the Social Credit Party and its purported anti-Semitic tendencies." It reported that "the matter is being very closely studied and efforts are being made to counteract the menace of the propaganda."[42] While Congress discussed, discussed, and discussed some more, others were unabashedly confronting Social Credit's anti-Semitism.

In February 1945 the Toronto-based Anglo-Jewish monthly *Today* published a damning article entitled "Prophets of Race Hate: Turning the Spotlight on Social Credit Leaders Who Have Imported Hitler's Program of Anti-Semitism into Canada." It examined what it called "the new gospel being spread throughout the country by prairie prophets who must be bringing joy to Hitler and his hard-pressed colleagues. They are a group of Social Credit leaders who light candles at the Nazi altar clothed in the mantle of Aberhart. They have developed a unique 'theory' of hate and confusion, distilled of fascist forgeries, medieval prejudices and Herr Goebbels' lies." *Today* cited several examples of Social Credit's anti-Semitism, including statements by Low, Jaques, James, Byrne, and the *Canadian Social Crediter* to prove that "a distinct group of the Social Credit leadership has discarded monetary reform and all other encumbrances to embrace a straight program of political anti-Semitism and race hate." It emphasized that Low and others "have not stopped at mere Jew-baiting. In recent months they have turned their anti-Semitic propaganda into an all-out attack – in the classical fascist manner – against other political parties, against the United Nations, against the Soviet Union, and against every step taken by the democratic powers to ensure a durable peace organization. They are no longer content to attack the Jews as such; they denounce the various important measures approved by the United Nations as a part of the alleged Jewish plot to dominate the world. They are now stumping the country with the cry that Canadians are confronted with only one task: combatting 'the great conspiracy against humanity.'"

Although *Today* acknowledged Manning's earlier repudiation of anti-Semitism, it declared: "It is not enough for Manning to oppose anti-Semitism *in a radio address*. He must clearly repudiate the line of the Low clique in the national leadership ... as provincial premier it is his job to exercise his constitutional authority to stamp out the anti-Semitic ramp in the province." The paper also demanded legal action: "It is time the federal government and the security authorities acted. Where are the Defence of Canada Regulations? What guarantee of national security can we have if a gang of politicians can circulate the illegal *Protocols of Zion* in public, talk blandly of war against one of our main allies, belittle our other allies, and smear the peace aims of the United Nations as a 'Jewish plot'? ... the situation calls for a government investigation to put an end to this campaign of hate and falsehood." To demonstrate its abhorrence of Social Credit's anti-Semitism graphically, *Today* included a cartoon depicting Nazi propaganda minister Joseph Goebbels pumping the poisonous well of anti-Semitism

This cartoon was published by the Anglo-Jewish monthly *Today* in February 1945 and republished in March 1947 by the *New Voice*, the monthly publication of the *Canadian Jewish Weekly*. It depicts Joseph Goebbels, Nazi minister of propaganda, pumping the poisonous well of anti-Semitism for Social Credit's national party leader, Solon Low, who attempts to force an unwilling Canada to take a drink. According to the two Jewish papers, Canadians were no longer willing to countenance Social Credit's anti-Semitism.

for Low, who was attempting to force an unwilling Canada to take a drink.[43]

Shortly after publication of the *Today* article, the *Toronto Daily Star* published a letter by one Edward Joseph, who similarly charged Low and other Social Credit leaders with "embark[ing] on a program of Jew-baiting and anti-United Nations propaganda." Joseph, who clearly had read the *Today* article, provided similar examples of Social Credit's anti-Semitism, including an article in the *Canadian Social Crediter* that argued that the international financial conspiracy was Jewish-controlled: "Let us have a look at the names of the key personalities in the Great Conspiracy against humanity, perpetrated through International Finance. Rothschild, Schiff, Warburg, Kahn, Cassel, Morgan, Goschen, Schuster, Samuels, Rathenau, Strakosch, Deutche, Ballin, Mendel, Sassoon, Niemeyer, Gugenheim, Baruch … they are or were all either German or of German origin. They are almost exclusively Jews racially, with one or two exceptions." Joseph cited an article by Jaques in which he quoted extensively from the *Protocols*. According to Jaques, the *Protocols* "were written before the end of the last Century and they are an exact blue print of the plans for a new world order which have been, and now are preparing behind closed doors. That is why they are called forgeries. And who are 'we'? Who else but Shylock and Marx? And what is their new plan? Disarmament, surrender of national sovereignty to an International Union, which means a world bank, a world gold standard, and a world police force … Do not believe any leader – religious, labour or political – who advocates surrender to world government, and 'police force' ... We are not pouring out blood and treasure to save the world from slavery by Hitler and Hirohito in order to hand it over to Shylock and Marx." Joseph also pointed to *Canadian Social Crediter* columnist James's allegations that the real objectives behind the Dumbarton "Hoax" Conference, the Bretton Woods Conference, and the "machinations" of the United Nations Relief and Rehabilitation Administration (UNRRA) were "the absolute Sovietisation of ... NATIONS," the consequence of which would be "the complete overthrow of Christianity and Democracy." From this evidence Joseph concluded that Social Credit's anti-Semitism was impeding the war effort: "In the midst of a war for survival these people are inciting the people of Canada to race hatred. Our boys overseas are suffering the tortures of being maimed, broken, killed because they know, we know that this is the only way civilization can be saved [and] Canada can remain a democratic country. Is their suffering to be in vain? The whole matter calls for vigorous action by the federal government. Otherwise there is a danger that in winning the war we shall yet lose the peace."[44]

In a published reply in the *Toronto Daily Star*, Low denied the charges put forward in Joseph's "vicious, scurrilous and libellous letter" and attacked *Today* for being part of that "powerful section of Canadian Jewry [which] is backing the mischievous activities of the Communist organization in the country." Low averred that he had "yet to see a single repudiation by any official Jewish paper of the vicious propaganda of these friends of communism."[45] The editor of *Today*, R.S. Gordon, in his own published reply in the *Star*, accused Low of attempting to sow anti-Semitism by using the spurious *Protocols* to make his case.[46] In a further published reply Low denied charges that he had invoked the *Protocols* to prove the existence of an international Jewish conspiracy, but added that the document was "an exact blue-print of what is been going on in the world since. To state that it is a forgery, is irrelevant – for its devilish predictions are being carried out to the letter." Low also criticized Gordon for editing "a paper which is violently pro-Jewish to the exclusion of all non-Jews ... its pages are full of pro-Communist propaganda." He complained that he could not state that "certain German Jewish bankers financed Hitler's advent to power" without being accused of attacking *all* Jews. "[Yet] I cannot believe that this reflects the attitude of Canadian Jewry," he stated in moral disbelief. "If it did, then not only I but many other people in Canada would be forced to revise our views on this question, for it would have some very ugly implications."[47] Low's insinuation, of course, was that if Canadian Jewry denied that German Jews were behind the Nazis, this would prove that *all* Canadian Jewry was part of the international conspiracy. Like his recent speech in Lethbridge, Low's repudiation of anti-Semitism merely resulted in its confirmation.

Congress observed the heated exchange between Low and the *Today* editor but did not enter the fray. Although public and private citizens alike were confronting Social Credit's anti-Semitism, Congress persisted in its passivity. It seemed more willing to wring its hands privately or attempt to persuade Social Crediters behind closed doors than to confront the problem publicly or even support others in their confrontations. While Congress had been stung by its previous attempts to confront Low, his duplicity and aggression did not prevent others from acting. Congress needed to amend its basic public relations orientation, and, given Social Credit's tactics, a no-holds-barred approach promised to be the most effective. But this was a posture Congress was not ready to adopt.

None the less, Congress was working diligently, albeit through traditional public relations methods, to conduct anti-defamation work, much of which was indirectly directed at Social Credit. If open confrontation was not the preferred tactic, that did not mean Congress was abdicating all responsibility. For example, in the spring of 1945, before the end of the war, the national JPRC distributed fifteen thousand copies of an article that had appeared in the January edition of the *American Mercury*. The article, "Memorandum on Anti-Semitism," was an eloquent piece on the ignorance and illogic of anti-Semitism. It showed the ludicrousness of the international Jewish conspiracy theory by quoting figures that proved that Jews did not, in fact, control "the banks, Wall Street, the newspapers, the movies, the theatre, radio, and so on." It discussed the myriad contributions of American Jews, including Allied soldiers, poets, writers, dramatists, journalists, radio and movie stars, musicians, philanthropists, and scientists. The JPRC distributed copies of the article "particularly in Alberta where Social Credit propaganda against the Jews is reported to be making some headway."[48] It is noteworthy, however, that Congress did not consider publishing and distributing its own pamphlet showing the ludicrousness of Social Credit's international financial Jewish conspiracy theory.

In late summer of 1945 Congress's national officers also circulated an internal memorandum regarding post-war public relations problems. The memo discussed whether the end of the war had changed the problem of anti-Semitism in Canada and whether new methods of dealing with anti-Semitism in the reconversion and rehabilitation period were being discovered. With respect to organized anti-Semitism in Canada, and specifically Social Credit, the memo stated: "What is the position of organized anti-semitism in Canada today? ... The Social Credit party in Canada has an anti-semitic plank. It is our duty to determine on a method how to discredit it. How? ... By systematic publicity by our press office ... By Radio publicity ... By further distribution of proper literature ... By further negotiations with the representatives of the members of the Alberta Legislature of all political parties."[49] Although still based on traditional anti-defamation tactics, this was the most definitive attempt Congress had taken thus far to create an effective policy towards Social Credit. It was a harbinger of things to come.

The end of the war brought the full realization of the near-complete destruction of European Jewry, and as early as the autumn of 1945 Congress was adopting a stronger position towards anti-Semitism. It realized that the non-Jewish world had done nearly nothing to stop the annihilation of European Jewry and that both Jews and non-Jews needed to be more vigilant in demanding and ensuring racial tolerance. Accordingly, Congress began adjusting its public relations stance to project a more forthright approach to Jewish protection. A report by its Committee on Social and Economic Studies reflected this changing attitude. It discussed the possibility of public relations studies that would combat anti-Semitism in the post-war period. Following the lead of similar studies conducted by the American Jewish Congress (AJC), the Committee on Social and Economic Studies posed the following questions: "Under what conditions is anti-semitism a more or less harmless individual prejudice and when does it lead to organized group action? (This is indeed one of the crucial problems of political anti-semitism in Canada a solution to which is necessary for the spotting of potential danger points and for determining the means for counter-action[)] ... How can the democratic forces within the Jewish and non-Jewish community be liberated and mobilized efficiently, not merely for the purposes of a negative 'defense' against anti-semitism, but for a productive positive relation of cooperative living?"[50] These were important questions that Congress would need to consider as its public relations philosophy evolved. Yet adopting a more assertive approach would be extremely difficult, especially with respect to Social Credit. Meaningless denials of anti-Semitism by Manning and duplicitous dealings by Low had already convinced Congress of the costs of exposing Social Credit's anti-Semitism. Even more problematic was that, in the immediate post-war period, Social Credit's anti-Semitism was increasing instead of decreasing. The Social Crediters would prove to be slippery foes, and, notwithstanding Congress's increased determination, there would be no quick solution to the Social Credit problem.

Social Credit

William Aberhart, ca 1930s
(Canadian Broadcasting
Corporation Collection, National
Archives of Canada, c16476)

John Blackmore
(Arthur Roy Collection, National
Archives of Canada, PA46993)

Réal Caouette, 1945
(Arthur Roy Collection, National
Archives of Canada, PA47058)

Major C.H. Douglas, ca 1937
(Detail, Douglas Social Credit
Bureau of Canada Collection,
National Archives of Canada,
PA126856)

Louis Even, ca 1974
(Fonds Robert Rumilly, Archives
nationales du Québec, P303, S8,
SS1, D2, P19)

Joshua Haldeman
(Saskatchewan Archives Board,
R-A7956)

Premier Ernest Manning (right) receives first Alberta Anthology from John
Patrick Gillese, 1967
(Provincial Archives of Alberta, PA4019)

Norman James, 1955
(Provincial Archives of Alberta,
PA770/1)

Norman Jacques
(Arthur Roy Collection, National
Archives of Canada, PA47281)

Solon Low, 1946
(Arthur Roy Collection, National
Archives of Canada, C700)

Premier Ernest Manning, ca 1955
(Alberta Government photograph,
Social Credit Association of Canada
Collection, National Archives of
Canada, C87204)

Canadian Jewish Congress

Samuel Bronfman, 1963
(Canadian Jewish Congress
National Archives)

Hannaniah Caiserman
(Canadian Jewish Congress
National Archives)

Joseph Fine
(Canadian Jewish Congress
National Archives)

L.M. Fradkin
(*Calgary Albertan*, 10 August
1959)

H.A. Friedman, ca 1960s
(*Who's Who in Canadian Jewry*)

S. Hart Green, 1926
(*The Jew in Canada*)

Saul Hayes, ca 1960s
(Canadian Jewish Congress
National Archives)

David Kirshenblatt, ca 1950s
(Geraldine Carpenter, private
collection)

Max Moscovich, ca 1960s
(*Who's Who in Canadian Jewry*)

Louis Rosenberg, ca 1960s
(Canadian Jewish Congress
National Archives)

SOCIAL CREDITER'S WHEEL CROSS

Social Crediters stand for a Christian way of life. Wherever Social Crediters go they wear a wheel-cross, a symbol of Christianity. The wheel-cross signifies harmony, unity, perfect balance, and equality. It is one of the earliest symbols used by man. At various times the wheel-cross has been a symbol of God, the Sun, the Earth. On the other hand it is most modern. The wheel is the greatest scientific invention of all time. Significantly it symbolizes the age of power and technology. The Cross, symbolic of the supreme sacrifice of Christ for Mankind, is, and always has been, the most exalted emblem of the Christian faith. The circle is a sign of infinity.

This explanation of the "Wheel Cross" symbol appeared in the 10 June 1948 issue of the *Canadian Social Crediter*. The Wheel Cross, defined as a specifically Christian symbol, was the national Social Credit party emblem, and appeared on party stationery, buttons, and other campaign material. Social Credit party members also formed the Wheel Cross with their thumbs and index fingers as a gesture of fraternity.

5 A Worsening Climate

By 1945 the Canadian Jewish Congress was facing a world of change. Canadian Jewry was forced to confront the tragic implications of Hitler's tyranny; Canadian public opinion on anti-Semitism and racism was slowly changing with acknowledgment of the Holocaust, and the future of a Jewish state in Palestine was hanging precariously in the balance. In the aftermath of war, Congress was most concerned with the problems of European Jewry, and specifically with the thousands of displaced persons who had escaped or survived the Holocaust. After several years of quiet but persistent negotiation with federal government officials, Congress had succeeded in persuading the government to allow in a paltry five thousand Jewish refugees.[1] Congress had to acknowledge that European Jewry had been nearly destroyed and the Canadian government had done virtually nothing to ameliorate the tragedy. Yet Congress continued to work tirelessly to persuade grudging federal government officials to allow in more Jewish refugees, while it helped to re-establish the remaining Jews of Europe in more hospitable areas. At the same time Congress remained committed to the creation of a Jewish national homeland in Palestine and was greatly concerned that Britain's own political considerations would postpone or even cancel fulfilment of the promises made by Lord Balfour in 1917. During the early post-war period the Palestine crisis intensified as the British government, no longer willing to partition Palestine, handed the issue to the UN in February 1947. Congress, along with other world Jewish organizations, watched with dismay as a wave of terrorism was unleashed by radical Zionists in Palestine.[2]

While Congress was occupied with the problems of European and Palestinian Jewry, domestically it focused on issues of post-war reconstruction and reconversion and their potential effects on Canadian Jewry. Although anti-Semitism appeared to be on the wane across Canada, Jewish refugees were not welcome, in spite of the widely published facts of what had happened in Europe's death camps during the war.[3] None the less, in the wake of the Nazi regime and the horrors of the Holocaust, the nation's "polite-company rule" was changing as its social and political discourse adopted a more tolerant tone.[4] All the while, Social Credit continued to rail against the international financial Jewish conspiracy. Much to Congress's alarm, Social Credit's anti-Semitism worsened as it became more paranoid about a post-war world dominated by the UN, Soviet communism, and Zionism, all of which were deemed part of the international financial Jewish, and now overwhelmingly communist and Zionist, conspiracy.

Because of the widening discrepancy between Social Credit's anti-Semitism and the nation's emerging tolerance, Congress became increasingly determined to end the Social Credit problem. Even before the end of the war it realized the need to adopt more assertive measures and work with other organizations to ensure that the race hatred and genocide of Nazi Germany did not occur in Canada. By the immediate post-war period Congress was augmenting its initial public relations philosophy with a more sophisticated approach, concluding that it was insufficient to convince non-Jews that Jews were indeed good people or simply to correct all the slanders and misinformation about Jews. It was more important to show that anti-Semitism, race hatred, and intolerance were harmful to all society. Accordingly, Congress began a large-scale program that attempted to persuade group after group – labour unions, business groups, church groups, farm groups – that anti-Semitism was dangerous for all Canadians, not only for Jews.[5]

The emphasis on the universality of race hatred and the importance of combating all forms of prejudice and discrimination was discussed at Congress's 1947 plenary session, where Rabbi Abraham Feinberg argued that after the war Congress began to understand the importance of championing all minority groups who suffered from racial or religious prejudice, not merely the Jews: "The French-speaking Catholic in Ontario, the Japanese deportee from British Columbia, the Negro economic pariah, are no less a Jewish obligation than we are a moral crisis for the Christian."[6] By the early post-war period the nature of Congress's public relations work was evolving and maturing so that it encompassed more than anti-defamation work and focused also on the broader social implications of prejudice and discrimination. Protecting the Jewish community against false reports and hostile propaganda was still important, but now Congress believed that anti-Semitism was less a Jewish problem than a total community problem, and that anti-Jewish manifestations, having their root in social problems, ultimately affected the community as a whole. Certainly, the horrific lessons of Nazi Germany and the Holocaust had shown Congress the necessity of a healthy society in which attacks on minorities were not accepted as an inevitable consequence of social, economic, and political dislocation. In short, Congress's public relations orientation was now that discrimination against any racial, religious, or ethnic group constituted a menace to the entire social structure and that the Jewish community should do its part, through co-operation with other religious, labour, and ethnic organizations, to protect the civil and human rights of all groups.[7]

Significantly, although Congress's public relations philosophy was shifting from education-oriented anti-defamation work to a broad-based appeal against all race hatred, it none the less remained an appeal – Congress still assumed that anti-Semitism could be combated by changing the attitudes of non-Jews.[8] This assumption would greatly impede its public relations work regarding Social Credit's anti-Semitism. Although Congress was becoming more assertive and confronted Social Credit in a series of incidents, its efforts were continually thwarted by Social Crediters' duplicity and intransigence. When Congress leaders attempted to convince Social Crediters that their anti-Semitism was harmful to Canadian society and Jewry, the latter agreed wholeheartedly and encouraged Congress to denounce the international Jewish conspiracy so that anti-Semitism would cease. These tactics made it difficult for Congress to make many inroads. Social Credit was determined to continue and expand its anti-Semitic attack, irrespective of any appeal. Indeed, as the following examples indicate, its anti-Semitism continued unabated during the early post-war period and became more vociferous regarding the UN, communists, and Zionists.

During the war Social Credit propaganda had vehemently opposed the creation of an international peacekeeping association like the UN. In the early post-war period it continued to attack the UN and its umbrella organizations. Specifically, the party organ condemned financier and American presidential adviser Bernard Baruch for his alleged manipulation of the United Nations Relief and Rehabilitation Administration (UNRRA). The *Canadian Social Crediter* complained that the first chairman of UNRRA, Herbert Lehman, had been "nominated by the [American] President on the recommendation of his adviser – the adviser of all Presidents of the U.S.A. since away back, and that is none other than Bernard Baruch." The fact that Baruch was a financier, a presidential adviser, and a Jew was *a priori* proof of his involvement in the international financial conspiracy. As for Lehman, "one time Governor of New York and connected with the Old Gang," his Jewishness also connected him to the ubiquitous international conspiracy.[9] In another instance, the *Canadian Social Crediter* criticized the UN's plans to control atomic energy and Baruch's formulation of American atomic policy: "It will be so reassuring to know that a group of men representing and controlled by the very international crooks and gangsters who promoted two world wars, plunged the world into economic chaos and have brought us to the brink of universal catastrophe, will have the sole monopoly of not only bombing us out of existence, but will be able to control atomic energy in the industrial field so that there will be plenty of hard labour for the slaves of the glorious World State."[10] The party organ also blamed Baruch and other "international German Jewish financiers" for the post-war world food shortage, which was the result of "the association of Mr. Bernard Baruch and other international financiers, predominantly German Jews, with the various international authorities." According to the party organ, Jews controlled the world food supply because of "the idea that the Jews are a Chosen People whose destiny it is to form the 'brain' of a collectivised world. The practical background is the power of International Finance, which is dominated by German Jews, operating at the moment from America."[11]

Its anti-Semitism aside, Social Credit's conspiratorial rhetoric about the UN revealed the persistence of its wartime isolationism and its current scepticism that any international organization could prevent a post-war depression such as had occurred after the previous war. Most noteworthy is that Social Credit propaganda viewed the architects of post-war planning as part of a maniacal international force bent on creating a world slave state. MLA James warned that "this international gang, with their sanctimonious hypocritical yap for international unity, have only one objective, and that is the 'Unity' of Slavery ... and *that* is the gang responsible for the slaughters of the past thirty odd years, and *they* are the gang who are still planning the subjugation of the world to *their* will, and *they* are the gang who should be hanged or shot, or drawn and quartered or boiled in oil." Although James conceded that "some of them are Jewish and some of them aren't ... the majority of these international criminals just happen to be Jews." However, he added innocently, "I'm not interested in their race or creed, but if their names happen to be Rothschild, Cohen, Loeb, or Baruch, am I to blame?"[12]

During the war, when tensions with the Soviet Union heightened and communism became increasingly unpopular (and illegal) in North America, Social Credit made various accusations against the Jews: that they were communist conspirators attempting to extend their activities in North America under the guise of refugee status; that they were behind Germany's war against the Allies; that they themselves were to blame for the Holocaust; and that the Holocaust was, in fact, a Jewish fabrication. By the early post-war period Social Credit embraced the prevalent Cold War mentality and, like extreme right-wing groups in the United States,[13] concluded that Jews and communists were co-conspirators in a plot for world control. During the war the *Canadian Social Crediter* had announced that "the 'high priest' of Socialism was Karl Marx. The 'high priest' of Communism was Frederick Engels. They were both German Jews ... They both attacked religion in general and Christianity in particular."[14] After the war the party organ continued to harp on Lenin's and Trotsky's so-called Jewishness (Lenin was not a Jew) to explain the spread of communism in Russia and Europe: "Both Lenin and Trotsky were racially Jews, as were the overwhelming majority of the first Soviet hierarchy ... a disproportionate number of active Communist leaders are racially Jews, though most of them being atheists, are not Jews by religion." In an attempt to pre-empt criticism, the paper added: "Now we must wait for a time for the screams of 'Jew-baiter!' 'Fascist' 'Hate-monger!' – and so on – to die down. But in the interim, it is worth pondering whether all this can be coincidence."[15]

When reports of the conditions in European death camps were widely publicized after the war, Social Credit propaganda continued to question the destruction of European Jewry. In early 1946 the *Canadian Social Crediter* used the case of Lieutenant-General Sir Frederick Morgan, then UNRRA's chief of displaced-persons operations in Germany, as a way of undermining the severity of the Holocaust. In late 1945 Morgan had made some extremely insensitive and incorrect statements regarding the extent of Jewish destruction in Poland (which was nearly 100 per cent)[16] and suggested that European Jews were using the rationale of the Holocaust to obtain refugee status in order to emigrate from Europe. As a result, Morgan was recalled and ordered to resign as UNRRA chief.[17] The *Canadian Social Crediter* commended Morgan for his fearless reporting of the "facts" and demanded that his statements should have been verified before he was forced to resign, since not verifying them would "serve only to convince anti-Semites all over the world that their beliefs are right."[18] When Morgan was finally replaced by Meyer Cohen as UNRRA chief, the fact that Cohen was a Jew proved that UNRRA was controlled by the international Jewish conspiracy: "General Sir Frederick Morgan has been relieved of his position and Mr. La Guardia [chairman of UNRRA] has appointed in his place none other than one Meyer Cohen. Operations seem to be proceeding to plan."[19] Compared to that of the general press, the *Canadian Social Crediter*'s coverage of Morgan was disproportionate to its importance. Indeed, the party organ's larger purpose was to question the nature and extent of the Holocaust and to suggest that the Jewish refugee situation and UNRRA itself were part of the broader international Jewish conspiracy.

In a similar attempt to undermine the Holocaust, the *Canadian Social Crediter* referred to the activities of Henry Morgenthau, secretary of the treasury under Franklin Roosevelt, architect of the Morgenthau Plan, and a Jew. Originally, the intention of the Morgenthau Plan was to cripple Germany's industrial potential by turning it into an agricultural country at the end of the war.[20] Although the plan was never executed, as late as 1946 the *Canadian Social Crediter* accused Morgenthau and others of wreaking more havoc in Germany than the Nazis: "They (the executors of the Morgenthau plan) have abused and starved to death more German babies than there ever were Jews in Germany; and finally they raped and debauched hundreds of thousands of German, Austrian, and Hungarian girls and women from eight to eighty. They brought to their death five times as many Germans in one year of peace as died during the five years of war!" The paper then asked the "$64 question": "Whose policy is responsible for the mass raping, looting, starvation and murder now rampant in Germany?" The answer: "The Morgenthau policy, the direct brain child of the financiers and particularly of Morgenthau – a policy so brutal that it is rarely mentioned, because we at home could not eat or sleep if we knew of it."[21] What the *Canadian Social Crediter* ignored was that the Morgenthau Plan had long been a dead letter – for reasons that had little to do with an international financial Jewish conspiracy but much to do with fears of an overly powerful Soviet Union.

In short, Social Credit propaganda attempted to indict Jews on a number of counts, the fabrication of their own destruction being the most offensive. Significantly, Social Credit's propensity for focusing on Jewish issues made its propaganda unique among Canada's political parties. Its interpretation of the Holocaust was noteworthy for its radical deviation from the facts. Before and certainly during the war, the Allied powers were fully aware of Nazi persecution of European Jewry, and in Canada all provincial and federal parties at least paid lip service to the condemnation of Germany, even if they did little to prevent the impending massacre. Yet for years *following* the war, Social Credit politicians and propaganda questioned whether Jews had been persecuted and suggested that Jewish refugees were the vanguard of an attempted communist revolution in Canada. This made Social Credit the only democratically elected party and government in Canada to engage in Holocaust denial.

Social Credit also focused on another issue of deep concern to world Jewry in the immediate post-war period – the creation of the state of Israel. In conjunction with its refusal to support assistance to European Jews both during and after the war, Social Credit consistently opposed the Zionist cause and spoke strongly against the establishment of a Jewish state. Although anti-Zionism is not by definition anti-Semitic, Social Credit's anti-Zionism was predicated on its anti-Semitism. The *Canadian Social Crediter* emphasized that Social Credit was not anti-Semitic because it supported the Arabs' cause in Palestine: "The Label anti-Semitic was unfounded in view of the fact that [Social Crediters] are interested in the Arab's cause and Arabs are predominantly a semitic people." The paper referred to its published list of international financiers, not all of whom were Jewish, which proved that Social Credit was not anti-Semitic: "Those people who go yapping anti-Semitism at us will take the time to read this article."[22] In a separate attempt to defend its anti-Zionism, the *Canadian Social Crediter* pointed to the mother country: "Social Crediters have ... taken a stand against political Zionism. Is this a sin? If so, one had better take the British government to task."[23] The party organ also reprinted an article from the *Australian Social Crediter*, which had taken a similar stance on international finance and Zionism: "An alien policy is being imposed on the British Empire from the United States of America ... [which] proceeds, not from the American people, but from the International Financiers, who are predominantly Zionist Jews, and who have their headquarters in the U.S.A. at the moment, and dominate its government."[24]

MP Jaques, one of the most vocal opponents of the creation of the state of Israel, argued that the "evil twins" of political Zionism and communism were the "only real threat to the peace of the world."[25] With respect to Zionist terrorism he noted that hundreds of British soldiers, sailors, police, and civil servants had been murdered and held hostage by Jewish terrorists in Palestine. He pointed to the bombing of Jerusalem's King David Hotel by Zionist terrorists in July 1946[26] as indisputable proof of an international Jewish conspiracy: "The terrorist outrages leading up to the David Hotel bombing were not the acts of a few fanatics, but the deliberate policy of the responsible Jewish agency ... Zionism is a political movement ... to dominate the world." In Jaques's mind, although Zionist officials and sympathizers denounced the terrorists, the latter none the less "always find a safe refuge among their fellow Zionists." Moreover, "Zionist terrorists" outside Palestine also protected these Jewish "gangsters," and agencies like the American Jewish Anti-Defamation League "'smear' with anti-Semitism anybody who ventures even the mildest criticism of Zionism." Everywhere Zionists and their Communist-Marxian Socialist comrades stir hatred against Britain and the British – the best friends the Jews had ever had."[27] Certainly, Jaques's condemnation of Zionist terrorism, given the activities of the Stern gang and the bombing of the King David Hotel, was neither unique nor perhaps unjustified. However, given his record of blatant anti-Semitism, the most salient aspect of his rhetoric was the twinning of Zionism with an international Jewish conspiracy. Like other Social Credit ideologues, Jaques was either unwilling or unable to separate anti-Zionism from anti-Semitism.

Such was the nature of Social Credit's anti-Semitism in the early post-war period. Jaques's anti-Semitism increased markedly during this time, which became apparent when he forged links with the Christian Nationalist Crusade, an American extreme right-wing group led by Gerald L.K. Smith.[28] Smith, the "dean of American anti-Semites," had been associated with Henry Ford and Huey Long (the "Kingfish" of Louisiana) in the 1930s. Jaques shared the same platform with Smith at meetings across the United States beginning in 1946, and he emulated the sentiments of many American extreme right-wing contemporaries such as William Dudley Pelley, founder of the Silver Shirts, and Gerald B. Winrod, leader of the pro-Nazi Defenders of the Christian Faith.[29] The connection between Jaques and Smith was first revealed when Jaques was invited to Detroit as the main speaker to the Christian Veterans Intelligence Bureau, a right-wing veterans' group that had close associations with Smith's Christian Nationalists.[30] In an open letter promoting the upcoming meeting, the Christian Veterans announced: "We are bringing to the City of Detroit one of Canada's outstanding anti-Communist leaders ... the Honorable Norman Jaques, MP, who ... was one of the members of Parliament responsible for helping to bring about the apprehension of Russian spies and other enemies of Christianity operating in Canada. He is a foe of Internationalism, all forms of Bolshevism, and is familiar with internationalist intrigue as it involves the international bankers and the corrupt money system the world around ... We veterans who believe in Christianity and hate atheistic Communism consider it a high honor to be able to present this distinguished statesman."[31]

On 25 April 1946 the *Canadian Social Crediter* proudly announced that "Norman Jaques, MP for Wetaskiwin, is probably the first Social Crediter in Canada to receive an invitation from a prominent United States Society to address them in body, with all expenses paid and a 'substantial honorarium' added." Jaques spoke to the Christian Veterans in Detroit and also at a rally of Smith's Christian Nationalists in St Louis. Upon returning home, Jaques remarked: "A few weeks ago it was my privilege and pleasure to address a meeting in Detroit organized by the Christian Veterans. On that occasion I met, for the first time, Mr. Gerald K. Smith ... Since then I have taken the opportunity to read many of their publications including twelve issues of their paper *The Cross and the Flag* and I wish to say that I am in sympathy with the ideas expressed therein."[32] Given that Smith was part of America's racist, anti-Semitic, extreme right wing and that his publication could be defined as hate literature, Jaques's admiration did not reflect well on himself or the Social Credit movement. Yet at the time there was little public or political reaction to his connections with Smith.

There was, however, a notable reaction from the Canadian Jewish press. The *Canadian Jewish Weekly*, the organ of the pro-labour United Jewish People's Order (UJPO), called Jaques and Smith "partners in hate" and discussed at length Jaques's concurrence with Smith's "discreditable" views:

Jaques is not an isolated phenomenon. He is part of a group of men, holding high office, the ruling body in the province of Alberta, the representative of the Alberta people in Ottawa that calculatingly employs anti-Semitism to further its rise to power, just as Hitler did in Germany and just as Smith is doing in the United States today ... No honest, sensible Canadian can blink his eyes to the sinister threat which the Social Credit movement, acting through such men as Norman Jaques, has become. Its ascendancy parallels that of the Nazis in many respects. It began as a democratic party, pledged to bring security and prosperity to the people of Alberta. The pledges have been forgotten ... it has resorted to unscrupulous racial slanders and falsehoods to increase membership and influence ... Like Hitler [Social Credit leaders] seek to climb the ladder to power by playing off the people, by dividing and seducing them into civil disruption and racial conflict. Thus would the enemies of democracy, disguised as its champions, go into power through a side-door.[33]

Clearly, the horrors of the war had affected Canadian Jewry's response to anti-Semitism, at least at this Jewish paper. Certainly, the *Canadian Jewish Weekly* was making a strong statement: in the post-Holocaust, post-war period, there would be little tolerance for Nazi-like rhetoric and behaviour. Obviously the paper had no compunction about engaging in a polemical attack against a government and party that it deemed inimical to the welfare of Canadian Jewry.

For its part, Congress was more circumspect. Rosenberg was fully aware of Jaques's activities in the United States and had been corresponding with the American Jewish Committee on the matter.[34] For the time being, however, Congress refrained from taking any action. Although the national Joint Public Relations Committee (JPRC) discussed Social Credit's anti-Semitism at its meeting in May 1946, one officer suggested that "nothing be put in the minutes or in writing to anybody about the discussions ... These matters have a habit of getting about and if anything is to be done it must be known to very few."[35] It seems that plans were being made to confront Social Credit, but publicly denouncing Jaques or trying to persuade him to abandon his activities was not entertained at this point.

If Congress was not completely passive, it still persisted in taking a traditionally quiet diplomatic approach towards Social Credit. But Rosenberg was attempting something more forthright. He assembled data on possible electoral support for Social Credit's anti-Semitism. In August 1946 he submitted a report to national headquarters that examined the 1945 federal election results to determine the extent of anti-Semitic prejudice in Canada.[36] He argued that this study was important because the national Social Credit party made anti-Semitic prejudice and propaganda an integral part of its program, and Social Credit's most anti-Semitic members, like Jaques, Low, and Blackmore, were elected to the House of Commons. By determining Social Credit's electoral support nationally, Rosenberg hoped to ascertain the degree of anti-Semitism in Canada. His method, of course, neglected the more complicated possibility that those who voted for Social Credit did not necessarily support the party's anti-Semitism. Whether supporters voted for Social Credit because or in spite of its anti-Semitism was not easily quantifiable, and Rosenberg never addressed this possibility.

However, his study was not without value. By determining levels of Social Credit support, he was at least able to isolate that bloc of the electorate and could then attempt to verify whether those voters agreed with Social Credit's anti-Semitic philosophy. He analysed the votes cast by summarizing the population of every federal constituency in Canada, the total number of votes polled, and the number of votes polled for Social Credit. His results showed that out of a total of 904 candidates nominated in 245 constituencies across Canada, 87 had been nominated by Social Credit.[37] Yet of the 245 constituencies, only 13 elected a Social Credit member to Parliament, all in Alberta. Every constituency in Alberta had nominated a Social Credit candidate, and only 4 did not elect a Social Credit member.[38] Rosenberg also noted that out of a total of over 4 million votes polled in the 1945 election, slightly more than 200,000 were for Social Credit candidates. This was 4 per cent of the Dominion-wide vote. He correctly concluded that "only a very small proportion of Canadian electors voted for Social Credit ... candidates, and a still smaller proportion of such candidates were elected to Parliament."[39]

Yet Rosenberg cautioned that a party that preached prejudice and intolerance posed a greater danger to Canadian unity and democracy than its small numbers implied. Although proportionately weak at the national level, Social Credit supporters had considerable strength in Alberta, where 36 per cent of all voters cast their ballots for Social Credit candidates.[40] In Rosenberg's view this was not an insignificant percentage, and he concluded that those who voted for Social Credit had "allowed themselves to be influenced by propagandists of prejudice and intolerance to such an extent as to vote for candidates pledged to their policies." He emphasized that Congress could no longer look upon Social Credit's prejudice as the irresponsible ranting of a "lunatic fringe" or assume that such prejudice would not win the support of the average voter. Social Credit had been able to elect thirteen members to the House of Commons, "where they are able to make use of the prestige, privileges and immunity and the forum which parliament affords them, to inject the poison of prejudice and racial and religious hatred into the stream of Canadian life." Clearly, the fate of the Weimar Republic was still fresh in Rosenberg's mind, and he was vehemently opposed to a democratically elected party with an anti-Semitic agenda gaining power in the House of Commons: "Events since 1933 have raised considerable doubt concerning the wisdom of such complacency."[41] Rosenberg distributed his report among Congress officers, but, although it served as a useful educational tool, Congress confined it to internal channels and did not use it in its public relations work. Perhaps this was not injudicious, for despite the rantings of a few Social Credit MPs, it was (and remains) difficult to prove that electors voted for Social Credit because of its anti-Semitism.

Other events in the early post-war period compelled Congress to respond more actively to Social Credit's anti-Semitism. In 1946 the Gouzenko affair erupted, resulting in the arrest and conviction of Fred Rose, Congress activist and Labour-Progressive MP for Montreal-Cartier. In September 1945 Igor Gouzenko, a cipher clerk at the Soviet Embassy in Ottawa, had defected, taking with him confidential documents that revealed the existence of several spy rings in Canada. His experience and the subsequent spy trials quickly became the touchstones of Canada's Cold War. Not surprisingly, Social Credit had an immediate and strong reaction to the spy trials and delighted in dramatizing the connection between Jews and communists and, even more incriminating, the connection between Jews and communist spies.

When Gouzenko's evidence of espionage by the Soviet embassy was publicized in February 1946, Prime Minister Mackenzie King immediately appointed a royal commission to inquire into Gouzenko's story and take testimony from him and others who had been implicated. The Kellock-Taschereau Commission submitted its final report in July 1946. The sensationalized spy trials took place throughout 1946, and one was held in 1949. Many scholars argue that they galvanized an already existing Cold War mentality. As David Bercuson notes, the Gouzenko affair "was dramatic evidence that all was not well with the wartime alliance and the USSR and the West might not, after all, share common interests on matters of post-war peace and security ... The Gouzenko defection did not ... push Canada completely into the Cold War, but it was the first definite shove in that direction."[42]

Despite the sensationalism of the Gouzenko affair, the number of Canadians arrested and convicted was small. The commission named thirty-six people in its report[43] and stated that twenty-one of them had been engaged in disclosing secret information to the Soviet embassy or were aware of its disclosure. Of the twenty-one, nineteen were eventually charged, and the other two disappeared before they could be detained. Eighteen Canadians were charged with conspiracy or offences under the Canadian Official Secrets Act, while Alan Nunn May was tried in the United Kingdom. Among the eighteen Canadians, eight were convicted and had their convictions sustained; two were discharged on grounds of insufficient evidence; and eight were acquitted. The two Canadians most heavily implicated in the Gouzenko affair were Fred Rose and Sam Carr, organizing secretary of the Labour-Progressive Party. Rose and Carr, both Jews, were exposed as senior liaison agents to Colonel Grant Zabotin, the Soviet military attaché in Ottawa and director of the espionage operation. The two men had acted as recruiters and transmitters of information – finding recruits, handing them their tasks, and carrying their information to Zabotin or his officers. Rose was sentenced to six years' imprisonment for conspiracy, and Carr, who escaped to the United States, was apprehended in 1949 and also sentenced to six years.[44]

In its final report, presented in July 1946, the royal commission attempted to explain how these people had become spies. It hypothesized that some were interested in the small amounts of money paid by the Soviets; a few were ideologically committed communists; others were Jews who looked to the USSR to help fight North American anti-Semitism; a small number were of Russian descent; while the rest had joined communist study groups simply to meet friends and been accidentally drawn into espionage. The commission noted that Russian agents deliberately used the spectre of anti-Semitism to entice Jews: "The evidence before us strongly suggests that anti-semitism and the natural reaction of persons of Jewish origin to racial discrimination, was one of the factors played upon by the Communist recruiting agents. It is significant that a number of the documents from the Russian Embassy specifically note 'Jew' or 'Jewess' in entries on their relevant Canadian agents or prospective agents, showing that the Russian Fifth Column leaders attached particular significance to this matter."[45]

Social Credit had followed the Gouzenko affair closely from the time the story broke in February 1946. In previous months the *Canadian Social Crediter* had implied that those involved in the spy trials were Jews, but by autumn all circumspection was abandoned and its headlines read, "Communists Use Jews as Spy Stooges." The party organ incorrectly announced that twenty-four persons were accused of espionage in Canada, of whom nineteen were Jews.[46] It surmised from the commission's report that communist traitors had duped unwitting Jews by using the threat of anti-Semitism in North America to force them to spy for Russia. Thus, Jews were not only the playthings of communist spies but hopelessly enmeshed with them: "The Communists, using fear as a weapon ... [saw] to it that Communist papers 'sympathized' with the Jews and that Communist heads were appointed to positions in leading Jewish organizations and ... Jewish publishing firms. The average Jewish citizen, who accepts anything blindly once it is offered to him in the name of protection, fell sucker!" In a moralizing attempt to encourage Jewish self-improvement, the paper suggested that the best way to combat anti-Semitism would be for Jews to denounce those communists who made up "Canada's spy ring." If they did not, thereby proving their preference for Russia to North America, "they should have the decency to leave for it, without staying here haranguing those who do try to build a better democracy." Yet the party organ doubted Jews would heed its message: "This will all fall on deaf ears, as far as Jewish leaders are concerned. But it may awaken some semblance of thought in the minds of Jewish readers of this paper (few though they are) who, after all, are the ones who pay in suffering and heartache for their blind trust."[47] What the *Canadian Social Crediter* wholly ignored was that not all those Canadians accused of espionage were Jews. But this was of little concern, for Social Credit was obsessed with the fact that *some* of the spies were Jews and that Canada's only Communist MP was both.

Yet the *Canadian Social Crediter* had cleverly tapped into a strong post-war impulse – anti-communism – and twinned it with its traditional anti-Semitic rhetoric to create a political lexicon Congress found very difficult to oppose. The situation was exacerbated by a nationwide stereotype of the communist Jew. During the 1930s and 1940s many Jews became involved with left-wing groups such as the Socialist Party of Canada, the Social Democratic Party, the Communist Party of Canada, and the Co-operative Commonwealth Federation (CCF). However, among ethnic groups in Canada, Finns and Ukrainians, not Jews, were most highly represented among socialists and communists.[48]

In her discussion of Jewish membership in the Communist Party, Erna Paris notes that "in the 1930s and 1940s, when the fascist threat loomed ominously both inside and outside Canada, Jews grew deeply attached to the Communist Party's official United Front against fascism. Jewish membership in the Party grew substantially during this period, but it never represented more than a fraction of the Jewish population." Moreover, the primarily Jewish voters of Montreal-Cartier did vote for Fred Rose, a communist, but after the Gouzenko affair "the support lost in Cartier was Jewish support and it never returned to the [Communist] Party."[49] In short, although the Gouzenko affair proved some connection between Jews and communists, Social Credit inflated the connection to mammoth proportions.[50]

Congress was painfully aware of Social Credit's reaction to the Gouzenko affair. It had observed the *Canadian Social Crediter*'s coverage of the spy trials and was in the very uncomfortable position of being unable to refute charges about the connection among Jews, communists, and spies. Yet for his part, Rosenberg attempted to rebut some of the party organ's allegations, specifically, the number of Jews implicated. The *Canadian Social Crediter* had stated that out of twenty-four persons accused of espionage, no fewer than nineteen were Jews. Rosenberg maintained that twenty-eight persons were named in the commission's report and thirteen were Jews. (In fact, the commission had named thirty-six persons and did not indicate who were Jews). Rosenberg divided the accused into four groups: agents; those suspected of activities but against whom no action was taken; those who procured false Canadian passports and other citizenship documents for agents' use; and those who acted as intermediaries. According to his information, only thirteen were Jews. There were seven Jewish agents: Samuel Sol Burman, Sam Carr, Harold Samuel Gerson, Israel Halperin, Freda Linton, Fred Rose, and David Shugar. Jack Isadore Gottheil and Arthur Steinberg were suspected of activities. Henry Harris and John Soboloff were involved in the false passport case. Germina Rabinovitch and an unidentified espionage assistant named "Gini" were named as intermediaries. In effect, Rosenberg was attempting to show that thirteen of the twenty-eight persons (or 46 per cent) involved in espionage were Jews. The *Canadian Social Crediter* calculated that 79 per cent were Jews.[51]

Yet because neither Rosenberg nor the *Canadian Social Crediter* ascertained the number of Jews among the thirty-six persons named in the commission report, neither calculation was that valuable. While Rosenberg intended to prove that far fewer Jews were implicated than the *Canadian Social Crediter* alleged, the latter was equally determined to show that nearly all those implicated were Jews. Most importantly,

Rosenberg failed to understand that determining the proportion of Jews was certainly futile, for even the implication of one Jew would have confirmed Social Credit's suspicions about Jews, communists, and espionage. In any case, Congress did not publicize Rosenberg's findings, and the *Canadian Social Crediter* spread its anti-Semitic propaganda on the Gouzenko affair with impunity. Admittedly, it would have been difficult for Congress to confront Social Credit over this issue. That even some Jews were guilty of espionage in no way facilitated its public relations work, and Congress had learned from previous experience that publicizing Social Credit's anti-Semitism could often boomerang.

Still, others with much less to lose believed that public exposure of Social Credit's anti-Semitism was both justified and necessary. Certainly this was the response of the general press in a subsequent incident, when it discovered that Social Credit was reprinting the spurious *Protocols* in the *Canadian Social Crediter* and *Vers Demain*. The latter was Social Credit's fortnightly French-language paper and official organ of the Union des Electeurs, the Social Credit organization in Quebec. The editor of *Vers Demain*, Louis Even, was head of the Union des Electeurs and a member of the national party organization, the Social Credit Association of Canada (SCAC). Established in 1939,[52] *Vers Demain* was a blatantly anti-Semitic paper that fully embraced Social Credit's theory of an international financial Jewish conspiracy. The *New Voice*, the monthly journal of the *Canadian Jewish Weekly*, described *Vers Demain* as "a fascist sheet ... Aping Streicher's *Stürmer*, it publishes cartoons demeaning, caricaturing, and slandering the Jews ... To *Vers Demain* ... [t]he 'international Jew' is responsible for everything wrong; the UN is a fiendish Jewish plot; UNRRA was a vehicle for Jewish domination of Europe; and the impeccably conservative B'nai Brith becomes ... a diabolical international network of Jewish freemasons plotting to destroy the Roman Catholic Church, the sanctity of marriage, [and] the sacred right of private enterprise to exploitation and profit."[53] These criticisms were not exaggerated. Perhaps the most grievous action by *Vers Demain* was its publication of the *Protocols* in serial form from 1 January to 15 August 1946.

Yet the *Canadian Social Crediter* was only slightly less culpable. While it never reprinted the *Protocols* in full, it none the less published articles that quoted from them. Between May and July 1946 it published a series entitled "Startling Facts of Recent History," which rehashed much of the material originally published in *The International Jew* by Henry Ford's *Dearborn Independent*. In December it published a reprint from the *Protocols* that stated: "The scrambles of what appear to be the major contestants for the prize of world control cloak the machinations of a concealed aspirant: the International Jew. His technique is, through money power and propaganda to dissolve all national institutions, and at the same time to build up his own international organisations of control."[54] Meanwhile, Social Credit politicians like Jaques quoted from or referred to the *Protocols* to prove the existence of the conspiracy, arguing that it was irrelevant whether the *Protocols* were authentic since their uncanny prediction of world events ultimately proved their veracity.[55]

Thus, contrary to general assumptions about French Canada's relatively greater anti-Semitism, although *Vers Demain* reprinted the *Protocols* in serial form, the *Canadian Social Crediter* was Social Credit's greatest disseminator of anti-Semitic propaganda. From its inception as *Today and Tomorrow* its anti-Semitism increased markedly, especially from 1945 to Manning's purge in late 1947. In contrast, *Vers Demain* published several consecutive issues during this period without slandering Jews. Only after Manning's purge and *Vers Demain*'s split from the official movement did it publish increasingly anti-Semitic propaganda.[56] Moreover, the *Canadian Social Crediter* further distinguished itself by establishing connections with British fascists in 1946, when it opened an office in London with the Holborn Publishing and Distributing Company, publishers of Sir Oswald Mosley's fascist propaganda.[57]

All these propaganda activities came to light when the *Saskatoon Star-Phoenix* published an editorial in December 1946 entitled "Home-Baked Fascism." Primarily intended to expose *Vers Demain*'s publication of the *Protocols*, "which inspired Hitler and the Nazi racist program," the editorial also pointed to Jaques and other Social Credit politicians "who openly avow their anti-semitism"; to Social Credit's anti-Semitic ideology; and to the similarity between Social Credit propaganda and Nazi techniques. The editorial also quoted from Douglas's book *Social Credit*, which stated: "The Jews are the protagonists of collectivism in all its forms, whether it is camouflaged under the name of Socialism, Fabianism, or 'big business,' and ... the opponents of collectivism must look to the Jews for an answer to the indictment of the theory itself. It should in any case be emphasized that it is the Jews as a group, and not as individuals, who are on trial, and that the remedy, if one is required, is to break up the group activity."[58] The editorial noted that "the similarity of Mr. Douglas' remedy with that put into effect by Hitler will need no explaining to the Canadian people, whose memory of the notorious concentration camps of Nazi Germany is still vivid." The editorial also provided a detailed explanation of the origins of the *Protocols* and the fact that they were a forgery. It concluded that Social Credit's conspiratorial, anti-Semitic philosophy was a "sinister threat" to Canadian democracy and, if not rejected, "will undermine and consume the nation, as it did in Germany."[59] The editorial was reprinted by the *People's Weekly* (the Alberta CCF party organ), the *Regina Leader-Post*, and even the *Canadian Social Crediter*, which used it as negative evidence of Social Credit's national success.[60]

But the editorial had placed Social Credit on the defensive, and the task of rebuttal fell to J.N. Haldeman, president of the Social Credit organization in Saskatchewan and chairman of the national council of the SCAC. In a published reply to the *Star-Phoenix* Haldeman declared that "Social Credit is absolutely opposed to anti-semitism. The evidence indicates that anti-semitism is a weapon of international finance and socialism to introduce totalitarianism ... The fact that Social Credit is attacked as being anti-semitic shows that it is an imposing obstacle to the schemes of Socialism and Finance." In Haldeman's mind, Social Credit was not anti-Semitic, because to be so would mean it had been duped by the international financiers. Regarding *Vers Demain*'s publication of the *Protocols*, he argued that when a Swiss court determined that the *Protocols* were a forgery in 1935, the defence was not permitted to give its case. Moreover, whether or not the *Protocols* were a forgery was not the issue: "The point is that the plan as outlined in these *Protocols* has been rapidly unfolding in the period of observation of this generation." Thus, publication of the *Protocols* was justified because their veracity was confirmed by current events.

Haldeman also attacked the "socialist Jewish conspiracy" in a bald attempt to shift responsibility for anti-Semitism away from Social Credit. He argued that socialists were "the chief promot[ers] of anti-semitism" for "giving to the Jewish race all the virtues and having Jews in key advisory and Government positions carrying out policies which centralize control in the hands of the state and subject the individual to control by the state. Because these policies prove disastrous and repugnant to people the reaction is to blame the entire Jewish race." Conceding that many Jews were not socialists, Haldeman appealed to Jewry to join Social Credit "in exposing the enemies of society whether they be Jew or Gentile." Satisfied that he had proven his point, he concluded: "Far from being anti-semitic, Social Credit is the greatest defender of freedom of the people and the rights of minorities as long as they do not impose policies of enslavement on others. Social Credit is vigorously pro-Christian and pro-Canadian."[61] Like Low's earlier statements, Haldeman's attempt at rebuttal simply confirmed Social Credit's anti-Semitism. Moreover, his definition of Social Credit as "pro-Christian" and "pro-Canadian" explicitly and implicitly excluded Jews, and suggested the same parochial and nationalistic tactics used by radical anti-Semites in the United States and Europe.

This time, Congress was determined to act. The *Protocols* were the centrepiece of all anti-Semitic propaganda, and Social Credit had blatantly promoted them. Yet it is noteworthy that, again, the impetus for action came from outside Congress. If the *Star-Phoenix* had not exposed Social Credit's activities, it is questionable that Congress would have. As long as Congress abdicated responsibility by letting others take the initiative, it would have little influence in determining how the battle was fought, won, or lost. None the less, at least Congress was attempting to create an active policy to ensure that Social Credit's anti-Semitism was exposed and eliminated. To that end, a national JPRC meeting in Montreal addressed the topic of "subversive movements" – specifically, Social Credit. National executive director Hayes reported on anti-Semitic manifestations in Canada and possible ways to counteract them. The national JPRC considered a variety of actions, including getting the post office to bar distribution of anti-Semitic publications, and especially Social Credit publications.[62] Although these plans were still embryonic, they foreshadowed Congress's later legislative-oriented public relations approach. For now, such discussions indicated a more forthright attitude, which many Congress officers and agents viewed as long overdue.

After reading the *Star-Phoenix* editorial, John Dower of Edmonton asked Congress to give newspaper editors an "up to the minute analysis" of Social Credit literature, since "it is obvious that Solon Low and the Social Credit Party have made up their minds not to stop at anything in the way of Anti-Semitic propaganda." Dower believed that Social Credit's propaganda "is so clearly a repetition of what Goebbels did in Germany that I think every Canadian newspaper will be aware of its significance."[63] Sam Godfrey of Toronto also asked Congress if distribution of the *Protocols* could in any way "be construed an illegal act on the part of the distributors?"[64] Clearly, the mood within Congress was changing. Publication of the notorious *Protocols* was unacceptable, and this time Social Credit's anti-Semitism had gone beyond the pale. National headquarters also appeared ready to respond. Hayes stated to Godfrey that "the reappearance of the *Elders of Zion* has caused us considerable grief and we have studied the implications and the possibility of actions on a wide variety of fronts," such as "conversations which have already been initiated with the leaders of the Social Credit Movement ... in a very informal and casual manner ... Examination of the post office regulations with a view to determining if the Postmaster General can bar these things from the mails ... Possibility of court action even if we lose the case but as long as we are able to publicize widely the evidence that the [P]rotocols are a forgery and a complete fraud." Hayes added: "I may be able to convince my officers that it would pay us to take action even knowing that the law wasn't on our side for the morale value involved. It is a difficult decision to take however."[65] In the years ahead Congress would unequivocally accept the necessity of legislative action to stop race hatred, but the road to such assertiveness would be a long and difficult one.

Indeed, events in late 1946 indicated that a more confrontational approach was not so easy to undertake. While Hayes was trying to create a policy to handle Social Credit's distribution of the *Protocols*, Alberta Congress agents, who were growing impatient with national headquarters' deliberations, undertook discussions with Social Credit leaders. However, the nature of these talks proved that openly confronting Social Credit was going to be a difficult, if not impossible task. In early December, Max Moscovich, a Congress agent and lawyer from Lethbridge, was travelling to Edmonton by train, on which were also several Social Credit politicians. In subsequent correspondence to Hayes, Moscovich described his experience. Seeing Social Crediters on the train, he walked into their coach and sat down with John Blackmore, MP for Lethbridge and former Social Credit leader in the House of Commons. "John," he said, "Saul Hayes has a great respect for you and feels that you are opposed to Anti-Semitic propaganda by your group." Blackmore responded: "Not only am I not Anti-Semitic – but I am definitely Pro-Jewish." After a brief discussion with Blackmore, Moscovich returned to his coach. Then national party leader Low came and sat next to him. Moscovich said: "Solon – I was with Saul Hayes on Monday – and he states that you had written stating you had no control over members of your group – and that you couldn't control their anti-semitic outbursts." Low replied: "Max – you've known me most of my life – I am definitely not anti-semitic. I have as my secretary – my daughter – who may marry a London Jew ... Jaques – is a definite fanatic – we resent his utterances – and we will certainly see that he does not get the nomination at next election ... Furthermore Manning ... and I are supervising the policy of the S[ocial] Credit Paper – so that antisemitic statements will be eliminated." Low then brought up his "pet hobby," anti-communism, and told Moscovich he would "love to see Canadian Jewry openly oppose Communism." Moscovich concluded that Blackmore was not anti-Semitic but in fact pro-Jewish and was "a sincere – honest devout Citizen – [but] a poor politician." In contrast, Low was "a shrewd aggressive politician." Yet Moscovich trusted Low's promises that Social Credit's anti-Semitism would diminish. In fact, he wrote Hayes that "if the Policy of the S. Credit paper does not alter – let me know and I will speak to Manning and Low. It may take a little while to change the policy – but outside of that B- Jaques I feel that S. Crediters of the West are anything but Anti-Semites – their past activities notwithstanding."[66]

Yet Hayes wondered how Congress could test the good faith of Low's statements, and he asked Moscovich: "Is there any way in which you can follow this up? Is it feasible to ask Low for a letter committing to writing what he is saying verbally? Is it feasible to ask him to have an editorial denouncing race prejudice in his next issue? Is it feasible for him to undertake to see the Union des Electeurs ... to have them stop the nonsense on the *Elders of the Protocols of Zion?*"[67] Moscovich skirted these questions but suggested that Hayes "write Solon Low an official letter from your office, and tell him that I saw you in Calgary where I joyfully disclosed his assurances to me ... Tell him, that your view is that Canadian Jews are opposed to Communism – and urge him to intervene and extirpate the anti-semitic propaganda in Quebec – and thank him officially for his pro-Jewish attitude as disclosed by myself."[68]

Hayes did not write to Low, perhaps because he received four separate memoranda from Rosenberg citing further examples of anti-Semitism in the *Canadian Social Crediter.*[69] Instead, he forwarded the examples to Moscovich, stating: "When you will look through [them] you will find many references which we do not like." Hayes conveyed his deep scepticism about Low's promises: "I would think that it is a bit early for Solon Low to fulfill his promise, but surely if this kind of stuff would be repeated in forthcoming issues [of the *Canadian Social Crediter*], we can once more take his promises for what they are worth – that is, sub-zero. I hope to goodness I am wrong and I particularly hope that your conversation with him might mean a new deal."[70]

Unfortunately for Congress, Hayes was not wrong. On 18 December 1946 Low gave a nation-wide broadcast over the CBC that, although not blatantly anti-Semitic, repeated all the covert anti-Semitic slurs. He accused the federal government of being a "socialist administration" whose foreign policy was "handing over Canada to the domination of international gangsters." In Low's mind, international gangsters controlled the League of Nations and the UN and ensured that "men in high places" favourable to "treason-mongering" allowed Russian espionage to occur in Canada. He also mentioned "Germina (Hermina) Rabionovitch" in his discussion of the Gouzenko affair. In a spate of rhetorical questions, he demanded: "Do you know that the same group of international gangsters who are today scheming for world revolution are the same people who promoted the world war? Do you know that these same men promoted and financed the Russian revolution? Are you aware that these arch-criminals were responsible for the economic chaos and suffering of the hungry thirties, for financing Hitler to power, for promoting World War Two with its tragic carnage? Do you know that there is a close tie-up between international communism, international finance and international political Zionism?" He concluded by sermonizing: "The world conflict is a conflict between the forces of good and the forces of evil – of Christianity versus anti-Christianity and paganism ... That is the challenge which Christmas 1946 will bring to each one of us. How will you meet the challenge?"[71]

Low's speech was typically Social Credit. He had not used the word "Jew" once, but given his own reputation and Social Credit's anti-Semitic record, his meaning could easily be inferred.[72] Yet reactions within Congress were not uniform. Rabbi Gordon of Saskatoon listened to Low's speech, and, according to Moscovitch in Lethbridge, "his impression was that Low['s] address was pronouncedly Anti-Semitic." Moscovich himself "completely disagreed," although he noted to Hayes that Low had used the name "Rabinovitch" with respect to the Gouzenko affair and the term "international political Zionism."[73] None the less, stated Moscovich, "outside of these two references his speech was chiefly Anti-Communistic and to sum it up vulgarly – consisted of unadulterated B.S. I doubt if it tended to stir up anti-Jewish feeling." He still believed that Low's earlier promises about quelling Social Credit's anti-Semitism were not yet broken and exhorted Hayes to give Low a second chance: "[Low] is a damned Hypocrite – true – but I feel his volunteered promises may ultimately be implemented. He told me that Jaques ... who is now addressing audiences with G.K. Smith – is a fanatic – and that he cannot discipline him ... Now Saul – with your permission I will approach Low ... and if the policy of the Social Credit Press in Canada still follows the same tune – I will see him and ask him point blank – *Why he has failed to keep his word* ... give me one chance to try to convince this man – and one or two other Federal and Provincial S. Crediters – that they are unjustly and uselessly hurting us – and if that does not bring results – you might try other remedies."[74]

Hayes was less optimistic. In response to Low's speech, Congress officers in Ontario were exerting considerable pressure on national headquarters to take action. Hayes summarized the situation for Moscovich from his own perspective in Montreal: "It appears that most people who heard the broadcast interpreted it as being anti-semitic and one using the same techniques which Germany made so popular from

1933 to the fateful days of '39. I refer of course to the suggestion advanced by Low that international Communism, international Capitalism and international Zionism (only Hitler said 'Jewry') are responsible for the world's ills and that if the mass of the population would only recognize these evils and extirpate them all would be well. This has an ominous and familiar ring. Whether it is strictly anti-semitism or not pales into an insignificance beside its dangerous demagoguery." Hayes wanted eventual court action against Low for his statements about international political Zionism, "knowing full well that we would lose the case," but suggested that for now Moscovich merely "ought to bump into [Low] (I mean hard) and charge him with hypocrisy and double talk."[75] Moscovich promised Hayes he would take up the matter of "international political Zionism" with Low and would "not mince words."[76]

Notwithstanding their compromise, Hayes and Moscovich fundamentally disagreed on Congress's approach to the Social Credit problem. Indeed, lack of consensus was a major hindrance in creating that ephemeral national public relations policy. Moscovich did not believe Low's speech caused prejudice or discrimination against Jews. He also did not believe the words "Rabinovitch" and "international political Zionism" had much impact on the broadcast's listeners. And although he certainly did not agree with Social Credit's anti-Semitism, he did not believe it posed a dangerous threat to Canadian Jewry. In contrast, Hayes believed Low's speech showed chilling parallels to Hitler's methods, by which democracy was subverted, hatred spread, and the welfare of certain citizens threatened under the guise of the defence of democracy. In short, although both men disapproved of Low's rhetoric, they had different interpretations of its potential threat. While Moscovich was not an alarmist, Hayes was determined to protect Canadian Jewry from a worse fate. Given recent events in Europe, his concern was understandable. The similarity between Social Credit and Nazi rhetoric was striking, and Congress's duty should have been to ensure that such propaganda was disallowed, whether or not it posed any real threat to Canadian Jewry. But Congress was unable to reach this level of responsibility because of lack of consensus. In the absence of a unified approach, Congress had difficulty establishing *any* effective policy towards Social Credit.

Yet Congress was more willing and able than ever to confront Social Credit, and Low's speech was a further catalyst for action. At the Eastern Region's JPRC meeting in January 1947 officers discussed the speech and contemplated a formal protest to the CBC. A draft letter was introduced, which some officers wanted publicized in the press. Another officer suggested that members of parliament be contacted to take up Low's speech on the floor of the House. Everyone agreed that the Eastern JPRC should issue a public statement condemning *Vers Demain* for its anti-Semitic policy and publication of the *Protocols*, and that the national JPRC should "study the Social Credit Party statements and its publications and if [it] found [them] anti-semitic ... issue a public condemnation in the Press." Hayes also suggested that legal methods be used, in this case to fight the anti-Semitic propaganda of the *Canadian Social Crediter* and *Vers Demain*: "Counter propaganda might be used as a defence; efforts might be renewed and strengthened to have legislation outlawing anti-semitism; influential people or even political parties could be contacted to combat those who spread anti-semitism. Legal counsel is now being obtained as to possible court action against the anti-semitic publications; though such action might not have chances of success, it might be of great value from an education point of view."[77]

Congress was certainly breaking new ground – strong, effective measures were finally being considered to fight Social Credit's anti-Semitism. Yet in many ways the JPRC meeting was also typical. A stronger stance towards Social Credit was discussed; actions were considered; plans were debated; motions were carried. Meanwhile, Social Credit's anti-Semitism continued unabated. However, this meeting *was* different in one important respect: the plan to send a formal letter of complaint to the CBC was actually executed, by none other than Congress's national president. On 23 January 1947 Samuel Bronfman wrote to the chairman of the board of governors of the CBC to "register a formal protest against some of the statements which Mr. Solon Low, National Leader of the Social Credit Party, was able to voice in a free time political broadcast over the Trans-Canada Network of the CBC on December 18, 1946." Bronfman quoted those excerpts that discussed "the international power maniacs who aim to destroy Christianity"; the "international gangsters who are to-day scheming for world revolution"; and the "close tie-up between international communism, international finance and international political Zionism."[78]

Bronfman conceded that Low's allegations were vague and lacked evidence; none the less, he argued, such statements contravened the CBC's regulations for broadcasting stations, pursuant to section 22 of the 1936 Canadian Broadcasting Act.[79] He added that Low's statements also violated the general policy of the CBC, "which is one of encouraging a fair presentation of controversial questions of public interest and concern." Citing passages from Nazi propaganda, including *Mein Kampf*, to show their similarity to Low's rhetoric,[80] Bronfman stated: "Mr. Low's method, this whipping up of international plots, to scare and frighten people into a confused way of political thinking (including its thinly veiled anti-semitic core) is just a little too redolent of certain European politicians now defunct, to be permitted to pass by the c.b.c. and the Canadian people ... This is the type of political rubbish, very dangerous rubbish, which used to come over Goebbels' radio stations. You will agree, I think, we should not allow these insidious methods to creep into Canadian broadcasting." Bronfman judiciously added that he assumed the CBC was already aware of Low's transgression and, if it had not already done so, would give "certain advice to the party leader who indulged in this type of speech making."[81] The president of the Canadian Jewish Congress had finally taken on Social Credit. It appeared that a new era in public relations might be under way.[82]

Indeed, this was not the end of Congress's confrontation of Low. Quite by accident, Rabbi Solomon Frank of Winnipeg met with Low in January when the latter addressed the Winnipeg Division of the Empire Club, of which Frank was a member. Informed that there were no members of the press present and unaware of the rabbi's presence, Low spoke "quite freely at the meeting." Frank noted that, "in the course of his discussion on the state of the British Empire [Low] launched a very vicious attack against the Zionist Movement which he called the number 2 enemy of the British Empire, the number 1 enemy being Communism." Immediately after the meeting the club's chairman introduced Frank to Low. "Mr. Low was obviously embarrassed and tried to soft-pedal his statements somewhat," but when Frank pressed him on the matter, Low invited him to have lunch the following day "to discuss all problems of mutual interest." Although the lunch was on a Saturday, the rabbi accepted the invitation, and the contents of their meeting were subsequently reported at a Western Division JPRC meeting:

In his discussion with the Social Credit leader Rabbi Frank pointed out how erroneous [Low's] attitude was, especially with regard to the alleged link-up between Zionism and Communism. He gave [Low] documentary evidence on the determined anti-Communist stand of nearly all Jewish groups in Palestine and ... Mr. Low was deeply impressed by his statements. He admitted that irresponsible elements in the Social Credit Party such as Mr. Norman Jaques, suggest by their behaviour that the Social Credit Movement is antisemitic. In actual fact this is not the case. Mr. Low asked Rabbi Frank for a number of documents ... He promised that he would do everything in his power to curb antisemitic tendencies within his Party.

Frank suggested to the committee that various documents be furnished to Low and that further developments be watched closely. He felt that if Low's intentions were sincere, "we have every reason to welcome the above development and to work in every possible way towards more understanding of our problems on the part of the followers of the Social Credit Movement."[83]

It will be recalled that, years earlier, Frank had met with Aberhart, who gave him similar promises. Perhaps the rabbi should have been less naïve; this was not the first time Low or other Social Credit leaders had denied anti-Semitism and promised to do everything in their power to curb anti-Semitism within their ranks. More seriously, as in past years, the JPRC did not use Low's statements or his discussion with Frank to its advantage. Instead, it agreed that no publicity whatsoever should be given to Frank's and Low's meeting.[84] Congress needed to take advantage of the gains that came its way, and this encounter resulted only in another lost opportunity. Still, the meeting between Frank and Low was productive in so far as it was another confrontation of Social Credit's anti-Semitism. Many Congress officers and agents believed that their organization needed to have more confrontations with Social Credit. If Congress exerted enough pressure on the movement, perhaps its anti-Semitism would diminish.

While others within Congress were confronting Low, Rosenberg undertook a "content analysis" of the *Canadian Social Crediter* and submitted his findings in a lengthy memorandum. He garnered examples of anti-Semitic statements from forty-three issues of the party organ, covering January 1945 to January 1947, and noted that "42 out of the latest 106 consecutive issues of the *Canadian Social Crediter* have carried anti-semitic articles." In other words, during the previous two years the party organ had published anti-Semitic propaganda about 40 per cent of the time. Rosenberg suggested that Congress charge Social Credit with one or all of the following: seditious libel, defamatory libel, or contravention of postal regulations.[85]

For the charge of seditious libel to be upheld, Rosenberg argued that the party organ's reprinting of the *Protocols* and its allegations of an international financial Jewish world conspiracy must be considered seditious, which was plausible given that the latter especially "tends to disturb the tranquility of this country by inciting ill-will between different classes of His Majesty's Subjects." Rosenberg wondered if a connection could also be established between Alberta Social Credit, Mosley's Fascists in England, and Gerald L.K. Smith, and if so, "would such evidence be acceptable as proof of seditious intention?" Regarding defamatory libel, Rosenberg questioned whether a libelous attack upon an entire group or class of citizens, namely the Canadian Jewish community, was considered defamatory libel under the Criminal Code since the relevant section referred only to "persons" being defamed.[86]

He also wondered if Congress could legally demand that the *Canadian Social Crediter* publish refutations of its allegations, or whether Congress could publicly warn booksellers and newsdealers that the paper contained defamatory material and advise them that if criminal proceedings were instituted, legally they would not be able to exculpate themselves.[87] Lastly, if Congress were to charge Social Credit with contravention of postal regulations, it would be important to know if any of the excerpts from the *Canadian Social Crediter* or the *Protocols* themselves was "'indecent, immoral, seditious, disloyal, scurrilous or libelous' within the meaning of the Postal Regulation." If they were, asked Rosenberg, did the Postmaster General have complete discretionary power to determine what was "indecent, immoral, seditious, disloyal, scurrilous or libelous" and hence unmailable, or were his decisions subject to review by the courts? Further, if Social Credit literature were deemed indecent and immoral, could future issues of the *Canadian Social Crediter* be banned from the mails or could the party itself be forbidden use of the mails "as the organization responsible for the publication of the *Canadian Social Crediter?*"[88]

Rosenberg knew that favourable answers to these questions would demand solid evidence that Social Credit was distributing anti-Semitic propaganda – evidence that he had been gathering for years. The question remained whether the law would support any charges Congress brought against Social Credit. Employing legal means was problematic at best; under the Criminal Code seditious libel and defamatory libel referred to individuals, not groups, and Rosenberg was well aware of the outcome of earlier lawsuits that had attempted group libel charges.[89] Moreover, he was concerned about the kind of proof required to establish a convincing case of seditious libel or defamatory libel and the types of defences that would be used if such charges were laid. Indeed, invoking the law was a double-edged sword; Social Credit could just as easily use freedom of speech and parliamentary privilege to show that it had not contravened any laws or regulations. Thus, although Rosenberg believed he had indisputable proof that Social Credit was spreading anti-Semitism, the real issue was whether it was feasible for Congress to pursue justice through the legal system.

Rosenberg's suggestions were indicative of Congress's changing stance. At its seventh plenary session, held later that spring, it was resolved that through its regional and local organizations Congress should conduct active public campaigns at the local, provincial, and national levels to outlaw "all forms of discrimination and ... provide legal guarantees for full equality of treatment and opportunity for all Canadians regardless of race, religion or national origin."[90] Yet unanimity continued to be a problem, and not everyone supported such legalistic measures. Rabbi Feinberg, for example, cautioned that legislation would never resolve group tensions within society, and thus it was essential for Jews to rally behind all oppressed groups: "When overt acts of discrimination occur, no matter at whom they are aimed, they constitute a threat to us. Every minority is imperilled by every oppression. Once we condone cruelty or gross violations of elementary liberties, we prepare the shackles for ourselves."[91] But Congress's public relations approach was evolving to include both legislative action and broad-based appeals against race hatred. Still, the shift to a more rights-oriented, legislative policy was a slow process, and Congress's actions lagged far behind its rhetoric. Consequently, although Rosenberg suggested various legal actions to deal with the *Canadian Social Crediter*'s anti-Semitism, Congress confined his suggestions to the realm of possibility.

Yet Rosenberg was not the only Congress officer committed to more assertive action. On 14 February 1947 Saul Hayes travelled to Ottawa, walked into the House of Commons, and sat outside the Social Credit caucus room. After about thirty minutes Low and other party members came out of caucus. Hayes told Low he wanted to speak with him; Low said he was on his way to an appointment and could spare no time. None the less, he asked Hayes what he wanted, and when the latter told him it was about Low's recent radio broadcast and other matters, Low invited him to his office and spoke with him for forty minutes. "Either he had no appointment or forgot to keep it," Hayes later commented in a memo to other executive officers.[92]

The two men discussed several issues during their impromptu meeting. First, Hayes raised the issue of Low's broadcast, which had referred to "international political Zionism." He told Low his statements "w[ere] not only a fantasy but grievously pained the Jewish Community," and explained that it was fantastic to link international political Zionism with communism because the two ideologies were antithetical.[93] According to Hayes,

[Low stated that] the radio speech was not intended to embarrass the Jewish community[;] he was careful not to talk of Jews since this would have been against all his instincts and viewpoints ... Low says he is a Zionist ... His quarrel is that Zionism ... has become a movement which cares not who is in its way and this new political Zionism is what he deplores and will fight ... His attack on international Zionism was not an attack on Jews or his concept of Zionism. He does not allege ... that political Zionism is in conspiracy with international finance and international Communism. His thesis is that there are three insidious forces today working independently but all three have one thing in common – a desire to break up the British Empire. Nowhere in his speech, says Low, does he state that the three are in conspiracy but that each is a link (in a chain presumably) with the end in view of destroying the British Empire. The tie-up he refers to in his speech is the tie-up of having common arms not in conspiracy.

As proof of his faith in Zionism, Low told Hayes of his membership in the Canadian Palestine Committee. Hayes did not consider it good tactics to tell him that the mandate of the Canadian Palestine Committee was the very thing Low called "international and political Zionism." Low promised Hayes he would not give offence to the Jewish community, stating sympathetically that he realized the Jews were inevitably oversensitive because they had suffered so much. As a Mormon, he added, he considered himself a spiritual brother of the Jews since the Mormons too had suffered for their faith. "Sooner or later," remarked Hayes deprecatingly, "I knew he would come to the point that some of his best friends are Jewish and sure enough he stated this." Indeed, Low emphasized that he did not want to hurt the Jewish people since among his friendliest contacts were a half-dozen Jewish residents of Alberta such as Moscovich, Dower, and Freedman.[94]

Throughout their conversation Low kept mentioning that a disproportionate number of Jews were communists. When Hayes finally asked him where he was getting his figures, Low stated that Rabbi Frank of Winnipeg had told him that 700 of Winnipeg's 1,800 Jews were communists. Low asked Hayes to agree that this was a very high figure and clearly showed where Jewish interests pointed. "I told him that he had quite obviously misunderstood Rabbi Frank," stated Hayes. "There were 18,000 not 1,800 Jews in Winnipeg and while I knew nothing of the figures certainly 4% of the total should induce far different conclusions than a 40% proportion." Hayes again explained how communism and Zionism were antithetical ideologies, and Low promised him that on this issue "he would exercise great care to prevent unwarranted statements to creep into his texts."[95]

The second issue Hayes raised was *Vers Demain*'s publication of the *Protocols*, at which point Low shook his head "sorrowfully," swore that their publication "was surely not done mischievously but thoughtlessly," and admitted that the paper's editorial force had made a mistake. He added that he could likely arrange an agreement with its editor, Louis Even, to ensure that such material was not published again. Low explained that discussions were underway to set up a national editorial board so that the *Canadian Social Crediter* and *Vers Demain* followed a common policy. He emphasized that, in contrast to *Vers Demain*, the *Canadian Social Crediter* would never have published the *Protocols*. Further, although he had never read the

Protocols, he assumed they were a forgery, but "whether they are true or not they are dangerous and it would be bad to publicize them." Hayes remained unimpressed with Low's declarations, believing they "sounded hollow in the light of all that had transpired and was said." None the less, Low suggested that a meeting be set up between Hayes and Réal Caouette, the newly elected Union des Electeurs MP for Pontiac, Quebec. Hayes agreed, and a meeting was planned for the third week of February.[96]

The last issue Hayes and Low discussed was Jaques, who had become closely associated with the notorious American anti-Semite Gerald L.K. Smith. "Apparently not only has the Canadian Jewish Congress trouble with Jaques but so has the Social Credit party," Hayes reported. "[Low] told me (barely above a whisper) that they could not control [Jaques], that he considered himself above party discipline and that he absents himself from all caucuses." But Hayes reminded Low that Social Credit's internal difficulties were not nearly as important as the fact that "Jaques is putting the hall-mark of anti-semitism on Social Credit." Low protested that official Social Credit remonstrances could not influence Jaques, but he none the less agreed to look into the matter further. Hayes reported: "Mr. Low … said if Smith was as bad as I said he was, he, Low, would denounce Jaques either in the *Social Crediter* and at a Social Credit public conference or convention or he would find some method of dissociating Jaques from the Party."[97]

Low seemed conciliatory towards Hayes and genuinely concerned about the issues he raised. Yet Hayes's overall impression of their meeting was ambivalent: "Mr. Low is quick to make promises. He has certain fixed ideas on money and credit which no amount of cross-conversation will dislodge. These views are ideologies and without them he could not be a Social Crediter. He sounds reasonable on other matters and *if* he makes good his promises much of the potential harm to us of Social Credit may not emerge. We will soon be in a position to judge these promises. Until then a period of watchful waiting would seem to be indicated."[98]

Hayes's meeting with Low was discussed at the next meeting of the national JPRC. Officers suggested that in future encounters with Social Credit leaders, such as the upcoming meeting with Low and Caouette, Congress should send more than one delegate. Yet one officer cautioned that "there was a danger in having delegations since a person, on delicate matters, might desire to speak only to one person." No one suggested that it was time Congress became less concerned about offending the sensibilities of Social Crediters and more concerned with openly confronting their anti-Semitism, and if this required an entire contingent of Congress delegates, then so be it. But the JPRC agreed that, henceforth, no fewer than two Congress representatives should meet with Social Credit leaders. Accordingly, for the upcoming meeting Rabbi Feinberg, Joseph Fine (co-chairman of the national JPRC), and Hayes would be Congress's delegates. They would be responsible for submitting a report to the JPRC and empowered to co-opt additional officers in preparing a policy of action regarding Social Credit. Yet even the idea of creating such a policy was not unanimously accepted. While some officers believed that Social Credit was Congress's "greatest single public relations problem" and that the national party and Alberta government should be "put on the defensive," one officer stated that an open battle with Social Credit should be undertaken only if the movement declared an anti-Semitic policy (as opposed to propaganda), or if it refused to abandon certain practices Congress found dangerous and anti-Semitic. Others did not believe Canadian Jewry should have to wait for anti-Semitic rhetoric to be turned into policy before taking action. Importantly, there were officers, including Hayes, who wanted Congress to formulate a national policy on Social Credit immediately. Hayes "felt that there was great need for the methods of possible attack to be discussed now, to be used when the need is apparent."[99]

Thus, although no formal plans were decided upon at the meeting, Congress's stance was clearly more resolute than it had been two years earlier. The experience of European Jewry during the war, the Canadian government's recalcitrance and inhumanity, the increase in anti-Semitic agitation since the 1930s, together with Social Credit's distinctive anti-Semitic campaign, all played a role in its growing assertiveness. As Social Credit became more vocal in its denunciations of Zionism, communism, and other manifestations of the Jewish world plot, Congress's knowledge of the recent horrors of Nazi-occupied Europe and Canada's refusal to provide refuge made such rhetoric increasingly intolerable. Congress was moving towards a public relations philosophy of "Never Again" – a philosophy that would consider Social Credit's rhetorical anti-Semitism to be as potentially dangerous as the genocidal policies of the Third Reich. For many within Congress, it was unthinkable that, in the shadow of the Holocaust, Jews anywhere should wait once again to see if rhetoric would be turned into policy and policy into annihilation. Congress finally was refusing to countenance the prejudices of a provincial government and national party within its own country.

Shortly after the meeting of the national JPRC, Hayes and Fine[100] met with Low, Blackmore, and Caouette. The meeting, which took place in Ottawa at the end of February 1947, was different from that between Hayes and Low two weeks earlier. The increase in numerical strength on both sides altered the nature of the discussions. The meeting was more formal: the Congress officers were more forthright, and the Social Credit leaders more intransigent. Hayes and Fine gave specific examples comparing the rhetoric of the Nazi Party to the propaganda published in the *Canadian Social Crediter* and *Vers Demain*. "We cited chapter and verse," Hayes later reported to the national executive. "Needless to say, we did not charge them with Nazism or Fascism but drew the conclusion that whatever the motivation on their part, the pattern was identical with the sordid, cynical, brutal one of recent years."[101]

During the meeting the Congress officers also pointed to Social Credit's publication of the *Protocols*, for which none of the Social Crediters accepted responsibility. The latter conceded that *Vers Demain* had published the *Protocols* but they offered no explanation. Hayes and Fine informed them that the *Protocols* purported to be "the outlines of a vast Jewish plan to dominate the world." Low and Blackmore admitted that had they been consulted, they would have counselled against publication. Low added that he had never seen the *Protocols* until two days before, when he got them out of the Parliamentary Library. Hayes noticed that "Mr. Low attached great importance to the fact that the Library had a copy. It would appear that he considered this an imprimatur or at least lending a verisimilitude of authenticity to the *Protocols*." For his part, Caouette was noncommittal but stated that he had never bothered to read the *Protocols* and paid no attention to their serialization in *Vers Demain*. He added that the paper reached 60,000 French Canadian homes and suggested that Congress contact its editor, Louis Even, to discuss why the *Protocols* had been published.[102]

The Congress officers also discussed various speeches and writings by Social Crediters that attacked Jews. Low and Blackmore agreed that Congress had cause for complaint about many of the examples. Concerning others, they argued that Jews in fact were implicated and that Social Credit was only stating the truth. Hayes and Fine informed them that "we were resentful of the accents Social Credit gave to these matters, e.g. if in their creed international finance is one of the cardinal sins, why single out Jewish bankers from among the giants of international finance and moreover, why attack them as Jews [?]." It was a question to which the Social Crediters did not respond. The Congress officers emphasized that Social Credit's methods "were anti-semitic in effect if not in motivation."[103]

For their part, the Social Crediters expressed resentment at a recent *Congress Bulletin* whose front page stated "Social Credit Party

Includes Anti-semitism on Platform."[104] They argued that it was not true, and moreover that the story was not consistent with its headline. Nowhere in the *Bulletin*'s article was there any discussion of the party's platform; instead the article focused on the two party organs. Blackmore was very offended by the *Bulletin*'s headline, and both he and Low challenged anyone to offer "one scintilla of evidence that the party platform includes anti-semitism." They also charged many Jews and Jewish papers with "glaring inaccuracies," and Low especially resented the "lies and defamatory libels" of R.S. Gordon, editor of *Today*.[105]

Hayes and Fine apologized for the *Congress Bulletin* story, as it was supposed to have been removed before the *Bulletin*'s issue. Yet they emphasized that they considered the *Canadian Social Crediter* and *Vers Demain* to be anti-Semitic literature. As Hayes reported: "We further stated that if [the anti-Semitic literature] continues, we must assume that the sc party wish[es] to use these means of appealing to the electorate … we [emphasized] … that we learned the lessons of 1923 to the war years and would not view this pattern with resignation or equanimity. We made it abundantly clear that if the signs were portentous we would do all in our power to safeguard the future rights and protect the Jewish community from attacks and onslaughts." Low agreed to examine Congress's examples of anti-Semitism from the *Canadian Social Crediter*.[106]

Over two hours later, as the meeting drew to a close, the Social Crediters made their final remarks. According to Hayes, Low "affirmed that he and his party will not tolerate anti-semitism and wherever it rears its head he and his colleagues will decapitate it. He avowed his firm principles and his appreciation certain of the complaints we made." Blackmore, "who was most sanctimonious, alleged that he and Low were the best friends the Jews ever had. This was due to Low and he being Latter Day Saints who in their creed are descendants of Ephraim. He said moreover that complaints were double edged swords and he pleaded for accuracy on [Congress's] part." Lastly, Caouette, who was a "laconic individual," said very little except that "he has Jewish friends and contacts and has not resorted to anti-semitism."[107]

In his report to the national executive Hayes summarized the Social Crediters' arguments: "The [Social Credit] leaders stated they recognized the dangers of anti-semitic propaganda … The appearance of the *Protocols* was not their responsibility though they stated that had they any part in the paper's policy, they would not have published the *Protocols* … They admitted it to be a mistake to single out Jews as the preponderant influences in the camps of their enemies – International

Communism and International Finance ... They agree that certain articles and copy was offensive ... They avow their hatred of anti-semitism
and their immunity from its taints ... They ask for accuracy from us
and they on their part will attempt to play fair and deal equitably with
us as a group."[108]

As for his own impressions of the meeting, Hayes believed it was
possible that Social Credit would be more careful about blaming Jews
for the world's ills but would continue attacking internationally known
Jews who were involved in international finance and communism.
Congress's one hope was that "Social Credit will refer to Kuhn, Loeb,
etc. without indicating it is Jewish and by associating it with the giants
of international finance. We can hope too that if Social Credit has to
attack international financiers and name the machinators it will be
accurate[,] in which case individual Jews will be outnumbered by their
Gentile confraternity." To expect more than that was harbouring an
illusion, concluded Hayes: "Social Credit from our point of view has
cast its die. It has sold its devotees a creed which, if not anti-semitic,
is one of the finest backgrounds for anti-semitism. It cannot retreat
very much even if Solon Low, Manning, Blackmore and others, protest
their goodwill at matins and vespers; Social Credit knows what the
Jewish community will do if it fails to reform itself. We must wait to
examine the future issues of the *Social Crediter*, and *Vers Demain*, the
speeches of the leaders, their attitude on men like Jaques, etc. and other
indices of their viewpoints."[109] Hayes's comments imply a much stronger stance than Congress was probably willing or ready to take.
Although he averred that "Social Credit knows what the Jewish community will do if it fails to reform itself," it is questionable if Congress
did. Although its public relations stance was evolving and maturing,
Congress still confined itself to meeting with Social Credit leaders and
trying to persuade them to abandon their anti-Semitism. Low had
proven his inability and unwillingness to deal fairly and honestly with
Congress, and he would prove it again. For Social Credit, no appeal
by the conspirators – or at least their lackeys – would convince it to
lay down its arms. Congress needed to understand this and move ahead
with more forthright measures.

The next step was for Hayes and the others to recommend a plan
of action to the national JPRC. To this end Hayes organized and led a
special JPRC subcommittee whose purpose was to "study ... [the] Social
Credit Party, its leaders, its program and its literature in relation to the
security and well being of the Jewish Community in Canada." Before
the subcommittee reported back, however, it arranged meetings with
three American Jewish defence organizations, the Anti-Defamation
League of B'nai Brith (ADL), the American Jewish Congress (AJC), and

the American Jewish Committee, to obtain advice regarding Social Credit's anti-Semitism and its threat to Canadian Jewry.* The American Jewish organizations, although operating independently, co-operated in protecting and promoting the rights of American Jewry, and their pro-active approach would serve as a model for Congress's public relations work. On 14 March 1947 in New York City, Hayes, Fine, and Feinberg met with representatives from the three organizations. Congress previously had provided each organization with complete documentation of Social Credit's anti-Semitism, including copies of literature, speeches, correspondence, and memoranda. At the meeting, the American organizations offered their recommendations for combating the Social Credit menace. While some suggestions were consistent, others were completely contradictory.[110]

The ADL, the AJC, and the American Jewish Committee unanimously agreed that Congress should publicly expose and discredit Social Credit's leaders and ideas. The ADL suggested that Congress "accumulate all data which sheds discredit on any of the Social Credit members, whether parliamentarians or rank and file, and expose those vulnerable." The AJC similarly stated that an exposé of the party leaders was necessary and that Congress "ought to be the instrument publicly to fight Social Credit on Jewish issues which Social Credit raise." Likewise, the American Jewish Committee instructed Congress to "discredit the party leaders ... Keep up a constant barrage of literature." As for specific measures against Jaques, the ADL suggested that Congress get the American government to "bar Jaques from the United States and use this widely for publicity purposes," and the AJC recommended that "Jaques ... be exposed and in the expos[é] tie him up at all times to the Social Credit Party ... Ascertain possibilities of formal censure of Jaques in the House of Commons ... [u]se American periodicals to make a frontal attack on Jaques and other vulnerable leaders."[111]

The three organizations also agreed that Congress should ally itself with Social Credit's "natural enemies" in order to execute a co-ordinated attack. The ADL suggested that Congress "seek out commentators who have a following and ascertain whether they have ... an interest in attacking the Social Credit doctrine ... see if the Canadian

---

* The memorandum that records the meeting with the three American Jewish defence organizations is unsigned, undated, and has the following statement at the top of it: "Please do not retain this memorandum after perusal. We would insist that you co-operate by destroying it." Clearly, Congress officers did not want this information to be leaked to the public, especially to Social Credit sources. Luckily for scholarly posterity, someone did not follow orders.

Legion will ... protest the Social Credit platform and policy ... use the Trade Unions as a weapon to prevent Social Credit from spreading ... obtain allies from church groups both clerical and lay." The American Jewish Committee also suggested that Congress "obtain allies in groups and among interests which would want to ensure the obliteration of Social Credit (church, trade unions, other political parties)."[112]

On other recommendations, the organizations were not as unanimous. Only the ADL and the AJC suggested that Congress assist opposition candidates in federal and provincial elections in order to defeat key Social Credit candidates. Specifically, the ADL suggested that Congress "have individuals make financial contributions to trusted individuals who will distribute the monies strategically to ensure defeat of particular candidates provincial and federal." The AJC emphasized that "the main objective would be to destroy the party in Alberta by an aggressive campaign, by way of expos[é] of leaders and support to opposition candidates in provincial and federal elections." In contrast, the American Jewish Committee, although suggesting that Congress through "infiltration arrange for disreputable characters to enter the party so that a successful smear campaign can be undertaken," strongly discouraged using opposition parties to oust the Social Credit government: "Do not attempt to aid and assist opposition candidates since these matters cannot long be kept confidential without resulting in a noxious boomerang."[113]

There were also contradictory recommendations regarding legal action. The AJC strongly supported legal action and suggested several options: first, Congress should determine whether action could be taken by groups aggrieved by Social Credit speeches, pamphlets, and other propaganda; second, a person *outside* Congress should prepare a content analysis of the *Canadian Social Crediter* so that in any projected lawsuit Congress would have "a complete objective and scientific study ... on hand"; third, because Social Credit attacked Zionists as conspirators, some prominent Zionists should sue Jaques, Low, or whoever else was making such attacks; finally, legal action should be taken against those Social Crediters who edited, published, and distributed the *Protocols*. The AJC implied that even if the lawsuits were not successful, the results would be beneficial because of the accompanying exposé of Social Credit. In contrast, the ADL was "doubtful" regarding the use of legal action, and the American Jewish Committee was "unalterably opposed," warning specifically: "By no means and under no circumstances engage in or encourage others to engage in libel action, damage action, [or] group libel action."[114]

After meeting with the three Jewish organizations, Hayes, Fine, and Feinberg provided their comments and conclusions in a confidential memorandum. They expressed no surprise at the nature of the recommendations, which were congruent with "the pattern of work to which the various agencies have dedicated themselves." The ADL urged fact-finding and smear campaigns; the AJC suggested legal action wherever possible, "even though successful verdict would be largely in doubt from the very start"; and the American Jewish Committee advised against legal action but suggested a "campaign of infiltration of disreputable people" into Social Credit. The Congress officers concluded that, given the response of the American organizations, organized Jewry in the United States also looked upon Social Credit "as a dangerous group which must be attacked." Yet they were not optimistic about potential action against Social Credit: "The problem is acknowledged to be a most difficult one and even with the implementation of the program outlined, there is little guarantee that an effective brake will be put on the Social Credit machine." However, they recognized that Congress must continue its fight against Social Credit: "Despite the difficulties and woeful prognostications every possible action must be taken and a long range plan to accomplish the desired ends be formulated and followed."[115]

It had been an important meeting with the American Jewish organizations. Of greatest significance is the AJC's recommendation that Congress become the public instrument to fight Social Credit's anti-Semitism. Until Congress could fulfill its mandate as *the* public defender and promoter of Canadian Jewry's interests, it would make little headway against Social Credit. Perhaps because of this knowledge, Congress officers were discouraged by the daunting task ahead of them. Despite years of efforts, Congress had experienced few successes in its battle against the Social Credit problem. The organization had carefully documented Social Credit's anti-Semitic propaganda; it had investigated several methods of action and implemented some; it had confronted Social Credit leaders on numerous occasions; and even the president of Congress had taken on Social Credit. Yet the party's anti-Semitic propaganda machine continued to churn. Since the end of the war Social Credit's anti-Semitism had increased, not decreased. It appeared that the national organization for Canadian Jewry was unable to stop hate propaganda against its people.

Congress's general secretary, H.M. Caiserman, was fully cognizant of the limitations of Congress's approach. He acknowledged the necessity of legal action against promoters of anti-Semitism and pointed to the superior methods in Great Britain, South Africa, and Switzerland, where anti-Semitism and racial discrimination were brought before the courts. Caiserman agreed that Congress not only must continue its traditional public relations work of prevention, research, educational literature, and co-operative good-will activities; it must also make authorities aware of all anti-Semitic and racist material distributed in Canada, and present legislative proposals to the Canadian government.[116] This was much easier said than done, and adopting an assertive philosophy was much easier than executing an effective policy. Yet Congress's public relations work was gradually shifting, and more confrontational methods were being considered, if not always implemented. Importantly, Congress was now seeking assistance from other Jewish defence organizations to solve its most serious public relations problem. The time was coming when Congress would assemble all its energy and resources to bring down Social Credit's anti-Semitism. Little did it know that Social Credit's anti-Semitic foundations were already beginning to crumble.

6 "Hamlet without the Ghost"

Throughout the spring of 1947 the Canadian Jewish Congress continued to attempt a stronger public relations approach towards Social Credit's anti-Semitism. Although it carefully examined the proposals of the American Jewish defence organizations, it was not ready to execute such bold measures. Congress's public relations philosophy was still rooted in the misconception that anti-Semitism could be combated by appeals to humanitarianism and justice. But Congress was also learning the perils of this kind of approach, especially since Social Credit leaders made promises and promptly broke them. Although the organization still hesitated to take the American organizations' advice and create a new policy, its philosophy at least was changing. Congress was adapting to a post-Holocaust world in which race hatred was viewed as obnoxious and potentially dangerous. A growing number of Congress officers and agents embraced this post-war, post-Holocaust mentality and were more determined than ever to execute congruent action. Not surprisingly, much of this initiative came from the Western Division of Congress, specifically from the Alberta branch.

In late February 1947 S. Hart Green of Winnipeg wrote to national executive director Hayes, stating that he and several Western Division Congress officers perceived Social Credit to be "our greatest enemy today" and that "all our efforts must be put forth to combat this evil." Regarding Hayes's recent meeting with Low in Ottawa, Green remarked that Low's comments were "the same bunk that he gave to Rabbi Frank here [in Winnipeg], and the same as Aberhart gave to

Rabbi Frank prior to his death some years ago." Green suggested that rather than meeting with national Social Credit leaders in Ottawa, the way to solve Social Credit's anti-Semitism was to confront it in Alberta. Years earlier Edmonton Congress officers had said "to leave the situation with them," yet they had obtained few results. Now, however, the Alberta branch had a plan that Green believed could be executed from Alberta and would obtain definite results. He suggested that Leonard Bercuson, director of the provincial department of education's correspondence school and western executive director of the Zionist Organization of Canada, use his public relations contacts to exert pressure on the Manning government. Green proposed that Bercuson "be put on this work for the next six months ... and that the Congress look after the necessary expense."[1] The plan was not revolutionary, but Green's idea that the Alberta branch could achieve quicker, more direct results was certainly worth trying. Importantly, it addressed the necessity of involving Alberta Jewry in creating a viable solution to the Social Credit problem.

Meanwhile, at the Western Division's Joint Public Relations Committee (JPRC) meeting in Edmonton in February 1947, officers discussed more aggressive measures against Social Credit. Some argued that the best tactic would be to defeat the Alberta government or at least some of its key personalities, and that the CCF was the only political party through which this could be accomplished. After some discussion, the western JPRC agreed that all assistance must go to the CCF. Committee member Wolfe Margolus, who was also treasurer of the Alberta CCF, had already obtained about $2,000 from Jews in Edmonton and Calgary that he put anonymously into CCF coffers. He also contacted Elmer Roper, leader of the CCF in Alberta, and informed him that the "Jewish people would be behind the CCF party in its attack on Social Credit." Roper indicated that he was prepared to use monies put into CCF coffers to pay five well-known CCF personalities to travel throughout Alberta on a three-month speaking tour. Margolus also asked Congress's national headquarters to send him at least $2,500 privately to be given to the CCF. In return he would supply Hayes with a detailed and confidential report of all CCF activities against Social Credit. Margolus emphasized that Social Credit "should be attacked by all means, fair or foul," and even suggested the possibility of employing private detectives to obtain material that would "blacken and expose" key Social Credit leaders who were guilty of dishonesty or "corrupt living." The minimum objective, he declared, should be the defeat of certain Social Credit leaders in their own constituencies.[2]

If these plans were quasi-subversive, Congress's Alberta branch may have felt compelled to respond to its repressive environment in a clandestine manner. In Margolus's view, Social Credit's activities were clearly anathema to Jewish welfare in Alberta and Canada. Given the pervasiveness of Social Credit's anti-Semitism, the Alberta branch believed the only solution was to remove Social Credit from power, by whatever means necessary. There is no evidence that Hayes or national headquarters sent Margolus $2,500; none the less, it is remarkable that Margolus had already given the CCF thousands of dollars and was looking for further funds. This was a calculated risk, for Social Credit politicians certainly would have attacked the CCF and Canadian Jewry as co-conspirators in a "Jewish-socialist plot" if they had discovered that Jews were secretly funnelling monies to the social-ist political opposition.

Bercuson, who had been called in to help the fight, was also con-vinced that removing the Social Credit government from power would solve the problem. He told Hayes that Edmonton Congress officers "are of the opinion that the [Social Credit] party constitutes a grave threat to the Jews of this country: more than that, we feel that its philosophy is a potential menace to all progressive forces in the country." Bercuson similarly believed that Congress must "defeat or greatly weaken the present Alberta government for it is from the prestige and the reputation of the Manning regime that the federal party derives its strength and sustenance." The only way to defeat the Social Credit government, he declared, was to support the CCF: "The rise or decline of this dangerous philosophy will be decided only in the political arena."[3]

It is clear that the Alberta branch wanted national headquarters and the Eastern Division to take both it and Social Credit's propaganda more seriously. Alberta Congress officers were aware that most Cana-dians "have looked upon Alberta with some amusement as an isolated, remote province carrying out an economic experiment doomed at its beginning to failure" and that many saw Social Credit "as a rather humorous effort to wring prosperity from 'funny money.'" Mean-while, the majority of Canadian Jewry in Toronto and Montreal "look upon the movement with smug unconcern." However, opined the Alberta branch, Social Credit was a dangerous and growing force that needed to be taken seriously by all Canadians, especially Jews: "Twelve years ago it was only a provincial party; today it has a voice in the Federal House, while neutral observers are amazed by its growth in Quebec and Ontario … It is time for Canadians to take stock of the situation; certainly the Jews of this country cannot waste another moment. The party philosophy is directed against Jews; the strongest plank in the platform is unquestionably anti-Semitism. A single glance at the party organ, *The Canadian Social Crediter* proves the point, for its pages are filled with propaganda and innuendoes against Hitler's first victims."[4]

The Alberta branch was determined that Social Credit not be allowed to rise to national prominence. In its view, the problem was still manageable; there were only thirteen Social Credit MPs and the national party depended on the Alberta government's support and reputation for its continued growth. Even the *Canadian Social Crediter*, which was ostensibly the national party organ, was published in Edmonton and focused predominantly on activities in Alberta. Consequently, stated the Alberta branch, "the most effective method of striking at the national movement is by hacking at the roots. Paradoxical as it may sound, the most telling way to stop the circulation of the *Protocols* in Quebec is to defeat Norman Jaques in Wetaskiwin, Alberta ... Social Credit must be checked in its home province. If its power in Alberta can be materially reduced or if the party can be defeated, Canadian Jewry's most direct threat will be averted."[5] The Alberta branch was making an important point. National headquarters had focused more on the national Social Credit party and less on the Alberta government: it had confronted Social Credit MPs in Ottawa, attempted to quash distribution of the *Protocols* by *Vers Demain*, and scrutinized Jaques's antics in the House of Commons. All these actions were important and necessary. However, according to the Alberta branch, it was time to start fighting Social Credit not from national headquarters in Montreal but from Alberta, where the problem resided. Not only did Social Credit need to be taken more seriously, but the Alberta branch must be listened to and included in any attempt to create a workable public relations approach.

In fact, without waiting for a response from national headquarters, Alberta Congress officers unilaterally created their own public relations policy to fight the Alberta government. Clandestine in nature, the policy was called the "educational program," and Social Credit politicians were known as the "educational leaders." It included an analysis of the 1944 Alberta provincial election that was presumably not unlike Rosenberg's analysis of the 1945 federal election; biographical data on Social Credit leaders; exposure of the "weak chinks" in Social Credit's armour; distribution of pamphlets and other media; and financial assistance to "educational leaders [Social Crediters] who oppose present ones where good chance of success possible." The policy was to be known to only a few in Alberta and even fewer in Montreal.[6] At the same time the Alberta officers elaborated their plans to back the CCF. They believed that the CCF was gaining support in Alberta (notwithstanding that it had won only two seats in the last provincial election)[7] and that general unrest with the government could be galvanized and swung behind Roper's group. If enough financing were given to the CCF and public expression given to Social Credit's misdemeanours (specifically its censorship of 16-mm movies[8] and Jaques's activities), perhaps the CCF could win the 1948 provincial election. The Alberta officers also made three recommendations for fighting Social Credit nationally: sponsor a radio commentator, such as Lorne Greene, to expose subversive activities in Canada "while emphasizing the concept of 'Canadians All'"; publish pamphlets that compared "in parallel columns the statements by Social Credit spokesmen and Nazi propagandists"; and bring Social Credit's anti-Semitic propaganda to the attention of editorial writers throughout Canada.[9]

Unquestionably, the Alberta branch was committed to removing Social Credit from power and was willing to use both traditional and non-traditional public relations methods to achieve its goals. In hindsight, the Alberta officers were overly optimistic regarding CCF party fortunes in the next Alberta election (see Table 4); none the less, they were at least determined to stop the Social Credit propaganda machine. Yet in executing their new plan, the Alberta officers were careful that no one discovered they were contributing funds to the CCF or undertaking an "educational program" against Social Credit. Again, their secrecy suggests the repressive climate in which they were forced to operate during the Social Credit regime and that greatly influenced their public relations work. Without the force of the law, government, or even public opinion behind it, the Alberta branch was confined to traditional public relations methods – education, anti-defamation, moral suasion – and any measure that exceeded these polite methods needed to be pursued clandestinely.

The Alberta branch's educational program was the most confrontational and assertive action suggested thus far, and significantly it was not condoned by national headquarters. Hayes had kept abreast of the Alberta branch's plans, and when he briefed the national executive, it expressed concern that "this Educational Program might prove a bit of a boomerang in that the person whom we are thinking of to implement it, might make statements to educational leaders and might be called to give an accounting in the event that the present educational leaders dislike the project."[10] Although cryptically expressed, the worry seemed to be that Social Credit leaders might confront the person leading the anti–Social Credit campaign (be it Bercuson or someone else) and ask him for whom he was working. When Hayes conveyed the national executive's concern to Bercuson, the latter assured him that Alberta officers would warn their man not to say anything that might reveal that Canadian Jewry was in any way attempting to bring about the defeat of the Alberta government.[11] Clearly, both national

Table 4
Alberta provincial election, 17 August 1948

Political party	Votes received	% of vote	Candidates nominated	Candidates elected
CCF	56,387	19.13	51	2
Independent	9,014	3.05	7	1
Ind. Citizen's Assoc.	3,969	1.35	2	0
Ind. Social Credit	2,958	1.00	3	1
Labour	3,579	1.21	1	0
Labour Progressive	1,372	0.47	2	0
Liberal	52,655	17.86	49	2
Social Credit	164,003	55.63	57	51
United Labour	856	0.30	1	0
TOTALS	294,793	100.00	173	57

Source: Statistics are from Alberta, A Report on Alberta Elections.

headquarters and the Alberta branch did not want Social Credit to know of these confrontational plans.

The national executive was also concerned that attempting to stop Social Credit's anti-Semitism by defeating the government would bring negative, not positive consequences. It expressed "great doubt ... at the wisdom of the Jewish community actively supporting political parties in opposition to Social Credit" because of the danger of leakage and a possible boomerang effect. Because of its serious reservations about the "educational program," the national executive refused to approve any plans to oppose the Alberta government until "considerable further thought be given it."[12] It appears that the Alberta branch was moving too swiftly for the old guard at national headquarters. Perhaps if Social Credit had formed the government in Quebec, Congress's national executive in Montreal would have been more motivated to implement an aggressive policy.

Yet the national executive was not alone in its disapproval of this new public relations approach. When the national JPRC met in July 1947 to discuss Social Credit, it reviewed the Alberta officers' "educational program" and their "investigations of the [Social Credit] party." The JPRC noted that Bercuson recently had made trips to Edmonton, Lethbridge, and Calgary "for the purposes of his investigations," which focused on "money wastage and corruption" in the Alberta government, and that, with only one exception, "the Jewish communal leaders of Western Canada had been consulted and had expressed their agreement with the plan." This was an important accomplishment: the Western Division had created a coherent, unified public relations policy. It was something national headquarters had yet to achieve. But the JPRC was not convinced by the Western Division's new strategy. One officer doubted that an exposé of graft in the Alberta government would have the desired effect on public opinion, "judging by the experience in the past in Western Canada and Alberta in particular." In contrast, other officers believed that such an exposé would in fact have an effect on public opinion, even in Eastern Canada.[13] Although reactions were mixed, most JPRC officers were sceptical that Alberta Jewry's plans would bring positive results.

Despite misgivings at the national level, at least Alberta Jewry had a definite plan, and when Bercuson asked for $500 so that "a responsible person [could] tour the province and assess the situation," the national executive authorized his request.[14] Yet before the Alberta branch was able to obtain any concrete results, Social Credit began to experience its own problems with anti-Semitism. Two events had sparked broad press and political reaction: the Alberta Social Credit Board's 1946 annual report, and Premier Manning's repudiation of anti-Semitism at the closing of the Alberta legislative session on 1 April 1947. These incidents would show that Social Credit's years of anti-Semitism were beginning to boomerang on their own. A growing constituency of Albertans was beginning to identify Social Credit's views as obnoxious, intolerant, and anti-democratic.

In March 1947 the Social Credit Board released its 1946 annual report to the Alberta legislative assembly. The report varied little from previous years – it described how the world dictatorship and the international financial tyranny were conducted by world plotters. However, the report differed in two important respects: it named several prominent Jews in the United States and Britain as proof to "those who still have lingering doubts regarding the existence and identity of a ruthless group of World Plotters"; and it questioned the validity of democratic measures such as majority rule, the secret ballot, and universal franchise.[15] Specifically, the report listed several prominent Jews, including Eugene Meyer, organizer of the World Bank, which was "controlled by individuals who are not responsible to national or international governments ... [and who] can wield incalculable economic power and determine the financial policies of every nation"; Herbert H. Lehman, first chairman of the United Nations Relief and Rehabilitation Association (UNRRA), who was "no doubt nominated by the President of the United States, acting on the advice of the adviser of all Presidents, Bernard Baruch"; Baruch, U.S. representative on the United Nations Atomic Energy Commission; Lord Rothschild, prominent British socialist peer, "who occupies a prominent place in the inner circle of International High Finance"; Sir Ernest

Cassel, contributor of endowment funds to the London School of Economics, "an institution devoted to the training of socialists"; and Harold Laski, "one of the star lecturers in the London School of Economics" who had instructed some sixty members of the current British Parliament. Meyer, Lehman, Baruch, Rothschild, Cassel, and Laski were used as evidence of "the close kinship which exists between the leading figures in the socialist ranks and those of international finance ... the forces of socialism and finance are both working with all their might to reach the same objective – the establishment of the totalitarian world state."[16]

In its discussion of the validity of majority rule, the report stated: "Majority rule is definitely not a democratic concept, though false propaganda has led many to accept it thoughtlessly ... If the majority of a group want three meals a day, there seems to be no sane reason why the minority should be compelled to eat three meals as well when they only want two." Regarding the secret ballot,

There must be something wrong with the system under which we live when individuals are so insecure and subservient to other individuals that they dare not let it be known how they marked their ballots. If the World Plotters *permitted* the secret ballot, then it was the political party system which they used to render it harmless to their vested interests. Meanwhile, the generality of people were deceived in the belief that they had made one more stride towards true democracy ... there seems to be no reason why a voter should not place an open *signed* ballot into the ballot box, thus openly declaring the results he wanted and automatically assuming responsibility for the policy adopted ... a voter would ... ponder carefully the manner in which he proposed to mark his ballot, knowing that, as a result of a wrong decision, he would suffer the consequences and moreover, be obliged to foot the bill.

With respect to universal franchise, the report stated: "We believe that the secret ballot and universal franchise are the labels which identify any genuine Democracy ... There are sound reasons why we should doubt the validity of these and other terms which have been so freely used to describe the Democratic ideal."[17]

Although the report's anti-democratic nature was obvious, its anti-Semitism was more covert. Not surprisingly, it did not use the word "Jew" but certainly implied that the "World Plotters" were Jewish. This transparent attack was not viewed positively by the Alberta press and political opposition. The *Edmonton Journal* criticized the board's chairman, A.V. Bourcier, for having allowed the publication of a government report that named several eminent Jews as world plotters: "One cannot read the report without receiving the impression that the board listed these names for the precise purpose of linking 'World Plotters' and 'Jews,' and the importance of the latter as leaders among the former. It is just possible, of course, that Mr. Bourcier did not write the report, but surely he read it before he signed it as chairman of the Alberta Social Credit Board." In response, Bourcier accused the *Edmonton Journal* of "uttering a deliberate falsehood," since "at no place in the report can one say there is one reference to any Jews or to world plotters led by eminent Jews."[18] Bourcier was correct. Jews were not mentioned, but it was a question of semantics. The board may not have labelled any Jews *as Jews*, but its intentions were clear. The *Calgary Herald* similarly criticized the board for offering "a warmed-over serving of the ideas of Major C.H. Douglas ... with all overt indications of Major Douglas's basic philosophy of anti-Semitism carefully deleted." Regarding the board's accusation that Baruch, United States representative on the UN Atomic Energy Commission, was a world plotter, the *Herald* remarked: "This is utterly meaningless unless one accepts Major Douglas's theory that every individual who is extremely wealthy and a Jew (and Bernard Baruch is both) is necessarily a ringleader in the plot to seize world power. Mr. Baruch's high ideals and outstanding record of public service make such a notion preposterous."[19]

In the Alberta legislature CCF leader Roper noted that the board's anti-Semitism was the same as Douglas's. He declared the report "absurd and a menace to democracy," and stated that the board did not have the right to issue official statements as an "arm of the government operating on public funds." In response, Premier Manning stated that the board was not an "arm of the government" but operated under the direct authority of the legislature and was "at liberty to function within that authority designated to it by this legislature."[20] Manning was obfuscating. In fact, the board *was* an arm of the Alberta government and operated only because Social Credit was in power. If Social Credit were to lose office, the board would cease to exist.

The Canadian Jewish press also condemned Social Credit's intolerance. In an article entitled "The Facts about Social Credit," the *New Voice*, the monthly journal of the *Canadian Jewish Weekly*, declared: "Social Credit has attracted into its ranks as motley an aggregation of democracy-hating individuals as can be found anywhere in the country ... Originally a farm protest movement, it has become an organ of bitter anti-democratic dimensions, an outspoken threat to Canadian democracy ... it is no longer a popular movement in its original sense. It is a high-powered machine, covered over by a veneer of religious fanaticism and obscurity." Interestingly, the *New Voice* reprinted the cartoon from the Anglo-Jewish monthly *Today* that depicted Nazi propaganda minister Joseph Goebbels and Low trying to force an unwilling Canada to drink from the poisoned well of anti-Semitism. Its recycling of the cartoon was clearly a retaliatory gesture; the *New Voice* desired to give in kind what Canadian Jewry had long been receiving from Social Credit. At the same time, the paper exhorted Jews and all Canadians to oppose Social Credit's anti-democratic tactics: "The democrat alone can defeat the fascist or the would-be fascist. That holds true for every country, Canada included. Jews in Canada must take their place firmly and affirmatively in the front ranks of democracy. That is a major duty which cannot be evaded."[21]

As a result of political and press criticism, the Alberta government decided to conduct damage control. On 1 April 1947, at the closing of the legislative session, Manning issued an official statement regarding Social Credit's anti-Semitism. He protested that recent criticism of the board and government was "a vicious campaign of deliberate misrepresentation" and argued that "a deliberate attempt is being made to associate the government and the Social Credit movement with various viewpoints and individual opinions which we, as a government and a movement, do not endorse and to which we do not subscribe." Manning then announced three resolutions regarding Social Credit's philosophy, including its stance on anti-Semitism:

1 We re-affirm our unswerving allegiance to the principles of Social Credit and our unshakable determination to ... fight for social and economic security with freedom initiated in this Province by the late Premier William Aberhart.

2 We condemn, repudiate and completely disassociate ourselves and the Social Credit movement in Alberta from any statements or publications which are incompatible with the established British ideals of democratic freedom or which endorse, excuse or incite anti-Semitism or racial or religious intolerance in any form.

3 We reiterate our intention to do everything in our power to unite the people of this Province and country irrespective of colour, race or creed in an all-out effort to end the present vicious financial monopoly and restore the effective control over money and credit to the people themselves.[22]

In reporting on Manning's statement, the *Calgary Albertan* castigated the premier for implying that there was an "underhanded campaign to slander [the government]." The paper concluded that Social Credit was indisputably anti-Semitic and gave the following examples as proof: MP Jaques and his association with "semi-fascist anti-Jewish organizations in the United States"; Douglas, "almighty omniscient

oracle of Social Credit, and one of Britain's most violent Jew-baiters";
the Australian Social Credit movement, which "takes its inspiration
from Major Douglas and to a lesser extent from the Alberta Social
Credit movement [and] pins most of its case on anti-Semitism"; and
the Union des Electeurs, "[which is] now busy circulating the *Protocols
of the Elders of Zion* ... [and] fast becoming the rallying point of the
numerous Jew haters in French Canada." As for the board's report, the
Albertan repeated the *Edmonton Journal's* comment that "one cannot
read the report without receiving the impression that the board listed
these names for the precise purpose of linking 'world plotters' and
'Jews,' and the importance of the latter as leaders among the former."
The *Albertan* further criticized Manning for not taking more responsibility for Social Credit's anti-Semitism. It accepted that Manning himself was probably not anti-Semitic, "but perhaps Mr. Jaques speaks
for the 'movement' more than Mr. Manning does." In conclusion,
"Mr. Manning more than anyone else can speak for the Alberta government, and if he says it is not anti-Semitic, he ought to be taken at
his word. But he must pardon a good deal of skepticism when he says
the 'Social Credit movement' is not anti-Semitic."[23] The *Lethbridge
Herald* also joined the fray, remarking that "Premier Manning of
Alberta has issued a statement condemning statements or publications
which endorse or excuse anti-Semitism. We hope he beamed it at the
Social Credit MP for Wetaskiwin [Jaques], and it wouldn't hurt to
include the father of the Social Credit theory, Major Douglas himself."[24]

Political responses to Manning's statement were equally negative,
and his opponents seized the opportunity to deride the premier's repudiation of anti-Semitism. CCF leader Roper noted that Manning's statements contradicted both Social Credit's actions and the views of
Douglas, Jaques, and Social Credit technical adviser Byrne. The Alberta
CCF party organ, *People's Weekly*, harshly criticized the board's report
and called Byrne "the chore boy and echo of Major Douglas." In
response, the *Canadian Social Crediter* declared that the CCF and the
communists were working in tandem and that the "Communists have
been given official orders to brand everyone who stands in their way
as 'anti-Semitic.'" The party organ also referred to the American Anti-
Defamation League (ADL) as a "sinister part" of the "smear bund,"
whose "victims are seldom anti-Semitic but are always anti-Communist."[25] While Manning and the party organ continued to deny vehemently that the movement was infected with anti-Semitism, evidence
to the contrary had clearly become a political liability. Social Credit
needed to extricate itself from its own progeny.

Congress watched these events closely but, in keeping with its
problematic approach, did not issue its own statement condemning the

board's report. Nor did it publicly support the press's denunciations. Moreover, despite Manning's announcement, most officers and agents were sceptical that Social Credit was about to discard its anti-Semitism. Rosenberg, now employed as Congress's national research director, noted that although Manning had repudiated anti-Semitism and racial or religious intolerance within the movement, "the *Canadian Social Crediter* continues to print not only anti-Semitic editorials and articles but also articles against the admission of refugees, against 'pleas for racial tolerance' and against the extension of full citizenship rights to Canadians of Japanese and Chinese origins."[26] Manning's declarations notwithstanding, Rosenberg had little faith that Social Credit's intolerance was about to diminish.

However, a turn of events in the spring of 1947 increased the pressure on Social Credit and offered new hope to Congress. This time the spotlight turned on Jaques's anti-Semitic activities. On 5 May 1947 the *Montreal Star* showed a picture of Jaques with Gerald L.K. Smith and his wife in Philadelphia, where Jaques had attended a meeting addressed by the notorious anti-Semite. On 7 May, in a telephone interview granted to the *Montreal Gazette*, Jaques revealed the close connection between his and Smith's ideas: "Gerald Smith is a truly great Christian gentleman who has been cruelly maligned. He stands for Christian nationalism. But of course the Communists have smeared him as anti-semitic ... Smith believes in America for the Americans and in the American way of life ... I have tried to do the same with the Canadian way of life and Canadian freedom and I will keep right on trying." The *New York Post* reported that the ADL had recently asked the state department in Washington to bar Jaques from entering the country. The ADL described Jaques as a "notorious anti-semite who has abused the privilege of entry into the United States by stirring up misunderstanding and tensions among racial and religious groups." To this allegation Jaques simply retorted: "I don't have to defend my actions," and added that the ADL was "part of the Zionist Terrorists who have been making such trouble in Palestine ... [and] part of the Communist front [which uses] blackmail and defamation of character [as] part of [its] work."[27]

In the House of Commons the next day, Jaques was less recalcitrant. He retracted his earlier statements and denied he was a disciple of the notorious Smith. Regarding the recent *Gazette* article, he swore that "most of the remarks, including the quotations attributed to me, are pure fabrications." However, he admitted stating that Smith "had done more to expose communist plots than any other public man in the United States of America" and that he, Jaques, "would do my best to expose communist plots here." To Jaques's recantations, the *Gazette* remarked: "Afterthought apparently convinced burly Norman Jaques ... that he had said either too much or too little when ... he frankly avowed himself a disciple of US Christian Front Leader Gerald L.K. Smith."[28]

Further denunciations of Jaques and Social Credit quickly followed. The *Montreal Star* stated: "Norman Jaques ... [has] denied a report that he was a disciple of the notorious American rabble-rouser, Gerald L.K. Smith ... Mr. Jaques may be no disciple of the Jew-baiting America Firster, but he acts like one ... Social Crediters in Canada have become professional anti-Semites; they have re-issued the fake *Protocols of the Elders of Zion* and under cover of an attack on communism preach racial hatred ... Little wonder, then, that when [Jaques] was reported to have described Gerald L.K. Smith as a 'truly Christian gentleman,' the public would be inclined to believe that he did. Smith has been discredited in the United States as neither a gentleman nor a Christian ... Mr. Jaques would be well advised to follow a less bespattered messiah."[29] The *Montreal Herald* similarly remarked: "Next time they have the opportunity, Canadian voters – and particularly those of Wetaskiwin, Alta., – should make it clear that the doctrines of Gerald L.K. Smith are not welcome in Canada ... Mr. Smith has been stirring up race hate, anti-Semitism and similar Nazi specialties, in the US for a considerable number of years. It's up to Canadian voters in general, because Mr. Jaques is one of the best known spokesmen of the Social Credit Party – and Social Credit doctrine trends toward the type of nationalism carried to the extreme by the notorious Smith."[30]

The *Montreal Gazette* likewise condemned Jaques for his association with Smith: "In avowing even partial or qualified support for the vociferated agitation of Mr. Smith, and his intention to promote similar views in this country, Mr. Jaques reveals himself the apostle of an un-Canadian gospel which has no proper place in the life of this country ... Canadians should realize the disruptive and repugnant import of Mr. Jaques' preachments and his association with Mr. Smith ... they should set themselves in both mind and deed decisively against allowing such alien concepts to take root in this democratic country."[31] It is interesting that the *Gazette* declared that Smith's nationalistic ideals had no place in Canada. Perhaps this was a post-war response to the extreme nationalism of wartime Germany. Yet is curious that Jaques preached an anti-Semitic gospel for years and was censured only when he associated himself with an American leader of dubious fame. Had he not become publicly involved with Smith, it is questionable whether the Canadian press would have bothered to take up the case. A Canadian politician who voiced anti-Semitism was small news, but one who became associated with a notorious American was much more newsworthy. Thus, perhaps the *Gazette*'s patriotic response was merely a traditional exercise of defining Canadian identity in anti-American terms.

In any case, as a result of this negative press coverage Jaques realized his reputation was at stake. In a second interview granted to the *Montreal Gazette* on 11 May he denied describing Smith as "a truly great Christian gentleman" but quickly added, "not ... that I deny that he is. But I just don't seem to remember having said it." Referring to himself as a "Canada First man" and "a Britisher through and through," Jaques promoted the principle of "Canada for Canadians" while emphasizing that "I am totally free of bias on all questions involving race, creed and/or religion." Yet he railed against Zionists as "poisonous propagandists," expressed his belief in the *Protocols*, and declared the Balfour Declaration to be "the root of the evil." When asked if he was going to organize a Christian Front in Canada along the lines of Smith's organization, he responded incriminatingly: "We believe ... that the Social Credit Party is already doing that work here. It defends Christian principles."[32]

If Jaques believed this second interview would help clear up the misunderstanding that had arisen from the first, he was clearly mistaken. The next evening, national Social Credit leader Low rose in the House of Commons and stated: "I want to make it clear that neither the social credit movement in Canada nor the group of social credit members in this house takes its lead from Gerald L.K. Smith, nor is associated with him in any way," and that "except for the meagre reports we have read in the press, thirteen of us know nothing about the work Mr. Smith is doing or about the movement called the 'Christian Front.'" As the *Montreal Gazette* noted, "[Low's] reference to '13 of us' was pointed since the Social Credit group in the House has 14 members." The *Gazette* accurately inferred that Low was sending a rebuke to Jaques and his "political indiscretions."[33]

To this rebuke Jaques responded most irrationally. Shortly thereafter, he stood in the House of Commons and announced he was threatened by "communist secret police" and that "some of their agents are working within our [Social Credit] movement." In a manner that would become the hallmark of Joseph McCarthy, Jaques waved a piece of paper in the air and declared that a communist agent "was detected a few years ago and among his papers was found a note" that read: "There always are certain individuals prominent in the social credit movement who will deserve careful attention. Jaques is one of them. In my opinion this man is most dangerous to our cause ... Despite our efforts we have never been able to unseat him. Watch him carefully, he has many followers." Jaques neither identified the agent nor explained the note's origins. However, he insisted that "this is not the first time that I have been threatened by the communist secret police." With a "we who are about to die, salute you" gesture, he proclaimed: "Sooner or later we must all stand up and be counted. I have many friends in the United States, fine, fearless people who are fighting the communist enemies of their country and of our country. I should be sorry not to meet them again. But my mind is made up; I am in a fight to a finish against the red communists and pink fellow travellers. I shall not be stopped by threats. My silence is not for sale at any price. You shall know the truth and the truth shall make you free."[34]

Jaques's behaviour was bizarre indeed. Most certainly he was the author of the note, which suggests that he suffered from paranoid anxiety or delusions of persecution.[35] Yet armchair analyses are hardly reliable; what is clear is that Jaques had believed in the existence of an international, financial, Jewish conspiracy since the beginning of his political career, if not earlier. In the wake of Manning's new pronouncements he was losing support, both publicly and politically. When Low deliberately distanced the national party and its members from any association with Smith, this was an implicit rebuff of Jaques. Marginalized from his fellow combatants, Jaques was forced to wage war against his long-time enemy – international Jewish finance – alone.

The Canadian press was not overly sympathetic to Jaques's plight. The *Ottawa Journal* was sceptical about the communist agent's note that had been left "lying handily around," and smirked that "it was something of a mystery just who might be threatening [Jaques's] life." Moreover, "while possibly fearing for his life, [Jaques's] concern up to this morning had not been sufficient to impel him to seek any special protection from either the RCMP or the Commons' Protective Staff." The *Montreal Star* similarly scoffed: "Just why anyone would threaten the life of Mr. Jaques is a deep mystery. Certainly he seldom is to be found speaking to a packed House of Commons." The *Montreal Gazette* called Jaques's address "the wildest speech of several sessions of Parliament."[36] The strongest denunciation of Jaques, however, came from the Alberta press. The *Calgary Albertan* declared:

Thousands of Social Crediters throughout Alberta are greatly pleased and relieved to hear that Solon Low and Premier E.C. Manning, their federal and provincial leaders, have repudiated almost everything Norman Jaques stands for. It now remains for the people of Wetaskiwin constituency, who elected Mr. Jaques to parliament, to repudiate him also. Although Mr. Jaques calls himself a Social Crediter, he has been devoting most of his time and talents to fostering a peculiar brand of anti-Jewish Fascism patterned on Gerald L.K.

Smith's "Christian Front" movement in the United States ... Since Mr. Jaques has declared that Social Credit is virtually identical with the Christian Front, Mr. Low and Mr. Manning seem obliged to go one step further and say Social Credit has nothing in common with Mr. Jaques.[37]

The *Wetaskiwin Times* revealed its own attitude towards its elected member of parliament:

Our Federal M.P. and his penchant for stirring up racial animosity has always been a source of embarrassment to his constituents, but we have overlooked this weakness in the hope that the rest of Canada would take his pet-peeve with a grain of salt as we do at home. The recent request of the Anti-Defamation League of B'nai B'rith that he be barred from entry into the United States puts things in a different light. This latest development is "the straw that breaks the camel's back" in the relations between Mr. Jaques and his constituents ... About the only time we see our federal member in Wetaskiwin is when he descends on us during an election to inform us of the dire plots against democracy which he has uncovered at Ottawa and other eastern points. He also makes an excellent job of impressing us with his high-sounding opinions on international finance ... We have no place and no time for Jew-baiting or any other racial isms in Western Canada. It is this very freedom that has kept the muzzle off Mr. Jaques for so many years. But we have had enough.[38]

If the press is a reflection of public opinion, the people of Wetaskiwin had spoken. They were no longer willing to countenance their MP's intolerant and anti-democratic views. It appeared that Jaques's political career was quickly coming to an end.

Congress followed the turn of events carefully and, during the exposé of Jaques, contacted the editorial staffs of the Montreal press. Hayes wrote to the *Montreal Gazette* and *Montreal Star* commending them for exposing Jaques's associations with Smith: "You render a public service in informing your readers of Mr. Jaques' connection with Mr. Smith. The more often the public is acquainted with these facts the better. Expos[é]s of this nature are important." Congress also provided one of the Montreal papers with material on Jaques to be used in future editorials.[39] Thus, while Congress was willing to co-operate privately with others in opposing Social Credit, it was still unable to enter the public realm on its own behalf. At no time did it publish its own denunciation of Jaques. For the time being at least, Congress seemed content to let the press handle the renegade MP. In a letter to the ADL (which was still working to get Jaques barred from the United States) Hayes expressed his pleasure at the recent exposure of Jaques: "The whole conjunction of developments is interesting, especially since we have been discussing with the editors of the *Montreal Gazette* just this sort of expos[é] of Jaques' anti-semitism. I think that we can all be pleased that a dangerous man stands exposed by his own words. The menace, however, that he and his group represent is far from dispelled and the Social Crediters will certainly continue to bear watching."[40] Certainly, Congress could feel more hopeful that public opinion would turn against Jaques and, by extension, Social Credit. If Social Credit's leading anti-Semite could be discredited, perhaps the entire movement would fall from grace.

Yet Rosenberg noted that, despite recent events, Social Credit continued to publish and promote anti-Semitic propaganda. In fact it had created a new avenue for promoting anti-Semitism, perhaps because of mounting criticism. The Basic Book Club was formed in the spring of 1947 and became Social Credit's unofficial agency for the advertisement and distribution of anti-Semitic literature. Roy Ashby, son of MP Patrick Ashby, established the Basic Book Club as a mail-order business independent of the movement. However, the Basic Book Club advertised regularly in the *Canadian Social Crediter*, and orders for its books went through the Social Credit Board and later through the party organ's offices. In a memorandum to Hayes, Rosenberg noted that although the mandate of the Basic Book Club was ostensibly to spread knowledge of Social Credit theory and principles and to distribute Social Credit literature, it rarely did so.[41] Instead, the club advertised explicitly anti-Semitic pamphlets and books such as *Know Your Enemy: The 'UNRRA' Infiltra(i)tors*; *An Editor on Trial*; *The 'Palestine' Plot*; and *Father of Lies*.

Know Your Enemy was a twenty-eight-page pamphlet published by Tidal Publications of Sydney, Australia, the official publishers of the Australian Social Credit movement, and was imported by the Basic Book Club. The pamphlet claimed to be an exposé of Jewish and communist control of the United Nations Relief and Rehabilitation Administration (UNRRA), and was "documented" with anti-Semitic quotations from various sources. Rosenberg gave the following appraisal of *Know Your Enemy*: "It consists of a series of extracts from an alleged memorandum written by an anonymous 'Former UNRRA Greece Mission Embassy–Passport Officer in 1946,' interlarded with quotations from anti-Semitic sheets published in Great Britain, and Canada, such as *Tidings* (Douglas Reed), *Housewives Voice*, and the annual report of the Alberta Social Credit Board."[42]

An Editor on Trial recounted the seditious libel case "Rex *vs* Caunt" tried in Liverpool, England, in November 1947. On 6 August 1947 James Caunt, editor of the *Morecambe and Heysham Visitor*, had written an article condemning Zionist terrorism in Palestine, attacking British Jews for their "face-saving propaganda" about peace in Palestine, and declaring that Britain's economic and political life was controlled by Jews. He had declared therein: "[British Jews] should disgorge their ill-gotten wealth in trying to dissuade their brothers in the United States from pouring out dollars to facilitate the entrance into Palestine of European Jewish scum, a proportion of whom will swell the ranks of the terrorist organisation and thus carry on the murderous work which British Jewry professes to abhor." After his trial and acquittal Caunt published *An Editor on Trial*, undoubtedly to vindicate himself and further promote his views. Needless to say, the pamphlet had nothing to do with Social Credit theories.[43]

The Basic Book Club boasted that *The 'Palestine' Plot* "throws a new light on the Palestine question. Are the Khazars in control of World Jewry through the Zionist Organization? This and many other questions will be answered when you read this book. It is documented." The book was in fact a vicious attack on Jews and Zionism filled with such excerpts as "'Ye are of Your Father the Devil' said Jesus of Nazareth to 'the Jews' of his own time. They were city dwellers and money-lenders, then as now, and their slum-world was, then as now, built on false and anti-natural (ungodly) foundations. For thousands of years the Father of Lies has raised his children, 'the Jews,' on the inverted and Satanic principles of the Talmud."[44]

Father of Lies was published in London by MCP Publications (the initials stood for Militant Christian Patriots), an organization that, according to Rosenberg, was composed of "bitter anti-Semitic and Fascistic propagandists." According to the Basic Book Club, *Father of Lies* was "a treatise on Judaism, Occultism, Freemasonry, and the Old Testament, Illustrated and complete with a wallet of charts and symbolism." The book argued that a score of pagan and occult religions, Judaism included, were working towards "world theocracy"; however, it focused preponderantly on Judaism's magical and occult characteristics, especially its perverse sexuality or "phallic cult."[45]

The tracts promoted by the Basic Book Club were the most offensively anti-Semitic of all Social Credit literature. Obviously, they had no relevance to the implementation of Social Credit theories in Alberta and Canada. Even more incriminating, the Basic Book Club imported and sold the *Protocols*. Indeed, it was the only Social Credit propaganda agency to do so, advertising them as follows: "The *Protocols*, claimed by the originators to be a forgery, is the best book on the policy of evil prevalent in the world today. Forgery means the act of fabricating an original document. No original document has been forthcoming to prove the fabrication of the *Protocols*."[46] It is worth emphasizing that although the Basic Book Club was officially independent of the Social Credit movement, its mailing address, advertising, and means of acquiring literature were none the less connected to the Social Credit provincial party organization and Alberta government. As Rosenberg remarked in a memorandum to Hayes, "while the Basic Book Club had been set up ostensibly to sell Social Credit literature, its real purpose was to sell literature which the Social Credit Party wanted distributed without having to accept responsibility for doing so."[47]

In addition to scrutinizing the activities of the Basic Book Club, Rosenberg pointed out to Hayes that the Social Credit Board and the *Canadian Social Crediter* continued to stock, advertise, and offer for sale "books and pamphlets which are definitely anti-Semitic and which frequently quote the *Protocols of the Elders of Zion* or reprint anti-Semitic canards previously published in Ford's *International Jew* and the Anti-Semitic Nazi literature of the Fichte Bunde." Moreover, "neither Mr. Solon Low nor Premier Manning or any other Social Credit member can deny knowledge of the anti-Semitic nature of the propaganda literature, for it is distributed and sold at all Social Credit meetings and all the members make frequent quotations from it."[48] Thus, despite Manning's official repudiation in the legislature, Social Credit's anti-Semitism had not diminished but actually had increased. Even worse, Congress remained unable or unwilling to capitalize on the exposure brought about by the board's report, Manning's repudiation, or Jaques's antics. The press and political opposition had come out against Social Credit's anti-Semitism. The time was ripe for Canadian Jewry's national organization to take its own stand. Yet Congress could not, or would not. What it needed most of all was *chutzpah*.

But Congress continued at its own pace and discussed various measures to solve the pernicious Social Credit problem. In July 1947 the national JPRC debated plans to assist Alberta Jewry in its fight against the Alberta government. It questioned whether the Mormon Church (of which Low was now a bishop, and Blackmore a member) or any other denominational churches had come out publicly on the matter of Social Credit's anti-Semitism. It was revealed that none had; accordingly, the JPRC discussed the possibility of approaching some. One officer stressed that if they were to try to obtain a statement from the Mormons, "it was incumbent on Congress to investigate this side of the question as much as possible and enlist the assistance of the American defense agencies to approach the center of this church in Salt Lake City."[49] Yet there is no evidence that Congress attempted to do so, perhaps because of traditional suspicions about the Mormon Church's prophecies of a Jewish-Mormon conciliation and subsequent Jewish conversion.[50]

Interestingly, however, the Mormon Church expressed its own disapproval of Blackmore and excommunicated him in December 1947, ostensibly because he had advocated the doctrine of plural marriage. In his own defence Blackmore stated: "I was charged with ... teaching and advocating the doctrine of plural marriage which is contrary to the present teaching of the church of Jesus Christ of Latter Day Saints. (Notice that I was not charged with advocating the practice of plural marriage; neither was I charged with practising plural marriage.) I deny the charge. I maintain that I have merely discussed and defended the doctrine of plural marriage as a biblical principle, not as a present-day practice."[51] Although the evidence is scanty, it is possible that the Mormon hierarchy used Blackmore's technical transgression to distance itself from his anti-Semitic, Social Credit connections. The Baptist Church also denounced Social Credit, independently of any intervention by Congress. In mid-July 1947 the *Canadian Baptist* published an article criticizing Social Credit's "two Mormon MP's" (Low and Blackmore) for their intolerant stance on evacuation of Japanese-Canadians; two weeks later it published another article condemning *Vers Demain* for its publication of the *Protocols*.[52]

At its July meeting the national JPRC also discussed a proposed press campaign against Social Credit. However, Hayes squelched this idea because "this had already in part been accomplished by the actions of Mr. Jaques himself by his open association with Gerald L.K. Smith, and the publicity given in general in the Canadian press to the letter of the [Anti-Defamation League] to the United States Secretary of State." Moreover, both the *Montreal Star* and the *Montreal Gazette* had reproached Jaques for "consorting with Fascists."[53] Hayes's stance was remarkably passive and incongruent with his previous efforts, yet no other officer emphasized the need to build on existing successes against Social Credit. Recent events had shown that the press and politicians were eager to discredit Social Credit's anti-Semitism, yet Congress remained in the shadows and refused to capitalize on existing gains.

Thus, despite *attempts* at a stronger policy, Congress had not *executed* any policy by the autumn of 1947. Not surprisingly, then, there were few advances on the Social Credit front. In August the American state department informed the ADL that there were no grounds on which it could bar Jaques from entering the country.[54] Later that autumn Congress's national headquarters attempted to link Jaques's anti-Semitism with a comparable anti-Catholicism based on his associations with Smith, in hopes of rallying French-Canadians against Social Credit.[55] However, the ADL informed Congress that there was "no anti-Catholic activity on the part of Gerald L.K. Smith or his cohorts with whom Norman Jaques consorted on his visit to the United States."[56] Bercuson in Alberta similarly informed national headquarters that "there seems little evidence of anti-Catholic agitation being combined with anti-Semitism. One or two educational leaders [Social Crediters] are known to hold anti-Catholic views, but their opinions are not reflected in any of the educational propaganda issued ... there is no merging of anti-Catholic and anti-Jewish attitudes."[57] Thus, any plans to "effectively fight the anti-semitism of Jaques ... by exposing the tie-up between Jaques and some of the American Nationalists who are just as vociferous in their anti-Catholicism as in their anti-Semitism"[58] came to naught. Still, Congress's attempt to show that Social Credit's anti-Semitism was dangerous to all Canadian society, not only Jews, was indicative of its evolution and maturation. If Social Credit's anti-Semitic campaign could be seen as more than a Jewish concern, perhaps public opinion would turn against it.

By the autumn of 1947, however, neither national headquarters nor the various JPRC committees were expending much effort against the Social Credit menace. For too many years there had been meetings, correspondence, expressions of good will, declarations by Social Credit leaders, promises by Alberta premiers – while Social Credit's anti-Semitism continued unabated. In fact, in the post-war period Social Credit's enhanced conspiracy theories about the UN, communism, and Zionism simply added to its repertoire of anti-Semitic propaganda.[59] Yet its most blatant anti-Semitism still emanated from standard accusations about the international financial Jewish conspiracy. In a nationwide radio address in September 1947, Low explained how "[Rothschild] and his henchmen set out to control the money of the globe. They succeeded even beyond their own fondest dreams. As a result, world or international finance has become a means of tyranny. Imperialism is its tool, the kind of imperialism which we now see emanating from Wall Street in New York City."[60] Several weeks later the *Canadian Social Crediter* announced that in addition to the "Big Three" world powers (presumably Britain, the United States, and Russia), there was a fourth *secret* world power – the Jewish nation – whose policy "derived from the mystic philosophy of the Jews – the belief that they are the Chosen People ... since this Power has no country, and no army ... [i]ts most important weapon is Finance – money-power." In the same issue the party organ's editor, John Patrick Gillese, explained how usury was the sole purview of Jews: "In common law the practice of taking increase was classed among the lowest crimes against public morals. So odious was it among Christians that the PRACTICE WAS CONFINED ALMOST WHOLLY TO THE JEWS, WHO DID NOT EXACT USURY OF THE JEWS, BUT OF CHRISTIANS."[61] Such was the nature of Social Credit's propaganda after Manning's repudiation of anti-Semitism.

For Congress, Social Credit's anti-Semitism must have seemed indefatigable. Yet even Social Credit supporters were beginning to tire of the conspiracy theories and confronted the movement. That autumn a Social Crediter from Malartic, Quebec, criticized the *Canadian Social Crediter* for its attacks on labour, socialism, communism, and Jews: "You show your true colours too often to fool even poor workers. You believe in tolerance? Then why does the Union des Electeurs and Jaques go up and down the country screeching at the Jews? ... There is much about Social Credit that I admire, but racial discrimination and disrespect for either Socialism or Communism is a poor way to advance your own cause." In response, the *Canadian Social Crediter* denied that any Social Crediter went "up and down the country screeching at the Jews." It admitted that it condemned political Zionism, "but so have many prominent Jews." Then, in a revealing statement, the party organ denied its anti-Semitism and simultaneously admonished the complainant for having been duped by the international Jewish conspirators: "Surely our correspondent knows that if we were anti-Semitic we would have courage enough to say so – and material enough to fill every edition of The *Canadian Social Crediter* for years to come. It is too bad that people will fall for the 'smear campaign.' We condemn anti-Semitism if for no other reason than that it has been used as an instrument against the people of the western world. If our correspondent is a thinker, let him think that one out."[62]

As long as Social Credit could spread its anti-Semitic propaganda with impunity, and, even more importantly, as long as Congress remained bound to a predominantly passive public relations approach, little could be done. Yet Social Credit was on the brink of an ideological revolution, one that neither Congress nor the movement itself could have predicted. Circumstances converged so that Manning's decision in November 1947 to shut down the Social Credit Board ended in a full-blown party rift and a major Cabinet shuffle. What ensued was an ideological housecleaning of the movement and a purge of the anti-Semites. Congress had no choice but to sit back and watch the dominoes fall.

Manning's purge of 1947–48 was largely the result of negative publicity emanating from the Social Credit Board's report and the premier's public repudiation of anti-Semitism. As early as April 1947 there had been stirrings in the Alberta government that a change was underway. Rumours abounded that Gillese, editor of the *Canadian Social Crediter*, was going to be reprimanded or even replaced. This was undoubtedly because of his anti-Semitic editorial policy, which he outlined in a "strictly confidential" memorandum to the party organ's contributors and directors of policy: "We have allowed our propaganda to become too *defensive*, rather than *offensive*. In too many cases, we are continually explaining that we are not anti-Semitic, that we are not fascist, that we meant one thing when we said another ... The enemy has manœuvred us into this position. We should concentrate on offensive action again, putting the enemy on the defensive. If it becomes necessary to refute any charges, close all arguments by raising a counter-charge against the enemy, which will again put him on the defensive."[63]

Gillese was also very jealous of his role as managing editor of the paper. In his view the *Canadian Social Crediter* was the party organ of the national movement, not the Alberta movement, and thus should take its orders from the former.[64] This was theoretically true, but as Manning himself noted to Saskatchewan Social Credit politician H.N. Haldeman, the *Canadian Social Crediter* was considered part of the Alberta movement: "In the public mind the Social Credit government of [Alberta] is bound to be associated with the viewpoints expressed in an organ which purports to be the official mouthpiece of the National Social Credit Movement."[65] This placed Manning in an awkward position: he had little *de jure* control over the national party organ but could exercise much *de facto* control. He indicated as much, stating: "I think my views with respect to the *Social Crediter*, under Gillese's editorship, are well known. I think I have advised pretty nearly every member of the National Executive that the *Canadian Social Crediter* for some considerable time has been a definite detriment to the Social Credit Movement and to our work as a Government in this Province. In spite of this fact the National Executive thus far has not taken any effective action to correct the situation." In Manning's opinion, "if the organ had remained under the provincial organization in this Province ... its policy would be very different from what it is today but I have refrained from interfering with a matter which is now under the jurisdiction of the National Executive."[66]

But in the wake of recent criticism about Social Credit's anti-Semitism, Manning would no longer allow the party organ to work to the detriment of Social Credit in Alberta and Canada. Accordingly, in May 1947 he advised the national party organization that unless the policy and subject-matter of the *Canadian Social Crediter* drastically changed, "we will have no alternative but to disassociate ourselves from the paper entirely and make it clear to the public that it does not in any way express our views or have our endorsation." Noting that the paper should have had a circulation of about fifty or sixty thousand by that time, when in fact it had only about eleven thousand, Manning remarked: "No one who values their name or their influence is going to get behind a publication which contains little but negative and destructive criticism flavored with 'Jew-baiting' and of a nature that tends to stir up discontent and discord instead of uniting the people of Canada in a positive, constructive crusade for social and economic justice and political and economic freedom."[67]

Meanwhile, the Social Credit Board's technical adviser, L.D. Byrne, informed Low that "matters were brought to a head as a result of the rumpus created by Roper ... over the s/c Board Report," and that he thought a serious schism was inevitable: "Apparently the intention was for the caucus to disassociate the Alberta organization from the national movement, the Liverpool Secretariat and Douglas. (I gather that, like me, you are considered just a nasty anti-Semite.) The s/c Board was also to be either abolished or the personnel changed."[68] By September the press was repeating these rumours, noting that because the board's report had "prompted widespread criticism even in Social Credit ranks," its fate would be decided "at a late fall caucus in Edmonton of government members of the [legislature]."[69] On 21 October the *Edmonton Journal* reported that at the upcoming caucus meeting "Social Credit members will discuss the future of the Social Credit board. It is possible the powers of the board will be drastically reduced." On 3 November the *Journal* rumoured that "the board soon would end its operations under the auspices of the government and that there would be a move to incorporate the board's activities into the Alberta Social Credit league." During this time Manning privately informed a fellow Social Crediter that "there was very severe criticism of the Board during the last Session, particularly of the unfortunate report which it issued and which, undoubtedly, did the Social Credit Movement, provincially and nationally, considerable harm. Whether the Board will be continued is a matter for the members of the Legislature to decide."[70]

As predicted, at the end of November Manning took control of the movement and began his purge. At a national council meeting of the Social Credit Association of Canada (SCAC) Manning announced that Gordon Taylor, MLA for Drumheller, would take over as managing editor of the *Canadian Social Crediter*. This had the intended result of ousting Gillese from his job, and he subsequently resigned.[71] Further, all writings by Douglas, Jaques, and any other writers advocating "anti-isms" would be banned from the *Canadian Social Crediter*.[72] At this meeting the national council drafted a new editorial policy for the party organ, which stated that it "must put the spotlight on the enemies of the people, but in no case hold any race or creed up to ridicule ... In spotlighting anyone, be extremely careful about calling him a Jew

or a Scotsman, etc., unless there is a very good reason for so doing ...
The editors have full scope with the aims of Political Zionism. Political
Zionism is tied up hand-and-glove with International Finance and
Communism. Invite the Jews to take a stand on Communism."[73] The
national council also decided that "the economic principles of Social
Credit as enunciated by Major C.H. Douglas [should] receive ...
whole-hearted endorsation but the political and personal views of
Major Douglas particularly in regards to Semitism and Holy Scripture
[are] definitely no part or parcel of the Social Credit Association of
Canada."[74]

At the Alberta Social Credit League's convention held shortly thereafter, Manning decreed that the Social Credit Board would be abolished at the end of the fiscal year (31 March 1948) and its activities
transferred to the Alberta Social Credit League and department of
economic affairs.[75] The new policy of the Alberta government and the
Social Credit League was that "we condemn, repudiate and completely
disassociate ourselves and the Social Credit movement in Alberta from
any statement or publication which are incompatible with the established British ideals of democratic freedom or which endorse, excuse,
or incite anti-Semitism or racial or religious intolerance in any form
... We re-iterate our intention to do everything in our power to unite
the people of this Province and country, irrespective of colour, race or
creed in an all-out effort to end the present vicious financial monopoly
and restore the effective control over money and credit to the people
themselves."[76] Manning's statement was a replica of his earlier repudiation, which had proven ineffective. Moreover, his repudiation still
raised the bogey of a "vicious financial monopoly." Thus, the crucial
question remained: was the vicious financial monopoly Jewish? The
Calgary Herald, which had been closely following the activities of the
national and provincial movement, had its own opinion. It questioned
whether there was a Manning brand of Social Credit distinct from the
Douglas brand, or "has the government so far departed from the true
philosophy that it can no longer countenance the very teachings that
gave it birth? Is it the heretics who are going to the scaffold – or the
true believers?"[77]

Congress was not convinced these latest histrionics would have any
real or lasting effect. Rosenberg in particular was highly sceptical,
although at the time he had little but supposition to go on. In a series
of lengthy memoranda to Hayes he offered his interpretation of Manning's purge. Rosenberg believed a split in Social Credit ranks was in
the offing long before Manning made his announcement. Ever since
the inception of the national Social Credit party in 1944 there had
been considerable friction between the national organization, the SCAC,

and the provincial organization, the Alberta Social Credit League. There were three reasons for this, claimed Rosenberg: first, the Alberta Social Credit League, with Manning at its head, considered itself to be the real centre of Social Credit in Canada. This was understandable since it had existed long before the SCAC; indeed, the latter owed its very existence to the Alberta Social Credit League's electoral successes. Moreover, the Alberta Social Credit League was head of the only Social Credit government in Canada. Accordingly, it believed that the SCAC and Social Credit MPs should take their direction from it and Manning. In contrast, national party members such as Low believed the SCAC should take its orders directly from Douglas's Social Credit Secretariat in England.[78]

The second reason for the split, explained Rosenberg, was that the Alberta Social Credit League believed it was the originator of Social Credit theories in Canada and saw the affiliation between the SCAC and provincial Social Credit organizations in Ontario and Quebec (namely the Union of Electors and Union des Electeurs) as an attempt by "eastern Canada" to usurp control of the movement. In addition, there were many members in the Alberta Social Credit League who, with their Protestant and English Canadian background, were opposed to the Catholic and French Canadian character of the Union des Electeurs. Often, Alberta Social Credit League members condemned the Union des Electeurs because it was "typically" fascist and anti-Semitic, meanwhile ignoring the anti-Semitism within their own organization. Thirdly, Social Credit's more "moderate" elements, including Manning, believed that anti-Semitic propaganda was neither advisable nor necessary. It was probable, argued Rosenberg, that these Social Crediters, like their more overtly anti-Semitic colleagues, believed in the predictions of the *Protocols* and the international financial Jewish conspiracy theory. However, unlike the "extremist" elements, the moderates did not consider it politically expedient to advertise those theories.[79]

As for Manning's latest repudiation, Rosenberg believed that it "should evidently be taken with much more than a grain of salt. There is no reason to believe in its sincerity, nor is there any evidence to warrant that it shows any change in policy on the part of Mr. Manning, the Social Credit Party in Alberta, the Social Credit members of the Dominion Parliament, or the *Canadian Social Crediter*." In fact, given "the previous tactics of the Social Credit Party and its leaders, the statement is intended to divert attention from its actual activities and to provide a statement which can be quoted in an attempt to prove its innocence while it continues to follow its anti-Semitic policy." What was worse, Rosenberg re-emphasized, was that Manning differed little from the anti-Semites whom he was ousting, since he "has several times made public statements over the radio and in the press concerning secret conspiracies of international bankers, etc., and the only difference in the wording of his statement and those of Solon Low or Norman Jaques is that he has been careful to eliminate the word 'Jewish' in talking about an international financial conspiracy."[80]

Rosenberg was also sceptical about the ban on Jaques's writings or Social Credit's elimination of anti-Semitic propaganda. He noted that the same issue of the *Canadian Social Crediter* announcing Manning's new policy also advertised "no fewer than 6 violently anti-Semitic books which quote from the *Protocols of the Elders of Zion* including the anti-Semitic books by the notorious Nesta Webster ... [and] *The Brief for the Prosecution* by Major Douglas."[81] Consequently, Manning's pronouncements "may give the impression that there has been a revolution in that party, that it has been purged of its anti-Semitic elements, and that from now onwards the Canadian Social Credit Party, its leaders, its propaganda literature and its members can be relied upon to follow a policy free from anti-Semitism." However, cautioned Rosenberg, "it would be dangerous and most inadvisable on our part to believe that the battle has been won and that the Social Credit Party and its activities may now be considered innocuous." In short, there "has been no actual change in the policy of the party towards anti-Semitism and anti-Semitic propaganda"; rather, "this may be a tactical manœuvre to put us off guard and absolve the Social Credit Party and its leaders from charges of anti-Semitism, distribution of the *Protocols of the Elders of Zion*, etc., and that the tactics will be resumed openly at a later period when the hue and cry dies down."[82]

Rosenberg concluded with a litany of evidence against Social Credit that he had been accumulating for years. He stated that belief in the *Protocols* and the theory of an international Jewish conspiracy were "not the result of personal idiosyncrasies of individual members such as Norman Jaques or John Patrick Gillese"; rather, these were "essential and indispensable parts of the Social Credit theory" to help Social Crediters explain why their monetary policies had not been implemented. In fact, declared Rosenberg, "Social Credit without anti-Semitism would be like Hamlet without the Ghost." Moreover, Jaques and Gillese were not the only Social Crediters employing anti-Semitic propaganda; the leaders of the party, including Low and other prominent MPs, used similar tactics. The *Canadian Social Crediter* and the Social Credit Board had published anti-Semitic attacks for years. In Rosenberg's opinion, "if all leaders and propagandists of the Canadian Social Credit Party who were anti-Semitic were to be repudiated ... it would involve a cleaning out of the party from top to bottom including

Solon Low, and Social Credit members of the House of Commons and even Premier Manning himself."[83]

Thus, according to Rosenberg, the real cause of Manning's purge was disagreement over strategy and tactics, not disagreement over fundamental Social Credit principles. Specifically, the movement disagreed over the extent to which anti-Semitic propaganda should be used in public pronouncements:

Some of the leaders of the party in Alberta, such as Premier Manning and the more "moderate" elements, while they believe in the mythical *Protocols* and international Jewish conspiracies, do not consider it advisable or necessary to emphasize the anti-Semitic angle, and would like to have it implicit rather than explicit. They believe in "discretion" rather than all out attack, and are, therefore, not very happy about the way in which Norman Jaques, Solon Low and others are continuously occupying the limelight with their anti-Semitic attacks. On the other hand the most active members within the Social Credit Party believe that anti-Semitism is a very useful and practical method of attracting members and gaining control in Canada, and feel that the more moderate group are too "milk and water."[84]

In sum, Rosenberg did not believe the party split was caused by a rift in Social Credit ideology. Social Crediters still believed in the existence of an international financial Jewish conspiracy. The real debate focused on the extent to which that ideological conviction should be advertised. Clearly, Rosenberg's interpretation of recent events was coloured and even skewed by years of scrutinizing Social Credit's anti-Semitic propaganda. However, given the movement's record of repudiations, denials, and reinvigoration of anti-Semitism, his subjectivity was certainly understandable and perhaps even merited.

The Alberta branch of Congress had its own interpretation of recent events. Regarding the *Canadian Social Crediter*'s new editorial policy, Bercuson informed Hayes that "Premier Ernest Manning has been increasingly embarrassed by the statements of the more rabid anti-Semites in his party ... It is apparent to Mr. Manning that his party derives no advantage from the line of argument pursued by propagandists like Mr. Jaques." Further, Social Credit's prestige had been damaged by the board's report, and a number of supporters, "particularly those who are deeply religious, have resented the scurrilous nature of much of the contents of the Canadian publication." Consequently, reported Bercuson, "Mr. Manning flatly insisted on the elimination of anti-Semitism from Social Credit publications ... [stating] that he would resign rather than be saddled by further embarrassment from propagandists." Bercuson believed that Manning's repudiation of anti-

Semitism and the new policy of the party organ were legitimate. Alberta Social Credit was heavily dependent on Manning for its continued prestige and popularity, as was the national party: "Consequently to keep him at the helm this reversal in policy has taken place." Bercuson predicted that in the future the *Canadian Social Crediter* "will in all probability be a different type of publication." Even more promising was that its new managing editor, Gordon Taylor, had a reputation for integrity and "freedom from any anti-semitic bias."* In a telling remark, Bercuson told Hayes that Manning had always held the power to stop Social Credit's anti-Semitism: "What has happened bears out a point that has been held by us in Alberta for a long time – namely, that if Mr. Manning insisted upon it, the Social Credit policy could be altered."[85]

Yet Bercuson's predictions were somewhat premature. In the short term, Rosenberg's scepticism was a clearer reflection of the situation. The *Canadian Social Crediter* continued to publish anti-Semitic propaganda, linking Zionism with the theory of an international financial Jewish conspiracy. It also continued to advertise anti-Semitic literature. Indeed, a few days after the party organ announced its new editorial policy, Congress successfully obtained a copy of the *Protocols* from the paper's offices.[86] Thus it seemed that Manning's purge had been merely cosmetic and Rosenberg was correct: the premier's actions were simply a political ploy to divert criticism. As the *Canadian Jewish Weekly* remarked on Christmas Day 1947, the party organ's new policy had wrought no real change in Social Credit policies: "It does not indicate any serious split; it is a case of a section of one of its groups being severely rapped over the knuckles for indulging in activities that are harmful to the movement. Some face-lifting is being undertaken. The show window is being cleaned up but the shelves inside are still piled with the same reactionary goods."

It was not clear to Congress whether Social Credit's anti-Semitism would actually be discarded. For those officers and agents committed to fighting the Social Credit menace, the past year had been both

---

* Notwithstanding Taylor's reputation for integrity, and despite his announcement that the *Canadian Social Crediter* would "no longer publish any articles of an anti-semitic nature or any 'anti-ism' material," Taylor had expressed anti-Semitic statements. In March 1947, in response to allegations that Social Crediters were anti-Semitic, Taylor (then party whip) declared that that "could not be further from the truth. We flay certain Jewish bankers for their world-planning Communistic tactics but we have never accused all Jews as being participants in a hideous world-plot to enslave the masses."[87]

frustrating and encouraging. Although their efforts had met with limited success, the Western Division, and especially the Alberta branch, had advocated and tried to execute a far more aggressive public relations approach. This was an important step in the long road to an effective public relations policy. Even more promising was the possibility that Social Credit's anti-Semitism would self-destruct. With Manning's new determination to purge anti-Semitism, perhaps Social Credit would succeed where Congress had not. Despite these promising developments, past disappointments overshadowed Congress's hopes for the new year. Too many times Social Credit leaders had made promises and declarations about stopping the anti-Semitism, while continuing to peddle their "reactionary goods." There was no guarantee that Manning's latest repudiation would bring any fundamental, lasting change. Consequently, Congress observed Social Credit's most recent posture with interest, caution, but most of all, scepticism.

7 A Period of Watchful Waiting

When Premier Manning began his purge of anti-Semitism in late 1947, three dissident groups emerged to challenge his authority as the true leader of Social Credit in Canada: the Quebec-based Union des Electeurs, the Ontario-based Union of Electors, and the Alberta-based Douglas Social Credit Council. They were hard-line followers of Douglas's anti-Semitic views, each declaring variously that the premier had converted to Zionism and that his movement was being run by communists, socialists, Freemasons, Jews, and even the Canadian Jewish Congress. However, these groups did not materialize overnight; two of the three had existed long before Manning's purge and operated within the mainstream movement for some time.

The Union des Electeurs was formed in Quebec in 1946 to act as a "political pressure-action group" committed to electing Social Credit members to power.[1] It acted as the grass-roots organizational body for the Quebec Social Credit organization, the Institut d'Action Politique. However, both the Union des Electeurs and the Institut d'Action Politique were led by Louis Even, editor of *Vers Demain*, and soon the Union des Electeurs was accepted as the province's official Social Credit organization. Although *Vers Demain* agreed to follow the policy set down by the Social Credit Association of Canada (SCAC) upon the latter's creation in 1944, Even did not agree with the SCAC's tactics or policy. Like Douglas, he believed party politics were corrupt and the only way to ensure that the government reflected the needs of the electorate was to abolish the party system and all political parties and replace them with a "union of electors." Within this union, elected members would be merely mouthpieces of their electors, reporting back regularly but making no decisions of their own. Party discipline and modern party politics would be abandoned.[2]

While Even's purist Social Credit ideas resonated with many Social Crediters, his non-democratic, authoritarian organizational methods, together with the anti-Semitism in *Vers Demain*, caused other Social Crediters to view him as an ambitious man who did not hesitate to use "communistic methods and morality and fascist propaganda."[3] The SCAC did not approve of Even's actions and resented that he had sent several of his organizers into Ontario to establish an Ontario Union of Electors, in spite of the existence there already of the officially sanctioned Ontario Social Credit League. Accordingly, the SCAC decided to rein in Even and his group. Its national council ruled that delegates to the next national convention (to be held in November 1947) must be elected by their provincial Social Credit organization, which meant that members of the Union des Electeurs could decide whether or not to send Even to the convention. Although this was in keeping with Even's concept of a union of electors, he did not agree with the ruling and subsequently resigned as the Quebec representative of the SCAC. Accordingly, when the SCAC held its convention in November, there were no Union des Electeurs representatives. It was at this convention that Manning began his purge. Shortly thereafter, J. Ernest Gregoire, who was sympathetic to Even and the Union des Electeurs, resigned as deputy national leader and vice-president of the SCAC.[4]

In the wake of Manning's actions, the Union des Electeurs embarked on an anti-Semitic, anti-Manning campaign. It alleged that the faction that had ousted Gillese from the *Canadian Social Crediter* was the same that had been won over to the cause of Zionism. Specifically, Even accused Manning of "selling out" to the Jews. In his opinion Manning and his group were "ambitious politicians, sellers of Social Credit," and two-thirds of Social Credit MPs in Ottawa were members of Freemasonry, which was "controlled by the Jews."[5] At a political rally in Quebec City, Réal Caouette similarly announced that "the Ottawa controllers are following the directives of those who aspire to establish a world Jewish and Freemasonary government."[6] *Vers Demain* postulated the theory of a "shadow government" that had taken over the Manning administration, with Jews and Freemasons at its head.[7] The organ also blamed Congress for the new policy of the *Canadian Social Crediter*. It quoted from a recent article in the *Canadian Jewish Chronicle* reporting an alleged meeting between Congress and Social Credit: "Leaders of the Social Credit Party have finally announced a ban on the publication of anti-Semitic articles in the organization's official organ, following conferences with Joseph H. Fine, chairman of the public relations committee of the Canadian Jewish Congress."[8] This was proof, *Vers Demain* crowed, that "un officier de la plus grande organisation juive du Canada a le privilège d'influencer les décisions de la faction qui s'est emparée du *Canadian Social Crediter* et de passer jugement sur les rédacteurs!"[9]

The second dissident organization, the Union of Electors in Ontario, was created in opposition to the officially sanctioned Ontario Social Credit League. The latter, headed by John J. Fitzgerald and William Ovens, did not have its own publication, but there was a section in the *Canadian Social Crediter* reserved for Ontario news. However, in late 1946 an Ontario Social Credit League member, Ronald Gostick, established the Union of Electors in Ontario in emulation of Even's Union des Electeurs. Gostick appointed himself president and founded the *Voice of the Electors*, which he designated the official organ of the new organization. Thus, by early 1947 two Ontario Social Credit organizations were co-existing uneasily. While the Ontario Social Credit League wanted to remain part of Manning's movement, the Union of Electors believed greater success would come from following Even's example. At a meeting in July 1947 an attempt was made to reconcile the two groups' differences. They decided to operate separately, but each would still work for the Social Credit cause. The *Voice of the Electors* would remain the official organ of the Union of Electors of Ontario but would be sponsored by the Ontario Social Credit League. Following the meeting, the *Canadian Social Crediter* cheerfully reported on the mutually beneficial agreement: "Under this new arrangement, everyone should be superbly happy. Those who favour the Social Credit party idea have open to them the Ontario Social Credit League. Those who believe in non-party action can support the Union of Electors, which seeks ... to restore, and maintain, power in the hands of the electors – power that will make elected representatives ... obedient servants of the people, rather than (as in Ottawa today) tools of a party machine which does not consult the people."[10]

However, this *modus vivendi* did not last very long. In October 1947 the Ontario Social Credit League called an emergency convention in Toronto to discuss the activities of the Union of Electors. Ben Kayfetz, director of the Central Division's JPRC, attended the convention incognito and reported what he believed was a "faithful, if abbreviated, account of as much of the proceedings as I witnessed."[11] According to Kayfetz, four major grievances were aired: first, the Union of Electors had been organizing in Ontario without the sanction of the Ontario League; second, Even and the Union des Electeurs had been supplying the Ontario Union of Electors with organizers and field-workers without the Ontario League's approval; third, Gostick and the Union of Electors were raising funds under the Social Credit party name but not channelling those funds to the party; lastly, Even had sent out a letter to *Vers Demain* readers urging them to reject the Ontario League and support the Union of Electors. As a result of these activities, the Ontario League considered the Union of Electors and Union des Electeurs to be infringing on its provincial autonomy.[12]

At the convention Ontario League president Fitzgerald also described the clash between himself and Gostick. During the summer of 1947 Gostick apparently had agreed to a reconciliation and unity of purpose, but then refused to sign the document outlining the new requirements, instead organizing the Union of Electors with even greater zeal. Consequently, at the convention a new constitution was adopted in which the Ontario League, with the backing of the SCAC, repudiated Gostick and the Union of Electors. Interestingly, this repudiation did not include any criticism – or even mention – of Gostick's anti-Semitic views, which would soon reach new heights.[13] Yet the break between the Ontario League and the Union of Electors was part of the emerging split within the Social Credit movement, which culminated in Manning's purge of the anti-Semites. After Manning's decision to abolish the Social Credit Board and sanitize the *Canadian Social Crediter*, Gostick's group worked closely with Even's Union des Electeurs. It engaged in similar anti-Semitic attacks, and the *Voice of the Electors* promoted the *Protocols* as "one of the most sensational documents ever published. A 'must' for every political student." The new organ also declared that because "political Zionists ... sow the seeds of anti-Semitism and bring hatred and persecution to the Jewish people," the solution "is obvious. The Jewish people must repudiate Political Zionism, International Communism, and the International Money Monopoly spawned by Amschel Mayer Rothschild." In another article the *Voice of the Electors* argued that Jews controlled the atom bomb: "The chairman of the U.S.A. Atomic Energy Commission is the Jew, David Lilienthal; the others are Wm. Waymack, L. Strauss (Jew), R. Bacher (Jew), and S.T. Pike. Three Jews out of five ... Behind them is the Jew Barney Baruch, whose official position in the business is U.S.A. member of the U.N.O. commission on Atomic Energy."[14]

The third dissident organization, the Douglas Social Credit Council (DSCC) in Alberta, emerged as a direct result of Manning's purge and was organized by alienated Douglasites planning their own counterattack. After his forced resignation from the *Canadian Social Crediter*, Gillese, who had been impressed with the Union des Electeurs as an electoral machine, decided to form his own union of electors. On the DSCC's executive were A.V. Bourcier (former chairman of the Social

Credit Board) as chairman, Gillese as vice-chairman, and Kenneth Burton (former associate editor of the *Canadian Social Crediter*) as secretary-treasurer. Roy Ashby of the Basic Book Club joined Gillese, and the Basic Book Club became the official distributing agency for the DSCC. It continued to advertise the same books and pamphlets by Douglas, Webster, and others, but added new anti-Semitic treatises to its repertoire.[15] Soon after its establishment the DSCC distributed a circular justifying its purpose, which was to take "militant action against the unchecked onslaught of the forces identified with so-called communism, monopoly finance, and state socialism which are centred in international Zionism seeking world domination ... For this purpose it has become necessary to set up a Canadian Social Credit Secretariat working in close conjunction with The Social Credit Secretariat of Major C.H. Douglas."[16] In another circular distributed among the Social Credit rank and file, the DSCC emphasized that it was not anti-Semitic but that its policy was to "fearlessly attack and expose the three evil enemies of genuine democracy – international finance, international communism and international political Zionism (which, for the most part, is controlled by atheists and is also an enemy of the common Jew and of cultural and religious Judaism)."[17]

The DSCC's organizational efforts were assisted by events in February 1948 that indicated Manning's purge was not yet complete. Because Manning had decided to abolish the Social Credit Board the previous November, L.D. Byrne's position as its technical adviser had become obsolete. Before "retiring," Byrne was responsible for writing a final report on behalf of the board. He had little to lose and flaunted Douglas's theories about the international financial socialist communist Jewish Zionist conspiracy. He declared that "*the issue* in the world at the present time is Christendom versus Zionism ... the present plight of the remnants of our civilization is the result of a deliberate and deep-seated conspiracy to enslave humanity under a World Police State ... The main agencies being used to advance the policy of Monopoly towards its goal of a World Slave State are international socialism, international communism, and international finance. These are all rooted in their parent body – International Zionism." Byrne also invoked the *Protocols* in an attempt to prove that an international Jewish conspiracy was aiming for world control: "The *Protocols*['] ... contents have been carried out faithfully by the protagonists of world Zionism – and by Zionism in the context of this report is meant a policy based on the claims by a group, and a powerful group, of internationalists of the racial superiority of the Jewish people and directed to the complete subjugation of all nations to the rule of a Jewish hierarchy supported by a Jewish plutocracy." Byrne also issued several directives to Manning's movement, which he assailed for losing sight of true Social Credit principles: "What is necessary ... is to bring out into the open the nature of the socialist-communist conspiracy, to reveal their connection with international big business and finance, to connect these with the parent body of Zionism, to make it plain what is going on and to name those responsible ... At the present time, outside the Quebec movement and the Union of Electors organization in Ontario, the Canadian [Social Credit] movement is pursuing a course of action which is, in itself, in conflict with the policy of Social Credit. This cannot fail to play into the hands of the enemy, and if persisted in, lead to the disruption of the movement."[18]

In addition to presenting his report to the Social Credit Board, Byrne also submitted a copy to the provincial Cabinet, which discussed its contents. At the Cabinet meeting, education minister R.E. Ansley agreed with the report and defended Byrne's position. As John Barr notes: "When the matter of Byrne came before cabinet, Ansley supported Byrne. Later, Manning called Ansley into his office and suggested that in light of the need for cabinet unanimity, perhaps Ansley should resign. Ansley stolidly replied that he couldn't see why this disagreement should be reason for his resignation. 'All right,' said Manning dryly, 'I'm asking you for your resignation. Now you've *got* a reason.'"[19] By 23 February the Alberta press was reporting that the premier had asked for the resignations of Byrne and Ansley.[20] Little wonder Manning decided they should be relieved of their duties. If he did not think Byrne's comments on "international Zionism" and the "Jewish hierarchy" were injudicious, he must certainly have taken exception to Byrne's criticisms that the movement was no longer pursuing true Social Credit principles. And in the wake of his recent pronouncement, he refused to countenance any Cabinet support of Byrne's anti-Semitic views. Thus, by sacking Byrne and Ansley, Manning was mopping up the residuals of his November purge.

The short-term result, however, was to bolster the cause of the DSCC. In the ensuing debacle MLA N.B. James, columnist for the *Canadian Social Crediter* and member of the Social Credit Board, quit writing for the party organ and joined the Alberta dissidents. Other Alberta Social Crediters who broke with Manning included MLA Ansley (who had been fired), MP Jaques (whose writings had been banned from the *Canadian Social Crediter*), and MP Patrick Ashby, a stolid defender of the Douglasite faith who refused to go along with Manning's "apostasy."[21] The DSCC quickly became the opposing organization to Manning's Alberta Social Credit League. Its politicians remained Social Credit in name, and some were re-elected on the Social Credit ticket in the 1948 provincial election (see Table 4, p. 127).[22] The DSCC published two propaganda organs, the *Social Credit Challenge* and the DSCC *Information Service*, which criticized Manning for his purge and claimed that he had fallen prey to the machinations of the international financial Jewish conspirators. Although circulation figures are unavailable, these organs were extremely limited in readership and irregular in their publication.[23] Accordingly, in an attempt to gain legitimacy they republished excerpts from Douglas's *Social Crediter* that harshly criticized the Alberta administration.

In one article reprinted by the DSCC, Douglas flayed Manning's group for not being a true Social Credit government: "The Social Credit Government, now headed by Mr. E.C. Manning, is where it is because some of the most powerful Forces in the world have failed in previous attempts to put it out ... the opposition met by the first three Social Credit Administrations ... was quite different in character to that now existing ... the change results from ... the fact that the Alberta electorate is Social Credit, but the Administration is not ... The Manning Administration is no more a Social Credit Administration than the British Government is Labour."[24] In another piece Douglas vehemently criticized Manning for refusing to implement Social Credit policies and for supporting Zionism: "To the extent that 'Social Credit has failed in Alberta,' i.e., has not been tried, the root cause has always been evident – a persistent determination not to recognise that when Mr. Aberhart won his first electoral victory, all he did was to recruit an army for A WAR. That war has not been fought; and Mr. Manning declares in the plainest terms that he will not lead that army into a fight. Perhaps reasonably, he prefers to ride at its head in ceremonial parades."[25] Clearly, Douglas was siding with his namesakes and had no more use for Manning, whom he considered to be a lackey of international Jewish finance. For its part, the DSCC happily used Douglas's statements to bolster its anti-Manning cause.

In sum, in the wake of Manning's purge, the Union des Electeurs, the Union of Electors, and the Douglas Social Credit Council acted as opposing forces to the official movement, each declaring that the premier had departed from the true Social Credit faith. These organizations shared three common characteristics that placed them in diametric opposition to the Manningites: their emphasis on non-party political action; their emphasis on simon-pure Social Credit monetary reform; but most importantly, their unwillingness to discard anti-Semitism.[26] These combined characteristics made their activities obnoxious enough to Manning and the moderates to cause a major party split. Yet despite their carping criticism, the dissident groups held little influence, and Manning's directive of November 1947 ultimately prevailed. In the interim, his purge actually contributed to an increase

in anti-Semitic propaganda: once expelled from the movement, renegade Social Crediters were free to publish increasingly anti-Semitic
statements, since their propaganda no longer had to pass any standards
of acceptability. But these groups lacked the legitimacy of the official
movement, and their support was very limited. Manning's directive
was eradicating anti-Semitism, and the fringe groups were just that –
marginal movements whose promotion of anti-Semitism remained
peripheral to the Social Credit mainstream.

Congress closely observed Social Credit's most recent drama. It
scrutinized the splinter groups' propaganda organs, observed press
coverage of the Social Credit split, and monitored the *Canadian Social
Crediter* for evidence of anti-Semitism. However, during the months of
the purge, from November 1947 to February 1948, Congress doubted
that Manning's pronouncements were exerting much influence. In early
1948, for example, the national JPRC reported that "anti-semitism [in
Canada] does not present today an immediate menace to the Jewish
community ... overt acts of anti-semitism are rarer today than they
have been since Hitler came to power in Germany." Yet, "however few
may be the manifestations of anti-semitism it has nevertheless seared
deeply into [the] Canadian soul. Anti-semitism has attained a measure
of recognition and respectability which are in themselves dangerous."
It then named several groups and organizations which continued to
cause it concern. Social Credit headed the list.[27]

The national JPRC also reported that Social Credit and the Union
des Electeurs "are today the only political parties whose programs
include planks which arouse anxiety in the Jewish community ...
Although Social Credit officially disavows the word anti-semitism ...
there remains a considerable measure of anti-Jewish propaganda by
indirection even if Jews are referred to only as political Zionists,
international bankers, Judaeo-communists and by other vague terms
... Social Credit literature in Canada echoes the mouthings of avowed
antisemites in Great Britain and in the United States. At one time the
organization in the Province of Quebec had actually disseminated the
Protocols of the Elders of Zion." The JPRC admitted that the situation
"remains quite unsatisfactory" but that "the problem is receiving the
constant attention of the Joint Public Relations Committee. We are
alert to antisemitic elements in Social Credit propaganda and from
time to time we conduct counter-propaganda efforts to correct specific
allegations to which they give currency."[28]

Thus, despite Manning's actions, the JPRC still considered Social
Credit to be its foremost public relations problem. Such concern
was not superfluous – during and even after the purge, the *Canadian
Social Crediter* continued to advertise, sell, and distribute anti-Semitic

propaganda. Although it had eliminated most anti-Semitic references in its columns, it continued to promote anti-Semitic literature by Douglas and Webster.[29] In Alberta, Bercuson was not surprised that such literature was still advertised and sold. He told national executive director Hayes, "Mr. Manning may have won his point with regard to the *Canadian Social Crediter*, but there still remains a virulent anti-semitic element in the Party which considers international finance the keystone of all Social Credit propaganda ... Whether Manning will attempt to quell this group is questionable."[30] Bercuson's suspicions were correct; Manning never succeeded in completely eradicating the various splinter groups, but he sufficiently sanitized Social Credit ideology to make anti-Semitism appear to be the purview of a fanatical few.

For his part, Rosenberg doubted the genuineness of Manning's most recent purge. Despite the fact that Byrne and Ansley had been fired and the DSCC created, Rosenberg was still "convinced that the split between the Manning group and the Jaques-Pat Ashby group does not involve any difference in principle, nor does it really mean that there are two groups within the Social Credit Party, one of which is anti-semitic and the other one is not anti-semitic; but rather that it represents a split in matters of policy; the Manning group believing that it is not expedient at the present time to continue an open anti-semitic line in public, while the dissident group ... believe[s] in the policy of open and militant anti-semitism."[31]

Bercuson disagreed with Rosenberg, at least initially. He maintained that "the rupture in the ranks is a definite one and represents a real division of opinion" and the firings were "the culminating step of a development long expected ... There appears to be a real division of opinion on fundamental matters. That is why I think we have gained considerably from these recent events." In other correspondence Bercuson reiterated: "I do not think we should under-estimate the significance of what has occurred. Manning's action in insisting on the resignation of two of the leading Douglasites has done the party no good. The statements of the leaders, including Mr. Low, are full of confusion. On the one hand it is realized that Manning's support is essential to the party; on the other hand it is also recognized that Social Credit without the Douglas theories is not Social Credit." Later, however, Bercuson vacillated. He admitted that just because Manning had publicly repudiated anti-Semitism and fired two key government members, "this does not mean that the Social Credit party has gone on record as condemning anti-semitism or as eliminating it from the party platform ... The fact remains that for years anti-semitism and international finance have been the keystones of the party's propaganda. Consequently, those of us who are close to developments never expected a complete repudiation of these fundamentals. As Mr. Rosenberg suggests, there has been no repudiation. The rank and file of the Social Credit movement will continue to be anti-semitic, having been indoctrinated along these lines for years." Thus, Bercuson concluded, "there is no open split in ideology; rather, the party members will continue to hold their old views while Mr. Manning or possibly Mr. Low may repudiate anti-semitism because it now seems expedient."[32]

Although Bercuson seems to have been unsure whether or not Social Credit was experiencing a fundamental split, Rosenberg believed unequivocally that the dissension was more affected than real. In a memorandum to Hayes he offered evidence to prove that Social Credit's seemingly dramatic changes were not so dramatic as they first appeared; in fact, there had been no real change in its anti-Semitic philosophy. First, Rosenberg argued, it was highly questionable whether the Social Credit dissidents were actually "rebels," since none of them had been formally expelled from the national party. Second, although the SCAC had ostensibly repudiated the Union des Electeurs, Even, and *Vers Demain*, the *Canadian Social Crediter* still carried Even's name on its masthead as the official Social Credit representative in Quebec. Finally, although Manning had publicly repudiated anti-Semitism and liquidated the Social Credit Board, the Alberta Social Credit League had taken over all the board's activities, including the advertisement and distribution of anti-Semitic literature in the *Canadian Social Crediter*. These facts, Rosenberg concluded, "justify the belief that the recent 'split' is not one which affects the principles of the movement, but is due to a difference of opinion as to whether it is opportune at the present time for the Social Credit movement to make open anti-semitic attacks."[33]

Despite Rosenberg's unflagging scepticism, most Congress officers and agents generally agreed that, for good or ill, Social Credit had conducted its own housecleaning and any residual anti-Semitism was peripheral to the official movement. But this acknowledgment had an unsettling effect on Congress's public relations goals because the organization no longer felt compelled to create ways to confront Social Credit. Although Congress continued to scrutinize both the official and splinter groups' activities, the days of meeting with Social Credit leaders and undertaking covert actions to undermine the Alberta government had come to an end. Yet this very passivity had prevented Congress from achieving an earlier solution. Neither its public relations philosophy nor its policy had evolved quickly enough to eliminate the Social Credit menace at its height; consequently, it was Social Credit, not Congress, that ultimately solved the Social Credit problem. None the less, the organization continued its tradition of monitoring Social

Credit's anti-Semitic tendencies and would do so long after Manning's purge.[34]

If Congress was no longer interested in direct confrontation, there were still opportunities to take a public stand on Social Credit's record of anti-Semitism. In December 1947, shortly after Manning began his purge, the *Vancouver News-Herald* argued that Social Credit had been "stigmatized as anti-Semitic" predominantly because of Jaques. Calling the MP a "lone wolf," the *News-Herald* stressed that "as a whole, the party is not anti-Semitic. Alberta's King's printer, Abe Shnitka, is, in fact, a Jew – appointed by the Social Credit government."[35] It also commended Manning for disavowing anti-Semitism and banning Jaques's writings from the party organ: "This reform of the *Canadian Social Crediter* was long overdue. Mr. Jaques ... has brought little credit to himself, his party, or to Canada. There is no place in any Canadian party for violent racial or religious intolerance, and it is to be hoped that the Social Credit party is completely sincere in dissociating itself from any such bigotry."[36]

Congress's national headquarters was not pleased with the *News-Herald*'s interpretation of recent events. Years earlier, in a discussion regarding Shnitka's appointment as King's Printer, Rosenberg had remarked to an Alberta Congress officer: "After all, 'one swallow doesn't make a summer,' neither does one King's Printer wash spreaders of antisemitic propaganda clean."[37] Congress's press officer David Rome agreed with Rosenberg's assessment; after reading the *News-Herald* article he recommended that a letter be sent to the paper challenging its interpretation. However, he suggested that the letter be sent by a Jew but not a Congress officer, and not necessarily for publication.[38] Hayes agreed with this remarkably passive approach, and a letter was written by A. Jacob Livinson of Montreal, a frequent letter writer to the *Montreal Star*. In accordance with Rome's suggestions, Livinson wrote that Jaques was not in fact a "lone wolf" with respect to anti-Semitism and that other Social Credit leaders, including Low, made similar statements about international Jewish financiers. Further, the Union des Electeurs, through its French-language paper, *Vers Demain*, had published the *Protocols*, and "this notorious document and other anti-semitic literature are still being sold by Social Credit book-distributing organizations." As for Shnitka being King's Printer, "too much importance may be attached to the appointment of a Jewish businessman to a governmental office ... It is a purely personal relationship, rather inconsistent with the general line of the party, but surely such an appointment does not exculpate anyone from anti-semitism." Livinson thanked the *News-Herald* for bringing Social Credit's anti-Semitism to the attention of Canadians: "Your editorial is an instance of the very great service which the press can render the Canadian tradition of working democracy by being vigilantly watchful on such important issues. I trust that you will continue this excellent work. The Social Credit Party must be urged to clean its house cleaner, for the common good of all peoples of Canada."[39]

Livinson's letter was not sent on behalf of Congress, and Rome urged that the editor be requested not to publish it. This was quintessential Congress, and simply another example of how problematic its public relations approach was at best, how grossly ineffective at worst. By late 1947 Manning had been forced to publicly disavow anti-Semitism and sanitize the party organ. Public opinion had swung away from Jaques, and press coverage exposed the connection between anti-Semitism and the Social Credit movement. Yet Congress continued to conduct its public relations work in a covert and passive manner. It could take little credit for Social Credit's new line on anti-Semitism and was failing to take full advantage of the gains that came its way. Congress had failed to fulfil its mandate as the national organization to protect and promote the interests and rights of Canadian Jewry. As matters turned out, the *News-Herald* did publish the letter,[40] and readers were presented with a Jewish perspective, although not explicitly Congress's.

Through 1948 Congress continued to monitor the ramifications of Manning's purge. It appeared that Gordon Taylor, the new editor of the *Canadian Social Crediter*, was following Manning's directive to the letter. In its 11 December 1947 issue the party organ had published part one of a two-part article entitled "Clues to the Determination of Certain Sections of Jewry to Secure Palestine as A Jewish State," which discussed how "Financial Jewry (both Zionist and non-Zionist) was furthering the aspirations of fanatical Zionism for its own ends, namely, in order to gain possession of the colossal Oil and Mineral resources of Palestine ... [so] they could be developed for the aggrandisement of Financial Jewry, preferably under the aegis of a Jewish State." However, in the paper's 18 December issue the following announcement appeared: "In strict accordance with our new editorial policy the second part of the article ... entitled 'Clues to the Determination of Certain Sections of Jewry ...' WILL NOT be published. – The Editors." In early January 1948 Taylor editorialized that Social Credit's philosophy was positive, not negative, and that "there is no room in the Social Credit movement for misfits and sadists who build their house on hate and intolerance and prejudice."[41] In a memorandum to Hayes, Rosenberg expressed interest in Taylor's statement because it "appears to be an attempt to put forward a 'positive' approach towards Social Credit as opposed to the 'negative' policy of attacking religious and racial groups." But Rosenberg remained sceptical: "Whether this new policy is merely an attempt to wriggle out of the difficult position in which the Social Credit movement has placed itself because of its previous anti-Semitic attacks, or is evidence of a real change of heart still remains to be seen."[42]

Rosenberg's scepticism was becoming overblown. In fact, Manning *was* enforcing the new line on anti-Semitism. In the months after his purge the DSCC attempted to solicit funds by stating that the provincial government had sold out to the Zionists and international communist financiers.[43] On 24 March 1948 Manning announced over his radio program, *The Social Credit Hour*, that his movement had not deviated from or repudiated any of the Social Credit principles as enunciated by Douglas (although this was plainly untrue). Moreover, in fighting to establish those principles, Social Credit "shall not be sidetracked by controversial abstract side issues and racial prejudices which have nothing whatever to do with the basic principles of a true Social Credit economy." Manning emphasized that the "self-styled" DSCC had "no connection whatsoever with the Alberta Social Credit League or with the Social Credit Association of Canada and can be regarded only as an organized attempt on the part of a few disgruntled individuals to create division in the Social Credit ranks." Dismissing the Douglasites in one moral sweep, Manning proclaimed: "There are always a few who will never learn that progress in the interests of the people as a whole is not brought about by childish quibblings over names or abstract theories or racial prejudices." He concluded: "We re-iterate our intention to do everything in our power to unite the people of this Province and country irrespective of color, race or creed in an all out effort to end the present vicious financial monopoly and restore the effective control over money and credit to the people themselves."[44] Manning had stayed true to his convictions: Social Credit must continue to fight the "vicious" international financial conspiracy, but it was not explicitly Jewish.

Not surprisingly, Rosenberg was deeply unimpressed with Manning's latest pronouncements and remarked to Hayes, "Evidently Mr. Manning is of the opinion that anti-semitism is merely 'a controversial abstract side issue,' and believes that it can be separated from Social Credit philosophy itself, whereas in actual fact all Social Credit literature and almost every book written by its founder Major C.H. Douglas is so steeped in anti-semitism that Major Douglas, Social Credit and anti-semitism are inseparable." In short, Rosenberg did not accept Manning's repudiation as genuine, given his profession of loyalty to Douglas's Social Credit principles and the party organ's continued advertisement of anti-Semitic literature. In Rosenberg's opinion, this "should be ample evidence to prove that the repudiation of anti-Semitism by Premier Manning is not sincere, but is merely intended to ward off attacks and lull opponents into a sense of false security."[45]

Rosenberg's scepticism was understandable but at this point not merited, and one wonders if he would ever have commended Manning for his efforts. In Rosenberg's mind, Manning had been and would continue to be just as culpable as his more overtly anti-Semitic colleagues. Whether Manning truly believed in a Jewish-financial-communist plot to enslave the world is debatable – the premier openly advocated the theory of an international financial conspiracy but demurred on its Jewish aspect. For years he had expressed no opposition to his colleagues' advocating the theory of an international financial Jewish conspiracy, and in fact made very similar comments. But now, in the post-war, post-Holocaust period, Manning was cleaning house. He was explicitly marginalizing those Douglasite Social Crediters who advocated anti-Semitism, and for this he must be given credit. It was undoubtedly because of Manning that, when the state of Israel was proclaimed on 14 May 1948, the *Canadian Social Crediter* was conspicuously silent. One can only imagine the paper's conspiratorial comments if this had occurred before Manning's dictum. Instead, in keeping with its more "positive" approach, the party organ focused on the upcoming fifth anniversary of Aberhart's death (23 May 1943) and paid extensive tribute to Alberta Social Credit's founder.[46]

Yet Rosenberg remained unwilling to credit Manning for the movement's transformation, perhaps because he could not accept that Social Credit's philosophy was in fact changing. He had monitored its anti-Semitic propaganda for years and become an expert on the movement. Although he was correct in stating that "Major Douglas, Social Credit and anti-semitism are inseparable," Rosenberg did not entertain the possibility that Manning could lead a movement that was Social Credit only in name. The Social Credit serpent was shedding its skin; anti-Semitism was being discarded, and Congress would have to adapt accordingly.

This shedding, however, was not occurring without a struggle. Through the spring of 1948 Douglas's Social Credit Secretariat in England continued to side with the DSCC and denounce Manning's government, not only for deviating from the founder's principles but for allowing Congress to dictate its policies. In one instance the English *Social Crediter* warned that the "Planners" for "Communist-Zionist world domination" would stop at nothing short of "murder" because they "cannot permit Social Credit in Alberta to succeed." According to the *Social Crediter*, Manning and his Cabinet members were the "target for perhaps the most venomous manoeuvres ever directed against administrative office holders ... A whole world is at stake and atomic or bacterial war are arguments only deferred until less troublesome inducements have failed."[47] Interestingly, the *Social Crediter*'s warning of "murder" was given Alberta-wide newspaper coverage and broadcast over local radio stations. The *Edmonton Bulletin* reported that Manning "was unperturbed by the warning [and] had no comment to make."[48]

However, some officers within Congress – significantly, those in the Alberta branch – believed a comment was necessary. Bercuson and other Edmonton officers believed that this "dangerous nonsense" could not go unchallenged. The policy of the Edmonton JPRC, stated Bercuson, was "to call public attention to statements which are obviously false and which are intended only to prejudice the position of the Jews." Accordingly, the committee prepared a public statement "explaining the absurdity of linking Communism and Zionism in a so-called plot." The statement, given radio and press coverage throughout Alberta, stressed that the most relentless foe of Zionism over the years had been communist Russia. In fact, "the purpose of Zionism is to establish for the Jews a Homeland in Palestine such as every other people possesses. It is sheer nonsense ... to claim that attacks against cabinet members in Alberta would be included in this program. This vicious rumor must be exposed immediately since its inventors cannot supply one iota of proof to substantiate the charges." Once again, the Alberta branch proved itself more willing and able than national headquarters to execute an aggressive public relations policy. Indeed, the actions of the Alberta branch were predicated on the conviction that it was Congress's *duty* to issue a public statement on this matter. Alberta officers believed a strong stance was necessary since, as Bercuson reported, the situation was "certainly confused" and "there is no clear cut distinction in the party between the Manningites and the Douglasites. Consequently the anti-semitic barrage still continues in one way or another."[49]

The Alberta branch was certainly correct about the confusion. In the post-purge period Social Credit's internecine warfare bewildered many rank and file supporters, who wrote the premier asking for clarification of Social Credit's philosophy and the purpose of the DSCC.[50] As one Social Credit supporter wrote: "Just a few lines to yourself Personally to ask you a straight Question. It is being Circulated and used for Political propaganda here that the *Social Credit Party* is *Anti-Jewish* or to use the exact words: is *Anti-Semetic*. Now *is this true* Mr. Manning *or is it not*. I want a definite statement from yourself. Is it true with the *Alberta* set-up of Social Credit or is it true with the *original frame work* of Social Credit as it was established in the Old Land. Let me Know by Return Mail."[51] Manning responded to each letter individually[52] and repeated what he said in his radio address: "There has not and will not be any repudiation of Social Credit principles and we ... shall not be sidetracked by abstract side issues and racial prejudices which have nothing whatever to do with the fundamental principles of a true Social Credit economy."[53]

There were other residual problems. Despite its marginal status, the DSCC continued to haunt Manning, and it took him several months to completely discredit the Alberta dissidents. Meanwhile, the Ontario Union of Electors, together with the Quebec Union des Electeurs, denounced his regime and published increasingly hard-core anti-Semitic propaganda. The Union des Electeurs also began campaigning in various constituencies across Quebec for the upcoming provincial election in July 1948.[54] Congress's national headquarters watched Even's activities closely, and with perhaps greater interest than it observed affairs in Alberta. Congress's assistant press officer, David Kirshenblatt (then Kirshnblatt) travelled to Trois-Rivières and Cap-de-la-Madeleine, where Union des Electeurs rallies were being held. Réal Caouette (now leader of the Union des Electeurs) and J. Ernest Gregoire spoke at Trois-Rivières and Cap-de-la-Madeleine respectively in early March. Kirshenblatt noted that, although neither "referred to, or mentioned directly, the word Jew," the "ward-heelers" who introduced them variously announced that "members in the House of Commons were under the control of 'high finance' that is international Jewry"; that "some fifty Jews control the finance of Canada"; and that "the agents presently at work preparing the ground-work for a revolution in Canada are 'high financiers, freemasons and Jews.'" Consequently, stated Kirshenblatt, "After such an introduction, Caouette and Gregoire had no need to describe whom they meant by bankers and high financiers." Kirshenblatt inferred that "the party leadership recognized the embarrassment entailed by leaving themselves open to direct accusations of anti-semitism. But this is inherent in the indoctrination given to members. Both men who referred to the abstractions of high finance, free-masonary and Jewry are not of a high intellectual calibre as they admitted in their speeches. However, *Vers Demain* is sowing a dangerous seed which growth the leadership will possibly be unable to control."[55]

Throughout the spring of 1948 Kirshenblatt kept abreast of Union des Electeurs activities. In May he travelled to Rouyn-Noranda, where he spoke with Julien Morissette, editor of *La Frontière* and a leading critic of Social Credit in Quebec.[56] Kirshenblatt learned not only that Social Credit was extremely strong in "remote and rural places" in Quebec but that "meetings of ... Social Credit in this area are definitely anti-semitic. Although the speakers do not make anti-semitism their topic the speeches are replete with references to Jewish finance, International Jewry, Jewish bankers, etc." The Union des Electeurs was also wooing farmers in these areas by "asking why the Government was able to assist them during the depression years and is not able to pay the $20 a month dividend now." However, Kirshenblatt learned that counter-propaganda, such as the condemnation of the Union des Electeurs by certain members of the Quebec clergy,[57] was having some effect. He suggested to Hayes that Congress indirectly support additional counter-propaganda aimed at farmers, proving why Social Credit economic theories were unworkable. The purpose of such a campaign would be to "expos[e] Social Credit for what they are. Although they are proven as a bunch of uneducated anti-semites ... the Social Credit speakers still have a strong case in that their doctrine has not been disproven in articles able to make the average layman understand why it is unworkable ... if we were to arrange for the ghost writing of such an article we could place it in various French Canadian newspapers who would be only too anxious to run something like it."[58] Kirshenblatt's initiative was apparently not emulated at national headquarters, since the latter did not sponsor any anti–Social Credit propaganda in French-language newspapers. In keeping with its insufficient public relations approach, national headquarters was content to rely on Morissette, who continued his anti–Social Credit campaign within the pages of *La Frontière*.[59]

As the Quebec election drew nearer, the Union des Electeurs increased its efforts. On 27 June 1948 Kirshenblatt travelled to Drummondville to hear Caouette speak at a Union campaign rally. Other speakers included Even and Gregoire. Kirshenblatt reported that there was only one anti-semitic speaker, Edmond Major, a Union candidate for Drummond County, who "lumped together financiers, trusts, freemasons and international Jewry in the category of seeking to dominate the world." Kirshenblatt inferred that the Union was hoping for a big win; he overheard one candidate optimistically projecting as many as "53 seats in the forthcoming election."[60] Yet when the election occurred on 28 July, the Union des Electeurs fared very poorly, and the votes polled were negligible.[61]

Meanwhile, the Union of Electors was attempting to take over Social Credit in Ontario. Congress watched the rival organization closely, especially its propaganda organ, the *Voice of the Electors*, which was increasingly anti-Semitic and anti-communist. In response, Congress forwarded copies of the *Voice of the Electors* to the Anti-Defamation League (ADL), which was familiar with similar American literature that linked anti-Semitism with Cold War anti-communism.[62] The ADL compared the *Voice of the Electors* with American extreme right-wing publications, only to discover striking similarities. The *Voice of the Electors* described the "anti-Semitic whining" of Jews who used the "ploy" of the Holocaust to accuse innocent people of "Hitlerian practices" and cautioned: "Let us not revive the 'Hitlerian cry' at every turn. After all, reports indicate that many of the Jews liquidated by Hitler have since entered the United States – most illegally."[63] The American fascist publication *Bible News Flashes* similarly stated: "Four million Jews which the Germans are supposed to have barbecued or executed in gas chambers in Europe are now walking the streets of America ... Since millions have evidently entered this country 'illegally,' this open violation of the laws of our land is evidently countenanced by the high New Deal officials in Washington."[64] Although neither the ADL nor Congress suggested any action against the *Voice of the Electors*, its parallels to American extremist sheets was duly recognized. Recognition of the problem, however, was not a solution, as Congress had learned from years of experience. None the less, the organization maintained its well-worn stance of not confronting what was now Social Credit's fringe anti-Semitism.

Although it did little more than monitor the splinter groups, Congress began to question whether Social Credit's factions, although disagreeing over policy, had any fundamental divergence over philosophy. (Indeed, the same question should have been posed to Congress regarding its public relations work.) In a memorandum to Hayes, Kirshenblatt expressed his belief that the Social Credit factions had disagreements but "it is not over ideology." During election campaigns "there appears to be understandings between both [the official Social Credit movement and the splinter groups]." Thus, "the verbal 'split' was merely a public relations scheme to satisfy all concerned." Yet Kirshenblatt emphasized that the DSCC and the Union of Electors "should receive closer attention than the more moderate Social Credit Association of Canada."[65] In short, although Kirshenblatt was sceptical about Social Credit's ideological differences, he was none the less cognizant of the more blatant anti-Semitic propaganda emanating from the renegade groups.

Yet the dissidents were not the only cause for concern – the official movement was still engaging in anti-Semitic polemics well after Manning's purge. In the 8 July 1948 issue of the *Canadian Social Crediter*, national leader Low discussed the recent rift in party ranks. In response to the English *Social Crediter*'s accusations that Manning "had become a Zionist, having been converted by Lady Reading or some such person from England," Low dismissed them as "a complete fabrication." However, he admitted, "it is perfectly true that Mr. Manning has not been a rabid enemy of the Jews, nor has he harped against Zionism. But he has been quite aware of the plotters and planners, and their nefarious schemes against the welfare of the people." In the 29 July 1948 issue Low stated: "The unholy trinity of rank materialism, namely International Communism, International Finance, and International Political Zionism got in their deadly work. They plotted to engulf the world in war. Having succeeded in this, they proceeded to spread confusion and chaos, and to engender fear and hatred and suspicion into the hearts of men."

After reading Low's statements, Rosenberg concluded to Hayes that "there has been no change in the policies and principles of the Social Credit movement in Canada. It is still anti-Semitic and anti-Zionist. It has not expelled from its ranks or repudiated such anti-Semites as Norman Jaques ... Pat Ashby ... or Solon Low, and the Alberta headquarters of the Social Credit Association and the *Canadian Social Crediter* still advertise and offer for sale all the anti-Semitic pamphlets and books by Major Douglas and ... Nesta Webster, which quote from the alleged *Protocols of the Elders of Zion*." In short, stated Rosenberg, "the main point of difference is merely a question of tactics. The Alberta Social Credit leaders do not appear to believe it wise to make open anti-Semitic statements. Its opponents ... believe that anti-Semitic statements are both desirable and useful."[66]

Other excerpts from the *Canadian Social Crediter* reinforced Rosenberg's suspicions. In its 15 July issue J.N. Haldeman, president of the Social Credit Association of Saskatchewan and vice-president of the SCAC, discussed the recent party split and attempted to discredit the Ontario and Quebec splinter groups. He criticized them for their non-democratic practices and compared their opposition to the official movement with Hitler's and Stalin's attempts to "set up puppet regimes to overthrow the democratic governments in Europe." He also recalled that previous attempts to splinter Social Credit had "proved disastrous." In cheerleading fashion, Haldeman exhorted: "Let us all get back to Social Credit and stick to it. There is room in the Social Credit Leagues for every true Social Crediter. We will consistently fight communism and fascism, political party machine politics, monopoly and international finance wherever we find them. We must uphold the Christian way of life and work to make governments and the money system serve the people. The situation is truly urgent. Let us unite in our fight for Social Credit."[67]

Rosenberg viewed Haldeman's statements with only slightly less cynicism. Convinced there had been no change in Social Credit philosophy, he told Hayes that he took great exception to those Congress officers who believed there had been a real "house-cleaning" within the movement: "There has been a tendency in some quarters to accept the statements of Mr. Solon Low, Premier Manning and Dr. J.N. Haldeman in which they disclaim anti-Semitism at their face value, and to believe that there are two kinds of Social Crediters in Canada, i.e., the 'kosher' kind ... who claim they are not anti-Semitic, and the 'non-kosher' variety ... who have been allegedly repudiated by Premier Manning and who hold fast by their anti-Semitic propaganda." In fact, declared Rosenberg, there was no difference between the "kosher" and "non-kosher" Social Crediters: "I knew the late Premier Aberhart and the present Premier Manning personally and heard them speak quite often, and despite the fact that they may and did claim that 'some of their best friends were Jews,' I can assure you that both of them were just as anti-Semitic as Norman Jaques is. The only difference between them is that Aberhart, Manning, Solon Low, Haldeman and the 'respectable Social Crediters' do not believe that it is expedient to make open avowal of anti-Semitism while Norman Jaques, Gregoire, Louis Even, and the Union of Electors believe that open anti-Semitism is a useful and practical way of getting into power." In short, "there has been no change of heart and no change of policy ... [and] no hope or possibility of any such change in the near or the distant future." Accordingly, Rosenberg cautioned Hayes, Congress should "be on guard against accepting any statements by Premier Manning, Solon Low, Dr. J.N. Haldeman or any other Social Credit agitator in Canada regarding anti-semitism at their face value."[68]

Rosenberg's opinions about Aberhart's and Manning's anti-Semitism are debatable; the evidence reveals that anti-Semitism had diminished within the official movement because of Manning, who was purposefully marginalizing the dissident factions. In November 1948, for example, when the national JPRC sent a non-Jew to observe the Ontario Social Credit League convention, it was informed that "there was no indication of any anti-semitic feeling or platform in the proceedings." In addition, Ontario Social Credit League president Fitzgerald "repudiated publicly any connection with the Ontario Union of Electors," which was now vehemently anti-Jewish.[69] The *Montreal Gazette* similarly reported that the League had "sever[ed] its connections with the Union of Electors of Quebec Province" and quoted Fitzgerald as saying there was a "sinister campaign ... stamping the Social Credit Party as an anti-semitic organization." He challenged "anyone, anywhere, to find one iota of anti-Semitism – or anti-anything for that matter – in the Social Credit League of Ontario."[70] Clearly, Manning's directive was exerting influence.

Yet the *Canadian Social Crediter* was still publishing inflammatory statements about international political Zionism, international finance, and other world plotters.[71] Significantly, Low was responsible for many of these statements. In November 1948 he submitted a "suggested manifesto" for the movement, which was published in the party organ. One of the manifesto's resolutions stated: "We are implacably opposed to and we shall combat by all legitimate means international communism and socialism, international finance and its commercial ramifications and international political zionism as instruments of a single central group pursuing a consistent policy directed against human freedom and towards the establishment of a world tyranny modelled on the communist dictatorship of the Union of Socialist Soviet Republics." At the 1948 Alberta Social Credit League convention held shortly thereafter, Low attempted to pass the manifesto in a resolution condemning "Communism, Socialism, and international political Zionism." Although claiming that international political Zionism sought to "enslave" the world, he distinguished between "religious Zionism" and "international political Zionism": "The first is a movement to establish a Jewish homeland by peaceful means, but the second is an attempt to set up a state forcibly in someone else's country ... World peace hangs on a very slender thread because of the way the forces of international political Zionism took over Palestine forcibly without waiting for the sanction of the [United Nations] Security Council." In another resolution, Low suggested that the Alberta Social Credit League establish a chair of history at the University of Alberta "so that the facts of history – not the fancies – are made available to the people." This government-controlled chair would help counteract "school histories," or what Low called "a group of bedtime stories," which kept the facts of international finance and economic domination from the people.[72]

Manning did not let Low's resolutions pass without amendment. He suggested that the phrase "international political Zionism" not be used alongside "international communism and socialism, or international finance," because opponents of Social Credit would accuse the movement of being anti-Semitic. Accordingly, the convention's delegates struck the phrase from the resolution so that that segment read: "We are implacably opposed to and we shall combat by all legitimate means international communism and socialism, international finance and its commercial ramifications." As various Alberta newspapers reported: "References to international political Zionism ... were deleted from the resolution because delegates felt it would prejudice the movement in the eyes of people who did not distinguish between the two forms of [political and religious] Zionism."[73]

Other incidents marked the Alberta Social Credit League convention. At one point it "exploded into a bitter battle" because the League executive denied membership to Bourcier, Gillese, and Burton, all members of the DSCC. Convention delegates hotly disagreed whether the executive had acted in a dictatorial fashion, but Manning's influence quelled the dissension and the Douglasites were refused membership.[74] Manning seemed determined to enforce the new party line: anti-Semitic Douglasites would be denied entry, and anti-Semitic propaganda would not form part of the convention's resolutions.

At Congress's national headquarters, Rosenberg greeted Manning's actions and the convention's amendment with incredulity. In his opinion these incidents merely highlighted the inconsistent nature of the purge. As he indicated to Hayes, notwithstanding the expulsion of Bourcier, Gillese, and Burton, "no official steps have been taken to expel Solon Low ... Norman Jaques ... and Pat Ashby ... from the national Social Credit Party, although they have repeatedly made statements ... concerning international Jewish financiers, international political Zionism and the *Protocols of the Elders of Zion.*" As for Low's distinction between "international political Zionism" and "religious Zionism," this was "a very feeble attempt to white wash his attacks, in a similar manner to which Solon Low has in the past claimed that the Social Credit Movement is not anti-Semitic because the Arabs are Semitic and he is not against the Arabs." As for deleting "international political Zionism" from the resolution, "the amendment as passed did not actually repudiate Mr. Low's anti-Semitic remarks and attitude, but was motivated largely by the desire of Premier Manning and the group in control of the Social Credit Movement in Alberta to avoid charges of anti-Semitism." In sum, concluded Rosenberg, Social Credit was still honeycombed with anti-Semitism, and the leader of the national party was leading the pack: "Solon Low ... speaking at the annual provincial convention of the Alberta Social Credit Association was responsible for the drafting and support of a resolution which was really a rephrasing of the anti-Semitic charge that the Jews are responsible for an international conspiracy on the lines charged in the alleged *Protocols of the Elders of Zion.*" Consequently, Social Credit's "pledge" of several months earlier to "keep [its] columns and propaganda clean from anti-Semitic propaganda and attacks" was meaningless.[75]

Meanwhile, Congress's Alberta branch had learned of Low's comments on "international political Zionism" and, in keeping with its more aggressive public relations approach, decided to take action. A few days after the League convention, Low was scheduled to speak in Medicine Hat. Congress agents in the small local Jewish community asked national headquarters to forward a draft letter for publication in the *Medicine Hat Daily News.* Jewish community leaders had already contacted the editor of the paper, asking him "to suppress publication of any similar outbursts against our people. We are assured of his co-operation and he will not give Mr. Low any front page publicity at all – except to report briefly on page 10 on his meeting."[76] Hayes agreed that Medicine Hat Jewry was "acting wisely and vigorously in making certain that Mr. Low's anti-semitic outbursts should not receive unduly great prominence before the public." Accordingly, he forwarded a draft letter to be published in the local paper.

The letter criticized Low for his "dangerous statements" and discussed how post-war anti-Semitism "carefully avoids attacking Jews by that name but continues to incite against the same people using the vaguer terms of 'Zionists and international financiers.'" It connected Social Credit's anti-Semitic statements with the *Protocols* and "similar nazi publications" and condemned Low for his comments about the teaching of history: "Mr. Low cast doubt upon the authority of the study of history and other subjects in our own University of Alberta and suggested that a chair of history be established where he calls 'the facts of history – not the fancies' will be taught. Here we have again an attempt at the disruption of academic institutions parallel to that which corrupted and disappointed the once noble universities of Germany and other European countries. It will be well if the public will be alert to the menace inherent in such agitation."[77] It was an effective and eloquent letter, and it suggested national headquarters' willingness to publicly confront Social Credit, but *only* in response to others' efforts. National headquarters, not the Alberta branch, should have initiated this action, just as the former should have provided a unified, coherent, national public relations policy. What national headquarters needed to do was act on issues of anti-Semitism, not react. In any case, the letter to the *Medicine Hat Daily News* became a moot point because the editor did not publish it. He also did not keep his word. Low's visit to Medicine Hat was the lead story on page one, although it focused mostly on his condemnation of Soviet Russia and its "centralizing" and "totalitarian" tendencies.[78]

Meanwhile, Low was resuming efforts to pass his manifesto at other Social Credit conventions. In early December 1948 the national council of the SCAC met in Winnipeg. Heading the convention in his capacity as national leader, Low submitted the manifesto. The only change was that "fascism" had been added to the list of world tyrannies, perhaps to extinguish any accusations of fascism against Social Credit. Thus, that portion of the manifesto read: "We are implacably opposed to and we shall combat by all legitimate means international communism and socialism, international finance and its commercial ramifications, international political zionism, fascism, and all other policies directed against human freedom." Social Credit's national council endorsed this and eight other points as the "basis for the new manifesto" to be submitted at its national convention the following April.[79]

Rosenberg noted the minuscule change between Low's original manifesto and that passed by the national council. He concluded to Hayes: "Evidently, Solon Low as national leader of the Social Credit Party is not as squeamish as Premier Manning and has no scruples against placing the National Social Credit Party squarely on record as being opposed to Zionism and coupling it with Communism and International Finance."[80] It seems that Manning did not exert as much influence over the national party as he did over his own provincial government. Certainly, it appears that Low had got his way, as his manifesto became part of the national party's resolutions. The *Canadian Social Crediter* sympathetically reported that Low "vehemently denied that anti-semitic sentiment exists in his movement," and Low himself stated: "In the Social Credit association there is not one particle or bit of anti-semitism. For that matter, there is no race prejudice or discrimination against anyone because of race, colour or creed."[81]

Such was the state of affairs within Social Credit at the end of 1948. Certainly, there was still much confusion regarding the place of anti-Semitism in the movement's philosophy and its stance on anti-Semitic propaganda. Dissident Social Crediters promoted the international financial Jewish conspiracy theory with even greater enthusiasm, while so-called loyal Social Crediters such as Low continued to express views that were just as anti-Semitic.[82] In its own assessment of Social Credit, Congress looked back on a year of complication and contradiction. It acknowledged that there had been many positive changes regarding the Social Credit problem, but there had been negative repercussions as well. Manning had completed his purge of anti-Semitism, but several splinter groups had emerged and achieved a small degree of success throughout the year. The official movement had attempted to disassociate itself from these splinter groups, only to have mainstream leaders declare the existence of a "Zionist-Communist plot" in terms strikingly similar to those of the dissidents.[83]

Congress's assessment of the year's events was accurate; however, a longer view of Manning's purge shows a marked decrease in Social Credit's anti-Semitic propaganda, notwithstanding challenges to the premier's authority. This trend would continue in the following months. By early 1949 Congress could safely relax its vigil on Social Credit. The movement continued to experience residual anti-Semitism, but essentially Manning's purge had been successful. Congress still monitored the activities of the splinter groups, which continued to spout anti-Semitism, but no serious occurrences compelled it to take action. Rather, the organization confined itself to observation, commentary, and distribution of information to its umbrella committees. In many ways this public relations work was easiest for Congress. Concerted action against Social Credit had always been difficult, and now that the eye of the storm had passed, Congress could return to its observation post with the assurance that the worst was over. However, the organization could take little comfort in the knowledge that Social Credit had eradicated its own anti-Semitism, since the party could just as easily revive it.

Yet by early 1949 the sanitation of Social Credit's philosophy was basically complete, and was confirmed when Congress obtained a copy of Byrne's final report to the Social Credit Board. Although it was an internal government report and not intended for publication, the DSCC published it in its October 1948 issue of the DSCC *Information Service*, which was distributed in January 1949.[84] After reading the report, Rosenberg merely stated to Hayes: "It is generally understood that this report was one of the reasons which led to the expulsion of Byrne and his supporters from the Social Credit Party in Alberta."[85] Congress now held the final evidence proving the full-blown anti-Semitism of Byrne and the Social Credit Board. The story behind Manning's purge was complete and on the record.

Another event in early 1949 symbolized the end of Social Credit's anti-Semitism and helped to ease Congress's concerns further. Norman Jaques died. The announcement of his death on 31 January did not go unnoticed by Congress, although its reaction was certainly reserved. Kirshenblatt merely wrote to Hayes: "It might interest you to know that Norman Jaques departed permanently from this world over the weekend while in Ottawa. For your information."[86] The Canadian Jewish press, however, was much less circumspect. The *Canadian Jewish Weekly* declared: "Norman Jaques ... was one of the first Canadian members of Parliament to openly proclaim his anti-Semitic views to the country. A Social Crediter, Jaques stunned Canadians when he used the House of Commons to air his bigoted opinions. Jaques split with some of his Social Credit associates over party ideology, but he never swerved in his hatred of the Soviet Union and in his attacks against Jews ... Jaques was connected with the most rabid anti-Semites in both the United States and Canada."[87]

The *Canadian Jewish Chronicle* similarly announced that Jaques "was one of Canada's most notorious Jew-baiters, a professional anti-semite, a crony of Gerald K. Smith, a spokesman for the mufti cause, and a juggler of the triple slander against Jewry – namely that there existed against the world a Jewish conspiracy made up of Communism, international finance, and Zionism." The *Chronicle* criticized Prime

Minister Louis St Laurent and national CCF leader M.J. Coldwell for describing Jaques as "sincere" in their condolence speeches in the House of Commons. Indeed, St Laurent had stated: "On many matters [Jaques] held strong views which most of us did not share, but no one could doubt his sincerity or his earnest desire to be of service to his fellow Canadians in the advocacy of those views ... I am sure he will be remembered as an earnest, painstaking and courtly gentleman who served his constituents and his fellow citizens with zeal and devotion." Coldwell made similar use of the term: "We often disagreed fundamentally, and sometimes violently, with the late member for Wetaskiwin. None the less we do know that the views he expressed in this house were held sincerely and arose from deep conviction, and for this we respected him, as we respect any member who speaks from sincerity and conviction."[88] The *Chronicle* was outraged that these two politicians, "caught between the requirements of condolence and the imperatives of truth, hit upon the same adjective to cast a glow of integrity over the reputation of the deceased." Whether Jaques was sincere or not was irrelevant, the paper vented: "We do not think that any will question Hitler's sincerity when he, too, entertained the same notions about 'international Jewry' ... Will Mr. St. Laurent say of Mr. Stalin, too, that he is sincere, – which, after his fashion, he no doubt is?"[89] Once again, the Canadian Jewish press had done what Congress always should have: it openly, publicly, pugnaciously confronted the blatancy of Social Credit's Jew-hatred. Instead, national headquarters had Rosenberg write a memorandum assessing the political reactions to Jaques's death and distribute it among national and regional officers.

In his memo Rosenberg fully agreed with the *Canadian Jewish Chronicle* and expressed dismay at St Laurent's and Coldwell's choice of words: "Since Norman Jaques was a notorious and rabid anti-Semite who had used his privileges as a member of the House of Commons to make it a sounding board for the most fantastic appeals to racial and religious prejudice, and had read into the official proceedings of the House of Commons many extracts from the *Protocols of the Elders of Zion* and other anti-Semitic propaganda, it is indeed disturbing, to say the least, to have the Prime Minister of Canada and the leader of the CCF make what appear to be testimonials to his 'sincerity,' 'zeal and devotion,' and characterize him as a 'courteous and courtly gentleman' in the words of the Prime Minister." Rosenberg feared (quite irrationally) that St Laurent's and Coldwell's remarks would be used by anti-Semites in Canada as a "testimonial" for anti-Semitism, "since the public in general will assume that to describe Norman Jaques as 'sincere' is equivalent to stating that his anti-Semitic attacks were true." Rosenberg was clearly stretching the limits of potential Jew-hatred, for it was extremely unlikely that St Laurent's and Coldwell's condolence remarks would encourage anti-Semitism. In any case, like the *Chronicle*, Rosenberg concluded that "Norman Jaques' sole claim to praise, if any, is that he was no hypocrite, and was an open and unashamed anti-Semite, rather than a concealed one. From the point of view of being open and unashamed advocates of the policies which they favour, Sir Oswald Mosley in England and Fred Rose in Canada might equally merit the description of 'sincere,' yet one cannot imagine parliamentary leaders in Canada or Great Britain applying those adjectives to them in statements to the House of Commons. Hitler, Goering and Goebbels may also have been without pretence and unfeigned in their hatred of Jews, but that would not merit them being eulogized as 'sincere' by democratic parliamentary leaders."[90]

Reactions of Social Crediters to Jaques's death are equally interesting. Bourcier, renegade Social Crediter and chairman of the DSCC, called Jaques "one of Canada's great Statesmen," and vilified the Manning faction while casting Jaques as a martyr:

Mr. Jaques dedicated his life to the cause of Christian Democracy and he fearlessly denounced those forces which are seeking to destroy Christianity and civilisation itself and rear up in their place a Godless world slave state ... The enemies of Christian civilization are devilishly cunning in the methods which they employ. Mr. Jaques committed the – to them – unpardonable offence of exposing the link which exists between international Communism, Socialism, High Finance and Political Zionism. The method used to silence him was the well-tried smear technique. Press, radio and party heelers labelled him "anti-semitic," "fascist," etc. Stupid people who did not take the trouble to learn the facts took up the hue and cry, and threw their bits of mud at the man who sacrificed his life to the cause of their God-given liberties. Perhaps the heaviest cross he had to bear was the fact that even within the ranks of his own party there were some who were misled by false propaganda and blindly took part in the campaign of abuse.[91]

Bourcier had perhaps unwittingly drawn an analogy between Jaques and Jesus Christ; in fact, Bourcier's tribute is strikingly similar to the story of Christ's crucifixion and his betrayal by the Jews. Like Christ, Jaques dedicated his life to a cause for which he was persecuted and betrayed by his enemies – and his friends.

R.E. Ansley, another dissident, likewise offered a glowing tribute in the Alberta legislature to the martyred Jaques: "The constituency of Wetaskiwin never had a more capable representative combined with the highest degree of sincerity and honesty of purpose ... Mr. Jaques' unimpeachable character made it impossible for the enemies of what he was advancing, or the conscious or unconscious stooges of those enemies, to deter him in his course. No one in our movement was so subjected to smear tactics engineered by the enemies of Christian democracy ... we have lost a great man. I feel that his spiritual strength will be even greater and, as the truth of the world picture becomes better understood, many of his critics will become his strong admirers."[92] Even Low, who had ostensibly remained loyal to Manning and shunned Jaques and other Douglasites, vindicated Jaques in the House of Commons: "My colleague was a man of deep convictions. His determination was unshakeable. These qualities, together with a high degree of personal courage, often drove him into vigorous debate as well as into strong denunciation of what he firmly believed to be social injustices or real threats to the peace and happiness of the people of the world. In spite of the fact that much personal criticism was directed to him, often amounting almost to character assassination, he stuck to his convictions, and to the very end continued in what he thought was his duty to humanity ... We, his colleagues in the Social Credit movement, mourn his passing. We have lost in him a devoted advocate and a warm personal friend."[93] For his part, Rosenberg told Hayes he found Low's statements ironic, since Low was part of that group that had banned Jaques's writings from the party organ and dissociated itself from Jaques's anti-Semitism.[94]

The *Canadian Social Crediter* also published an unusually warm tribute to Jaques, given the circumstances of his being barred from the paper. Indeed, it nearly defended Jaques's career of anti-Semitic agitation. It stated that the "people of Wetaskiwin have lost a steadfast representative who acted according to his views, and, who regardless of what his opponents might say or think, always tried to do his honest best." In an attempt to defend Jaques's activities, it added: "Born of English yeoman stock, Mr. Jaques never deserted his forbears or their love of freedom. He detested communism and all totalitarian concepts and only aroused bitter enmity among Jewish peoples when he unrestrainedly attacked what he called international political Zionism. He blamed it for most of the world's ills ... Those who condemn him for his alleged anti-Semitism are apt to overlook the good work he did in combatting communism in high places and low, and generally in pushing the cause of the common citizens – who are the people." The paper simultaneously apologized for and defended its decision to bar Jaques from its pages: "In paying tribute to the manifold good qualities of Mr. Jaques, it should be made clear that, contrary to oft-expressed views, he was not 'barred' from the columns of the *Canadian Social Crediter*. What was barred was anything of an anti-religious or anti-racial nature, or what might be construed as such. With that proviso, the writings of the late member were subject to no more disbarment than those of any other."[95]

It was a fitting way for the party organ to bid farewell to its leading anti-Semite. Its eulogy expressed ambivalence about purging Jaques from its pages, an ambivalence that had always existed within Social Credit. For years Social Credit politicians had consistently denied that their movement was anti-Semitic and protested that they were not responsible for Jaques's remarks, even as his anti-Semitic attacks received front-page billing in the *Canadian Social Crediter*. Even after his banishment from the party organ, no Social Credit leader officially repudiated him.[96] Thus, while Manning may have conducted his purge, the statements and activities of the dissidents and not-so-dissidents proved that Social Credit's anti-Semitic philosophy had deep roots and potential legacies. For the party organ to have published such a eulogy showed that Social Credit's central philosophy connecting Jews, finance, communism, and international political Zionism was not entirely defunct. Such ambivalence was best described by Jaques's daughter over forty years later, when she was asked about her father's anti-Semitism: "He believed what he said; he thought it was real, the threat … the world closed in on him … he was completely ostracized … I'm sure he was probably wrong … in the end."[97]

If the death of Jaques may be seen as the symbolic end of Social Credit's anti-Semitism, then by 1949 the worst had been eliminated. Smaller incidents cropped up through the 1950s and 1960s, and James Keegstra's activities in the 1970s and 1980s revealed the legacy of Social Credit's Jew-hatred.[98] But most scholars do not consider these later incidents to be part of Social Credit's record nor a continuation of the movement's earlier anti-Semitism. By 1949 the Social Credit drama had seemingly come to an end. Congress could now consider the Social Credit problem solved. But the victory was not sweet. Congress did not stop Social Credit's anti-Semitism; the movement's intolerance crumbled under its own weight and from circumstances largely separate from Congress's efforts. Canada's political culture was changing; there was much less room for publicly espoused intolerance, and Manning was well aware of the political and economic liabilities of spouting anti-Semitic propaganda.

Indeed, it must be emphasized that the reasons for Manning's purge were not ideological, for the difference in ideology between the Manningites and the Douglasites was merely one of degree. Rather, political and economic considerations caused Manning to act. As Howard Palmer notes:

Manning's expulsion of the Douglasites had many causes and was not simply a reaction to their anti-semitism. Some of them had criticized Manning's government for its failure to implement Social Credit policies and were thus challenging his leadership from within the party. In addition, the Social Credit Board's 1946 report was not only more openly anti-semitic than previous reports, but it also followed Major Douglas in criticizing the secret ballot ... Combined with these notions, the board's anti-semitism appeared to be just one more aspect of an ideology which was veering toward fascism. Further, Douglasite opposition to Zionism ... was incompatible with the world-view of many Alberta Protestants who saw the return of the Jews to Palestine as a fulfillment of prophecy and one of the key "signs of the times" foretelling the imminence of Christ's second coming. Finally, the anti-semitism of Douglas and his followers had, upon the revelations in 1946 of the mass destruction of Jews by Nazi Germany, become intolerably incompatible with the sympathies of democratic countries.[99]

While Manning's religious views prevented him from stating that the conspiracy was Jewish, it is unlikely that religious considerations were the primary motive for his purge. There is stronger evidence that political and economic motives compelled him to denounce the anti-Semitic Douglasites. By the post-war period, Alberta's political climate had been altered by several events, all world-wide in their implication: the Second World War, the near-destruction of European Jewry, Zionism and the birth of Israel, and the growth of communism and the ensuing Cold War. Although Social Credit propaganda questioned the conspiratorial, totalitarian motives of the Allied powers, doubted the extent of Jewish persecution before, during, and after the war, declared Zionism part of the international financial Jewish conspiracy, and equated Jews with communism, most Albertans viewed these events with more equanimity. The Alberta press covered extensively and often empathetically the Jewish refugee crisis, Nazi atrocities, the Nuremberg war crimes trials, and the problem of anti-Semitism in Canada. Although most Canadians still opposed Jewish immigration in the early post-war period, as did most Americans,[100] a Canadian Gallup poll in early 1946 revealed that 49 per cent of respondents agreed that Jews should "be allowed to settle freely in Palestine," and a further 20 per cent agreed that Jews should be allowed to settle there in limited numbers. Only 7 per cent opposed further Jewish settlement, and 24 per cent were undecided. Yet as David Bercuson notes, "It is likely that the poll reflected a mixture of motives ... there can be little doubt that some Canadians favoured Jewish immigration to Palestine because they did not want Jews coming to Canada."[101] A Gallup poll in 1948 revealed that 58 per cent expressed no opinion on the Palestine issue; 19 per cent sympathized with the Jews; and 23 per cent sympathized with the Arabs. Thus, most Canadians were either neutral or sceptical about the Palestine issue,[102] and this can probably be extended to the majority of Albertans.

Moreover, by the early post-war period Cold War paranoia was crystallizing, and the fear of communism superseded Canadians' and Albertans' concerns about "the Jewish question." This was also the case within Social Credit, which had already shifted its emphasis from the international financial conspiracy to the international communist conspiracy. Those Social Crediters who embraced Douglas's views touted both conspiracies as Jewish-controlled. For his part, Manning supported the Douglasites' anti-communist rhetoric but not their anti-Semitism. More importantly, in his view international communism had replaced international finance as the epitome of evil; consequently, the enemy had to be fought on the political front, not the economic front. As Manning stated to the Alberta Social Credit League in 1949: "Things are different now from 1935 … and the Social Credit movement's approach to them must be different, too."[103] In addition, Manning's war against international socialism and communism was political ammunition against the contending CCF. As C.B. Macpherson notes, as early as the 1944 provincial election "the struggle against socialism conveniently replaced the struggle for social credit."[104] By using the bogey of socialism, Social Credit could attack the CCF by associating it with the international socialist-communist conspiracy.

Thus, by the post-war period Manning, like the Douglasites, was a bona fide Cold Warrior, but in keeping with his religious convictions – and in direct contrast to the Douglasites – he supported Zionism and the establishment of the state of Israel and avoided explicitly anti-Semitic rhetoric. While the Douglasites veered off into anti-Semitic, anti-Zionist anti-communism, Manning confined his conspiracy theorizing to socialists and communists. For Manning, the Social Credit ideologues' continued emphasis on the Jewish-financial aspect of the international conspiracy was obsolete, and their anti-Semitism had become a political liability in a post-Holocaust world. For Manning, theories of an international Jewish conspiracy were passé; the real threat came from the conspiracy of international communist plotters.

Alberta's post-war economic climate was also an incentive for Manning to purge the Douglasites. On 13 February 1947 Alberta became the "Promised Land"[105] as the Leduc No. 1 oil well blew. The oil discovery unarguably had a profound impact on Alberta's economic culture. From its inception Social Credit had been eager to entice outside capital in the search for oil, and accordingly compartmentalized its views on international finance when seeking foreign investors.[106] When the strike came at Leduc, "nothing in Social Credit's past equipped it for the onslaught of prosperity brought on by oil." The province's public sector became enormously wealthy; the yearly income from oil enabled the government to provide a high level of services and public facilities without high taxation.[107] As C.B. Macpherson states, Alberta's post-war prosperity cancelled the need to "subdue the financiers or otherwise implement social credit principles."[108] Alvin Finkel notes that the Alberta government had, in effect, shifted gears: big business and big banking interests were no longer the enemy; labour and socialism were the new evils.[109] Walter Young cleverly comments that "the quest for Douglasite prosperity was shelved; oil and free enterprise succeeded where the 'monetization of unused capacity' and the 'A plus B theorem' had not ... The enemy-in-chief became socialism."[110] As the *Manitoba Commonwealth* remarked on the government's unabashed wooing of American investors after the oil strike, "Yesterday's Enemy is Today's Friend."[111]

Thus, by the time Manning conducted his purge in 1947–48, Social Credit was already Social Credit only in name. Douglas's theories had proven both unworkable and unnecessary, and his ideologues had become political and economic liabilities. Economic and political powerlessness had enabled Social Credit to come to power in 1935, but by 1947 Alberta was no longer powerless. In sum, it is highly debatable that Manning conducted his purge because of religious predilections and support for ethnic tolerance. It is much more plausible that he effected the purge to secure Alberta's economic and political fortunes.

For Congress, the post-war, post-Holocaust, post-purge period was a different world. The pervasive anti-Semitism of earlier years was receding; the horrors of the Holocaust had shocked many Canadians and made race hatred noxious, and Jews in Palestine had engaged in a dramatic struggle to create their own state.[112] Upon emerging from this era of rampant anti-Semitism, Congress embraced the philosophy learned from European Jewry's horrifying experience – "Never Again." For Congress, never again should Canada's and Alberta's political culture embrace such intolerance. Never again would Congress allow it. Accordingly, in the post-war period Congress modified its public relations philosophy to embrace a zero-tolerance approach to intolerance. It acknowledged that its previous public relations philosophy had been inadequate because it dealt only with one aspect of Jewish status – the attitude of non-Jews towards Jews. In the post-war period Congress realized that more salient factors had and would have the power to affect the status of Jews: political and economic discrimination, persecution and genocide, the precarious future of Jewish refugees in displaced persons camps, and the creation of a Jewish homeland in Palestine. Congress now accepted that Jewish protection involved more than altering the mental abstractions of non-Jews. Its public relations work must ensure that the rights to which Jews were entitled in a democratic society were respected, enforced, and guaranteed. In this way, Congress's new philosophy advocated the most complete form of democracy for all groups in Canada.[113]

Congress's new approach was self-respecting, even pugnacious. The organization now held that Jewish rights were not to be begged or pleaded for or accepted with thanks, but could and should be demanded and fought for legitimately. Jews' status would not be protected by influencing the attitudes of non-Jews or filling them with good-will. Jewish protection would come from enactments of public policy, legislation, administrative practices, and judicial precedents that would make the practice of discrimination impossible. Congress did not abandon good-will propaganda or educational campaigns in the post-war period, and the efficacy of this kind of public relations work was still accepted. However, Congress realized that previous public relations measures had basically left the root problem untouched – that the Canadian democratic system had allowed racism and discrimination to form part of the social, political, and economic fabric of the nation.[114] It was this problem that Congress began to address in the post-war period.

The national JPRC, for example, relied less on educational programs and other means of "intellectual persuasion" to help end anti-Semitic prejudice, and accepted that "it was actually easier to keep people from translating prejudice into discrimination." The committee became less concerned with people's private hatreds and focused more on ensuring that expression of that hatred would be met with the force of the law. As the director of the national JPRC, E.M. Rosenzweig, stated in 1950: "Prejudices may not damage anyone but the person who entertains them; it is only when the prejudiced mind walks over the bridge of action, and puts the prejudice into effect, that the real danger ensues." To this end, the JPRC focused its energies on legislation that would halt employment discrimination, resort discrimination, education discrimination, restrictive covenants, and discrimination in public services.[115] As Irving Abella notes, "Quiet diplomacy had been tried and found wanting ... only direct lobbying and public agitation and education would work. [Jewish leaders'] strategy was to fight to remove restrictions not only against Jews but against all minorities." Congress's reliance on legal action was strengthened with the passage of human rights legislation in Saskatchewan in 1947 and fair employment and housing legislation in Ontario and other provinces. "As these legal protections were put into place," states Abella, "an emboldened Canadian Jewry showed that it was no longer willing to accept the anti-semitism of an earlier period without a struggle."[116]

Yet Congress never completely abandoned its earlier public relations approaches, and in many ways its final philosophy was an amalgam or montage. In 1948 the JPRC re-emphasized the importance of a basic program of education that "will put the Canadian public on guard against the fomentors of anti-semitism and will ensure that the integration of Canadian Jewry into Canadian life is so complete that anti-semitism will be discredited as the impossible nonsense that it is in reality."[117] In its overview of anti-Semitism in Canada in 1949, Congress reported that its battle against prejudice continued in the realm of actual cases of anti-Semitism, educational programs aimed at "clearing prejudice from the minds of Canadians," constitutional gains, and developing relationships with the several ethnic groups in Canada.[118] Thus, by the post-war period Congress's initial public relations philosophy had been enhanced, not replaced. Congress continued to emphasize education work and pro-Jewish propaganda; it still attempted to cultivate harmonious Jewish-Gentile relations. But now these measures worked in tandem with more rights-oriented and legislative-directed measures designed to protect all minorities.

In the following decades Congress solidified its new public relations approach. However, critics contended that Congress had not gone far enough and that it had never been militant enough in pursuing and protecting Jewish interests. Harold Troper and Morton Weinfeld note that "this charge is retrospectively levelled against Congress for its actions before and during World War II. Communal leaders, past and present, have been accused of toadying to the state power, selling out the community in the process. 'Quiet diplomacy' has had a bad press in the post-Holocaust era ... Thus splinter groups have occasionally sprung up with more militant postures."[119] Indeed, throughout the post-war period a number of Jews became increasingly impatient with establishment-oriented Jewish organizations like Congress and "preferred to take up activist positions rather than docilely follow traditional community procedures. This was particularly true of small groups in Montreal and Toronto who were ready to deal physically, if necessary, with Nazi-type anti-Semitic Canadian organizations ... they ... sought to make it patently clear to anti-Semites that Jews would not sit idly by in their own self-defense: that every anti-Semitic action would be met with a forceful Jewish reaction."[120]

Yet despite such criticisms, past and present, Congress's public relations philosophy had evolved and matured considerably. H.M. Caiserman's biographer makes an insightful comment about Congress's post-war mentality: "In the years to come the great function of the Congress was to fit Canadian Jewry more effectively into the pattern of the post-war world. Before this was to develop Caiserman and his fellow-workers in the program of anti-defamation became self-taught but veritable experts in the theory, mechanics and defence of democracy ... Painfully they learned that informing Ottawa of a wrong is not sufficient for its cure; that a letter of protest or of denial to a newspaper only repeats the falsehood and sets the journalist to its defence with the advantage of the last word[;] ... that polemic with a hatemonger provides him with the meat of his life and prosecution exalts him with the virile blood of martyrdom."[121] Instead, Congress would fight to ensure that Jews' and all minority groups' rights were protected and promoted within the dominant, majority culture. In the post-war world Congress became an *actor* in the broader Canadian polity.

Intolerance in Canada during the 1930s and 1940s – the increase in anti-Semitic and fascist agitation, the federal government's refusal to accept Jewish refugees, and the extensive anti-Semitic propaganda campaign by Social Credit – signalled the need for Congress to create a more effective public relations philosophy and policy. Moreover, the indescribable experience of European Jewry convinced Congress of the necessity of protecting Canadian Jewry from a similar fate. But in a climate of governmentally, politically, and publicly sanctioned intolerance, executing an effective public relations policy was extremely difficult. Clearly, Social Credit's anti-Semitism alone did not make Canada a politically intolerant nation, but such propaganda contributed to the extensive intolerance engendered during this period. Similarly, Social Credit's campaign of Jew-hatred was not the only factor persuading Congress to redefine its public relations work, but it certainly provided ample reason.

8 Conclusion

The history of the Social Credit movement is incomplete without an examination of the response of organized Canadian Jewry. Although the history of Social Credit in Alberta and Canada is not solely an account of anti-Semitism, this facet of the movement's history has been inadequately addressed. This book has shown that anti-Semitism formed an integral part of C.H. Douglas's economic and political theories. These theories were absorbed and perpetuated by the Alberta movement, in part because of the ambiguous statements of Premiers Aberhart and Manning but more because both leaders allowed anti-Semitic propaganda to be disseminated with impunity. Anti-Semitic treatises by Douglas, Nesta Webster, and lesser-known anti-Semites formed a central component of Social Credit propaganda and were distributed through the movement's party organs and government and party agencies. The party organs themselves were filled with diatribes about the Jewish world plot. The extension of Social Credit into the federal field only encouraged further distribution of this propaganda. National party members like Low, Blackmore, and Jaques became leading spokesmen for Social Credit's anti-Semitic theories. Gostick, Even, and others outside Alberta also became leading proponents of anti-Semitism. When Manning decided to purge Social Credit of its anti-Semitism, his actions tore the movement apart.

During these years the Canadian Jewish Congress was relatively powerless in its battle against Social Credit's anti-Semitism. Its public relations philosophy, although evolving, was neither adequate nor effective in solving "the Social Credit problem." Notwithstanding the concerted efforts of many officers and agents, especially within the Western Division and the Alberta branch, Congress was unable to execute a policy that would stop Social Credit's hate propaganda. Yet examining Congress's response and the difficulties it experienced offers a new perspective on both Congress and Social Credit. Perhaps most importantly, analysing the response of that ethnic group most directly affected and potentially threatened by Social Credit's anti-Semitism shows the necessity of examining the past from "the other side."

This "other" perspective is not often included in works on racism and anti-Semitism. It is more common for studies to focus on the aggressor and to overlook the reaction, role, and responsibility of the aggrieved. However, it is imperative that the object of vilification provide its own story. Only when this previously dehumanized and objectified party gives a human, *subjective* voice to its experience can the full effects of such prejudice be revealed. Social Credit's extensive anti-Semitic propaganda campaign may not have physically harmed one Jew, but it adversely affected the entire Canadian Jewish community at a time when it feared for the fate of its European brethren and ultimately its own. The impact of Social Credit's anti-Semitism does not become clear until and unless the response of Canadian Jewry is expressed.

An examination of Congress's response to Social Credit shows the detrimental effects of publicly and politically sanctioned intolerance on this organization's ability to protect and promote its constituents' rights and interests. Congress experienced great difficulty in adopting a coherent, assertive, national public relations policy, and its task was made even more difficult by the hostility, duplicity, and irresponsibility of Social Credit politicians. This occurred at a time when Jewish refugees and immigrants were not welcome in Canada and anti-Semitism was an acceptable part of public discourse. This was not a conducive environment for the defence and promotion of Canadian Jewish rights.

Although Social Credit must bear responsibility for its anti-Semitism, Congress too must acknowledge its own role and responsibility in this affair. Its ineffective and passive stance greatly contributed to its failure to quell the Social Credit menace. Congress's main handicap was lack of confidence, a fear that if it were too vocal or public in its denunciation of Social Credit, further anti-Semitism would ensue. The result was a covert, reticent, *insecure* approach to Jewish rights, an approach that did not work in Congress's or Canadian Jewry's best interests. However, that Congress faced obstacles such as governmental restriction of immigration and politically sanctioned anti-Semitic propaganda says much about the nation's existing culture of intolerance. It is not surprising that in such a climate Congress lacked confidence.

The consequence was that Congress itself was never able to solve the Social Credit problem. Instead, the spoils of victory fell to Ernest Manning, whom posterity has vindicated for eliminating anti-Semitism within Social Credit. What is less well acknowledged is that Manning's understanding and promotion of the international financial conspiracy dovetailed with the anti-Semitism of the Douglasites to make anti-Semitism a mainstay of the movement's philosophy and propaganda. When Manning finally decided to exercise his power and expel the Douglasites, he did so primarily for political and economic reasons, not ethical or humanitarian ones. Throughout the Second World War, when Canadian Jewry was in dire need of government and public support, this democratically elected provincial government and national party undertook a propaganda campaign comparable to those of radical anti-Semites in the United States and Europe. The Canadian government's response to the Jews of Europe was not an honourable one, and Social Credit contributed in its own way to this record of intolerance.

Yet Manning's purge of anti-Semitism altered Social Credit's philosophy none the less. With the full revelations of the horrors of the Nazi death camps, Social Credit's allegations of a diabolical Jewish world plot were inappropriate and ill-timed. Manning sanitized Social Credit's philosophy in response to changing political and public opinion, which, in the post-Holocaust period, found the movement's intolerance increasingly obnoxious and undemocratic. A more compelling reason for Manning's purge was that anti-Semitic propaganda had become passé. In the post-war period condemnations of the international Jewish financier were less effective than anti-communist, Cold War rhetoric. Accordingly, Social Credit now focused on the conspiratorial machinations of Russian communists and quickly discovered that vilification of the Red Menace was more politically rewarding.

Another impetus for eliminating Social Credit's anti-Semitism in the post-war period came from improved economic conditions. Especially after the 1947 Leduc oil strike, there was little need for conspiracy theories about oppressive Jewish-controlled banks and governments. Albertans were embarking on a period of great economic prosperity, and in the absence of economic privation, scapegoats were no longer needed. Thus, by 1949 Congress could report that the *Canadian Social Crediter* occasionally published unfriendly comments about Jews, but such anti-Jewish material, when it appeared, was seldom of a feature or campaign character: "Usually it is a snide little item about Jews, almost as a filler, or else it is injected almost off hand in much longer treatment of a totally unrelated character."[1] Perhaps this was all

Congress could hope for from Social Credit – residual, banal, age-old anti-Semitic slurs.

Congress itself was compelled to adapt to post-war trends of increased political and public tolerance. Prime Minister Mackenzie King's platitudes about the nation's absorptive capacity were the first of many grudging steps towards a multicultural Canada. This changing climate helped Congress to adopt a more effective public relations approach than it had during the war. Its efforts were augmented by Diefenbaker's passage of the Canadian Bill of Rights in 1960 and the subsequent relaxation of restrictions on immigration. At the grass-roots level a changing economic, political, and social reality, in which immigrants were a more integral part of the Canadian landscape, also contributed to Congress's increased confidence. In this enhanced context of ethnic pluralism and legal safeguards for minorities, Congress became more active in protecting and advancing the rights of Jews and all minority groups. Congress's broader focus eventually made it the champion not only of Jewish rights but of all human rights in Canada.

External developments in the post-war period also helped Congress to protect and promote Jewish rights in a more forthright manner. The creation of the state of Israel in 1948 and the Six-Day War in 1967 were especially influential. Both events instilled greater confidence in Canadian Jewry: the first because it was fulfilment of a millennia-old promise and offered a future sanctuary should there be another lapse in the world's conscience; the second because it sent a message to the nations of the globe that Jews were not ready victims and had the military might to prove it. The growing strength of world Jewry enabled Congress to deal more effectively with issues of Canadian Jewish concern such as Holocaust denial, neo-Nazism, and war crimes trials, and it subsequently achieved a more visible profile on the national political scene.

Changes in Canada's political and public climate in the post-war period and the increased political strength of Congress seem to confirm Canada's reputation as a tolerant nation. While Canada's threshold for intolerance was remarkably high before and during the Second World War, since then Canada has developed a posture of multicultural tolerance that at times is more rhetorical than real. None the less, the nation *is* less racist and intolerant than it was fifty years ago, and legal and constitutional developments, together with the current trend of political correctness, have ensured that public prejudice is considered to be in poor taste at least, and discrimination is officially disallowed.

Congress's activist public relations work has contributed to these achievements. In the post-war period Congress began to advocate legal measures to disallow discrimination, and continues to champion these measures today. There appears to be no effective way to end a society's prejudices, but through advocacy of legal and governmental measures, Congress has ensured that such prejudices remain just that – personal, idiosyncratic hatreds, confined to individual minds. In this way the lessons of the Holocaust have been indelibly etched on Congress's psyche. It works to ensure that prejudice will "Never Again" be allowed to be translated into discrimination, then policy, then annihilation.

If Congress's response to Social Credit's anti-Semitism is placed within the broader historical context of its own evolving and maturing public relations work, the experience convinced Congress of the need to establish a stronger presence within the Canadian polity. Through the numerous, mostly unsuccessful battles with Social Credit, Congress was compelled to acknowledge the futility of attempting to alter Social Crediters' convictions about Jews and money and their conspiratorial mindsets about Jewish world plots. Although timing was such that the Social Credit movement itself solved the Social Credit problem, Congress realized in hindsight that it could stop such hatred *not* by attempting to alter hostile attitudes but by preventing such attitudes from reaching public expression. Seen in this light, Congress's frustrating and negative experience with Social Credit became a powerful motive to create new solutions to one of Jewry's oldest problems.

APPENDIX A

Social Credit Career Sketches

WILLIAM ABERHART

William "Bible Bill" Aberhart, the founder of the Social Credit movement in Alberta, was born 30 December 1878 at Huron County, near Seaforth, Ontario. He was educated at Egmondville, Seaforth, and Mitchell, Ontario, and attended Chatham Business College, Hamilton Normal College, and Queen's University, where he received a BA in 1906. Aberhart was a lay preacher and school teacher, teaching first in Brantford, Ontario, and then from 1910 to 1915, in Calgary. From 1915 to 1935 he was principal of Calgary's Crescent Heights High School. Aberhart founded the Calgary Prophetic Bible Conference in 1918 and opened the Calgary Prophetic Bible Institute in 1927, with Ernest Manning as his first pupil. In 1932 Aberhart began disseminating Social Credit theories through the Prophetic Bible Institute and his weekly Sunday radio broadcast, *Back to the Bible Hour*. In 1935 Aberhart's religious-political crusade won the Alberta election with fifty-six out of sixty-three seats, and 54.25 per cent of the popular vote. Aberhart did not run in the election; he was elected by acclamation in a by-election in November 1935. He served as MLA for Okotoks–High River 1935–40; one of five MLAs for Calgary 1940–43; minister of education 1935–40; and minister of education and attorney general 1940–43. Aberhart died 23 May 1943 while still in office.

R.E. ANSLEY

Ronald Earl Ansley was born 20 March 1908 in Killam, Alberta. He was educated at Killam and Camrose, and received a first-class teacher's certificate. He was an insurance agent, lecturer on economics, teacher, and principal of

Blackfalds School from 1928 to 1933. Ansley served as Social Credit MLA for Leduc 1935–52, and as an Independent Social Credit MLA for Leduc 1952–63. He was appointed to the Alberta Social Credit Board in 1941 and made chairman in 1943. Ansley was minister of education from 1944 until Manning's purge of the Douglasites in 1948, when he was fired from the Cabinet for supporting technical adviser L.D. Byrne, whom Manning also fired. Thereafter Ansley joined the dissident Douglas Social Credit Council and became an Independent Social Crediter. He died in Canmore, Alberta, 6 December 1965.

PAT ASHBY

Patrick Harvey Ashby was born 17 October 1890 in Sussex, England. He came to Canada in 1905, attended Coaticook High School in Quebec, McGill University, Oxford University, and the University of Alberta. He served in the First World War, and in 1922 became a farmer at Ellerslie, near Edmonton. A member of the Alberta Farmers' Union, the Canadian Legion, the Freemasons, and the Army and Navy Veterans' Association, Ashby was Social Credit MP for Edmonton East 1945–49. He split from Manning during the purge of 1947–48 over Manning's refusal to adhere to pure Douglasite principles and his firings of Ansley and Byrne. Ashby subsequently helped to organize the dissident Douglas Social Credit Council in Alberta. His son was Roy Ashby, director of the Basic Book Club, and his son-in-law was J.P. Gillese, editor of the *Canadian Social Crediter*. Ashby retired from farming in 1967 and moved to Campbell River, BC, where he died 29 January 1985.

FLOYD BAKER

Floyd Milton Baker was born 1 December 1891 in Stevensville, Ontario, and was educated there. He came out west in 1907. He was a tinsmith by trade but engaged in business as a hardware merchant and dealer in farm implements, oil, and automobiles at Spruce Grove and Fort Saskatchewan, Alberta, from 1915. Baker was Social Credit MLA for Clover Bar 1935–67 and editor of the Social Credit party organ, *Today and Tomorrow*. He was secretary-treasurer of the Alberta Social Credit League and a member of the Alberta Social Credit Board 1942–46. Baker was superintendent of the United Church Sunday school in Fort Saskatchewan, chairman of the Fort Saskatchewan school board, and an active member of the Boy Scouts Association. He died in Edmonton 2 April 1986.

JOHN BLACKMORE

John Horne Blackmore was born 27 March 1890 at Sublett, Idaho. He came to Canada in 1892 with his parents, who had joined a Mormon emigration to Alberta. He attended public school in Cardston, Normal School in Calgary, and the University of Alberta, where he received a BA in 1913. He taught school at Mountain View, Woolford, and Cardston, Alberta, and was principal at Raymond, Alberta. Blackmore was Social Credit MP for Lethbridge 1935–58 and was the first house leader of the Social Credit group in parliament in 1935. In 1944, when the national Social Credit party was created, he was replaced by Solon Low as national party leader. A vociferous anti-communist and defender of Joseph McCarthy, Blackmore was also an outspoken advocate of the sugar beet industry in Alberta and championed the battle for improved irrigation in southern Alberta. He spoke on behalf of the native bands in southern Alberta and in 1945 was named honorary chief of the Blood Indian tribe. In 1947 Blackmore was excommunicated from the Mormon Church for advocating the doctrine of plural marriage. He was nominated to stand as Social Credit candidate for Lethbridge in the 1962 federal election, but was defeated. Blackmore died in Cardston 2 May 1971.

A.V. BOURCIER

Albert Vital Bourcier was born 25 August 1901 in Northbridge, Massachusetts. He came to Canada in 1912, was educated at Edmonton Separate School and Edmonton Normal School, and became a school teacher and principal from 1920 to 1935. Bourcier served as Social Credit MLA for Lac Ste Anne 1935–52. He was appointed a member of the Alberta Social Credit Board in 1941 and was chairman 1944–46. Bourcier was one of the Douglasite dissidents who broke from Manning during the purge of 1947–48, and he became chairman of the Douglas Social Credit Council. Yet he continued to run as a Social Credit candidate and won his seat in the 1948 provincial election. Bourcier died in Edmonton 8 February 1982.

RÉAL CAOUETTE

David Réal Caouette was born 26 September 1917 in Amos, Quebec. He was educated at the public and high schools in Amos, and attended St Alexandre College, Limbour (Gatineau), Quebec, and Sacred Heart Commercial College, Victoriaville, Quebec. He became a businessman and automobile dealer at Rouyn, Quebec, and was president of Garage Joyal Lteé. A member of the Union des Electeurs, he ran as a Social Credit candidate for Abitibi-West in the 1944 Quebec provincial election, but was defeated. He ran as a Social Credit candidate for Pontiac in the 1945 federal election, but was also defeated. On 16 September 1946 Caouette was elected Social Credit member for Pontiac in a federal by-election. When Manning conducted his purge in 1947–48, Caouette remained part of the Social Credit movement. In the 1949 federal election he ran as Union des Electeurs candidate for Villeneuve, but was defeated. In the 1956 Quebec provincial election he was defeated as a Liberal candidate for Abitibi-East. In the 1957 and 1958 federal elections Caouette ran as a candidate for the Union des Electeurs for Villeneuve but was again defeated. In July 1961 he was chosen deputy leader of the national

Social Credit party at a national convention in Ottawa. In the 1962 and 1963 federal elections he was elected Social Credit member for Villeneuve. In October 1963 Caouette withdrew from the national Social Credit party and became leader of Le Ralliement des Créditistes. This launched him on his successful career as the charismatic Créditiste leader of Quebec. In the 1965 federal election Caouette was elected Ralliement Créditiste member for Villeneuve, and in the 1968 federal election for Témiscamingue. In the 1972 and 1974 federal elections he was elected Social Credit member for Témiscamingue. Caouette died 16 December 1976 while still in office.

C.H. DOUGLAS

Clifford Hughes Douglas, the founder of the Social Credit movement, was born 20 January 1879 in Stockport, England. He studied engineering at Pembroke College, Cambridge University, and became chief engineer in India for the British Westinghouse Electric Company. Later he became assistant superintendent of the Royal Aircraft Works at Farnborough. During the First World War, Douglas served as a major in the Royal Flying Corps. His theories of economic and political reform were initially published in the English periodicals *Organiser*, *English Review*, and the *New Age* from 1917 to 1919, and in his first book, *Economic Democracy* (1920). Douglas established Social Credit as a movement in England in the early 1920s, when he founded the Social Credit Secretariat in Liverpool. In 1938 he founded the weekly journal the *Social Crediter*, which became the standard for other Social Credit newspapers in the British Commonwealth, including Canada, Australia, and New Zealand. Until his death Douglas acted as advisory chairman of the Social Credit Secretariat in England. In 1934 he visited Edmonton, and from 1935 to 1936 acted as reconstruction adviser to the Aberhart government. After a Cabinet crisis in the Aberhart government in 1937, Douglas sent two emissaries, G.F. Powell and L.D. Byrne, to act as Social Credit's technical advisers. Douglas devoted his career to speaking and writing about Social Credit's economic and political theories, which were predicated on the paranoid assumption that an international, financial, Jewish conspiracy controlled the world's economic and political systems. He disseminated these ideas in a number of books and pamphlets, which the Canadian Social Credit movement imported and sold. Douglas died in Fearnan, Scotland, 29 September 1952.

LOUIS EVEN

Louis Even was born in 1885 in France. He came to North America in 1903, and in 1906 began teaching at St François-Xavier School in Montreal. He spent over three years with the Jesuit missions of the Rocky Mountains, teaching Indian boys. In 1911 he joined Garden City Press as a typographer. Even became one of the leading founders of the Social Credit movement in Quebec. In May 1936 he helped to found La Ligue du Crédit Social de la Province de

Québec, and began publishing *Cahiers du Crédit Social* irregularly. In 1939, together with Mrs Gilberte Côté-Mercier, he created the bi-monthly newspaper *Vers Demain*, with himself as editor. In 1942 Even helped to incorporate the Institut d'Action Politique as an arm of *Vers Demain*. He became the Quebec representative of the national party organization, the Social Credit Association of Canada, in 1944, and in 1946 he helped to found the Union des Electeurs, which replaced the Institut d'Action Politique as the Social Credit organization in Quebec. The Union des Electeurs became increasingly alienated from the Social Credit Association of Canada, and in late 1947 Even and the Union broke from the Social Credit movement. Even continued to edit *Vers Demain* and renewed its focus on anti-Semitic rhetoric. He maintained his leadership position and control over the Quebec Social Credit movement until the late 1950s, when Réal Caouette emerged as leader of its forces in Quebec. Even turned his attention to creating two extreme right-wing groups, Les Pèlerins de Saint-Michel and Les Bérets Blancs. He died 27 September 1974.

J.P. GILLESE

John Patrick Gillese was born in 1920 and raised on a farm near Rochfort Bridge, Alberta. A freelance writer from the age of seventeen, in 1944 Gillese became editor of the Social Credit party organ, the *Canadian Social Crediter*, previously known as *Today and Tomorrow*. Gillese held this position until he was forced to resign in late 1947 during Manning's purge of the anti-Semitic Douglasites. He then organized the dissident Douglas Social Credit Council and published two anti-Semitic, anti-Manning sheets, the *Social Credit Challenge* and the DSCC *Information Service*. Gillese went on to a successful career as a writer, and in 1971 became director of Alberta Culture's Film and Literary Arts Branch, where he set policies and programs for the first provincial government literary arts council in Canada. The most successful program he initiated was the Alberta "Search for a New Novelist" competition. Gillese retired from the directorship in 1985 and continued to write and teach until 1992. He died in October 1999.

RON GOSTICK

Ronald Gostick was born in 1918 and raised near Gadsby, Alberta. He was a former high school student of William Aberhart and the son of Edith Gostick, Social Credit MLA for Calgary from 1935 to 1940 and later provincial librarian. Gostick served during the Second World War. In 1946 he helped to organize the Union of Electors in Ontario as a rival group to the Ontario Social Credit League, the official Social Credit organization in that province. Gostick appointed himself president of the Union of Electors and founded the propaganda organ *Voice of the Electors*. In late 1947 he and the Union of Electors broke with Manning. In 1950 Gostick moved to Flesherton, Ontario, where he eventually became one of Canada's most notorious anti-Semites; leader of the Canadian League of Rights, an extreme right-wing organization established in 1968; and publisher of two libellous broadsheets called the *Canadian Intelligence Service* and *On Target*. Former Alberta high school teacher James Keegstra used Gostick's propaganda in his classroom to promote the theory of an international Jewish conspiracy. Gostick returned to Alberta in 1989 and continued to publish racist, anti-Semitic propaganda from High River, under the name Canadian Intelligence Publications.

J. ERNEST GREGOIRE

Joseph Ernest Gregoire was born in July 1886 at D'Israeli, Quebec. He was educated at Sherbrooke Seminary and Laval University, and was a graduate of the University of Louvain, Belgium, and the University of Lille, France. A barrister, Gregoire also taught political economy at Laval University. He was a recipient of the Chevalier de la Legion d'Honneur (France) in 1934 and the Order of the British Empire in 1935. Gregoire was MLA for Montmagny, Quebec, 1935–39, first as a National Liberal Action party member and, after 1936, as a Union Nationale member. He also served as mayor of the city of Quebec from 1934 to 1938. Gregoire was elected vice-president of the Social Credit Association of Canada in 1944 and was one of the leaders of the Union des Electeurs, established in 1946. He resigned as national vice-president in January 1948 after Manning's purge of the Douglasites. Gregoire led the Union des Electeurs in the 1948 Quebec provincial election and was a candidate in the riding of St Maurice. He, like every Union des Electeurs candidate, was defeated. Gregoire died 17 September 1980.

J.N. HALDEMAN

Joshua Norman Haldeman was born 25 November 1902 in Pequot, Minnesota, and moved to Saskatchewan with his parents in 1907. He was educated in Saskatchewan and Iowa, and attended the Manitoba Agricultural College, the University of Chicago, and the Palmer School of Chiropractic in Davenport, Iowa, where he graduated in 1926 and did post-graduate studies. Haldeman had been a rodeo performer, farmer, and construction worker, and during the Great Depression lost a large farm in the Saskatchewan dustbowl. In 1936 he set up a chiropractic practice in Regina and was a member of several chiropractic organizations in the United States and Canada. Haldeman was chairman of the national council of the Social Credit Association of Canada and president of the Saskatchewan Social Credit League. In the 1945 federal election he ran as Social Credit candidate for Prince Albert but was defeated; in the 1948 Saskatchewan provincial election he ran as Social Credit candidate for Yorkton and was defeated; and in the 1949 federal election he ran as Social Credit candidate for Lake Centre and was once again defeated. Haldeman moved to Pretoria, South Africa, in 1951 and opened a chiropractic clinic. An experienced pilot, he died in a plane crash in Pretoria on 13 January 1974.

ANTHONY HLYNKA

Anthony Hlynka was born 28 May 1907 in Halychyna, Western Ukraine. In 1910 he came to Canada with his parents and settled on a farm near Delph, Alberta. Hlynka attended public school at Delph and Edmonton, and attended the Edmonton Technical School and Alberta College. A writer and journalist, in 1935 Hlynka became editor of a Ukrainian-language paper entitled *Klych* (*The Call*), and wrote a number of articles in the journal *Suspil'nyï Kredyt* (*Social Credit*), where he exploited traditional Ukrainian antipathies towards Jews. Hlynka was Social Credit MP for Vegreville 1940–49, and near the end of his life began writing a political treatise on Ukrainians in Canada, published posthumously as *Anthony Hlynka, Member of the Canadian House of Commons, 1940–1949*. An ardent Ukrainian nationalist and anti-communist, in 1946 Hlynka travelled throughout the displaced persons' camps in Germany, then returned and raised $40,000 to establish Ukrainian refugees in Canada. Hlynka died in Edmonton 25 April 1957.

ALF HOOKE

Alfred John Hooke was born 25 February 1905 at Whitecroft, England. He came to Canada in 1913 and was educated at Stettler, Alberta, the University of Manitoba, the University of Alberta, and LaSalle University, Chicago. Hooke was a school teacher in Alberta from 1926 to 1935, during which time he was principal at Trochu for one year and at Rocky Mountain House for five years. He also served in the Second World War. Hooke was Social Credit MLA for Red Deer 1935–40 and MLA for Rocky Mountain House 1940–71. He was secretary of the Social Credit caucus, deputy speaker of the House, Social Credit whip, and chairman and member of the Alberta Social Credit Board. Hooke was provincial secretary 1943–48 and 1955–59; minister of economic affairs 1945–55; minister of public works 1952–55; minister of municipal affairs 1955–67; and minister of public welfare 1967–71. Although Hooke was part of the group of original Douglasites who attempted a party revolt under Aberhart in 1937, when Manning conducted his purge of the Douglasites in 1947–48, Hooke was not among those repudiated. He wrote a book on his career in the Social Credit government entitled *30 + 5: I Know, I Was There*. Hooke died 17 February 1992.

N.B. JAMES

Norman Bloomfield James was born 4 August 1872 at Wandsworth, England. He was educated in Croydon, England, attended Aberystwyth University, Wales, and came to Canada in 1893, where he worked as a cowboy near Calgary for several years and then farmed in Youngstown district, near Lethbridge. James served in England during the First World War. He was director of the Canadian Institute for the Blind and honorary vice-president of the Army and Navy Veterans' Association. James was Social Credit MLA for Acadia 1935–40 and one of five MLAS for Edmonton 1940–48. He was appointed secretary of the Alberta Social Credit Board 1942–46. James wrote a weekly column, "Main Street," for the *Canadian Social Crediter* until Manning's purge of the Douglasites in 1947, when he broke with Manning's movement. In 1947 he wrote his autobiography, entitled *The Autobiography of a Nobody*. James died in Edmonton 12 December 1963.

NORMAN JAQUES

Norman Jaques was born 29 June 1880 in London, England. He attended Eastborne College, Sussex, England, and came to Canada in 1901, where he became a farmer at Mirror, Alberta. He attempted to establish a horse-breeding farm but later abandoned the project. Jaques was Social Credit MP for Wetaskiwin 1935–49. He was long considered to be the most notorious anti-Semite in the Social Credit movement and used his parliamentary privilege in the House of Commons to oppose international political Zionism vehemently. In late 1947 Jaques's anti-Semitic writings were barred from the Social Credit party organ, and he was marginalized by Manning and other Social Credit members. He was none the less renominated as Social Credit candidate for Wetaskiwin in December 1948 for the next federal election. Jaques died in Ottawa 31 January 1949 while still in office.

SOLON LOW

Solon Earl Low was born 8 January 1900 in Cardston, Alberta, and was raised on a farm near there. He was educated in Cardston and attended Calgary Normal College, the University of Alberta, and the University of Southern California. He became a teacher at Arrowwood and Raymond, Alberta, and in 1934 became principal at Stirling, Alberta. He was Social Credit MLA for Warner 1935–40, for Vegreville 1940–44, and for Warner 1944–45. He was provincial treasurer 1937–43, provincial treasurer and minister of education 1943–44, and minister without portfolio 1944–45. Low served as president and national leader of the Social Credit Association of Canada from 1944 to 1958. In 1945 he resigned as MLA for Warner and served as Social Credit MP for Peace River 1945–58. He was defeated in the 1958 federal election and resumed teaching until 1961, when he was appointed a family and juvenile court judge in Lethbridge. A member of the Mormon Church, Low expressed extremely anti-Semitic statements throughout his career. When Manning conducted his purge of the anti-Semitic Douglasites in 1947–48, Low technically followed Manning's directive but continued to espouse anti-Semitism. In the 1950s, however, Low visited Israel and became an ardent proponent of Zionism. He died at Shelby, Montana, 22 December 1962.

ERNEST MANNING

Ernest Charles Manning was born 20 September 1908 at Carnduff, Saskatchewan. He was raised near Rosetown, Saskatchewan, where he attended public school, and in 1927 he travelled to Calgary to attend William Aberhart's Prophetic Bible Institute. He lived in the Aberhart home and in 1929 was the Institute's first graduate. Soon after he became the Institute's executive secretary and Aberhart's religious and political protégé. Manning was elected MLA for Calgary in the 1935 Alberta election and was appointed minister of trades and industry that year, making him the youngest Cabinet minister in the British Commonwealth. He was also provincial secretary 1935–43. After Aberhart's death in May 1943, Manning took over his mentor's religious radio broadcast, the *Back to the Bible Hour*, and was sworn in as premier, serving in that capacity until his retirement in 1968. Manning was provincial treasurer 1944–54, minister of mines and minerals 1952–68, and attorney general 1955–68. Manning was summoned to the Senate in 1970 and retired in 1983. He acted as a key adviser to his son, Preston Manning, after the founding of the Reform Party of Canada in 1987. Manning was granted honorary degrees by several universities, including an LLD from McGill University in 1967, and was named a Companion of the Order of Canada. In 1981 he was the first recipient of the Alberta Order of Excellence, and in 1982 received the National Humanitarian Award from B'nai Brith Canada. Manning died in Calgary 19 February 1996.

LUCIEN MAYNARD

Lucien Paul Maynard was born 17 February 1908 in Montreal. He was educated at Edmonton Jesuit College, and received a BA from Laval University and an LLB from the University of Alberta. He was admitted to the Alberta Bar in 1932, practised law in St Paul, and was a member of the Association of French Canadians of Alberta. Maynard served as Social Credit MLA for Beaver River 1935–48 and for St Albert 1948–55. He was minister without portfolio in 1936, minister of municipal affairs 1937–43, and attorney general 1943–55. Maynard owned and edited *Today and Tomorrow* from 1935 to 1943, when the Alberta Social Credit League made it the official Social Credit party organ. In 1955 he resumed law practice in Edmonton and was thereafter appointed provincial justice. Maynard died in Edmonton 7 February 1996.

GORDON TAYLOR

Gordon Edward Taylor was born 20 June 1910 in Calgary. He was educated at Drumheller public and high schools, Calgary Normal School, Drumheller

Business College, the Banff School of Fine Arts, and the University of Alberta. Initially a school teacher, after 1946 he operated a real estate and insurance business in Drumheller. Taylor served in the RCAF during the Second World War. He was Social Credit MLA for Drumheller 1940–79, and Social Credit whip in the Alberta legislature 1943–50. He replaced Gillese as editor of the *Canadian Social Crediter* after the former's resignation in December 1947. Taylor was minister of railways and telephones 1950–59, minister of highways and transport 1951–71, and minister of youth 1970–71. He was also chairman of the Alberta Research Council 1953–58, a member of the St Mary's Boys Home Advisory Board 1968–69, honorary chairman of the Badlands Passion Play project, and founder and president of Camp Gordon, a camp for underprivileged boys' holidays. Established in 1930 at Pine Lake, Alberta, Camp Gordon is still in operation, and Taylor remains president. A long-time politician, Taylor served as Conservative MP for Bow River, Alberta, 1979–88. In 1986 he drew nation-wide attention for his vocal opposition to homosexuals in the RCMP.

WILLIAM TOMYN

William Tomyn was born 4 September 1905 at Warwick, Alberta, the son of pioneer settlers. He was educated at Plain Lake, Vegreville, Edmonton, and Calgary Normal School, where he received a first-class teacher's certificate. He began teaching in 1926 at Plain Lake and later was a high school teacher in Willingdon. In 1949 he became an insurance underwriter in Edmonton. Tomyn served as Social Credit MLA for Whitford 1935–40, for Willingdon 1940–52, and for Edmonton-Norwood 1959–71. He was a member of the Alberta Social Credit Board 1942–44 and vice-chairman of the board 1944–48. Tomyn was a member of Ukrainian Catholic Unity, the Ukrainian Canadian Pioneers' Association, and the Ukrainian Professional and Businessmen's Club. He died in Edmonton 5 October 1972.

APPENDIX B

Canadian Jewish Congress
Career Sketches

SAM BRONFMAN

Samuel Bronfman was born 4 March 1891 in Brandon, Manitoba. He was educated in the public and high schools of Brandon and Winnipeg, and received honorary LLDs from the University of Montreal in 1948, the University of Waterloo in 1961, and the University of Alberta in 1969. He entered the hotel business in 1909 in Winnipeg, and operated a large hotel there from 1912 to 1915. In 1924 he founded Distiller's Corporation Ltd in Montreal and in 1928 acquired Joseph E. Seagram and Sons Ltd of Waterloo, Ontario. He merged the two into Distiller's Corporation–Seagrams Ltd, and his company eventually became the world's largest distilling firm and a billion-dollar financial family empire. Bronfman was president of the Canadian Jewish Congress 1938–62 and was heavily involved in nearly all areas of organized Canadian Jewish life, including anti-defamation, immigration, Jewish political rights, and fund-raising campaigns, as well as the war effort. He was honorary vice-president of the Zionist Organization of Canada; vice-president of the World Jewish Congress and chairman of its North American section; and a founder and honorary president of the Combined Jewish Appeal of Montreal. Bronfman sat on the executive of dozens of community, national, and international organizations. A well-known philanthropist, Bronfman supported the development of new agricultural fields, art centres, museums, universities, hospitals, and national charities. He was named a Companion of the Order of Canada in 1967 and was elevated in 1969 by Queen Elizabeth to the rank of Knight of Grace of the Order of St John of Jerusalem. Bronfman died in Montreal 10 July 1971.

H.M. CAISERMAN

Hannaniah Meir Caiserman was born 6 March 1884 in Piatra, Romania, and immigrated to Montreal with his parents in 1910. Educated in the public and high schools of Montreal, Caiserman worked in a Montreal clothing factory and became heavily involved in organizing Montreal's clothing workers. He was a journalist and poet, and contributed to nearly all the Jewish papers in Canada. Caiserman was one of the founders of the Canadian Jewish Congress in 1919 and was employed as its general secretary first in 1919 and again from 1934 to 1950. He was one of Congress's leading advocates before 1919 and was among those most responsible for its reconstitution in 1934. Caiserman was one of the founders of the World Jewish Congress and the Jewish Immigrant Aid Society; a leader in the Poale Zion organization; an officer in the Canadian Association for Labor Palestine; founder of the J.L. Peretz Schools, the Jewish People's Schools in Montreal, and the Jewish Public Library; and national organizer of the Zionist Organization of Canada. The author of a volume on Jewish poets in Canada, he wrote numerous articles on literary subjects. After the Second World War, Caiserman visited Poland and then toured Canada, the United States, and South America, addressing Jewish communities on the condition of the surviving Jews in Poland. While in South America he reorganized the Jewish relief administration along the lines of the United Jewish Refugee and War Relief Agencies. Caiserman has been called an "architect of modern Canadian Jewish history." He died in Montreal 24 December 1950.

JOHN DOWER

John David Dower was born 15 October 1887 in Kossmach, Austria, and came to Canada in 1900. His family settled in Alberta, where he became an industrialist and president of Dower Brothers Ltd, Northwest Manufacturing Company, Sterling Shoes Ltd, Paramount Shoes Ltd, and other enterprises in Edmonton. Dower was an executive officer of several local, provincial, and national organizations, including Jewish organizations. He was national vice-president of the Zionist Organization of Canada, vice-president of the Red Cross Society, Alberta branch, president of the Edmonton Chamber of Commerce, and director of the Edmonton Community Chest. During the Second World War he was chairman of the War Services Council of Central and Northern Alberta, and in 1945 he won the Edmonton Junior Chamber of Commerce citizenship award. Dower died in Edmonton in 1959.

A.L. FEINBERG

Rabbi Abraham L. Feinberg was born 14 September 1899 in Bellaire, Ohio. He received a BA at the University of Cincinnati in 1921, and attended Hebrew Union College, Cincinnati, where he was ordained in 1924. He also did post-graduate work at the University of Chicago and Columbia University.

Feinberg served as a rabbi in Niagara Falls, New York, and Wheeling, West Virginia. In 1927 he was called to Temple Israel in New York, the city's second-largest Reform Jewish congregation. In 1930 he left the rabbinate and became a famous radio crooner, Anthony Frome, but in 1935 he returned as rabbi of Mount Neboh Temple in New York City and in 1938 as a rabbi in Denver, Colorado. In 1943 Feinberg was called to Holy Blossom Temple in Toronto, the largest and most influential Reform Jewish congregation in Canada. Selected in a *Saturday Night* poll as one of Canada's seven greatest preachers, in 1957 Feinberg was the first rabbi to receive an honorary LLD from the University of Toronto. He was chairman of the Central Division of the Joint Public Relations Committee of the Canadian Jewish Congress, and co-chairman of the national Joint Public Relations Committee. Feinberg retired from the active rabbinate in 1961 and was appointed Rabbi Emeritus of Holy Blossom Temple for life. A writer, singer, radio personality, and theatre performer, after retiring he wrote and campaigned for world peace, disarmament, and social justice. Feinberg died in Reno, Nevada, 5 October 1986.

JOSEPH FINE

Joseph H. Fine was born 7 November 1896 in Romania. He was educated at City College in New York, where he received a BA in 1917. In 1931 he received an LLM from the University of Montreal, and he was named King's Counsel in 1947. Active in many national and Montreal Jewish organizations, Fine was national treasurer of the Canadian Jewish Congress 1948–62, co-chairman of the national Joint Public Relations Committee of Congress 1944–51, chairman of the Eastern Region, United Jewish Relief Agencies of Canada, and member of the Joint Public Relations Committee of the Zionist Council of Canada and Congress 1945–62. Fine died in Montreal 11 June 1980.

L.M. FRADKIN

Louis Manly Fradkin was born in 1897 in the Russian province of Chernigov. He came to Calgary in 1908 and attended Central School and Central High School there. He became a barrister and was admitted to the Alberta bar in 1923 and appointed King's Counsel in 1949. A prominent lawyer and long-time resident of Calgary, Fradkin was president of the Calgary branch of the Zionist Organization of Canada and of B'nai Brith, chairman of the Board of Education of the Calgary Hebrew School, and a member of the House of Jacob congregation. He died in Calgary 9 August 1959.

SOLOMON FRANK

Rabbi Solomon Frank was born 5 January 1900 in New York City. He moved to Buffalo with his parents in 1904 and was educated in the public schools of Buffalo, obtaining a BSC and LLB from the University of Buffalo in 1922 and 1923. He was subsequently ordained at Hebrew Union College. Frank came to Canada in 1926 and obtained an MA and PhD from the University of Manitoba in 1929 and 1943. He served as rabbi of Shaarey Zedek Synagogue in Winnipeg 1926–47, and of the Spanish and Portuguese Synagogue (Congregation Shearith Israel) in Montreal 1947–70. Frank was national vice-president of the Canadian Jewish Congress 1935–37; western director of Congress's Joint Public Relations Committee; president of the Winnipeg lodge of B'nai Brith; grand chancellor of the Knights of Pythias; president of the Winnipeg branch of the League of Nations Society; and editor of the *Canadian Jewish Chronicle*. A chaplain for various hospitals and institutions in Montreal, Frank was best known for his Sunday messages over CJAD radio for twenty-five years. He died in Montreal 21 October 1982.

H.A. FRIEDMAN

Harry A. Friedman was born 16 August 1890 in Buffalo, New York. He moved with his family to St Catharines, Ontario, where he received his public education. He graduated from Osgoode Hall, University of Toronto, in 1913, and was called to the Ontario bar that year. The same year Friedman was the first Jewish lawyer to be called to the bar of Alberta. He set up a law practice in Edmonton shortly thereafter with M.I. Lieberman. Friedman was appointed King's Counsel in 1928. President and director of several companies, he was also a member of the Alberta Liberal party and president of the Edmonton Bar Association 1929–30. He was co-founder of Beth Israel Synagogue and president of the Edmonton Hebrew Association, the Edmonton Talmud Torah, and the Edmonton lodge of B'nai Brith, and for several years a member of the council of the Zionist Organization of Canada. Friedman retired in 1950 and died in 1956.

S. HART GREEN

Solomon Hart Green was born 23 October 1885 in St John, New Brunswick, a descendant of one of the first pioneering Jewish families to settle in that city. He was educated at St John High School; King's College, Windsor, Nova Scotia; and St John Law School, where he received a BCL in 1906. He was called to the New Brunswick bar in 1906 and the Manitoba bar in 1907. Green was the first Jew to take a seat in any legislature in Canada, serving as Liberal MLA for Winnipeg North 1910–14, and was the youngest member of the Manitoba legislature at the time. From 1916 to 1921 he was Crown prosecutor of the Assize Court in Winnipeg. In 1927 Green was the first Jewish lawyer in western Canada to be named King's Counsel. He was president of the Winnipeg Talmud Torah and Jewish Welfare Fund; founder and president of Winnipeg B'nai Brith; president of the Hebrew Immigrant Aid Society in Winnipeg; honorary vice-president of the Zionist Organization of Canada; and founder of the Glendale Country Club in Winnipeg. Green died in 1969.

SAUL HAYES

Saul Hayes was born 28 May 1906 in Montreal. He was educated at McGill University, where he received his BA, MA, and BCL in 1927, 1928, and 1932 respectively. He received an honorary LLD from Sir George Williams University in 1970, and an honorary LLD from McGill University in 1974. He was called to the Quebec bar in 1932 and appointed King's Counsel in 1940. Hayes left active law practice to serve as national executive director of the Canadian Jewish Congress 1940–59 and national executive vice-president 1959–74. He was also executive director of the United Jewish Refugee and War Relief Agencies of Canada after 1940. Hayes represented world Jewry at the council of UNRRA in 1944, and represented Canadian Jewry at the first UN assembly in San Francisco in 1945 and at the Paris Peace Conference in 1946. He appeared before numerous government commissions regarding immigration, industrial relations, fair employment practices, amendments to the Criminal Code, and hate propaganda. He also led a Canadian Jewish delegation to the first Jerusalem Conference in 1953. Hayes was a lecturer in the School of Social Work at McGill University and a frequent delegate to international meetings regarding world Jewry. A Fellow of the Royal Society of Arts, he was awarded the Coronation Medal in 1953, the Centennial Medal in 1967, and was named an Officer of the Order of Canada in 1974. Known as "Mr Canadian Jewish Congress," Hayes was considered to be Jewish Canada's ambassador to Ottawa. He died in Ste Adèle, Quebec, 12 January 1980.

SAM JACOBS

Samuel William Jacobs was born 6 May 1871 in Lancaster, Ontario. He attended high school in Montreal and received a BCL from McGill University in 1893 and an LLM from Laval University in 1894. He was called to the Quebec bar in 1894 and became a prominent Montreal lawyer of the firm Jacobs, Phillips & Sperber. He was appointed King's Counsel in 1906. Jacobs was retained in a wide variety of criminal cases, played a leading part in civil rights cases, and was the author and joint editor of two legal treatises. He was also an influential figure in the Liberal party and served as Liberal MP for Montreal-Cartier 1917–38. Jacobs was Canadian director of the Jewish Colonization Association of Paris, honorary president of the Jewish Immigrant Aid Society and the Montefiore Hebrew Orphans' Home, and honorary vice-president of the Jewish Publication Society of America. He was president of the Baron de Hirsch Institute 1912–14, and of the Canadian Jewish Congress 1934–38. During the 1930s Jacobs fought tenaciously for Jewish legal rights and for the admittance of German Jewish refugees into Canada. He died 21 August 1938 while still in office as MP and president of the Canadian Jewish Congress.

BEN KAYFETZ

Ben (B.G.) Kayfetz was born 24 December 1916 in Toronto. He graduated from the University of Toronto in 1939 with a BA in modern languages and taught in various high schools in Toronto. From 1943 to 1945 he worked for the Wartime Information Board, and from 1945 to 1947 with the Control Commission for Germany, British Army of the Rhine. In 1947 Kayfetz was hired as director of public relations for the Canadian Jewish Congress's Central Division, and in 1955 he was made national director of Congress's Joint Community Relations Committee (previously the Joint Public Relations Committee). He was also the Canadian correspondent for the *Jewish Chronicle* in London, England, and the Jewish Telegraphic Agency. A frequent contributor to several publications, Kayfetz was a recipient of the Order of Canada and the Samuel Bronfman Medal. He retired in 1985 and continues to reside in Toronto.

DAVID KIRSHENBLATT

David Kirshenblatt (originally Kirshnblatt) was born 29 October 1927 in Quebec City. He was educated in Quebec City, and later graduated with a BA from Sir George Williams College in Montreal. Kirshenblatt worked as a journalist for the *Quebec Chronicle-Telegraph*, and in 1946 began working as assistant press officer to David Rome at the Canadian Jewish Congress's national headquarters in Montreal. He later worked for the British United Press in Montreal. Kirshenblatt received his BCL from McGill University in 1955 and the same year was called to the bar of Montreal. He practised law with M.S. Yelin in Montreal and was appointed Queen's Counsel in 1976. Kirshenblatt continues to reside in Montreal.

MOE LIEBERMAN

Moses Isaac Lieberman was born 16 June 1891 in Toronto. He was educated at public schools in Kingston and Toronto and attended the University of Toronto, where he received an engineering degree in 1911 and a BSC in 1912. He came to Calgary in 1912 and moved to Edmonton in 1914, graduating from the Law School of Alberta in 1917. He was called to the Alberta bar that year and set up practice in Edmonton with H.A. Friedman. He was appointed King's Counsel in 1934. A player for the Edmonton Eskimos football club from 1919 to 1921, Lieberman was manager in 1921 and president 1955–56, achieving Hall of Fame status in the Canadian Football League. Active in many Edmonton and Jewish community affairs, Lieberman was president of the Edmonton Little Theatre, vice-president of the Western Canada Rugby Union, co-founder and president of Beth Shalom Synagogue, and president of the Edmonton chapter of B'nai Brith. Lieberman died in Edmonton 27 May 1985.

WOLFE MARGOLUS

Wolfe Margolus was born 13 May 1910 in Toronto. His family moved to Edmonton, where he received a Bachelor of Commerce degree in 1935 from the University of Alberta and became vice-president of Sealy Mattress (Western Canada) Ltd. Margolus was national vice-president of the Zionist Organization of Canada, one of the founders of Beth Shalom Synagogue in Edmonton, and president of the Edmonton Jewish Community Council. He was also a member of the Alberta Co-operative Commonwealth Federation and served as its treasurer. Margolus died 30 December 1972.

MAX MOSCOVICH

Max Enoch Moscovich was born 15 May 1901 in Stockport, England. In 1908 he came to Lethbridge, Alberta, with his parents as pioneer settlers. Moscovich was educated at the public and high schools in Lethbridge and at McGill University, where he received an Honours BCL in 1921. He was called to the Alberta bar in 1924 and set up a law practice in Lethbridge that year. In 1939 he was named King's Counsel. A member of the council of the Canadian Bar Association from 1928 to 1959, Moscovich was president of the Lethbridge Bar Association, the Canadian Friends Hebrew University, Lethbridge, and the Lethbridge Jewish Congregation. He was a member of the Lethbridge B'nai Brith, the Zionist Organization of Canada, and the Canadian Friends Alliance Israelite Universelle. Moscovich died in Lethbridge 19 October 1973.

HARRY OLYAN

Harry Olyan was born 1 November 1884 in Odessa, Russia. He came to Edmonton in 1913, and in 1916 settled in Vegreville, where he headed a wholesale grocery business. An active participant in community affairs, Olyan was a member of the Vegreville School Board 1931–51 and served as its chairman for ten years. He was president and chairman of the National Affairs Committee of the Vegreville Chamber of Commerce; president of the Vegreville Hebrew Association; and a member of the Zionist Organization of Canada, B'nai Brith, and Workmen's Circle. Olyan was also one of the founders of the Dominion Council of the Canadian Jewish Congress. In 1959 he was honoured by Congress for forty years of dedicated service. Olyan died in Vegreville 17 March 1974.

DAVID ROME

David Rome was born 10 August 1910 in Vilna, Lithuania. He came to Vancouver with his family in 1921. He was educated at the University of British Columbia, where he received a BA in 1936, and did post-graduate work at the University of Washington in Seattle 1936–38. He graduated from the McGill Library School in 1939 and received his MA from the University of Montreal in 1961. Rome became the Canadian Jewish Congress's first press officer in 1942, and was the English-language editor of the Toronto *Daily Hebrew Journal* as well as the first national director of the Labor Zionist Organization. In 1942 he was appointed secretary to a Canadian Jewish Congress committee on Jewish–French Canadian relations, and in the early 1950s he founded the Cercle Juif de la Langue Française, the first francophone Jewish cultural group in Canada. In 1953 Rome became director of the Jewish Public Library in Montreal, and in 1972 he returned to the Canadian Jewish Congress as its archivist. In his later years he was historian for the Canadian Jewish Congress National Archives. Rome was one of Canada's most prominent historians, bibliographers, and librarians, publishing over sixty volumes and contributing greatly to the social, economic, and demographic study of Canadian Jewry. In 1987 he was named Knight of the Order of Quebec, and in 1991 he received an honorary LLD from Concordia University, Montreal. Rome died in Montreal 16 January 1996.

LOUIS ROSENBERG

Louis Rosenberg was born 7 June 1893 in Poland and was educated at the University of Leeds and the London School of Economics, receiving a BA in 1913. He came to Canada in 1915, where he started out in the field of education, first as a teacher and then as a principal, and from 1938 to 1939 as chairman of the Regina School Board. From 1919 to 1940 Rosenberg served as manager for western Canada of Jewish farm settlements for the Jewish Colonization Association. He was a member of the executive committee of the Western Division of the Canadian Jewish Congress 1934–40; member of the national executive council of the Canadian Jewish Congress in 1936; chairman of the Bureau of Social and Economic Research, Western Division of Congress, in 1936; vice-president of the Western Division of Congress 1937–39; and executive director of the Western Division of Congress 1940–45, as well as secretary of the Western Division's Joint Public Relations Committee. In 1945 Rosenberg was hired as national research director of Congress's Bureau of Social and Economic Research. He authored hundreds of publications, the most famous of which were *Canada's Jews* and a series of booklets published as *Canadian Jewish Population Studies*. He also authored a book, *Who Owns Canada*, under his pseudonym, Watt Hugh McCollum. Rosenberg was a leading member of the League for Social Reconstruction, the braintrust of the Co-operative Commonwealth Federation, and helped to draft the 1933 Regina Manifesto. One of the world's most prominent Jewish sociologists and a leader in the study of Jewish demography in Canada, Rosenberg was a fellow of the Royal Statistical Society, the Royal Economics Society, and the American Sociological Society. He died 13 September 1987.

Notes

CHAPTER ONE

1 In February 1947 substantial oil reserves were discovered at Leduc, south of Edmonton. As Alvin Finkel notes, the oil strike "provided the province with its major ticket out from its previous 'have-not' status. By the end of the period of Social Credit rule in 1971, the oil and gas industries directly accounted for almost 40 per cent of all value added in the province. Royalties from oil and gas gave the Alberta government the highest per capita revenue in the country." Finkel, *The Social Credit Phenomenon in Alberta*, 100.

2 On the Canadian government's poor humanitarian record towards Jews in the 1930s and 1940s, see Abella and Troper, *None Is Too Many*.

3 See Stingel, "Revising the Historiography of the Social Credit Movement in Alberta," 91–107.

4 See Abella, *A Coat of Many Colours*; Belkin, *Through Narrow Gates*; Brown, *Jew or Juif?*; Brym, Shaffir, and Weinfeld, *The Jews in Canada*; Chiel, *The Jews of Manitoba*; Elazar and Waller, *Maintaining Consensus*; Frager, *Sweatshop Strife*; Godfrey and Godfrey, *Search Out the Land*; Gutkin, *Journey Into Our Heritage*; Hart, *The Jew in Canada*; Horowitz, *Striking Roots*; Kage, *With Faith and Thanksgiving*; Paris, *Jews*; Rhinewine, *Looking Back a Century*; Sack, *History of the Jews in Canada*; S. Rosenberg, *The Jewish Community in Canada*; Speisman, *The Jews of Toronto*; Tulchinsky, *Taking Root*; Weinfeld, Shaffir, and Cotler, *The Canadian Jewish Mosaic*; Wolff, *The Jews of Canada*.

5 See Canadian Jewish Congress, *Pathways to the Present*, and *Seventy Years of Canadian Jewish Life*.

6 Theories of deconstruction, poststructuralism, and postmodernism, although jargon-laden and exclusionist, are helpful in determining the nature of ethnic groups' dialogues within dominant, majority cultures. For a discussion of these theories in the historical discipline, see Bloom, *Deconstruction and Criticism*; Niranjana, *Siting Translation*; Topolski, *Historiography between Modernism and Postmodernism*.

7 For historical studies of racism and discrimination in Canada, see Abella and Troper, *None Is Too Many*; Anctil, *Le Devoir, les Juifs et l'immi-gration*; Anctil and Caldwell, *Juifs et réalités juives au Québec*; Bolaria and Li, *Racial Oppression in Canada*; Betcherman, *The Swastika and the Maple Leaf*; Davies, *Antisemitism in Canada*; Delisle, *The Traitor and the Jew*; Ferguson, *A White Man's Country*; Hillmer, Kordan, and Luciuk, *On Guard For Thee*; Huttenback, *Racism and Empire*; Kallen, *Label Me Human*; McLaren, *Our Own Master Race*; Palmer, *Patterns of Prejudice*; Robin, *Shades of Right*; Roy, *A White Man's Province*; Thompson, *Ethnic Minorities during Two World Wars*; Troper, *Only Farmers Need Apply*; Walker, *Racial Discrimination in Canada*; Ward, *White Canada Forever*. For studies on theories of race and ethnic hierar-chy in Canada, see A. Anderson and Frideres, *Ethnicity in Canada*; K. Anderson, *Vancouver's Chinatown*; Berger, *The Sense of Power*; Coward and Kawamura, *Religion and Ethnicity*; J. Elliott and Fleras, *Unequal Relations*; Hill, *Human Rights in Canada*; Hughes and Kallen, *The Anatomy of Racism*; Li, *Race and Ethnic Relations in Canada*; Porter, *The Vertical Mosaic*; Ramcharan, *Racism*; Sunahara, *The Politics of Racism*; Tarnopolsky, *Discrimination and the Law in Canada*.

8 For discussions of racism and discrimination in Canada from the per-spective of the "objectified party," see Adams, *Prison of Grass*; Head, *Adaption of Immigrants in Metro Toronto*, and *The Black Presence in the Canadian Mosaic*; Helling, *The Position of Negroes, Chinese and Italians in the Social Structure of Windsor, Ontario*; Henry, *The Carib-bean Diaspora in Toronto*; Henry, *Perception of Discrimination among Negroes and Japanese-Canadians in Hamilton*.

CHAPTER TWO

1 In the 1950s Richard Hofstadter offered a revisionist interpretation of American Populism that showed its anti-Semitic, nativistic, and anti-democratic tendencies. Peter Argersinger calls this Populism's "scalier side." Argersinger, *Populism and Politics*, 58; Hofstadter, *Age of Reform*, 61–2ff.

2 Lipset, *Agrarian Socialism*, 122.

3 Elliott and Miller, *Bible Bill*, 102; Young, *Democracy and Discontent*, 94.

4 Burnet, *Next-Year Country*, 20.

5 Ibid., 13, 78; Lipset, *Agrarian Socialism*, 18.

6 Palmer, *Man Over Money*, 3; Brinkley, *Voices of Protest*, 74.

7 Parsons, *The Populist Context*, 147; Young, *Democracy and Discontent*, xii, 106; Richards and Pratt, *Prairie Capitalism*, 17; Macpherson, *Democracy in Alberta*, 216; Brinkley, *Voices of Protest*, 150.

8 Morton, *The Progressive Party in Canada*, 36.

9 Young, *Democracy and Discontent*, 4.

10 For an excellent exposition of how Alberta's tradition of non-party protest caused the eventual collapse of the Liberal party in the province, see L.G. Thomas, *The Liberal Party in Alberta*. On western Canada's opposition to the CPR, see Chodos, *The CPR*; Darling, *The Politics of Freight Rates;* Fowke, *The National Policy and the Wheat Economy*; Morton, *The Progressive Party in Canada*. The history of the National Progressive party and the UFA is covered in Morton, *The Progressive Party in Canada*. On the UFA see Betke, "Farm Politics in an Urban Age," in Thomas, *Essays on Western History*, 175–89; Betke, "The United Farmers of Alberta"; Foster, "John Edward Brownlee" and "The 1921 Alberta Provincial Election"; Laycock, *Populism and Democratic Thought in the Canadian Prairies*; Macpherson, *Democracy in Alberta*; Rolph, *Henry Wise Wood of Alberta*.

11 Hofstadter, *The Age of Reform*, 62; Minogue, "Populism as a Political Movement," in Ionescu and Gellner, *Populism*, 206; Palmer, "Ethnic Relations and the Paranoid Style," 26.

12 Laycock, *Populism and Democratic Thought in the Canadian Prairies*, 211.

13 On the transboundary nature of Populism's anti-Semitism, see Lipset, *Agrarian Socialism*; Palmer, "Ethnic Relations and the Paranoid Style"; Richards and Pratt, *Prairie Capitalism*; Sharp, *The Agrarian Revolt in Western Canada*; Stingel, "In the Presence of Mine Enemies," 14–21; Young, *Democracy and Discontent*.

14 Betke, "Farm Politics in an Urban Age," in Thomas, *Essays on Western History*, 175–89.

15 Hesketh, *Major Douglas and Alberta Social Credit*, 39.

16 "Social Credit: An Explanation for New Readers," 1946 (CJCNA, ZC, SC); Memo, Kirshnblatt to Hayes, 5 Apr. 1948 (CJCNA, CD, box 7, file 11P).

17 Irving, *The Social Credit Movement in Alberta*, 4–5.

18 Pinard, *The Rise of a Third Party*, 10–11.

19 Peterson, "Social Credit: A Critical Analysis," 1937 (PAM, JHSWC Collection, MG14, B44, box 15, file 2).

20 On Douglas's economic views and Social Credit's English origins, see Finlay, *Social Credit*; Hesketh, *Major Douglas and Alberta Social Credit*. Keynes's views are cited in Stein, *The Dynamics of Right-Wing Protest*, 33; Richards and Pratt, *Prairie Capitalism*, 33.

21 Macpherson, *Democracy in Alberta*, 125.

22 Douglas, *The Realistic Position of the Church of England*, 14; Memo, Rosenberg to Hayes, 19 July 1948 (CJCNA, ZC, SC).

23 Macpherson, *Democracy in Alberta*, 94.

24 Hesketh argues that Aberhart understood Douglas's Social Credit theories but did not know how to implement them. Perhaps this says more about their intrinsic fallacy than about Aberhart's comprehension. Hesketh, *Major Douglas and Alberta Social Credit*, 7.

25 Elliott and Miller, *Bible Bill*, 201, 252.

26 Mann, *Sect, Cult, and Church in Alberta*, 22, 120.

27 In his study of nineteenth-century American Populism, Lawrence Goodwyn describes "the complex process through which insurgent democratic movements (1) form, (2) recruit a mass base, (3) achieve a heretofore culturally unsanctioned level of economic analysis, and (4) find a way to express this new economic understanding through autonomous politics acts." This process creates a "movement culture." *The Populist Moment*, 164.

28 Elliott and Miller, *Bible Bill*, 113, 127; Irving, *The Social Credit Movement in Alberta*, 271.

29 Macpherson, *Democracy in Alberta*, 146; Laycock, *Populism and Democratic Thought in the Canadian Prairies*, 216.

30 Young, *Democracy and Discontent*, 90.

31 In 1933 the minister of public works in the UFA government was involved in a divorce trial in which there was evidence of "wife-swapping." Shortly after, Premier Brownlee was charged with having hired, seduced, and forcibly engaged in sexual relations a female government stenographer. Brownlee was convicted in 1934 and resigned as premier. Palmer with Palmer, *Alberta*, 255–6.

32 Betke, "Farm Politics in an Urban Age," in Thomas, *Essays on Western History*, 189; Mann, *Sect, Cult, and Church in Alberta*, 156; Irving, *The Social Credit Movement in Alberta*, 230, 232, 273.

33 Barr, *The Dynasty*, 57.

34 Elliott and Miller, *Bible Bill*, 198.

35 Young, *Democracy and Discontent*, 93; Barr, *The Dynasty*, 85; Irving, *The Social Credit Movement in Alberta*, 250–1.

36 For analyses of Social Credit's class composition, see O. Anderson, "The Alberta Social Credit Party"; Bell, "The Petite Bourgeoisie and Social Credit," 45–65, and *Social Classes and Social Credit in Alberta*; Grayson and Grayson, "The Social Base of Interwar Political Unrest in

Urban Alberta," 289–313; Macpherson, *Democracy in Alberta*; Malliah, "A Socio-Historical Study of the Legislators of Alberta"; Mann, *Sect, Cult, and Church in Alberta*; Palmer with Palmer, *Alberta*, 266.

37 Palmer with Palmer, *Alberta*, 269–70; *Time* (Canada), 8 Mar. 1948; *Maclean's*, 15 Oct. 1944.

38 Finkel, *The Social Credit Phenomenon in Alberta*, 43; Hesketh, *Major Douglas and Alberta Social Credit*, 128. Aberhart's reforms in the fields of education, health, and labour led Howard Palmer to argue that the premier began laying the foundation for a social welfare state in Alberta. Palmer with Palmer, *Alberta*, 269.

39 *Financial Post*, 23 June 1962; Peterson, "Social Credit: A Critical Analysis," 1937 (PAM, JHSWC Collection, MG14, B44, box 15, file 2); Elliott, "Anti-Semitism and the Social Credit Movement," 80.

40 Hesketh, *Major Douglas and Alberta Social Credit*, 5–6.

41 Cohn, *Warrant For Genocide*, 159; Ford, *The International Jew*.

42 Cohn, *Warrant For Genocide*, 158–62, 230–1; *The Protocols and World Revolution*; *The Times* (London), *The Truth about "The Protocols"*; Sigmund Livingston, "Protocols of the Wise Men of Zion, a spurious and fraudulent document manufactured to deceive and to engender religious and racial hatred," n.d. (PAM, JHSWC Collection, P4428, file 17); Memo, Rosenberg to Hayes, 5 Feb. 1947 (CJCNA, CA, box 33, file 306; CJCNA, ZC, SC); "Protocols Decision Washed Out," n.d. (PAM, JHSWC Collection, P4428, file 17); *Manitoba Commonwealth*, 8 Jan. 1947; *Regina Leader-Post*, 3 Jan. 1947; *Saskatoon Star-Phoenix*, 6 Dec. 1946; *Winnipeg Free Press*, 21 Apr. 1934.

43 Douglas, *Social Credit*, 30, 146; "Social Credit and Anti-Semitism," c. 1941 (CJCNA, ZC, SC); Memo, Rosenberg to Cohen et al., c. 1941 (CJCNA, ZC, SC); Flanagan and Lee, "From Social Credit to Social Conservatism," 212.

44 Douglas, *The Big Idea*, 6–7, 12, 14, 20, 42, 45, 48–50, 54, 63–4; Memo, Rosenberg to Hayes, 1 Apr. 1948 (CJCNA, ZC, SC).

45 Douglas, *The Land for the (Chosen) People Racket*, 7, 10, 21–2, 27–8, 38. Upon reading this pamphlet, Rosenberg noted that Douglas had changed the popular English political slogan "The Land for the People" into "The Land for the (Chosen) People," thus implying that Jewish plotters were attempting to hand over Britain's land to Jews as the "chosen people." Memo, Rosenberg to Hayes, 28 May 1947 (CJCNA, ZC, SC).

46 Douglas, *Programme for the Third World War*, 27–8; Memo, Rosenberg to Hayes, 20 May 1947 (CJCNA, ZC, SC).

47 Douglas, *The Brief for the Prosecution*, 8, 17, 20–1, 57, 62–3, 65, 67 *passim*, 81, 158; Douglas, *The Brief for the Prosecution*, cited in

"Social Credit: An Explanation for New Readers," 1946 (CJCNA, ZC, SC); Memo, Rosenberg to Hayes, 12 Dec. 1947 (CJCNA, ZC, SC).

48 Barr, *The Dynasty*, 158.

49 Elliott and Miller, *Bible Bill*, 176, 319.

50 Finkel, *The Social Credit Phenomenon in Alberta*, 83; Hesketh, *Major Douglas and Alberta Social Credit*, 48; Macpherson, *Democracy in Alberta*, 203; Palmer, *Patterns of Prejudice*, 158.

51 Elliott and Miller, *Bible Bill*, 301; Elliott, "Anti-Semitism and the Social Credit Movement," 83.

52 Palmer, "Politics, Religion and Anti-Semitism in Alberta," in Davies, *Antisemitism in Canada*, 175.

53 "The Province of Alberta and the Social Credit Government: An Interview with Premier Aberhart," n.d. (PAM, JHSWC Collection, P4428, file 1).

54 Elliott, "Anti-Semitism and the Social Credit Movement," 82–3; Elliott and Miller, *Bible Bill*, 117.

55 Laycock, *Populism and Democratic Thought in the Canadian Prairies*, 206.

56 Elliott and Miller, *Bible Bill*, 301.

57 Palmer, *Patterns of Prejudice*, 155.

58 Elliott, "Antithetical Elements in William Aberhart's Theology and Political Ideology," 58.

59 Palmer, *Patterns of Prejudice*, 158.

60 Ibid., 156–7; Elliott, "Anti-Semitism and the Social Credit Movement," 83; Hesketh, *Major Douglas and Alberta Social Credit*, 50; Palmer, "Politics, Religion and Anti-Semitism in Alberta," in Davies, *Antisemitism in Canada*, 175.

61 *Today and Tomorrow*, 14 Sept. 1944.

62 Ibid., 9 Dec. 1943.

63 Ibid., 16 Dec. 1943.

64 Hesketh, *Major Douglas and Alberta Social Credit*, 14–15.

65 Finkel, *The Social Credit Phenomenon in Alberta*, 65–6, 74–5; *Calgary Herald*, 24 Jan. 1948; *Canadian Social Crediter*, 17 July 1947.

66 Hesketh, *Major Douglas and Alberta Social Credit*, 49.

67 "Congress Issues Official Jewish Population Figures," n.d. (CJCNA, ZA 1944, box 2, file 35); "Draft on Anti-Semitism in Canada," c. 1949 (CJCNA, ZA 1945, box 2, file 31; CJCNA, ZA 1948, box 1, file 3); *The Facts*, May 1949 (CJCNA, ZA 1949, box 3, file 26; NA, CJC Collection, MG28, vol. 13, V, 101, reel M-5461); Rosenberg, *The Jewish Population of Canada*, 9, 15, 18.

68 Rosenberg, *Jewish Communities in Canada*, 21–3, and *The Jewish Population of Canada*, 18; "Social and Economic Problems of Western Canadian Jewry," n.d. (NA, CJC Collection, MG28, vol. 13, V, 101, reel M-5461).

69 In 1906 the colony of Rumsey was founded in the Trochu Valley north-east of Calgary. It was ostensibly the wealthiest Jewish colony in western Canada in its time, having been favoured with frequent good crops. However, in the period following the First World War, many of the farmers faced insurmountable debts and subsequently abandoned their farms. In 1921 thirteen Jews resided in Rumsey; ten in 1931; three in 1941; and four in 1951. Gutkin, *Journey into our Heritage*, 64; Leonoff, *Pioneers, Ploughs and Prayers*, 11; Belkin, *Through Narrow Gates*, 82; Rosenberg, *Jewish Communities in Canada*, 23.

70 Elazar and Waller, *Maintaining Consensus*, 71.

71 Figler and Rome, *Hannaniah Meir Caiserman*, 113; Rosenberg, "The Canadian Jewish Congress, 1919–1969: Fifty Years of Organized Jewish Community Life," c. 1969 (PAM, JHSWC Collection, P58, file 21); Speisman, *The Jews of Toronto*, 272; Tulchinsky, *Taking Root*, 274–5.

72 Tulchinsky, *Taking Root*, 275.

73 On the Montreal schools question, see Behiels, *Quebec and the Question of Immigration*; Tulchinsky, *Taking Root*, 138–44, 243–8, 273–4.

74 Although Quebec journalist Adrien Arcand is often associated with the introduction of fascism to Canada, it had been present in Canada long before. In the early 1920s Mussolini used the Italian consulates to plant *fasci* in the Italian communities of Montreal and Toronto, and after 1933 the German consular service sponsored the Deutscher Bund Canada to spread the doctrines of the National Socialist German Workers' Party to German immigrants and persons of German descent. Native fascist parties arose in Canada in the early 1930s, including the Winnipeg-based Canadian Nationalist Party, the Canadian Union of Fascists (purportedly a nation-wide federation with headquarters in Toronto), and Arcand's movement, the Parti National Social Chrétien, which became a virulently anti-Semitic French-Canadian nationalist party. In March 1938 Arcand and other fascist leaders formed the National Unity Party/Parti unité nationale, with Arcand at the helm. For discussions of Arcand and his party, see Betcherman, *The Swastika and the Maple Leaf*; Robin, *Shades of Right*; Thompson with Seager, *Canada, 1922–1939*, 323–4; Zucchi, *Italians in Toronto*.

75 Anctil, "Interlude of Hostility," in Davies, *Antisemitism in Canada*, 135–65; Betcherman, *The Swastika and the Maple Leaf*, 8–9, 11; Canadian Jewish Congress, *Pathways to the Present*, 5; Paris, *Jews*, 42–8.

76 The two notable exceptions were the Co-operative Commonwealth Federation and the United Church of Canada, both of which pushed for the admission of Jewish refugees. Betcherman, *The Swastika and the Maple Leaf*, 132–3. The story of Canada's darkest period of humanitarian effort has been expertly told by Abella and Troper in *None Is Too Many*.

77 Betcherman, *The Swastika and the Maple Leaf*, 32–3; Caiserman, "Anti-Semitism in Canada," c. 1938–39 (NA, CJC Collection, MG28, vol. 13, V, 101, reel M-5461); Canadian Jewish Congress, *Pathways to the Present*, 5. On Abbé Groulx's support of the *achat chez nous* movement, see Delisle, *The Traitor and the Jew.*

78 Abella, *A Coat of Many Colours*, 179.

79 Tulchinsky, "The Contours of Canadian Jewish History," in Brym, Shaffir, and Weinfeld, *The Jews in Canada*, 10.

80 Christie Pits, a playing-field in a working-class district of Toronto, was the scene of violence between Jews and non-Jews. The major incidents took place in the summer of 1933, when the Swastika Club of Toronto erected swastikas at the East End Beaches and harassed Jewish bathers. At a baseball game at Willowvale Park (commonly known as Christie Pits), non-Jewish youths waved swastika flags and yelled "Heil Hitler" and "Kill the Jews." Violence erupted as a result of these anti-Semitic provocations, with Jewish youths battling non-Jewish youths. Betcherman, *The Swastika and the Maple Leaf*, 57–60; Levitt and Shaffir, *The Riot at Christie Pits* and "The Swastika as Dramatic Symbol," in Brym, Shaffir, and Weinfeld, *The Jews in Canada*, 77–96; Speisman, *The Jews of Toronto*, 332–5.

81 Abella and Troper, *None Is Too Many*, 36–7; Betcherman, *The Swastika and the Maple Leaf*, 65, 101–2, 126.

82 Caiserman, "Anti-Semitism in Canada," c. 1938–39 (NA, CJC Collection, MG28, vol. 13, V, 101, reel M-5461); Abella and Troper, *None Is Too Many*, 10; Tulchinsky, *Taking Root*, xix.

83 Abella, *A Coat of Many Colours*, 188; Caiserman, "Anti-Semitism in Canada," c. 1938–39 (NA, CJC Collection, MG28, vol. 13, V, 101, reel M-5461); Canadian Jewish Congress, *Pathways to the Present*, 6; Rosenberg, *Two Centuries of Jewish Life in Canada*, 37; Rosenberg, *The Jewish Community in Canada*, vol. 2, 43; Speisman, *The Jews of Toronto*, 331.

84 The Western Division comprised that part of Canada situated west of and including Port Arthur; the Central Division included Ontario as far west as Port Arthur; and the Eastern Division included Quebec and the Maritime provinces. Abella and Troper, *None Is Too Many*, 10; "Constitution and Resolutions, Second General Session," 27–9 Jan. 1934 (Glenbow, Shumiatcher Papers, M1107, box 4, file 38).

85 Rosenberg, *Two Centuries of Jewish Life in Canada*, 37–8.

86 "Constitution and Resolutions, Second General Session," 27–9 Jan. 1934 (Glenbow, Shumiatcher Papers, M1107, box 4, file 38); Schneiderman, *The American Jewish Year Book, 1934–35*, vol. 36, 151.

87 The United Jewish Refugee and War Relief Agencies was set up in 1939, and worked closely with the American Joint Distribution Committee to

rescue Jewish refugees during the war and to help settle Jewish displaced persons in the post-war period. "The Canadian Jewish Congress and the United Jewish Relief Agencies in Canada," n.d. (CJCNA, ZA 1948, box 10); Rosenberg, *The Jewish Community in Canada*, vol. 2, 44, 46; Letter, Hayes to Shumiatcher, 4 Nov. 1942 (Glenbow, Shumiatcher Papers, M1107, box 8, file 57).

88 Canadian Jewish Congress, *Pathways to the Present*, 7–9; Troper and Weinfeld, *Old Wounds*, 50.

89 "Constitution and Resolutions, Second General Session," 27–9 Jan. 1934 (Glenbow, Shumiatcher Papers, M1107, box 4, file 38).

90 B'nai Brith, a fraternal organization based on the foundations of service, brotherhood, and education, was first organized in New York City in 1843. The first Canadian B'nai Brith lodges were set up in Toronto in 1875 and Montreal in 1881. In 1960 there were more than fifty B'nai Brith lodges in Canada, a number of women's lodges, and chapters of the B'nai Brith Youth movement. Today, B'nai Brith is Canadian Jewry's largest membership organization. It is best known for its Anti-Defamation League in the United States and its League for Human Rights in Canada, both active lobbying groups for civil rights and justice for minority groups. Phillips, "The B'nai B'rith in Canada," in Hart, *The Jew in Canada*, 433–7; Rosenberg, *Two Centuries of Jewish Life in Canada*, 40; Selick, *History of B'nai B'rith in Eastern Canada*, 7–8; Troper and Weinfeld, *Old Wounds*, 52.

91 Abella, *A Coat of Many Colours*, 203; "Constitution and Resolutions, Second General Session," 27–9 Jan. 1934 (Glenbow, Shumiatcher Papers, M1107, box 4, file 38); Grossman, *Canadian Jewish Year Book, 1939–1940*, vol. 1, 127.

92 "Resolution, Joint Committee of Winnipeg B'nai Brith and Congress," 2 Aug. [1938] (CJCNA, ZA 1938, box 2, file 20).

93 "The Canadian Jewish Congress and the United Jewish Relief Agencies in Canada," n.d. (CJCNA, ZA 1948, box 10); "Summary of Committee Reports for the Sixth Annual Regional Conference, Toronto," 22 Sept. 1940 (Glenbow, Shumiatcher Papers, M1107, box 7, file 50).

94 "Summary of Activities of the National Joint Public Relations Committee of the Canadian Jewish Congress and the B'nai B'rith," c. 1948 (CJCNA, ZA 1948, box 10).

CHAPTER THREE

1 In 1938 an unnamed officer of Congress infiltrated one of Arcand's National Unity Party meetings at St Thomas Aquinas Church Hall in Montreal. He reported that Arcand was organizing a 900-signature petition to the Canadian government requesting that 400 Jewish refugees

recently arrived at the Port of Montreal be returned to the countries from which they came. At the meeting Arcand reportedly stated that "as soon as his party assumes power he will enforce his own laws and these will see to it that all fortunes accumulated by Jewish thieves will remain [in Quebec]." He declared that the Jews would be forced to remain in Quebec to receive their "just punishment" and that he would "send his friends, Rabbi Harry J. Stern, A.J. Freiman and H.M. Caiserman and others, to Bordeaux to cut stones." The Congress officer also noted that *The Key to the Mystery*, a compilation of anti-Semitic texts edited by one of Arcand's assistants, was distributed at the meeting free of charge. Significantly, this booklet was also distributed at Social Credit party meetings and was available through the Alberta Social Credit Board. Betcherman describes *The Key to the Mystery* as "undoubtedly the most vicious defamation of the Jewish people ever published in Canada." Betcherman, *The Swastika and the Maple Leaf*, 91; Congress memo, 25 Apr. 1938 (CJCNA, ZA 1938, box 2, file 28).

2 Stember, *Jews in the Mind of America*, 110–11. On the activities of American fascists, isolationists, and anti-Semitic right-wingers in the interwar period, see Bennett, *Party of Fear*; Brinkley, *Voices of Protest*; Ribuffo, *The Old Christian Right*.

3 "Proceedings of the Seventh Plenary Session," 31 May–2 June 1947 (PAM, JHSWC Collection, MG6 B3).

4 Caiserman, "Anti-Semitism in Canada," c. 1938–39 (NA, CJC Collection, MG 28, vol. 13, V, 101, reel M-5461); Rosenberg, *The Jewish Population of Canada*, 1–2.

5 One of the most effective measures Congress undertook at this time was against Adrien Arcand in Quebec. In 1939 a Congress delegation met with Minister of Justice Ernest Lapointe and handed him a heavily documented brief on Arcand's activities. Thanks to Congress's efforts, Arcand was deemed a threat to security, interned, and remained in prison for the duration of the war. Rosenberg, *The Jewish Community in Canada*, vol. 2, 44. On Congress's anti-defamation work in Quebec during this period, see Betcherman, *The Swastika and the Maple Leaf*, 40–1, 94–5.

6 *Canadian Jewish Review*, 7 June 1935 (Glenbow, Shumiatcher Papers, M1107, box 4, file 38).

7 Ibid., 24 May 1935.

8 *Calgary Herald*, 7 Aug. 1939; Minutes, Third Session of the Third Regional Congress Conference, Western Division, 6 Aug. 1939 (Glenbow, Shumiatcher Papers, M1107, box 5, file 44).

9 "Report of the Executive Director of the Western Division, Sixth Western Conference," 23–4 May 1943 (Glenbow, Shumiatcher Papers, M1107, box 8, file 58).

10 In 1938 Rosenberg gave a statistical analysis of the economic stratification of Canadian Jewry. He reported that there were six Jewish farmers in Canada for every Jew engaged in financial occupations and that only two of every thousand Jews gainfully occupied were engaged in finance, as compared with three of every thousand among the total population of all origins, and four of every thousand among those of British origin. He reported that there was not and had not been for forty years in Canada a single Jewish director of a chartered bank, railway, ocean or air transportation company, telephone or telegraph company, public utility corporation, or pulp and paper corporation, and that the membership lists of the Montreal and Toronto stock exchanges "are as clear of Jewish names as the register of an exclusive country club." Other statistics showed that, occupationally, Jews were disproportionately represented in the manufacturing industry, trade, and clerical occupations in Canada. In 1941, for example, 31.24 per cent of Jews were engaged in manufacturing, as compared to 16.73 per cent of all other origins; 34.86 per cent of Jews were engaged in trade, as compared to 8.54 per cent of all other origins; and 14.2 per cent of Jews were engaged in clerical occupations, as compared to 8.04 per cent of all other origins. Conversely, only 1.19 per cent of Jews were engaged in agriculture, as compared to 25.24 per cent of all other origins. Only 0.28 per cent of Jews were engaged in finance, which was almost equal to the 0.29 per cent of all other origins. Rosenberg, "Canada's Jewish Citizens," in *Social Welfare*, 3 Sept. 1938 (PAM, JHSWC Collection, MG10, file 3 / MG8, file 6); Rosenberg, *The Jewish Population of Canada*, 32; National JPRC, "Some Figures on the Jewish Population of Canada," c. 1951 (PAM, JHSWC Collection, MG10, file 3 / MG8, file 3).

11 Rosenberg, "Jews in Canadian Industry and Finance," 15 June 1936 (PAM, JHSWC Collection, P600 A).

12 Caiserman, "Anti-Semitism in Canada" (NA, CJC Collection, MG 28, vol. 13, V, 101, reel M-5461).

13 "Summary of Committee Reports for the Sixth Annual Regional Conference," 22 Sept. 1940 (Glenbow, Shumiatcher Papers, M1107, box 7, file 50).

14 "Report to the Fifth Plenary Session of the Canadian Jewish Congress, Montreal," 10–12 Jan. 1942 (Glenbow, Shumiatcher Papers, M1107, box 7, file 54).

15 Rosenberg, "Jews in Canadian Industry and Finance," 15 June 1936 (PAM, JHSWC Collection, P600 A); Letter, Silcox to Rosenberg, 12 Dec. 1935 (CJCNA, ZC, SC).

16 Letter, Caiserman to Rosenberg, 14 Apr. 1941 (CJCNA, ZC, SC).

17 Memo, Rosenberg to Cohen et al., c. 1941 (CJCNA, ZC, SC).

18 Canada, Commons, *Debates*, 9 July 1943, 4569–71, 4614–16; 12 July
   1943, 4660–3; 24 July 1943, 5396–401; 17 Dec. 1945, 3706–10;
   31 Aug. 1946, 5744–8; 7 Feb. 1947, 223–5; 17 July 1946, 3553;
   14 May 1947, 3086–9; 24 June 1947, 4569; 4 July 1947, 5114–16;
   19 Feb. 1948, 1391–5; 31 May 1948, 4579–83; 19 June 1948, 5552–6.
19 Streit, *Union Now* and *Union Now With Britain*.
20 *Today and Tomorrow*, 27 Apr. 1944.
21 *Western Producer*, 30 Jan. 1941.
22 Letter, McCollum [Rosenberg] to the editor, *Western Producer*, 18 Feb.
   1941 (CJCNA, ZC, SC).
23 Ibid.
24 Letter, Rosenberg to Cohen, 25 Mar. 1941 (CJCNA, ZC, SC); Letter,
   Rosenberg to Olyan, 21 Apr. 1941 (CJCNA, ZC, SC).
25 Letter, n.d., attached to letter, Olyan to Rosenberg, 11 Apr. 1941
   (CJCNA, ZC, SC).
26 Rosenberg's oft-used pseudonym was short for Watt Hugh McCollum
   (said quickly it is "what you m'call 'em"). He justified the pseudonym
   by stating: "I am, as a rule, not a believer in writing letters to the Editor, and I have therefore signed it with a pen name." Letter, Rosenberg
   to Cohen, 25 Mar. 1941 (CJCNA, ZC, SC); Weintraub, *City Unique*, 145.
27 Letter, Rosenberg to Cohen, 25 Mar. 1941 (CJCNA, ZC, SC).
28 Balduf told Rosenberg that Streit's ancestors "came to this country
   before the Revolution, and are partly German and partly Irish. There is
   no trace anywhere in his genealogy of Jewish blood, 'assuming there is
   such a thing as Jewish blood.' Mr. Streit, does not of course share the
   Nazi attitude toward Jews and does not regard the imputation that he
   is part Jewish as an 'accusation.' It is simply a falsehood indulged in by
   Nazis and Americans with pro-Nazi leaning." Letter, Balduf to Rosenberg, 25 July 1941 (CJCNA, CD, box 7, file 11P).
29 Letter, Rosenberg to Balduf, 28 July 1941 (CJCNA, CD, box 7, file 11P).
30 *Western Producer*, 17 July 1941, 9 Oct. 1941; Memo, Public Relations
   Committee, Western Division, 28 July 1941 (CJCNA, ZC, SC).
31 *Today and Tomorrow*, 17 June 1943; Memo, Rosenberg to Hayes,
   5 Feb. 1947 (CJCNA, CA, box 33, file 306; CJCNA, ZC, SC).
32 Letter, Manning to Jukes, 20 May 1947 (PAA, Alberta Social Credit
   League, file 1472).
33 *Today and Tomorrow*, 27 Apr. 1944.
34 Ibid., 8 Oct. 1942.
35 Ibid., 30 Sept. 1943.
36 Ibid., 6 Aug. 1942.
37 Ibid., 31 Aug. 1944; *Canadian Social Crediter*, 17 July 1947; Memo,
   Rosenberg to Hayes, 7 Aug. 1947 (CJCNA, DA2, box 3, file 4).
38 *Canadian Social Crediter*, 18 Sept. 1947.

39 *Today and Tomorrow*, 22 July 1943, 27 Jan. 1944.

40 Sir William Beveridge, one of Great Britain's foremost economists, directed the London School of Economics from 1919 to 1937. He was responsible for helping to shape Britain's post-war welfare-state policies and institutions through his 1942 report *Social Insurance and Allied Services*, also known as the Beveridge Report or Beveridge Plan. See also J. Beveridge, *Beveridge and His Plan*; Harris, *William Beveridge*.

41 Dr Leonard Marsh was a Canadian economist who studied at the London School of Economics and became director of an interdisciplinary social-science research program at McGill University from 1930 to 1941. An early member of the group of social reformers who eventually formed the League for Social Reconstruction, he was a major contributor to the League's influential book *Social Planning for Canada*, published in 1935. He was also research adviser for the federal Committee on Postwar Reconstruction from 1941 to 1944, and published his influential *Report on Social Security for Canada* in 1943, also known as the Marsh Report. See also Research Committee of the League for Social Reconstruction, *Democracy Needs Socialism*.

42 *Today and Tomorrow* noted that McGill principal Cyril James had been appointed chairman of the seven-man Committee on Reconstruction, which went to Britain in early 1942 to consult with authorities regarding post-war reconstruction. The paper then remarked: "Everybody realizes the disaster of losing the war, now we had better understand the penalties of winning it if the arch-intriguers of International Finance have their way. Our choice is between German gangsters, and International racketeers. Nearly everyone believed we are fighting to save democracy, but, according to Dr. James, democracy is to be replaced by world dictatorship and the rule of gold" (12 Mar. 1942, 31 Aug. 1944).

43 Ibid., 12 Mar. 1942, 1 Apr. 1943, 31 Aug. 1944, 21 Sept. 1944; *Edmonton Bulletin*, 14 Oct. 1944.

44 See Chernow, *The Warburgs*.

45 *Today and Tomorrow*, 27 Jan. 1944, 27 Apr. 1944; *Canadian Social Crediter*, 3 Jan. 1946; "Content Analysis of the *Canadian Social Crediter*," c. 29 Jan. 1947 (CJCNA, ZC, SC).

46 *Today and Tomorrow*, 27 Jan. 1944, 27 Apr. 1944.

47 Ibid., 18 Nov. 1943.

48 See Pinder, *Fifty Years of Political and Economic Planning*.

49 *Today and Tomorrow*, 13 May 1943.

50 Ibid., 27 Apr. 1944, 31 Aug. 1944.

51 Ibid., 2 Jan. 1941.

52 Ibid., 29 Jan. 1942.

53 Ibid., 21 May 1942.

54 Ibid., 29 Jan. 1942, 27 Jan. 1944.

55 Letter, Fradkin to Friedman, 4 Feb. 1942 (CJCNA, ZC, SC).

56 Letter, Friedman to Fradkin, 6 Feb. 1942 (CJCNA, ZC, SC).

57 Letter, Frank to Friedman, 10 Feb. 1942 (CJCNA, ZA 1948, box 1, file 7); Letter, Frank to Fradkin, 10 Feb. 1942 (CJCNA, ZC, SC).

58 Ibid.

59 Letter, Fradkin to Friedman, 18 Feb. 1942 (CJCNA, ZC, SC); Letter, Friedman to Fradkin, 25 Feb. 1942 (CJCNA, ZC, SC).

60 Specifically, Rosenberg contacted Fradkin of Calgary and Friedman of Edmonton, and asked the latter to forward clippings from *Today and Tomorrow* that had "an anti-Semitic tinge." It appears that Rosenberg began scrutinizing the party organ regularly at this time. Letters, Rosenberg to Fradkin, 26 Aug. 1942, 8 Sept. 1942 (CJCNA, ZC, SC); Letter, Fradkin to Rosenberg, 5 Sept. 1942 (CJCNA, ZC, SC); Letter, Rosenberg to Friedman, 18 Sept. 1942 (CJCNA, ZC, SC).

61 Memo, Hayes to Rosenberg, 22 Apr. 1943 (CJCNA, ZC, SC).

62 Letter, Rosenberg to Hayes, 28 Apr. 1943 (CJCNA, ZC, SC).

63 Ibid.

64 Letter, Hayes to Rosenberg, 3 May 1943 (CJCNA, ZC, SC).

65 Barr, *The Dynasty*, 102–4; Elliott and Miller, *Bible Bill*, 256–61; Finkel, *The Social Credit Phenomenon in Alberta*, 59–62; Hesketh, *Major Douglas and Alberta Social Credit*, 145–6; Macpherson, *Democracy in Alberta*, 171–2.

66 On Powell's involvement with the libellous "Bankers' Toadies" pamphlet, see Elliott and Miller, *Bible Bill*, 273–4; Hesketh, *Major Douglas and Alberta Social Credit*, 170.

67 Macpherson, *Democracy in Alberta*, 210.

68 In *Secret Societies* Webster examined the Knights Templars, Freemasonry, German Templarism, French Illuminism, Jewish Cabalists, Bavarian Illuminati, Pan-Germanism, Communism, and "the real Jewish peril." These movements were all ostensibly Jewish-controlled, which proved "the immense problem of the Jewish Power, perhaps the most important problem with which the modern world is confronted." Webster, *Secret Societies*, xiii, 369; Memo, Rosenberg to Hayes, 17 June 1947 (CJCNA, ZA 1947, box 1, file 7). In *The Surrender of an Empire* Webster described how, since the First World War, Jews had undermined and dismembered the British Empire. She argued that a secret group of international-Jewish-German-financial-capitalist-communist-revolutionary-political-Zionist plotters was the governing force behind the German imperialists before the First World War, the Bolsheviks, the Irish revolutionaries, the Indian nationalist Swaraj, the Egyptian Wafd, the Kuomintang in China, and the Zionists in Palestine. One excerpt stated: "For the purpose of weakening England, the German Nationalists pursued their usual policy of co-operation with the International

Communists. This was carried out mainly through the Fraina-Ruthenberg group of American-Jewish Communists, who were in touch with Moscow on one hand and with the revolutionary elements in England and Ireland on the other" (137); Memo, Rosenberg to Hayes, 17 June 1947 (CJCNA, ZA 1947, box 1, file 7). *The Socialist Network* discussed hundreds of communist, socialist, trade union, and peace organizations in the United States, Britain, and Europe that constituted the "socialist network." Webster denounced movements ranging from the America Civil Liberties Union to the Nudity Movement and invoked numerous Jewish names in her denunciation. She also included a twelve-page "Index of Persons" who made up the socialist network (145–57). After reading this book, Rosenberg pointed out: "There is not the slightest mention of monetary theories, Social Credit, or farmers' problems in the book and at first glance the book would appear most unsuitable for distribution by a Canadian political party which forms the government of a predominantly agricultural Canadian province." Memo, Rosenberg to Hayes, 25 June 1947 (CJCNA, ZA 1947, box 1, file 7). Similarly, in *World Revolution* Webster attempted to explain the hidden force behind all the revolutions in the world, from the French Revolution of 1789 to the Russian Revolution of 1917, concluding that all were the result of a Jewish conspiracy to attack Christianity and the social and moral order. For the most part she blamed the "Jewish-controlled Illuminati" for the revolutions and warned that this same conspiracy was now threatening British civilization. She appended a large and complicated chart of all the world revolutions, showing the connections between the "open revolutionary forces" and the co-operating "hidden forces" of the secret societies. Memo, Rosenberg to Hayes, 7 Aug. 1947 (CJCNA, ZC, SC).

69 Memo, Rosenberg to Hayes, 31 Mar. 1948 (CJCNA, ZA 1948, box 1, file 7).
70 *Today and Tomorrow*, 13 May 1943; Memo, Rosenberg to Hayes, 27 June 1947 (CJCNA , ZA 1947, box 1, file 7).
71 Macpherson, *Democracy in Alberta*, 210.
72 *Today and Tomorrow*, 13 May 1943; Memo, Rosenberg to Hayes, 27 June 1947 (CJCNA, ZA 1947, box 1, file 7).
73 *Canadian Tribune*, 29 May 1943.
74 Letter, Fradkin to Rosenberg, 8 June 1943 (CJCNA, ZC, SC); Letter, Rosenberg to Fradkin, 31 May 1943 (CJCNA, ZC, SC).
75 Letter, Fradkin to Lieberman, 8 June 1943 (CJCNA, ZC, SC).
76 Letter, Lieberman to Fradkin, 9 June 1943 (CJCNA, ZC, SC).
77 Ibid.
78 Letter, Rosenberg to Olyan, 13 July 1943 (CJCNA, ZC, SC).
79 Letter, Jaques to Reidell, 10 May 1943 (CJCNA, ZC, SC); Letter, Reidell to Bernstein, 10 June 1943 (CJCNA, CA, box 33, file 306).

80 Letter, Rosenberg to Reidell, 16 Aug. 1943 (CJCNA, ZC, SC); Letter, Caiserman to Rosenberg, 5 Aug. 1943 (CJCNA, CA, box 33, file 306).

81 Letter, Rosenberg to Coldwell, 24 Aug. 1943 (CJCNA, ZC, SC); Letter, Rosenberg to Caiserman, 17 Aug. 1943 (CJCNA, CA, box 33, file 306).

82 Memo, Rosenberg to Fine et al., 17 Aug. 1943 (CJCNA, ZC, SC).

83 Letter, Jaques to Steiner, 13 Sept. 1943 (CJCNA, CA, box 33, file 306).

84 Abella and Troper, *None Is Too Many*, 145–7.

85 Letter, Rosenberg to Caiserman, 16 Nov. 1943 (CJCNA, ZA 1945, box 7, file 100).

CHAPTER FOUR

1 Memo, Caiserman to Members of the Public Relations Committee, 1 Feb. 1944 (CJCNA, ZC, SC).

2 Letter, Rosenberg to Caiserman, 11 Feb. 1944 (CJCNA, ZC, SC).

3 Letter, Caiserman to Morosnick, 11 Jan. 1944 (CJCNA, ZA 1944, box 2, file 42).

4 Letter, Morosnick to Caiserman, 24 Jan. 1944 (CJCNA, ZA 1944, box 2, file 42).

5 Letter, Caiserman to Morosnick, 23 Feb. 1944 (CJCNA, ZA 1944, box 2, file 42).

6 Letter, Morosnick to Caiserman, 29 Feb. 1944 (CJCNA, ZA 1944, box 2, file 42).

7 Letter, Caiserman to Morosnick, 9 Mar. 1944 (CJCNA, ZA 1944, box 2, file 42).

8 Ibid.

9 Hesketh, *Major Douglas and Alberta Social Credit*, 208–20.

10 *Today and Tomorrow*, 2 Mar. 1944.

11 Letter, Rosenberg to Lappin, 14 Mar. 1944 (CJCNA, ZA 1945, box 7, file 100); Letter, [Rosenberg] to Fradkin, 13 Mar. 1944 (CJCNA, ZA 1945, box 7, file 100).

12 *Today and Tomorrow*, 27 Apr. 1944.

13 Memo, Rosenberg to Hayes et al., 9 May 1944 (CJCNA, ZA 1945, box 7, file 100). For a biographical exposition of William Dudley Pelley, see Ribuffo, *The Old Christian Right*.

14 The Ontario legislation, entitled "An Act to prevent the Publication of Discriminatory Matter Referring to Race or Creed," was assented to on 14 Mar. 1944 and was known as "The Racial Discrimination Act, 1944." On 20 Mar. 1944 in the House of Commons, CCF MP Angus MacInnis introduced Bill 37 to amend the Criminal Code of Canada. The purpose of the amendment was "to prevent public utterances or the dissemination of material calculated or likely to cause discrimination or

disharmony on account of race or religion. The utterance for publication of such statements tends to set race against race and religious groups against religious groups. The intention is to make such action illegal in the interest of unity and harmony among the people of Canada, irrespective of race or religion." MacInnis's motion was agreed to and the bill was read the first time, but it subsequently died on the order table. Ontario, *Statutes of the Province of Ontario*, 1944, 231–2; Canada, *Debates*, 20 Mar. 1944, 1626.

15 *Today and Tomorrow*, 4 May 1944.
16 Memo, Rosenberg to Hayes et al., 15 May 1944 (CJCNA, ZA 1945, box 7, file 100).
17 Letter, Caiserman to Rosenberg, 18 May 1944 (CJCNA, ZA 1945, box 7, file 100).
18 Letter, Hayes to Lappin, 19 May 1944 (CJCNA, ZA 1945, box 7, file 100).
19 Bretton Woods was the informal name for the United Nations Monetary and Financial Conference at Bretton Woods, New Hampshire, from 1 to 22 July 1944. The purpose of the conference was to make financial arrangements for the post-war world. It was attended by experts representing forty-four states or governments, who drew up proposals for the International Bank for Reconstruction and Development and the International Monetary Fund, which were ratified and constituted in 1945 and 1946 respectively. Dumbarton Oaks was a conference held at the Dumbarton Oaks mansion in Georgetown, Washington, DC, from 21 August to 7 October 1944, and attended by representatives from China, the Soviet Union, the United States, and the United Kingdom. The Dumbarton Oaks proposals for a world organization, called the Proposals for the Establishment of a General International Organization, together with the agreements reached at the Yalta Conference in February 1945, formed the basis of the negotiations at the San Francisco Conference in 1945, out of which came the Charter of the United Nations. Schild, *Bretton Woods and Dumbarton Oaks*; *Edmonton Bulletin*, 14 Oct. 1944.
20 *Today and Tomorrow*, 3 June 1943.
21 Ibid., 18 Nov. 1943.
22 Ibid., 9 Dec. 1943.
23 *Canadian Social Crediter*, 12 Oct. 1944; *Maclean's*, 1 Sept. 1944.
24 Letter, Caiserman to Feinberg, 2 Aug. 1944 (CJCNA, ZA 1944, box 2, file 24).
25 *Fellowship*, May 1944 (CJCNA, ZF Fellowship [CCCJ], file PR 210.1).
26 *Edmonton Bulletin*, 14 Oct. 1944.
27 Ibid.

28 Ibid., 28 Nov. 1944.

29 Letters, Lappin to Rosenberg, 28, 30 Nov. 1944, 28 Dec. 1944 (CJCNA, ZC, SC); Letters, Rosenberg to Lappin, 1, 5 Dec. 1944 (CJCNA, ZC, SC); Letter, Rosenberg to Friedman, 1 Dec. 1944 (CJCNA, ZC, SC).

30 *Canadian Social Crediter*, 2 Nov. 1944.

31 *Canadian Tribune*, 2 Dec. 1944.

32 *Canadian Social Crediter*, 14 Dec. 1944.

33 Letter, Friedman to Hayes, 3 Jan. 1945 (CJCNA, ZA 1945, box 7, file 100).

34 Low, cited in letter, Lieberman to Fradkin, 19 Jan. 1945 (CJCNA, ZC, SC).

35 *Lethbridge Herald*, 10 Jan. 1945; *Canadian Social Crediter*, 11 Jan. 1945.

36 In a letter accepting to become a member of the Canadian Palestine Committee, Low wrote: "It is true that I have kept myself up to date on the history of the Jewish people and have always felt that the Balfour Declaration and the League of Nations mandate to Great Britain should be fulfilled to the letter, so far as they refer to the creation of a National home in Palestine. Under the circumstances I would be pleased to associate myself with the Committee and would appreciate receiving up to date information as it becomes available." Letter, Low to Dower, 17 Mar. 1944 (CJCNA, ZA 1947, box 2, file 7E); "List of members of Canadian Palestine Committee," 28 Mar. 1944 (CJCNA, ZA 1944, box 2, file 29).

37 Letter, Green to Moscovich, 16 Jan. 1945 (CJCNA, ZC, SC).

38 Letter, Lieberman to Fradkin, 19 Jan. 1945 (CJCNA, ZC, SC).

39 Letter, Fradkin to Rosenberg, 20 Jan. 1945 (CJCNA, ZC, SC).

40 Memo, Rosenberg, 30 Jan. 1945 (CJCNA, ZC, SC).

41 Letter, Caiserman to Rosenberg, 5 Feb. 1945 (CJCNA, ZC, SC).

42 Letter, Green to Moscovich, 16 Jan. 1945 (CJCNA, ZC, SC); Letter, Lieberman to Fradkin, 19 Jan. 1945 (CJCNA, ZC, SC); Minutes, JPRC Meeting, 1 Mar. 1945 (CJCNA, ZA 1945, box 2, file 19); Minutes, Dominion Council Eastern Division Meeting, 15 Feb. 1945 (CJCNA, ZA 1945, box 2, file 19).

43 *Today*, Feb. 1945.

44 *Toronto Daily Star*, 24 Feb. 1945; *Canadian Social Crediter*, 21 Sept. 1944, 19 Oct. 1944, 14 Dec. 1944.

45 *Toronto Daily Star*, 13 Mar. 1945.

46 Ibid., 22 Mar. 1945.

47 Ibid., 2 Apr. 1945; *Canadian Social Crediter*, 5 Apr. 1945; "Content Analysis of the *Canadian Social Crediter*," c. 29 Jan. 1947 (CJCNA, ZC, SC).

48 Memo, CJC Dominion Council, 23 May 1945 (CJCNA, ZA 1945, box 2, file 33); *American Mercury*, Jan. 1945.

49 Fine and Caiserman, "Public Relations Problems after the End of the War," 14 Sept. 1945 (CJCNA, ZA 1945, box 2, file 19).

50 Blumenstein, "Report of the Committee on Social and Economic Studies," c. Oct. 1945 (CJCNA, ZA 1945, box 2, file 20); Letter, Saalheimer, 24 Sept. 1945 (CJCNA, ZA 1945, box 2, file 20).

CHAPTER FIVE

1 Abella and Troper state that "between 1933 and 1945 Canada found room within her borders for fewer than 5,000 Jews; after the war, until the founding of Israel in 1948, she admitted but 8,000 more. That record is arguably the worst of all possible refugee-receiving states." Abella and Troper, *None Is Too Many*, xxii.

2 Bercuson, *Canada and the Birth of Israel*, 52, 58–9.

3 In 1943 Swedish journalist Arvid Fredborg published *Behind the Steel Wall*, which detailed the genocide of the Nazi death camps. Throughout the war Allied nations were aware of the extent of Nazi genocide, and certainly, by war's end, any Canadian who read a newspaper was cognizant of this fact. Yet a Gallup Poll in October 1946 asked Canadians to choose the immigrant group they found most undesirable. The question stated: "if Canada does allow more immigrants are there any of these nationalities [on a supplied list] you would like to keep out?" The results were as follows: Japanese, 60 per cent; Jewish, 49 per cent; German, 34 per cent; Russian, 33 per cent; Negro, 31 per cent; Italian, 25 per cent; Chinese, 24 per cent; Middle European, 16 per cent; Ukrainian, 15 per cent; Polish, 14 per cent; Others, 3 per cent; None, 18 per cent; No Answer, 3 per cent. As Abella and Troper note, "Second on the list was not Canada's prime European enemy, Germans, but Jews. Almost half of those questioned, forty-nine per cent, checked off Jews as undesirable immigrants." Abella and Troper, *None Is Too Many*, 231–2, 323; Fredborg, *Behind the Steel Wall*.

4 Generally speaking, the "polite company" rule is a barometer of a society's political correctness and gauges what remarks may be made in front of polite guests and not be deemed offensive.

5 "Proceedings of the Seventh Plenary Session," 31 May–2 June 1947 (PAM, JHSWC Collection, MG6 B3).

6 Ibid.

7 National JPRC, "Public Relations in Theory and in Practice," c. 1950, and "Declaration of Policy," c. 15 Aug. 1950 (PAM, JHSWC Collection, MG10, file 3 / MG8, file 3).

8 "Proceedings of the Seventh Plenary Session," 31 May–2 June 1947 (PAM, JHSWC Collection, MG6 B3).

9 *Canadian Social Crediter*, 29 Aug. 1946.

10 Ibid., 8 Aug. 1946; "Content Analysis of the *Canadian Social Crediter*," c. 29 Jan. 1947 (CJCNA, ZC, SC).

11 *Canadian Social Crediter*, 26 Sept. 1946; "Content Analysis of the *Canadian Social Crediter*," c. 29 Jan. 1947 (CJCNA, ZC, SC).

12 *Canadian Social Crediter*, 10 Oct. 1946; "Content Analysis of the *Canadian Social Crediter*," c. 29 Jan. 1947 (CJCNA, ZC, SC).

13 Social Credit's views on the connection between Jews and communism were similar to those of American right-wing extremists like William Dudley Pelley, Gerald B. Winrod, Gerald L.K. Smith, and Father Charles Coughlin. See Bennett, *The Party of Fear* and *Demagogues in the Depression*; Brinkley, *Voices of Protest*; Jeansonne, *Gerald L.K. Smith*; Marcus, *Father Coughlin*; Ribuffo, *The Old Christian Right*; Sargent, *Extremism in America*.

14 *Canadian Social Crediter*, 14 Dec. 1944.

15 Ibid., 4 July 1946; "Content Analysis of the *Canadian Social Crediter*," c. 29 Jan. 1947 (CJCNA, ZC, SC).

16 Ben-Sasson, *A History of the Jewish People*, 1023–9.

17 Morgan was quoted as stating: "Trainloads of Jews were arriving in Berlin Alshost [sic] daily from Poland ... the pockets of most of the Jews were well lined with money, and they were well fed and well clothed. Their stories of persecution of Jews in Poland ... were notable for their similarity ... The stories invariably were that the atrocities 'occurred in the next town' ... Some motivating force or promise ... is influencing the Jews to give up comfortable living in Poland, as evidenced by their physical condition, dress and money when they reach Berlin." The *Edmonton Bulletin* reported that "Morgan said he was becoming more and more convinced that reports of pogroms and atrocities against the Jews in Poland were based less and less on fact" (2 Jan. 1946). *Canadian Social Crediter*, 10 Jan. 1946. On the life and career of Morgan, see Woodbridge, UNRRA; Morgan, *Overture to Overlord*.

18 *Edmonton Bulletin*, 2 Jan. 1946; *Canadian Social Crediter*, 10 Jan. 1946; "Content Analysis of the *Canadian Social Crediter*," c. 29 Jan. 1947 (CJCNA, ZC, SC).

19 *Canadian Social Crediter*, 29 Aug. 1946.

20 The purpose of the Morgenthau Plan was to eliminate permanently Germany's capacity for making war. It was abandoned largely because the Allies believed German military strength was needed to counter the expansionist impulses of the Soviet Union. On Henry Morgenthau and the Morgenthau Plan, see Blum, *From the Morgenthau Diaries* and *Roosevelt and Morgenthau*.

21 *Canadian Social Crediter*, 22 Aug. 1946; "Content Analysis of the *Canadian Social Crediter*," c. 29 Jan. 1947 (CJCNA, ZC, SC).

22 *Canadian Social Crediter*, 16 May 1946; "Content Analysis of the *Canadian Social Crediter*," c. 29 Jan. 1947 (CJCNA, ZC, SC).

23 *Canadian Social Crediter*, 19 June 1947; Memo, Rosenberg to Hayes, 27 June 1947 (CJCNA, ZA 1947, box 1, file 7).

24 *Canadian Social Crediter*, 16 May 1946; "Content Analysis of the *Canadian Social Crediter*," c. 29 Jan. 1947 (CJCNA, ZC, SC).

25 *Canadian Social Crediter*, 6 June 1946; "Content Analysis of the *Canadian Social Crediter*," c. 29 Jan. 1947 (CJCNA, ZC, SC).

26 In September 1945 three Jewish underground groups in Palestine – the Haganah (Defence), the LEHI (Stern Gang), and the Irgun Zvai Leumi (National Military Organization) – all commanded by Menahem Begin, put aside their differences and joined together in a rebellion against British rule. They sabotaged railway lines, police stations, and radar traps attempting to capture illegal Jewish immigrants. On 22 July 1946 they bombed the King David Hotel in Jerusalem, which housed Britain's military and government offices. The bombing left ninety-one dead and forty-six injured. See Clarke, *By Blood and Fire*.

27 *Canadian Social Crediter*, 26 Sept. 1946, 18 Sept. 1947; Memo, Rosenberg to Hayes, 21 Oct. 1947 (CJCNA, ZA 1947, box 1, file 7A); "Content Analysis of the *Canadian Social Crediter*," c. 29 Jan. 1947 (CJCNA, ZC, SC).

28 On the life and career of Gerald L.K. Smith, see Jeansonne, *Gerald L.K. Smith*; Ribuffo, *The Old Christian Right*.

29 Bennett, *Party of Fear*, 244–7, 252–3. For an excellent biographical exposition of Smith, Pelley, and Winrod, see Ribuffo, *The Old Christian Right*.

30 *Canadian Social Crediter*, 25 Apr. 1946.

31 Letter, Asman, Christian Veterans, n.d. (CJCNA, ZC, SC).

32 *Canadian Social Crediter*, 18 July 1946.

33 *Canadian Jewish Weekly*, 8 Aug. 1946.

34 Letter, Rosenberg to Maller, 3 May 1946 (CJCNA, ZC, SC); Letter, Maller to Rosenberg, 20 May 1946 (CJCNA, ZC, SC).

35 Letter, Green to Hayes, 12 May 1946 (CJCNA, ZA 1947, box 1, file 7C).

36 "Results of the General Election of 1945 as an Index of the Extent and Prevalence of Anti-Semitic Prejudice in Canada," c. 29 Aug. 1946 (CJCNA, ZA 1945, box 2, file 31); Memo, Rosenberg to Hayes, 29 Aug. 1946 (CJCNA, ZA 1946, box 1, file 8).

37 Seventeen candidates out of a total of seventeen constituencies were nominated in Alberta; nine out of sixteen in British Columbia; nine out of twenty-one in Saskatchewan; eight out of seventeen in Manitoba; six out of eighty-two in Ontario; forty-three out of sixty-five in Quebec;

and one out of ten in New Brunswick. Prince Edward Island, Nova Scotia, and the Yukon did not nominate any Social Credit candidates. It should be noted that an error exists in Rosenberg's report. On page 2 he states that in British Columbia, three out of sixteen constituencies nominated Social Credit candidates. In fact *nine* BC constituencies ran Social Credit candidates. He rectifies this in Table I, "Number of Constituencies and Votes Polled at the General Elections, 1945", where he cites nine BC constituencies. "Results of the General Election of 1945 as an Index of the Extent and Prevalence of Anti-Semitic Prejudice in Canada," c. 29 Aug. 1946 (CJCNA, ZA 1945, box 2, file 31); *History of the Federal Electoral Ridings*, vol. 1 (BC) 24, 92, 127, 173, 178, 198, 207, 216, 228.

38 The only four constituencies in Alberta that did not elect a Social Credit member in the 1945 federal election were Athabasca (Liberal), Calgary East (Progressive Conservative), Calgary West (Progressive Conservative), and Edmonton West (Liberal). *History of the Federal Electoral Ridings*, vol. 1 (AB) 1–182.

39 "Results of the General Election of 1945 as an Index of the Extent and Prevalence of Anti-Semitic Prejudice in Canada," c. 29 Aug. 1946 (CJCNA, ZA 1945, box 2, file 31).

40 It may appear surprising that, with only 36 per cent of the popular vote, Social Crediters won thirteen out of seventeen seats from Alberta in the 1945 federal election. But rural ridings with small populations carried the same weight as urban ridings with larger populations. Indeed, every rural riding save Athabasca elected a Social Credit MP. As Alvin Finkel states: "Alberta, like all Canadian provinces, assigns seats on the basis of contests in constituencies rather than on the basis of a portion of the provincial vote. It is this policy that makes Alberta appear to be a single-minded province." *The Social Credit Phenomenon in Alberta*, 93.

41 "Results of the General Election of 1945 as an Index of the Extent and Prevalence of Anti-Semitic Prejudice in Canada," c. 29 Aug. 1946 (CJCNA, ZA 1945, box 2, file 31).

42 Bercuson, *Canada and the Birth of Israel*, 38; Bothwell and Granatstein, *The Gouzenko Transcripts*, 1. On the Gouzenko affair and Canada's involvement in the Cold War, see Gouzenko, *This Was My Choice*; Granatstein and Stafford, *Spy Wars*; Sawatsky, *Gouzenko*; Smith, *Diplomacy of Fear*; Weisbord, *The Strangest Dream*.

43 The Kellock-Taschereau Report named nineteen Canadian agents and seventeen members of the Soviet embassy staff who had engaged in espionage. Canada, *Report of the Kellock-Taschereau Commission*, 4–5, 85–6.

44 Bothwell and Granatstein, *The Gouzenko Transcripts*, 13–14; Granatstein and Stafford, *Spy Wars*, 62; Paris, *Jews*, 171; Smith, *Diplomacy of Fear*, 135–6.

45 Canada, *Report of the Kellock-Taschereau Commission*, 81–3; Granatstein and Stafford, *Spy Wars*, 61.

46 The figures used by the Social Credit party organ were unsubstantiated; in fact, the commission named thirty-six persons in total, nineteen of whom were *Canadian agents*. It never stated how many were Jews. Canada, *Report of the Kellock-Taschereau Commission*, 4–5, 85; *Canadian Social Crediter*, 12 Sept. 1946; Memo, Rosenberg to Hayes, 19 Sept. 1946 (CJCNA, ZC, SC).

47 *Canadian Social Crediter*, 12 Sept. 1946.

48 Avery, *Dangerous Foreigners*, 13, 117; Bercuson, *Canada and the Birth of Israel*, 18.

49 Paris, *Jews*, 145, 181. Fred Rose resigned his Montreal-Cartier seat in January 1946 and was replaced by Labour-Progressive candidate Michael Buhay. In a federal by-election in March 1947, three-quarters of the constituency's electors voted against Buhay, and Liberal candidate Maurice Hartt became the new MP. *Montreal Gazette*, 1 Apr. 1947.

50 *Canadian Social Crediter*, 12 Sept. 1946.

51 Memo, Rosenberg to Hayes, 3 Oct. 1946 (CJCNA, ZC, SC); Canada, *Report of the Kellock-Taschereau Commission*, 4–5, 85–6; *Canadian Social Crediter*, 12 Sept. 1946.

52 *Canadian Social Crediter*, 14 Nov. 1946; Memo, Rosenberg to Hayes, 16 Dec. 1946 (CJCNA, ZC, SC).

53 *New Voice*, Mar. 1947.

54 *Canadian Social Crediter*, 5 Dec. 1946.

55 Ibid., 9 May–4 July, 1946, 5 Dec. 1946; Memo, Rosenberg to Hayes, 5 Feb. 1947 (CJCNA, CA, box 33, file 306; CJCNA, ZC, SC).

56 Kirshnblatt, "Report on Anti-Semitism," 15 Sept. 1947 (CJCNA, CD, box 7, file 11P; CJCNA, ZA 1948, box 1, file 3); Letter, Rosenberg to Schaffer, 28 Apr. 1947 (CJCNA, CD, box 7, file 11P; CJCNA, ZC, SC); Memo, Kirshnblatt, 25 June 1947 (CJCNA, ZA 1949, box 3, file 31).

57 *Canadian Social Crediter*, 14 Nov. 1946; *Manitoba Commonwealth*, 18 Jan. 1947; *People's Weekly*, 4 Jan. 1947; CJC memo, n.d. (CJCNA, ZA 1947, box 1, file 7B); Memo, Rosenberg to Hayes, 16 Dec. 1946 (CJCNA, ZC, SC).

58 Douglas, *Social Credit*, 30.

59 *Saskatoon Star-Phoenix*, 6 Dec. 1946.

60 *People's Weekly*, 28 Dec. 1946; *Regina Leader-Post*, 3 Jan. 1947; *Canadian Social Crediter*, 2 Jan. 1947.

61 *Saskatoon Star-Phoenix*, 21 Dec. 1946; *Regina Leader-Post*, 14 Jan. 1947; *Canadian Social Crediter*, 2 Jan. 1947; Memo, Zimmerman to Hayes, 28 Jan. 1947 (CJCNA, ZC, SC); "Content Analysis of the *Canadian Social Crediter*," c. 29 Jan. 1947 (CJCNA, ZC, SC).

62 Minutes, National JPRC Meeting, 8 Dec. 1946 (CJCNA, ZA 1945, box 2, file 19); 23 Feb. 1947 (CJCNA, ZA 1947, box 9, file 104).

63 Letter, Dower to Hayes, 7 Jan. 1947 (CJCNA, ZA 1947, box 2, file 7E).

64 Letter, Godfrey to Hayes, 17 Dec. 1946 (CJCNA, ZA 1947, box 2, file 7E).

65 Letter, Hayes to Godfrey, 23 Dec. 1946 (CJCNA, ZA 1947, box 2, file 7E).

66 Letter, Moscovich to Hayes, 6 Dec. 1946 (CJCNA, ZA 1947, box 2, file 7E).

67 Letter, Hayes to Moscovitch [sic], 11 Dec. 1946 (CJCNA, ZA 1947, box 2, file 7A).

68 Letter, Moscovich to Hayes, 15 Dec. 1946 (CJCNA, ZA 1947, box 2, file 7E).

69 The memos discussed the *Canadian Social Crediter*'s reprinting of articles from Social Credit papers in Great Britain and Australia that were blatantly anti-Semitic; the party organ's coverage of Jaques's activities with Gerald L.K. Smith in the United States; the recent meeting of the national council of the SCAC; the use of the "Wheel-Cross" as the official symbol of the national Social Credit party; and the party organ's linkage between Judaism and the Ba'hai religion, both of which supposedly advocated "one world." Memos, Rosenberg to Hayes, 11, 12, 16 Dec. 1946 (CJCNA, ZC, SC).

70 Letter, Hayes to Moscovich, 16 Dec. 1946 (CJCNA, ZA 1947, box 2, file 7E).

71 "The Nation's Business," CBC Radio broadcast, 18 Dec. 1946 (CJCNA, ZA 1947, box 1, file 7A).

72 Low's views on Jews and international political Zionism were explained by Kirkland Lee, a Mormon and Social Crediter from Cardston, Alberta, who was on friendly terms with Low and had recently been debating Zionist theory with him. Lee explained that "Social Crediters who follow Jaques – believe that when the Jews were first driven from Palestine – 2 classes came into existence – Those who returned to Palestine – and those who were dispersed elsewhere. Those dispersed – are the 'International Political Zionists.'" Consequently, "some who oppose International Political Zionism do so with the feeling that there are two classes of Jews. Good Jews who returned from captivity under the reign of King Darius about 536 B.C. and those who are bad Jews who are not of this group but were to be scattered about the earth and destroyed. In the bad group have been classified the International Zionists. From

such a point of view you can see how these exponents claim to be both Anti and Pro Semetic." Lee added that this theory "does not voice the opinion of myself or the belief of our [Mormon] church." Low had also told Lee "he holds no prejudice or animosity towards the Jews," and that his recent radio broadcast discussing "international political Zionism" referred only to "those people who strive for a complete autonomous state in Palestine without proper recognition to minority groups." Letter, Lee to Moscovich, 28 Dec. 1946 (CJCNA, ZA 1947, box 2, file 7E); Letters, Moscovich to Hayes, 26, 30 Dec. 1946 (CJCNA, ZA 1947, box 2, file 7E).

73 Letter, Moscovich to Hayes, 18 Dec. 1946 (CJCNA, ZA 1947, box 2, file 7E); Letter, Dower to Hayes, 4 Jan. 1947 (CJCNA, ZA 1947, box 2, file 7E).

74 Letter, Moscovich to Hayes, 18 Dec. 1946 (CJCNA, ZA 1947, box 2, file 7E).

75 Letter, Hayes to Moscovich, 23 Dec. 1946 (CJCNA, ZA 1947, box 2, file 7E).

76 Letter, Moscovich to Hayes, 26 Dec. 1946 (CJCNA, ZA 1947, box 2, file 7E).

77 Minutes, Eastern Region JPRC Meeting, 23 Jan. 1947 (CJCNA, ZA 1945, box 2, file 19).

78 Letter, Bronfman to Dunton, 23 Jan. 1947 (CJCNA, ZC, SC).

79 Canada, *Acts of the Parliament of the Dominion of Canada*, 1936, 148; *Consolidated Regulations of Canada*, vol. 4, 2559.

80 One of the passages from *Mein Kampf* that Bronfman used stated: "For while the Zionists try to make the rest of the world believe that the national consciousness of the Jew finds its satisfaction in the creation of a Palestinian state ... all they want is a central organization for their international world swindle." Hitler, *Mein Kampf*, 324–5; Letter, Bronfman to Dunton, 23 Jan. 1947 (CJCNA, ZC, SC).

81 Letter, Bronfman to Dunton, 23 Jan. 1947 (CJCNA, ZC, SC).

82 Congress had further dealings with the chairman of the CBC board of governors. In early 1947 national executive director Hayes met with Dunton personally, although no record of their meeting could be found. Minutes, national JPRC meeting, 23 Feb. 1947 (CJCNA, ZA 1947, box 9, file 104).

83 Memo, Zimmerman to Hayes, 5 Mar. 1947 (CJCNA, ZA 1947, box 2, file 7E); Report, Winnipeg JPRC Meeting, 17 Feb. 1947 (CJCNA, ZA 1947, box 2, file 7E).

84 Ibid. Frank refused to write a report on his discussions with Low because he considered the matter too confidential and "nothing could be committed to writing." When the rabbi reported to the Western Division JPRC on 17 February 1947, it was to a so-called "inner

committee," and the secretary was instructed not to take any minutes. Immediately following the meeting, executive director Zimmerman wrote a report.

85 "Content Analysis of the *Canadian Social Crediter*," c. 29 Jan. 1947 (CJCNA, ZC, SC); Memo, Rosenberg to Hayes, 5 Feb. 1947 (CJCNA, CA, box 33, file 306; CJCNA, ZC, SC).

86 "Content Analysis of the *Canadian Social Crediter*," c. 29 Jan. 1947 (CJCNA, ZC, SC); Harvey, *Tremeear's Annotated Criminal Code*, 1944, sections 133–5, 317, pp 138–42, 367.

87 "Content Analysis of the *Canadian Social Crediter*," c. 29 Jan. 1947 (CJCNA, ZC, SC); Harvey, *Tremeear's Annotated Criminal Code*, 1944, sections 323, 330, pp 368, 370.

88 "Content Analysis of the *Canadian Social Crediter*," c. 29 Jan. 1947 (CJCNA, ZC, SC); Canada, *Revised Statutes of Canada*, 1927, vol. 3, section 7(d), 3079–80.

89 Specifically, Rosenberg referred to the Plamondon libel case of 1910, involving a Quebec notary who invoked the "ritual murder" charge against Jews. Leading figures in the Quebec Jewish community launched a libel action against Joseph Plamondon, but because "the law of libel did not cover group defamation, and, since Plamondon was not accusing any *particular* Jew of these abominations, the court found for the defendant." Tulchinsky, *Taking Root*, 253; "Content Analysis of the *Canadian Social Crediter*," c. 29 Jan. 1947 (CJCNA, ZC, SC).

90 "Proceedings of the Seventh Plenary Session," 31 May-2 June 1947 (PAM, JHSWC Collection, MG6 B3).

91 Ibid.

92 Memo, Hayes to National Executive Officers Only, 18 Feb. 1947 (CJCNA, ZC, SC).

93 Ibid. Hayes told Low communism and Zionism were not friendly ideologies because "Zionism was counterrevolutionary in the U.S.S.R., that Palestine is being built by private enterprise and by the Histadrut [the General Federation of Hebrew Workers] both of which considered Communism their mortal enemy and that the largest proportion of Jews are anxious to see Zionism succeed which means that a tie-up or alliance with Communism is not only untrue but impossible and a fantastic conclusion."

94 Ibid.

95 Ibid.

96 Ibid.

97 Ibid.

98 Ibid.

99 Minutes, National JPRC Meeting, 23 Feb. 1947 (CJCNA, ZA 1947, box 9, file 104).

100 The records do not indicate why Feinberg was not part of this meeting.
101 Memo, Hayes to National Executive, 4 Mar. 1947 (CJCNA, ZC, SC).
102 Ibid.
103 Ibid.
104 *Congress Bulletin*, Dec. 1946 (CJCNA, *Bulletins*); reprint of article, attached to letter, Gillese to Low, 26 Mar. 1947 (Glenbow, Solon Low Papers, M695, file 173).
105 Memo, Hayes to National Executive, 4 Mar. 1947 (CJCNA, ZC, SC).
106 Ibid.
107 Ibid.
108 Ibid.
109 Ibid.
110 Congress memo, n.d. (CJCNA, ZA 1947, box 1, file 7D).
111 Ibid.
112 Ibid.
113 Ibid.
114 Ibid.
115 Ibid.
116 Caiserman, "National Plan of the Public Relations Work to be Carried on in Canada by the Joint Public Relations Committee of the Canadian Jewish Congress and B'nai B'rith of Canada," c. 1947 (PAM, JHSWC Collection, P600 A).

CHAPTER SIX

1 Letter, Green to Hayes, 24 Feb. 1947 (CJCNA, ZA 1947, box 2, file 7E); Letter, Jacks to Hayes, 27 Feb. 1947 (CJCNA, ZA 1947, box 2, file 7E).
2 Memo, Zimmerman to Hayes, 5 Mar. 1947 (CJCNA, ZA 1947, box 2, file 7E); Report, Edmonton JPRC Meeting, 7–8 Feb. 1947 (CJCNA, ZA 1947, box 2, file 7E).
3 Letter, Bercuson to Hayes, 23 Apr. 1947 (CJCNA, ZA 1947, box 1, file 7D).
4 "The Social Credit Movement and Canadian Jewry," 22 May 1947 (CJCNA, ZA 1947, box 1, file 7C).
5 Ibid.
6 "Report of Hayes's interview with Bercuson," 21 May 1947 (CJCNA, ZA 1947, box 1, file 7C).
7 In the 1944 Alberta provincial election the CCF won 70,307 votes, amounting to 24.92 per cent of the popular vote, but won only two seats in the legislature. Alberta, *A Report on Alberta Elections*, 14.
8 In 1946 Alfred Hooke, provincial secretary and former chairman of the Alberta Social Credit Board, announced that the Alberta government would ban "communist propaganda" films. Accordingly, the government

extended its censorship laws to cover 16 mm films, which were often believed to contain communist material. As Finkel notes, "Within a year several 16 mm films had been banned for political reasons, including a British Information Office film that gave unreserved support to the United Nations and warned strongly against race hatred." *The Social Credit Phenomenon in Alberta*, 108.

9 "The Social Credit Movement and Canadian Jewry," 22 May 1947 (CJCNA, ZA 1947, box 1, file 7C).

10 Letter, Hayes to Bercuson, 13 June 1947 (CJCNA, ZA 1947, box 1, file 7C); Letter, Bercuson to Hayes, 2 June 1947 (CJCNA, ZA 1947, box 1, file 7C).

11 Letter, Bercuson to Hayes, 23 June 1947 (CJCNA, ZA 1947, box 1, file 7D).

12 Minutes, National JPRC Meeting, 9 July 1947 (CJCNA, ZA 1947, box 9, file 104).

13 Ibid.

14 Ibid.; Letter, Bercuson to Hayes, 23 June 1947 (CJCNA, ZA 1947, box 1, file 7D).

15 Annual Report, Alberta Social Credit Board, 1946 (CJCNA, ZA 1947, box 2, file 8).

16 Ibid.

17 Ibid.

18 *Edmonton Journal*, 1 Apr. 1947.

19 *Calgary Herald*, 28 Mar. 1947.

20 *Edmonton Journal*, 28 Mar. 1947.

21 *New Voice*, Mar. 1947.

22 *Canadian Social Crediter*, 3 Apr. 1947.

23 *Calgary Albertan*, 5 Apr. 1947.

24 *Lethbridge Herald*, 16 Apr. 1947.

25 *Canadian Social Crediter*, 17 Apr. 1947; *People's Weekly*, 5 Apr. 1947; Memo, Rosenberg to Hayes, 25 Apr. 1947 (CJCNA, ZA 1947, box 1, file 7B; CJCNA, ZC, SC).

26 Memo, Rosenberg to Hayes, 25 Apr. 1947 (CJCNA, ZA 1947, box 1, file 7B; CJCNA, ZC, SC); *Canadian Social Crediter*, 13 Mar. 1947.

27 *New York Post*, 7 May 1947; *Montreal Star*, 7 May 1947.

28 *Montreal Gazette*, 9 May 1947; Canada, Commons, *Debates*, 8 May 1947, 2872.

29 *Montreal Star*, 9 May 1947.

30 *Montreal Herald*, 9 May 1947.

31 *Montreal Gazette*, 10 May 1947.

32 Ibid., 12 May 1947.

33 Ibid., 13 May 1947; Canada, Commons, *Debates*, 12 May 1947, 2982.

34 Canada, Commons, *Debates*, 14 May 1947, 3089; *Montreal Star*, 15 May 1947; *Montreal Gazette*, 15 May 1947; *Ottawa Journal*, 16 May 1947; *Windsor Daily Star*, 15 May 1947.

35 Rycroft, *A Critical Dictionary of Psychoanalysis*, 28–9, 111.

36 *Montreal Gazette*, 15 May 1947; *Ottawa Journal*, 16 May 1947; *Montreal Star*, 15 May 1947.

37 *Calgary Albertan*, 15 May 1947.

38 *Wetaskiwin Times*, 21 May 1947.

39 Letter, Hayes to West, 12 May 1947 (CJCNA, CA, box 33, file 306); Letter, West to Hayes, 13 May 1947 (CJCNA, CA, box 33, file 306); Letter, Peters to Hayes, 9 May 1947 (CJCNA, CA, box 33, file 306); Bulletin, Hayes to National and Regional Public Relations Committees, 15 May 1947 (CJCNA, CA, box 33, file 306).

40 Letter, Hayes to Forster, 19 May 1947 (CJCNA, ZA 1947, box 1, file 7B).

41 Memo, Rosenberg to Hayes, 10 June 1948 (CJCNA, ZC, SC); Memo, Rosenberg to Hayes, 14 Oct. 1948 (CJCNA, ZA 1949, box 3, file 28; CJCNA, ZC, SC).

42 Memo, Rosenberg to Hayes, 15 July 1948 (CJCNA, ZA 1948, box 7, file 83; CJCNA, DA2, box 3, file 4).

43 Caunt, *An Editor on Trial*, 3–4; Basic Books Advertisement, Sept. 1948 (CJCNA, ZA 1949, box 3, file 28; CJCNA, ZC, SC); Memo, Rosenberg to Hayes, 14 Oct. 1948 (CJCNA, ZA 1949, box 3, file 28; CJCNA, ZC, SC).

44 Jensen, *The "Palestine" Plot*, 7; Basic Books Advertisement, September 1948 (CJCNA, ZA 1949, box 3, file 28; CJCNA, ZC, SC); Memo, Rosenberg to Hayes, 14 Oct. 1948 (CJCNA, ZA 1949, box 3, file 28; CJCNA, ZC, SC).

45 Weston, *Father of Lies*, 12, 14, 143; Basic Books advertisement, 30 July 1947 (CJCNA, ZC, SC); Memo, Rosenberg to Hayes, 7 Aug. 1947 (CJCNA, ZC, SC); Memo, Rosenberg to Hayes, 29 Oct. 1947 (CJCNA, ZA 1947, box 1, file 7).

46 Basic Books advertisement, c. Nov. 1947 (CJCNA, ZA 1947, box 1, file 7A; CJCNA, ZC, SC); Memos, Rosenberg to Hayes, 2 Dec. 1947, 12 Dec. 1947 (CJCNA, ZC, SC).

47 Memo, Rosenberg to Hayes, 7 Aug. 1947 (CJCNA, ZC, SC); Memo, Rosenberg to Hayes, 2 Dec. 1947 (CJCNA, ZA 1947, box 1, file 7A; CJCNA, ZC, SC); Basic Books advertisement, 3 May 1947 (CJCNA, ZC, SC).

48 Memo, Rosenberg to Hayes, 20 May 1947 (CJCNA, ZC, SC).

49 Minutes, National JPRC Meeting, 9 July 1947 (CJCNA, ZA 1947, box 9, file 104).

50 Shupe, *Wealth and Power in American Zion*, 229–33.

51 *Lethbridge Herald*, 27 Dec. 1947; *Montreal Star*, 29 Dec. 1947; *Montreal Gazette*, 29 Dec. 1947; *Montreal Standard*, 27 Dec. 1947.

52 *Canadian Baptist*, 15 July 1947, 1 Aug. 1947; Memo, Kayfetz to Hayes, 18 July 1947 (CJCNA, ZA 1947, box 1, file 7B); Memo, Kayfetz to Rome, 5 Aug. 1947 (CJCNA, CD, box 7, file 11P).

53 Minutes, National JPRC Meeting, 9 July 1947 (CJCNA, ZA 1947, box 9, file 104).

54 Letter, Haering to Forster, 14 Aug. 1947 (CJCNA, CA, box 33, file 306).

55 Apparently, years earlier Smith was opposed to the Catholic Church. Congress hoped that French Canadians could be rallied against Social Credit once Smith's and Jaques's anti-Catholic biases were confirmed. In this way, an exposure of Social Credit's anti-Catholicism would help to broaden the base of its opposition. Memo, Kirshnblatt to Hayes, 8 Sept. 1947 (CJCNA, ZA 1947, box 1, file 7B); Letter, Kirshnblatt to Sheinberg, 9 Sept. 1947 (CJCNA, ZA 1947, box 1, file 7B); Letter, Kirshnblatt to Bercuson, 9 Sept. 1947 (CJCNA, ZA 1947, box 1, file 7B); Letter, Kirshnblatt to Birkhead, 9 Sept. 1947 (CJCNA, CA, box 33, file 306); *Montreal Gazette*, 12 May 1947.

56 Letter, Sheinberg to Kirshnblatt, 11 Sept. 1947 (CJCNA, CA, box 33, file 306).

57 Bercuson did not mention which Social Credit politicians held anti-Catholic views, and there is little evidence of any anti-Catholicism within Social Credit. In fact, Social Credit MLAs A.V. Bourcier (Lac Ste Anne), W.F. Gilliland (Peace River), Lucien Maynard (St Albert), and J. William Beaudry (St Paul) represented franco-Albertan minorities. Letter, Bercuson to Kirshnblatt, 26 Sept. 1947 (CJCNA, ZA 1947, box 1, file 7B).

58 Memo, Kirshnblatt to Hayes, 8 Sept. 1947 (CJCNA, ZA 1947, box 1, file 7B).

59 *Canadian Social Crediter*, 23, 30 Oct. 1947, 11, 18 Dec. 1947.

60 *Canadian Social Crediter*, 18 Sept. 1947; Memo, Rosenberg to Hayes, 20 Oct. 1947 (CJCNA, ZA 1947, box 1, file 7A).

61 *Canadian Social Crediter*, 13 Nov. 1947; Memo, Rosenberg to Hayes, 21 Nov. 1947 (CJCNA, ZA 1947, box 1, file 7).

62 *Canadian Social Crediter*, 30 Oct. 1947; Memo, Rosenberg to Hayes, 7 Nov. 1947 (CJCNA, ZA 1947, box 1, file 7).

63 Gillese, "To Contributors and Directors of Policy," c. 1946 (Glenbow, Patrick Ashby Papers, box M31, file 6).

64 Letter, Gillese to Low, 13 May 1947 (Glenbow, Solon Low Papers, box M695, file 173).

65 Letter, Manning to Haldeman, 21 May 1947 (PAA, Alberta Social Credit League, file 1472).

66 Letter, Manning to Jukes, 20 May 1947 (PAA, Alberta Social Credit League, file 1472).

67 Ibid.; Letter, Manning to Haldeman, 21 May 1947 (PAA, Alberta Social Credit League, file 1472).

68 Letter, Byrne to Low, 14 Apr. 1947 (Glenbow, Solon Low Papers, box M695, file 35).

69 *Edmonton Journal*, 11 Sept. 1947; *Montreal Star*, 12 Sept. 1947; *Montreal Gazette*, 12 Sept. 1947.

70 Letter, Manning to Jukes, 2 Oct. 1947 (PAA, Alberta Social Credit League, file 1472).

71 Minutes, National Council Meeting of the Social Credit Association of Canada, 29–30 Nov. 1947 (Glenbow, Solon Low Papers, box M695, file 469); Letter, Gillese to Haldeman, 15 Dec. 1947 (Glenbow, Solon Low Papers, box M695, file 173).

72 *Calgary Albertan*, 15 Dec. 1947; *Edmonton Bulletin*, 13 Dec. 1947; *Edmonton Journal*, 15 Dec. 1947; *Lethbridge Herald*, 15 Dec. 1947; *Montreal Gazette*, 16–17 Dec. 1947; *Wetaskiwin Times*, 17 Dec. 1947; Memo, Rosenberg to Hayes, 12 Jan. 1948 (CJCNA, ZC, SC).

73 Minutes, National Council Meeting of the Social Credit Association of Canada, 29–30 Nov. 1947 (Glenbow, Solon Low Papers, box M695, file 469).

74 Ibid.; "Those Who Have Ears – Let Them Hear!" attached to letter, Taylor to Low, 23 Dec. 1947 (PAA, Alberta Social Credit League, file 1472).

75 World News Services, "Anti-Semites Curbed In Social Credit Appeal For Support of Electors," c. Dec. 1947 (CJCNA, ZC, SC).

76 Report of the Thirteenth Annual Provincial Convention of the Alberta Social Credit League, 27–28 Nov. 1947 (PAA, Alberta Social Credit League, file 1472); *Canadian Social Crediter*, 4 Dec. 1947.

77 *Calgary Herald*, 17 Dec. 1947.

78 Memo, Rosenberg to Hayes, 16 Dec. 1947 (CJCNA, ZC, SC).

79 Ibid.

80 Memo, Rosenberg to Hayes, 21 Nov. 1947 (CJCNA, ZA 1947, box 1, file 7); Memo, Rosenberg to Hayes, 12 Dec. 1947 (CJCNA, ZC, SC).

81 Memo, Rosenberg to Hayes, 12 Dec. 1947 (CJCNA, ZC, SC); *Canadian Social Crediter*, 4 Dec. 1947.

82 Memo, Rosenberg to Hayes, 16 Dec. 1947 (CJCNA, ZC, SC).

83 Ibid.

84 Ibid.

85 Letter, Bercuson to Hayes, 17 Dec. 1947 (CJCNA, CD, box 7, file 11P).

86 *Canadian Social Crediter*, 11 Dec. 1947; Memo, Rosenberg to Hayes, 19 Dec. 1947 (CJCNA, ZC, SC); Memo, Kirshnblatt to Hayes, 31 Dec. 1947 (CJCNA, ZC, SC).

87 *Edmonton Journal*, 4 Mar. 1947.

CHAPTER SEVEN

1 *Calgary Herald,* 24 Jan. 1948.
2 *Canadian Social Crediter,* 20 Feb. 1947; Memo, Kirshnblatt to Hayes, 3 Nov. 1947 (CJCNA, ZA 1949, box 3, file 31). For a discussion of the Union des Electeurs and the Social Credit movement in Quebec, see Stein, "Social Credit in the Province of Quebec," in Clark et al., *Prophecy and Protest,* 347–65; Stein, *The Dynamics of Right-Wing Protest*; Pinard, "One-Party Dominance and Third Parties," 358–73, and *The Rise of a Third Party.*
3 *Le Soleil,* 10 Dec. 1948; *Montreal Herald,* 12 Mar., 10 Dec. 1948; *Winnipeg Citizen,* 13 Mar. 1948; Letter, Kirshnblatt to Aronsfeld, 3 Sept. 1948 (CJCNA, ZA 1948, box 1, file 7).
4 Letter, Kirshnblatt to Aronsfeld, 3 Sept. 1948 (CJCNA, ZA 1948, box 1, file 7); Memo, Kirshnblatt to Hayes, 19 Feb. 1948 (CJCNA, ZA 1949, box 3, file 31); *Canadian Social Crediter,* 4 Dec. 1947.
5 *L'Evenement Journal,* 12 Jan. 1948; *Lethbridge Herald,* 12 Jan. 1948; *Montreal Daily Star,* 12 Jan. 1948.
6 Memo, Kirshnblatt to Hayes, 10 Feb. 1948 (CJCNA, ZA 1949, box 3, file 31).
7 *Vers Demain,* 15 Feb. 1948; Memo, Kirshnblatt to Hayes, 19 Feb. 1948 (CJCNA, ZA 1949, box 3, file 31).
8 *Canadian Jewish Chronicle,* 9 Jan. 1948; Memo, Kirshnblatt to Hayes, 19 Feb. 1948 (CJCNA, ZA 1949, box 3, file 31).
9 *Vers Demain,* 15 Feb. 1948. The *Canadian Social Crediter* denied any meeting between Social Credit leaders and Congress: "It is with some dismay we learn [of the] article published in the *Canadian Jewish Chronicle* ... The Social Credit Association of Canada is not anti-semitic and we wish to inform our readers that we know nothing of the above-alleged meeting. This paper will not carry 'anti-semitic' articles, not because of any conference with the Canadian Jewish Congress but because this is the policy of the Social Credit Association of Canada." Interestingly, Congress recorded no meeting between Fine and Social Credit either. *Canadian Social Crediter,* 4 Mar., 22 Apr. 1948; Memo, Rosenberg to Hayes, 29 Apr. 1948 (CJCNA, ZC, SC).
10 *Canadian Social Crediter,* 17 July 1947; Letter, Wax to Kirshnblatt, 11 June 1948 (CJCNA, ZA 1947, box 1, file 7D); Memo, Rosenberg to Hayes, 4 Aug. 1947 (CJCNA, ZA 1947, box 1, file 7).
11 The emergency convention of the Ontario Social Credit League was held at the King Edward Hotel in Toronto on 1–2 Oct. 1947. Memo, Kayfetz

to Kirshnblatt, 3 Oct. 1947 (CJCNA, ZA 1947, box 1, file 7C); *Canadian Social Crediter*, 9, 16 Oct. 1947.

12 Memo, Kayfetz to Kirshnblatt, 3 Oct. 1947 (CJCNA, ZA 1947, box 1, file 7C); Letter, Kirshnblatt to Wax, 4 June 1948 (CJCNA, ZA 1947, box 1, file 7D); Letter, Kayfetz to author, 22 Jan. 1999.

13 Letter, Wax to Kirshnblatt, 11 June 1948 (CJCNA, ZA 1947, box 1, file 7D); Memo, Kayfetz to Kirshnblatt, 3 Oct. 1947 (CJCNA, ZA 1947, box 1, file 7C); *Canadian Social Crediter*, 9 Oct. 1947; Letter, Kayfetz to author, 22 Jan. 1999.

14 *Voice of the Electors*, 1 May 1948, 1 July 1948, 31 Jan. 1949 (CJCNA, ZA 1947, box 1, file 7D); Memo, Kayfetz to Feinberg, 11 May 1948 (CJCNA, ZA 1947, box 1, file 7D).

15 New anti-Semitic treatises included Gerald L.K. Smith's *Is Communism Jewish?* whose title is self-explanatory, and a pamphlet entitled *Does it Fit the Facts?* which was a reprint of correspondence between Douglas and a Reverend Salis Daiches discussing the authenticity of the *Protocols of the Learned Elders of Zion*. Smith, *Is Communism Jewish?* n.d. (CJCNA, ZA 1948, box 7, file 83); "Does it Fit the Facts?" n.d. (CJCNA, ZC, SC); Basic Books advertisements, 3 May 1948, June 1948 (CJCNA, ZC, SC); Letter, Basic Books, Sept. 1948 (CJCNA, ZA 1949, box 3, file 28); Memos, Rosenberg to Hayes, 12 Apr. 1948, 10 June 1948 (CJCNA, ZC, SC); Memo, Kirshnblatt to Hayes, 16 Dec. 1947 (CJCNA, ZA 1947, box 1, file 7B).

16 "To All Canadian Social Crediters – Mobilization for Action," n.d. (Glenbow, Norman James Papers, box M574, file 6).

17 Douglas Social Credit Council circular, n.d. (PAA, Alberta Social Credit League, file 1830).

18 DSCC *Information Service*, Oct. 1948 (CJCNA, ZA 1949, box 3, file 28); Memo, Rosenberg to Hayes, 21 Jan. 1949 (CJCNA, ZC, SC); Memo, Rosenberg to Hayes, 7 Feb. 1949 (CJCNA, DA2, box 3, file 4).

19 Barr, *The Dynasty*, 130.

20 *Calgary Albertan*, 23 Feb. 1948; *Calgary Herald*, 23 Feb. 1948; *Edmonton Bulletin*, 23 Feb. 1948; *Edmonton Journal*, 23 Feb. 1948; *Lethbridge Herald*, 23 Feb. 1948; *Medicine Hat Daily News*, 23 Feb. 1948; *Peace River Record-Gazette*, 26 Feb. 1948.

21 Letter, Kirshnblatt to Aronsfeld, 3 Sept. 1948 (CJCNA, ZA 1948, box 1, file 7); Letter, Wax to Kirshnblatt, 11 June 1948 (CJCNA, ZA 1947, box 1, file 7D); DSCC *Information Service*, Sept. 1948 (CJCNA, ZA 1949, box 3, file 28); Memo, Kirshnblatt to Hayes, 24 Sept. 1948 (CJCNA, ZA 1949, box 3, file 28); Memo, Rosenberg to Hayes, 15 Jan. 1948 (CJCNA, ZC, SC); *Canadian Jewish Weekly*, 25 Dec. 1947; *Lethbridge Herald*, 23 Feb. 1948; *Montreal Daily Star*, 11 Dec. 1947; *Time* (Canada), 8 Mar. 1948; *Victoria Daily Times*, 11 Dec. 1947.

22 R.E. Ansley, MLA for Leduc, was re-elected in the Alberta provincial election on 17 Aug. 1948, as was A.V. Bourcier, MLA for Lac Ste Anne. At the federal level, Norman Jaques was renominated as Social Credit candidate for Wetaskiwin in 1948, but died before the 1949 general election. *Canadian Parliamentary Guide,* 1949 ed., 423–8.

23 The DSCC had difficulty publishing regular issues of the *Social Credit Challenge,* ostensibly because of financial problems but also because of strong criticism by Manning's movement. Before the 1948 provincial election, for example, the DSCC suspended publication of the *Challenge* because of conflict between it and the Alberta Social Credit League. At other times the DSCC published only the DSCC *Information Service* bulletin. Letter, Douglas Social Credit Council, 12 Sept. 1948 (CJCNA, ZA 1949, box 3, file 28); DSCC *Information Service,* Sept. 1948 (CJCNA, ZA 1949, box 3, file 28).

24 Ibid.; Letter, Basic Books, Sept. 1948 (CJCNA, ZA 1949, box 3, file 28).

25 Douglas, "Social Credit in Alberta," cited in DSCC *Information Service,* Sept. 1948 (CJCNA, ZA 1949, box 3, file 28); Letter, Kirshnblatt to Frank, 15 July 1948 (CJCNA, ZA 1949, box 3, file 28); Memo, Kirshnblatt to Hayes, 24 Sept. 1948 (CJCNA, ZA 1949, box 3, file 28).

26 Memo, Kayfetz to Feinberg, 11 May 1948 (CJCNA, ZA 1947, box 1, file 7D).

27 "Summary of Activities of the National Joint Public Relations Committee of the Canadian Jewish Congress and the B'nai B'rith," c. 1948 (CJCNA, ZA 1948, box 10).

28 Ibid.

29 *Canadian Social Crediter,* 11, 18, 25 Dec. 1947, 1, 8 Jan. 1948, 4 Mar. 1948, 15, 22, 29 July 1948; Memos, Rosenberg to Hayes, 6, 12, 15 Jan. 1948 (CJCNA, ZC, SC).

30 Letter, Bercuson to Hayes, 2 Jan. 1948 (CJCNA, CD, box 7, file 11P).

31 Memo, Rosenberg to Hayes, 11 Mar. 1948 (CJCNA, ZA 1948, box 1, file 7).

32 Letter, Bercuson to Hayes, 22 Mar. 1948 (CJCNA, ZA 1948, box 1, file 7); Letter, Bercuson to Kirshnblatt, 24 Feb. 1948 (CJCNA, ZA 1948, box 1, file 7); Letter, Bercuson to Hayes, 24 Feb. 1948 (CJCNA, CD, box 7, file 11P).

33 Memo, Rosenberg to Hayes, 31 Mar. 1948 (CJCNA, ZA 1948, box 1, file 7).

34 Congress continued to inform other Jewish organizations of Social Credit developments. In early 1948 it sent nearly a dozen "content analyses" of the *Canadian Social Crediter* to the Commission of Law and Social Action of the American Jewish Congress for its perusal. Letter, Kirshnblatt to Sultan, 28 Jan. 1948 (CJCNA, ZA 1948, box 7, file 83).

35 *Vancouver News-Herald*, 27 Dec. 1947. Congress was not pleased that a Jew was the Alberta government's official printer. As Rosenberg explained: "Shnitka is a Jew, formerly a poor and struggling job printer of the city of Calgary, who was one of Wm. Aberhart's early disciples, and was rewarded by being appointed King's Printer. In spite of the rank anti-Semitism displayed by the Social Credit Party, Shnitka has no scruples about printing these anti-Semitic pamphlets and allowing his name to be used as alleged proof that the Social Credit Movement is not anti-Semitic, since the Social Credit Party has appointed a Jew as its King's Printer." Rosenberg pointed specifically to the pamphlet *Battle for Freedom*, published by the Social Credit Board and printed by the King's Printer. As will be recalled, this was a reprint of Byrne's anti-Semitic address to the Rocky Mountain House Board of Trade in 1943. Memo, Rosenberg to Hayes, 27 June 1947 (CJCNA, ZA 1947, box 1, file 7); *Today and Tomorrow*, 13 May 1943.

36 *Vancouver News-Herald*, 27 Dec. 1947.

37 Letter, Rosenberg to Fradkin, 13 Mar. 1944 (CJCNA, ZA 1945, box 7, file 100).

38 Memo, Rome to Hayes, 5 Jan. 1948 (CJCNA, CD, box 7, file 11P).

39 Letter, A.J. Livinson to editor of *Vancouver News-Herald*, 12 Jan. 1948 (CJCNA, CD, box 7, file 11P).

40 *Vancouver News-Herald*, 3 Feb. 1948.

41 *Canadian Social Crediter*, 15 Jan. 1948.

42 Memo, Rosenberg to Hayes, 23 Jan. 1948 (CJCNA, ZC, SC).

43 Gillese, Douglas Social Credit Council circular, n.d. (PAA, Alberta Social Credit League, file 1830).

44 *Canadian Social Crediter*, 25 Mar. 1948; Memo, Rosenberg to Hayes, 1 Apr. 1948 (CJCNA, ZC, SC).

45 Memo, Rosenberg to Hayes, 12 Apr. 1948 (CJCNA, ZC, SC); Memo, Rosenberg to Hayes, 1 Apr. 1948 (CJCNA, ZC, SC).

46 *Canadian Social Crediter*, 20 May 1948.

47 *Social Crediter* (Liverpool), 27 Mar. 1948, cited in *Edmonton Bulletin*, 16 Apr. 1948.

48 *Edmonton Bulletin*, 16 Apr. 1948; Letter, Bercuson to Hayes, 20 Apr. 1948 (CJCNA, ZA 1948, box 1, file 7).

49 Letter, Bercuson to Hayes, 20 Apr. 1948 (CJCNA, ZA 1948, box 1, file 7); Letter, Bercuson to Hayes, 26 Apr. 1948 (CJCNA, CD, box 7, file 11P); *Edmonton Bulletin*, 21 Apr. 1948.

50 Letters, Bridges to Manning, 6 May 1948, 6 June 1948; Letter, Heslop to Manning, 10 Oct. 1948; Letter, Olson to Manning, 5 Mar. 1948; Letter, Wasse to Manning, 27 Feb. 1948 (PAA, Alberta Social Credit League, file 1830).

51 Letter, Downey to Manning, 10 June 1948 (PAA, Alberta Social Credit League, file 1830).

52 Letters, Premier to Bridges, 13 May 1948, 24 June 1948; Letter, Premier to Heslop, 13 Oct. 1948; Letter, Premier to Johnson, 15 Mar. 1948; Letter, Premier to Lindsey, 11 Mar. 1948; Letter, Premier to McIntyre, 29 Dec. 1948; Letter, Premier to McKinney, 12 Mar. 1948; Letter, Premier to Meeres, 11 Mar. 1948; Letter, Premier to Menzies, 11 Mar. 1948; Letter, Premier to Oddson, 15 Mar. 1948; Letter, Premier to Olson, 11 Mar. 1948; Letter, Premier to Parsons, 12 Mar. 1948; Letter, Premier to Payne, 12 Mar. 1948; Letter, Premier to Robson, 12 Mar. 1948; Letter, Premier to Shaw, 15 Mar. 1948; Letter, Premier to Wasse, 12 Mar. 1948; Letter, Elliott [executive secretary] to Downey, 16 June 1948 (PAA, Alberta Social Credit League, file 1830).

53 Letter, Manning to Lindsey, 11 Mar. 1948 (PAA, Alberta Social Credit League, file 1830).

54 The Union des Electeurs ran ninety-two candidates in ninety-two constituencies in the 1948 Quebec provincial election, a number equal to the Liberals and greater than the Union Nationale, which ran ninety-one. *Statistiques Électorales du Québec*, 2nd ed., 631.

55 Memo, Kirshnblatt to Hayes, 8 Mar. 1948 (CJCNA, ZA 1949, box 3, file 31).

56 Julien Morissette, a French Catholic journalist, used *La Frontière* (whose motto was "conservons notre héritage français") as a forum to denounce the Social Credit Party and, specifically, the Union des Electeurs. *La Frontière*, 29 Apr. 1948, 27 May 1948, 3, 10, 17, 24 June 1948, 1, 8, 15 July 1948, 5 Aug. 1948.

57 The Quebec Catholic hierarchy was concerned with what it perceived to be the anti-clerical and demagogic nature of the Union des Electeurs. Monseigneur Joseph Desmarais, bishop of Amos, publicly criticized the Union and believed it important to "alert ... our faithful against the danger of bad shepherds who could possibly lead them onto the road of perdition." He also instructed parish priests in northwestern Quebec not to permit Union des Electeurs meetings in their parish halls. *Canadian Social Crediter*, 15 July 1948; *Montreal Herald*, 4 May 1948; Memos, Kirshnblatt to Hayes, 30 Mar. 1948, 13 Apr. 1948 (CJCNA, ZC, SC).

58 Memo, Kirshnblatt to Hayes, 27 May 1948 (CJCNA, ZA 1949, box 3, file 31).

59 Throughout the spring and summer of 1948, in addition to publishing anti–Social Credit articles, *La Frontière* also published a series of "lettres ouvertes" to members of the Union des Electeurs castigating them for their materialism, affront to Church doctrine through lack of Christian charity, totalitarian and dictatorial measures that smacked of communism, and concomitant insistence that Social Credit was the only

solution to the spread of communism. *La Frontière*, 27 May 1948, 3, 10, 17, 24 June 1948, 1, 8, 15 July 1948, 1 Aug. 1948.

60 Memo, Kirshnblatt to Hayes, 29 June 1948 (CJCNA, ZA 1949, box 3, file 31).

61 In the 1948 Quebec election the Union des Electeurs won 140,050 votes out of a total of 1,531,899, a paltry 6.9 per cent of the popular vote. No members were elected on a Union des Electeurs ticket. *Statistiques Électorales du Québec*, 14.

62 It should be emphasized that in post-war America the extreme right wing, not the mainstream, directly connected anti-Semitism and anti-communism. In national opinion polls conducted from 1950 to 1954, "the image of the 'Jewish Communist' did not grow in prevalence during this period of increasingly militant anti-Communism ... The majority of Americans during the early 1950s plainly refused to consider Jews as a group communistic, and this refusal was in tune with the facts." Stember et al., *Jews in the Mind of America*, 157–69. On the extreme right wing in post-war America, see Bennett, *Party of Fear*; Hixson, *Search for the American Right Wing*; Sargent, *Extremism in America*.

63 *Voice of the Electors*, 1 May 1948.

64 Memo, Belack to Forster, 28 June 1948 (CJCNA, ZA 1947, box 1, file 7D).

65 Memo, Kirshnblatt to Hayes, 24 Sept. 1948 (CJCNA, ZA 1949, box 3, file 28); Letter, Kirshnblatt to Aronsfeld, 3 Sept. 1948 (CJCNA, ZA 1948, box 1, file 7).

66 Memo, Rosenberg to Hayes, 15 July 1948 (CJCNA, ZA 1947, box 1, file 7A).

67 *Canadian Social Crediter*, 15 July 1948; Memo, Rosenberg to Hayes, 23 July 1948 (CJCNA, ZA 1948, box 7, file 83).

68 Memo, Rosenberg to Hayes, 27 July 1948 (CJCNA, ZC, SC).

69 Memo, Kayfetz to Feinberg, 15 Nov. 1948 (CJCNA, ZC, SC).

70 *Montreal Gazette*, 9 Nov. 1948.

71 *Canadian Social Crediter*, 15, 22, 29 July 1948; Memo, Wax to Hayes et al., c. July 1948 (CJCNA, ZC, SC).

72 *Canadian Social Crediter*, 18 Nov. 1948; *Lethbridge Herald*, 25 Nov. 1948; *Montreal Daily Star*, 25 Nov. 1948; Memo, Rosenberg to Hayes, 30 Nov. 1948 (CJCNA, ZC, SC).

73 *Lethbridge Herald*, 25 Nov. 1948; *Medicine Hat Daily News*, 26 Nov. 1948; *Montreal Daily Star*, 25 Nov. 1948; Memo, Rosenberg to Hayes, 26 Dec. 1948 (CJCNA, ZC, SC).

74 *Montreal Daily Star*, 25 Nov. 1948; *Montreal Gazette*, 25 Nov. 1948; *Medicine Hat Daily News*, 25–26 Nov. 1948; *Canadian Social Crediter*, 2 Dec. 1948.

75 Memo, Rosenberg to Hayes, 30 Nov. 1948 (CJCNA, ZC, SC).

76 Letter, Raber to Congress, 25 Nov. 1948 (CJCNA, CD, box 7, file 11P).

77 Letter, Hayes to Raber, 1 Dec. 1948 (CJCNA, CD, box 7, file 11P).

78 *Medicine Hat Daily News*, 30 Nov. 1948.

79 *Canadian Social Crediter*, 16 Dec. 1948; Memo, Rosenberg to Hayes, 26 Dec. 1948 (CJCNA, ZC, SC).

80 Memo, Rosenberg to Hayes, 26 Dec. 1948 (CJCNA, ZC, SC).

81 *Canadian Social Crediter*, 16 Dec. 1948.

82 Low remained closer in views to the dissident Douglasites than to Manning. Years later, in an interview conducted by the CBC, Low continued to defend his view that there was a "close tie-up between international communism, international finance, and international political Zionism." Yet he did not consider this to be anti-Semitic, since "international political Zionism was not a movement composed entirely of Jewish people. They had a policy just the same as international communism had a policy." When asked point-blank if he was anti-Semitic, Low replied: "Not at all. As a matter of fact, I personally have a tolerant mind and attitude toward all groups and races of people. I have no prejudice in my mind against any particular racial group." Dominion Network [CBC], "Extract from Press Conference Interviewing Solon E. Low," 19 Nov. 1951 (PAM, JHSWC Collection, MG6 B3).

83 "Anti-Semitism in Canada – A Brief Review of 1948," 24 Dec. 1948 (CJCNA, ZA 1948, box 1, file 3).

84 DSCC *Information Service*, Oct. 1948 (CJCNA, ZA 1949, box 3, file 28); Speech, R.E. Ansley, MLA, Alberta Legislature Throne Debate, 1 Mar. 1949 (CJCNA, ZA 1949, box 3, file 28).

85 Memo, Rosenberg to Hayes, 21 Jan. 1949 (CJCNA, ZC, SC); Memo, Rosenberg to Hayes, 7 Feb. 1949 (CJCNA, DA2, box 3, file 4).

86 Memo, Kirshnblatt to Hayes, 1 Feb. 1949 (CJCNA, CA, box 33, file 306); Memo, Kirshnblatt to Sheinberg, 2 Feb. 1949 (CJCNA, CA, box 33, file 306).

87 *Canadian Jewish Weekly*, 3 Feb. 1949.

88 Canada, Commons, *Debates*, 31 Jan. 1949, 69; Memo, Rosenberg to Hayes, 11 Feb. 1949 (CJCNA, DA2, box 3, file 4).

89 *Canadian Jewish Chronicle*, 11 Feb. 1949.

90 Memo, Rosenberg to Hayes, 11 Feb. 1949 (CJCNA, DA2, box 3, file 4).

91 Speech, A.V. Bourcier, MLA, Alberta Legislature Throne Debate, Feb. 1949 (CJCNA, ZA 1949, box 3, file 28); Memo, Kayfetz to Rosenberg, 25 Apr. 1949 (CJCNA, ZC, SC).

92 Speech, R.E. Ansley, 1 Mar. 1949 (CJCNA, ZA 1949, box 3, file 28); Memo, Kayfetz to Rosenberg, 25 Apr. 1949 (CJCNA, ZC, SC).

93 Canada, Commons, *Debates*, 31 Jan. 1949, 70.

94 Memo, Rosenberg to Hayes, 11 Feb. 1949 (CJCNA, DA2, box 3, file 4).

95 *Canadian Social Crediter*, 3 Feb. 1949; Memo, Rosenberg to Hayes, 14 Feb. 1949 (CJCNA, DA2, box 3, file 4).

96 Memo, Rosenberg to Hayes, 23 Oct. 1947 (CJCNA, ZA 1947, box 1, file 7A); Bert Marcuse, "Is the Social Credit Movement Anti-Semitic?" c. 1949 (PAM, JHSWC Collection, P5128, file 20.5); Canada, Commons, *Debates*, 1947–49.

97 Telephone interview with Nanette McKay (née Jaques), Cobble Hill, BC, 19 Apr. 1992. When it was announced in Dec. 1947 that Jaques's writings would be barred from the *Canadian Social Crediter*, Nanette Jaques was a stenographer working for the party organ. She resigned along with Gillese and Burton. *Montreal Gazette*, 17 Dec. 1947; Memo, Kirshnblatt to Hayes, 17 Dec. 1947 (CJCNA, CD, box 7, file 11P).

98 On Social Credit's later incidents of anti-Semitism, see Bercuson and Wertheimer, *A Trust Betrayed*; Stingel, "Beyond the Purge: Reviewing the Social Credit Movement's Legacy of Intolerance," forthcoming in *Canadian Ethnic Studies*.

99 Palmer, "Ethnic Relations and the Paranoid Style," 24.

100 Abella and Troper, *None Is Too Many*, 231–2, 323; Stember et al., *Jews in the Mind of America*, 144–50, 216.

101 Bercuson, *Canada and the Birth of Israel*, 41.

102 Kay, *Canada and Palestine*, 148.

103 *Calgary Herald*, 28 Nov. 1949.

104 Macpherson, *Democracy in Alberta*, 206.

105 Francis, "'Rural Ontario West': Ontarians in Alberta," in Palmer and Palmer, *Peoples of Alberta*, 140.

106 Richards and Pratt, *Prairie Capitalism*, 78.

107 Barr, *The Dynasty*, 132, 157.

108 Macpherson, *Democracy in Alberta*, 209.

109 Finkel, "The Cold War, Alberta Labour, and the Social Credit Regime."

110 Young, *Democracy and Discontent*, 98.

111 *Manitoba Commonwealth*, 27 Sept. 1947.

112 Abella, *A Coat of Many Colours*, 213.

113 "Proceedings of the Seventh Plenary Session," 31 May–2 June 1947 (PAM, JHSWC Collection, MG6 B3).

114 Ibid.

115 National JPRC, "Public Relations in Theory and in Practice," c. 1950; "Declaration of Policy," c. 15 Aug. 1950 (PAM, JHSWC Collection, MG10, file 3 / MG8, file 3).

116 Abella, *A Coat of Many Colours*, 213–15.

117 "Summary of Activities of the National Joint Public Relations Committee of the Canadian Jewish Congress and the B'nai B'rith," c. 1948 (CJCNA, ZA 1948, box 10).

118 "Draft on Anti-Semitism in Canada," c. 1949 (CJCNA, ZA 1945, box 2, file 31; CJCNA, ZA 1948, box 1, file 3); *The Facts*, May 1949 (CJCNA, ZA 1949, box 3, file 26; NA, CJC Collection, MG28, vol. 13, V, 101, reel M-5461).
119 Troper and Weinfeld, *Old Wounds*, 51.
120 Rosenberg, *The Jewish Community in Canada*, vol. 2, 50–1.
121 Figler and Rome, *Hannaniah Meir Caiserman*, 254–5.

CHAPTER EIGHT

1 "Draft on Anti-Semitism in Canada," c. 1949 (CJCNA, ZA 1945, box 2, file 31; CJCNA, ZA 1948, box 1, file 3); *The Facts*, May 1949 (CJCNA, ZA 1949, box 3, file 26; NA, CJC Collection, MG 28, vol. 13, V, 101, reel M-5461).

Bibliography

PRIMARY SOURCES

Archival Sources

CANADIAN JEWISH CONGRESS NATIONAL ARCHIVES,
MONTREAL (CJCNA)
Central File Collection
Documentation Collection
Staff and Departmental Files

GLENBOW-ALBERTA INSTITUTE, CALGARY (GLENBOW)
Patrick Ashby Papers
John Blackmore Papers
Norman James Papers
Solon Low Papers
Abraham Isaac Shumiatcher Papers
Social Credit Board Papers

NATIONAL ARCHIVES OF CANADA, OTTAWA (NA)
Canadian Jewish Congress Collection
Canadian Jewish Congress Inter-Office Information Bulletins
   (National Library)
Jewish Historical Society of Western Canada Collection
Jewish Immigrant Aid Services Western Division Collection
Louis Rosenberg Papers

ONTARIO JEWISH ARCHIVES, TORONTO (OJA)
Joint Community Relations Committee Papers

PROVINCIAL ARCHIVES OF ALBERTA, EDMONTON (PAA)
William Aberhart Papers
Alberta Social Credit League Papers
Premiers Papers

PROVINCIAL ARCHIVES OF MANITOBA, WINNIPEG (PAM)
Abraham J. Arnold Collection
Canadian Jewish Congress Western Division Collection (Series II)
Jewish Historical Society of Western Canada Collection

Government Documents

ALBERTA
Alberta. *A Report on Alberta Elections, 1905–1982.* Edmonton: Office of the Chief Electoral Officer 1983.

CANADA
Canada. *Acts of the Parliament of the Dominion of Canada.* Ottawa: King's Printer 1936.
– *The Canada Year Book.* Ottawa: Dominion Bureau of Statistics, Department of Trade and Commerce 1936–50.
– *The Canadian Directory of Parliament, 1867–1967.* Ottawa: Public Archives of Canada 1968.
– Commons. *Debates.* Ottawa: King's Printer 1941–49.
– *Consolidated Regulations of Canada.* Vol. 4. Ottawa: Statute Revision Commission 1978.
– *Report of the Kellock-Taschereau Commission.* Ottawa: King's Printer 1946.
– *Revised Statutes of Canada, 1927.* Vol. 3. Ottawa: King's Printer 1927–28.

ONTARIO
Ontario. *Electoral History of Ontario.* Toronto: Office of the Chief Election Officer 1984.
– *Statutes of the Province of Ontario.* Toronto: King's Printer 1944.

QUÉBEC
Statistiques Électorales du Québec, 1867–1985. 2nd ed. Québec: Bibliothèque de l'Assemblée nationale 1986.

SASKATCHEWAN
Saskatchewan. *Provincial Elections in Saskatchewan, 1905–1986.* 3rd ed. Regina: Chief Electoral Office, Province of Saskatchewan 1987.

UNITED STATES
United States. Congress. House of Representatives. *Congressional Record,*
1931–32.

Newspapers and Periodicals

American Mercury
Calgary Albertan
Calgary Herald
Canadian Baptist
Canadian Jewish Chronicle
Canadian Jewish Weekly
Canadian Social Crediter
Canadian Tribune
Edmonton Bulletin
Edmonton Journal
Edmonton Ukrainian News
L'Evenement Journal
Financial Post
La Frontière
Globe and Mail
High River Times
Lethbridge Herald
Maclean's
Manitoba Commonwealth
Medicine Hat Daily News
Montreal Star
Montreal Gazette
Montreal Herald
Montreal Standard
New Voice
New York Post
Ottawa Journal
Peace River Record-Gazette
People's Weekly
Planning (P.E.P.)
Red Deer Advocate
Regina Leader-Post
Saskatoon Star-Phoenix
Saturday Night
Le Soleil
Time (Canada)
The Times (London)

Today
Today and Tomorrow
Toronto Daily Star
Vancouver News-Herald
Vers Demain
Victoria Daily Times
Western People
Western Producer
Wetaskiwin Times
Windsor Daily Star
Winnipeg Citizen
Winnipeg Free Press

SECONDARY SOURCES

Abella, Irving. *A Coat of Many Colours: Two Centuries of Jewish Life in Canada.* Toronto: Lester & Orpen Dennys 1990.

Abella, Irving, and Harold Troper. *None Is Too Many: Canada and the Jews of Europe, 1933–1948.* Toronto: Lester Publishing 1991.

Adams, Howard. *Prison of Grass: Canada from a Native Point of View.* Saskatoon: Fifth House Publishers 1989.

Anctil, Pierre. *Le Devoir, les Juifs et l'immigration: De Bourassa à Laurendeau.* Québec: Institut québécois de recherche sur la culture 1988.

Anctil, Pierre, and Gary Caldwell. *Juifs et réalités juives au Québec.* Québec: Institut québécois de recherche sur la culture 1984.

Anderson, Alan B., and James S. Frideres. *Ethnicity in Canada: Theoretical Perspectives.* Toronto: Butterworths 1981.

Anderson, Kay J. *Vancouver's Chinatown: Racial Discourse in Canada, 1875–1980.* Montreal and Kingston: McGill-Queen's University Press 1991.

Anderson, Owen. "The Alberta Social Credit Party: An Empirical Analysis of Membership, Characteristics, Participation and Opinion." PhD, University of Alberta 1972.

Arendt, Hanna. *The Origins of Totalitarianism.* New York: Harcourt, Brace 1941.

Argersinger, Peter H. *Populism and Politics: William Alfred Peffer and the People's Party.* Lexington: University Press of Kentucky 1974.

Avery, Donald. *Dangerous Foreigners: European Immigrant Workers and Labour Radicalism in Canada, 1896–1932.* Toronto: McClelland and Stewart 1979.

Barkun, Michael. *Religion and the Racist Right: The Origins of the Christian Identity Movement.* Chapel Hill: University of North Carolina Press 1994.

Barr, John. *The Dynasty: The Rise and Fall of Social Credit in Alberta.* Toronto: McClelland and Stewart 1974.

Barrett, Stanley R. *Is God a Racist? The Right Wing in Canada*. Toronto: University of Toronto Press 1987.

Baruch, Bernard M. *Baruch: My Own Story*. New York: Henry Holt 1957.

Behiels, Michael D. *Quebec and the Question of Immigration: From Ethnocentrism to Ethnic Pluralism, 1900–1985*. Ottawa: Canadian Historical Association 1991.

Belkin, Simon. *Through Narrow Gates: A Review of Jewish Immigration, Colonization and Immigrant Aid Work in Canada, 1840–1940*. Montreal: Canadian Jewish Congress and the Jewish Colonization Association 1966.

Bell, Daniel. *The Radical Right: The New American Right Expanded and Updated*. Garden City: Doubleday 1964.

Bell, Edward. "The Petite Bourgeoisie and Social Credit: A Reconsideration." *Canadian Journal of Sociology* 14, no. 1 (Winter 1989): 45–65.

– "Reply to Peter R. Sinclair." rejoinder to Peter R. Sinclair. *Canadian Journal of Sociology* 14, no. 3 (Summer 1989): 393–4.

– *Social Classes and Social Credit in Alberta*. Montreal and Kingston: McGill-Queen's University Press 1993.

Benedict, Ruth. *Race: Science and Politics*. New York: Viking Press 1970.

Bennett, David H. *Demagogues in the Depression: American Radicals and the Union Party, 1932–1936*. New Brunswick, NJ: Rutgers University Press 1969.

– *The Party of Fear: From Nativist Movements to the New Right in American History*. Chapel Hill: University of North Carolina Press 1988.

Ben-Sasson, H.H. *A History of the Jewish People*. Cambridge: Harvard University Press 1976.

Bercuson, David J. *Canada and the Birth of Israel: A Study in Canadian Foreign Policy*. Toronto: University of Toronto Press 1985.

Bercuson, David, and Douglas Wertheimer. *A Trust Betrayed: The Keegstra Affair*. Toronto: Doubleday Canada 1985.

Berger, Carl. *The Sense of Power: Studies in the Ideas of Canadian Imperialism, 1867–1914*. Toronto: University of Toronto Press 1970.

Berman, Hyman. "Political Antisemitism in Minnesota during the Great Depression." *Jewish Social Studies* 38 (1976): 247–64.

Betcherman, Lita-Rose. *The Swastika and the Maple Leaf: Fascist Movements in Canada in the Thirties*. Toronto: Fitzhenry & Whiteside 1975.

Betke, Carl Frederick. "The United Farmers of Alberta, 1921–1935: The Relationship between the Agricultural Organization and the Government of Alberta." MA, University of Alberta 1971.

Beveridge, Janet. *Beveridge and His Plan*. London: Hodder and Stoughton 1954.

Beveridge, Sir William. *Social Insurance and Allied Services*. New York: MacMillan 1942.

Bicha, Karel. *The American Farmer and the Canadian West, 1896–1914*. Lawrence, Kan.: Coronado Press 1972.

Blais, André. "Third Parties in Canadian Provincial Politics." *Canadian Journal of Political Science* 6, no. 3 (Sept. 1973): 422–38.

Bloom, Harold. *Deconstruction and Criticism*. New York: Continuum 1988.

Blum, John Morton. *From the Morgenthau Diaries: Years of War, 1941–1945*. Boston: Houghton Mifflin 1967.

– *Roosevelt and Morgenthau*. Boston: Houghton Mifflin 1970.

Bolaria, B. Singh, and Peter S. Li. *Racial Oppression in Canada*. 2nd ed. Toronto: Garamond Press 1988.

Bothwell, Robert, and J.L. Granatstein, eds. *The Gouzenko Transcripts*. Ottawa: Deneau Publishers 1982.

Bothwell, Robert, Ian Drummond, and John English. *Canada since 1945: Power, Politics, and Provincialism*. Toronto: University of Toronto Press 1989.

Boudreau, Joseph A. *Alberta, Aberhart and Social Credit*. Toronto: Holt, Rinehart and Winston 1975.

Brinkley, Alan. *Voices of Protest: Huey Long, Father Coughlin and the Great Depression*. New York: Alfred A. Knopf 1982.

Brown, Michael G. *Jew or Juif? Jews, French Canadians, and Anglo-Canadians, 1759–1914*. Philadelphia: Jewish Publication Society 1986.

Brym, Robert J., William Shaffir, and Morton Weinfeld, eds. *The Jews in Canada*. Toronto: Oxford University Press 1993.

Burnet, Jean. *Next-Year Country: A Study of Rural Organization in Alberta*. Toronto: University of Toronto Press 1951.

Burnet, Jean R., with Howard Palmer. *Coming Canadians: An Introduction to a History of Canada's Peoples*. Toronto: McClelland and Stewart 1989.

Burton, David H. *Cecil Spring Rice: A Diplomat's Life*. Toronto: Associated University Presses 1990.

Caldarola, Carlo., ed. *Society and Politics in Alberta: Research Papers*. Agincourt: Methuen Publications 1979.

Canadian Jewish Congress. *Pathways to the Present: Canadian Jewry and the Canadian Jewish Congress*. Toronto: Canadian Jewish Congress 1986.

– *Seventy Years of Canadian Jewish Life*. Montreal: Canadian Jewish Congress 1989.

Canadian Parliamentary Guide. Toronto: Info Globe 1936–95.

Canadian Who's Who. Toronto: Who's Who Canadian Publications 1936–75.

Carlsen, A.E. "The Evolution of Social Credit Economic Thought." *Queen's Quarterly* 70 (Autumn 1963): 374–85.

Cashman, Anthony W. *Ernest C. Manning: A Biographical Sketch*. Edmonton: Alberta Social Credit League 1958.

Caunt, James. *An Editor on Trial: Rex v. Caunt, Alleged Seditious Libel*. Morecambe and Heysham, England: Morecambe Press, c. 1947.

Chernow, Ron. *The Warburgs: The Twentieth-Century Odyssey of a Remarkable Jewish Family*. New York: Random House 1993.

Chiel, Arthur A. *The Jews of Manitoba: A Social History.* Toronto: University of Toronto Press 1964.

Chirol, Valentine. *Cecil Spring Rice In Memoriam.* London: John Murray 1919.

Chodos, Robert. *The CPR: A Century of Corporate Welfare.* Toronto: James Lewis & Samuel 1973.

Clark, S.D. "The Religious Sect in Canadian Politics." *American Journal of Sociology* 51, no. 3 (Nov. 1945): 207–16.

– *Church and Sect in Canada.* Toronto: University of Toronto Press 1948.

Clark, Samuel D., J. Paul Grayson, and Linda M. Grayson, eds. *Prophecy and Protest: Social Movements in Twentieth-Century Canada.* Toronto: Gage Educational Publishing 1975.

Clarke, Thurston. *By Blood and Fire: The Attack on the King David Hotel.* Toronto: Academic Press Canada 1981.

Cohen, Zvi. *Prominent Jews of Canada.* Toronto: Canadian Jewish Historical Publishing Company 1933.

Cohn, Norman. *Warrant for Genocide: The Myth of the Jewish World-Conspiracy and the Protocols of the Elders of Zion.* New York: Harper & Row 1967.

Coit, Margaret L. *Mr. Baruch.* Boston: Houghton Mifflin 1957.

Conway, J.F. "Populism in the United States, Russia, and Canada: Explaining the Roots of Canada's Third Parties." *Canadian Journal of Political Science* 11, no. 1 (Mar. 1978): 99–124.

Cook, Ramsay, ed. *Politics of Discontent.* Toronto: University of Toronto Press 1967.

Corti, Egon Caesar. *The Rise of the House of Rothschild.* London: Victor Gollancz 1928.

Coward, Harold, and Leslie Kawamura. *Religion and Ethnicity.* Waterloo: Wilfrid Laurier University Press 1978.

Darling, Howard. *The Politics of Freight Rates: The Railway Freight Rate Issue in Canada.* Toronto: McClelland and Stewart 1982.

Davies, Alan, ed. *Antisemitism in Canada: History and Interpretation.* Waterloo: Wilfrid Laurier University Press 1992.

Delisle, Esther. *The Traitor and the Jew: Anti-Semitism and Extremist Right-Wing Nationalism in Quebec from 1929 to 1939.* Montreal and Toronto: Robert Davies Publishing 1993.

Denny, Ludwell. *America Conquers Britain.* New York: Alfred A. Knopf 1930.

Dinnerstein, Leonard, ed. *Antisemitism in the United States.* Montreal: Holt, Rinehart and Winston 1971.

– *Uneasy at Home: Antisemitism and the American Jewish Experience.* New York: Columbia University Press 1987.

Directory of Members of Parliament and Federal Elections for the North-West Territories and Saskatchewan, 1887–1966. Regina and Saskatoon: Saskatchewan Archives Board 1967.

Dobbin, Murray. *Preston Manning and the Reform Party.* Toronto: James Lorimer 1991.

Douglas, C.H. *Economic Democracy.* London: C. Palmer 1920.

– *The Policy of a Philosophy.* London: K.R.P. Publications, c. 1937.

– *Social Credit.* London: Eyre & Spottiswoode 1937.

– *The Big Idea.* London: K.R.P. Publications, c. 1942.

– *The Land for the (Chosen) People Racket.* Liverpool: K.R.P. Publications, c. 1943.

– *Programme for the Third World War.* Liverpool: K.R.P. Publications, c. 1943.

– *The Brief for the Prosecution.* London: K.R.P. Publications 1946.

– *The Realistic Position of the Church of England.* Liverpool: K.R.P. Publications 1948.

Elazar, Daniel J., and Harold M. Waller. *Maintaining Consensus: The Canadian Jewish Polity in the Postwar World.* Lanham: Jerusalem Center for Public Affairs and University Press of America 1990.

Elliott, David R. "Antithetical Elements in William Aberhart's Theology and Political Ideology." *Canadian Historical Review* 59, no. 1 (1978): 38–58.

– "The Devil and William Aberhart: The Nature and Function of His Eschatology." *Studies in Religion* 9, no. 3 (Summer 1980): 325–37.

– "Anti-Semitism and the Social Credit Movement: The Intellectual Roots of the Keegstra Affair." *Canadian Ethnic Studies* 17, no. 1 (1985): 78–89.

– ed. *Aberhart: Outpourings and Replies.* Calgary: Alberta Records Publication Board, Historical Society of Alberta 1991.

Elliott, David R., and Iris Miller. *Bible Bill: A Biography of William Aberhart.* Edmonton: Reidmore Books 1987.

Elliott, Jean Leonard, and Augie Fleras. *Unequal Relations: An Introduction to Race and Ethnic Dynamics in Canada.* Scarborough: Prentice-Hall 1992.

Feingold, Henry L. "Finding a Conceptual Framework for the Study of American Antisemitism." *Jewish Social Studies* 47 (1985): 313–26.

Ferguson, Ted. *A White Man's Country: An Exercise in Canadian Prejudice.* Toronto: Doubleday Canada 1975.

Figler, Bernard. *Sam Jacobs: Member of Parliament.* Gardenvale, Que.: Harpell's Press 1970.

Figler, Bernard, and David Rome. *Hannaniah Meir Caiserman: A Biography.* Montreal: Northern Printing 1962.

Finkel, Alvin. "Social Credit and the Unemployed." *Alberta History* 31, no. 2 (Spring 1983): 24–32.

– "Populism and the Proletariat: Social Credit and the Alberta Working Class." *Studies in Political Economy* 13, no. 2 (Spring 1984): 109–35.

– "Alberta Social Credit Reappraised: The Radical Character of the Early Social Credit Movement." *Prairie Forum* 11, no. 1 (Spring 1986): 69–86.

– "Social Credit and the Cities." *Alberta History* 34, no. 3 (Summer 1986): 20–6.

- "The Cold War, Alberta Labour, and the Social Credit Regime." *Labour / Le Travail* 21 (Spring 1988): 123–52.
- *The Social Credit Phenomenon in Alberta*. Toronto: University of Toronto Press 1989.
- "Populism and Gender: The UFA and Social Credit Experiences." *Journal of Canadian Studies* 27, no. 4 (Winter 1992–93): 76–97.

Finlay, John L. *Social Credit: The English Origins*. Montreal and London: McGill-Queen's University Press 1972.

Flanagan, Thomas, and Martha Lee. "From Social Credit to Social Conservatism: The Evolution of an Ideology." *Prairie Forum* 16, no. 2 (Fall 1991): 205–23.

Flanagan, Thomas E. "Ethnic Voting in Alberta Provincial Elections, 1921–1971." *Canadian Ethnic Studies* 3, no. 2 (Dec. 1971): 139–64.

Flanagan, Tom. *Waiting for the Wave: The Reform Party and Preston Manning*. Toronto: Stoddart Publishing 1995.

Fleming, Donald, and Bernard Bailyn, eds. *Perspectives in American History*. Vol. 9. Cambridge: Charles Warren Center for Studies in American History, Harvard University 1975.

Ford, Henry. *The International Jew*. n.p.: n.p. 1920.

Foster, Franklin Lloyd. "The 1921 Alberta Provincial Election: A Consideration of Factors Involved with Particular Attention to Overtones of Millennialism within the U.F.A. and Other Reform Movements of the Period." MA, Queen's University 1977.

- "John Edward Brownlee: A Biography." PhD, Queen's University 1981.

Fowke, V.C. *The National Policy and the Wheat Economy*. Toronto: University of Toronto Press 1957.

Frager, Ruth A. *Sweatshop Strife: Class, Ethnicity, and Gender in the Jewish Labour Movement of Toronto, 1900–1939*. Toronto: University of Toronto Press 1992.

Francis, R. Douglas, and Herman Ganzevoort, eds. *The Dirty Thirties in Prairie Canada: Eleventh Western Canada Studies Conference*. Vancouver: Tantalus Research 1980.

Fredborg, Arvid. *Behind the Steel Wall: A Swedish Journalist in Berlin, 1941–43*. New York: Viking Press 1944.

Friesen, Gerald. *The Canadian Prairies: A History*. Toronto and London: University of Toronto Press 1984.

Glass, William R. "Fundamentalism's Prophetic Vision of the Jews: The 1930s." *Jewish Social Studies* 47, no. 1 (1985): 63–76.

Glock, Charles Y., and Rodney Stark. *Christian Beliefs and Anti-Semitism*. New York: Harper and Row 1966.

Godfrey, Sheldon J., and Judith C. Godfrey. *Search Out the Land: The Jews and the Growth of Equality in British Colonial America, 1740–1867*. Montreal and Kingston: McGill-Queen's University Press 1995.

Goodwyn, Lawrence. *The Populist Moment: A Short History of the Agrarian Revolt in America*. Toronto: Oxford University Press 1979.

Gottesman, Eli, ed. *Who's Who in Canadian Jewry*. Montreal: Jewish Institute of Higher Research, Central Rabbinical Seminary of Canada 1965.

Gouzenko, Igor. *This Was My Choice*. Toronto: J.M. Dent & Sons 1948.

Graeber, Isaacque, and Stewart Henderson Britt. *Jews in a Gentile World: The Problem of Anti-Semitism*. New York: MacMillan 1942.

Granatstein, J.L., and David Stafford. *Spy Wars: Espionage and Canada from Gouzenko to Glasnost*. Toronto: Key Porter Books 1990.

Grant, James. *Bernard M. Baruch: The Adventures of a Wall Street Legend*. New York: Simon and Schuster 1983.

Grayson, J. Paul, and L.M. Grayson. "The Social Base of Interwar Political Unrest in Urban Alberta." *Canadian Journal of Political Science* 7, no. 2 (June 1974): 289–313.

Groh, Dennis. "The Political Thought of Ernest Manning." MA, University of Calgary 1970.

Grossman, Vladimir, ed. *Canadian Jewish Year Book*. Vol. 1, *1939–1940*; vol. 2, *1940–41*; vol. 3, *1941–42*. Montreal: Canadian Jewish Year Book, 1939, 1940; Canadian Jewish Publication Society 1941.

Gutkin, Harry. *Journey into Our Heritage: The Story of the Jewish People in the Canadian West*. Toronto: Lester & Orpen Dennys 1980.

Halleday, Hugh. "Social Credit as a National Party in Canada." MA, Carleton University 1966.

Hallett, Mary. "The Social Credit Party and the New Democracy Movement, 1939–1940." *Canadian Historical Review* 47, no. 4 (Dec. 1966): 301–25.

Hannant, Larry. "The Calgary Working Class and the Social Credit Movement in Alberta, 1932–35." *Labour / Le Travail* 16 (Fall 1985): 97–116.

Harper, Donald Calvin. "Secularization and Religion in Alberta." MA, University of Alberta 1970.

Harris, José. *William Beveridge: A Biography*. Oxford: Oxford University Press 1977.

Harrison, Trevor. *Of Passionate Intensity: Right-Wing Populism and the Reform Party of Canada*. Toronto: University of Toronto Press 1995.

Hart, Arthur Daniel, ed. *The Jew in Canada: A Complete Record of Canadian Jewry from the Days of the French Regime to the Present Time*. Montreal: Jewish Publications 1926.

Harvey, Alan Burnside. *Tremeear's Annotated Criminal Code*. 5th ed. Calgary: Burroughs 1944.

Head, Wilson. *The Black Presence in the Canadian Mosaic: A Study of Perception and the Practice of Discrimination against Blacks in Metropolitan Toronto*. Toronto: Ontario Human Rights Commission 1975.

– *Adaption of Immigrants in Metro Toronto: Perceptions of Ethnic and Racial Discrimination*. Downsview: York University 1980.

Helling, Rudolf. *The Position of Negroes, Chinese and Italians in the Social Structure of Windsor, Ontario*. Windsor: n.p. 1965.

Henry, Frances. *The Caribbean Diaspora in Toronto: Learning To Live with Racism*. Toronto: University of Toronto Press 1994.

Henry, Franklin. *Perception of Discrimination among Negroes and Japanese-Canadians in Hamilton*. Hamilton: McMaster University 1965.

Hertzberg, Arthur. *The French Enlightenment and the Jews. The Origins of Modern Anti-Semitism*. New York: Shocken Books 1968.

Hesketh, Bob. "Major Douglas and Alberta Social Credit Ideology, 1932–1948." PhD, University of Alberta 1993.

– *Major Douglas and Alberta Social Credit*. Toronto: University of Toronto Press 1997.

Higham, John. *Strangers in the Land: Patterns of American Nativism, 1860–1925*. 2nd ed. New York: Atheneum 1981.

Hill, Daniel G. *Human Rights in Canada: A Focus on Racism*. Ottawa: Canadian Labour Congress 1977.

Hiller, Harry H. "A Critical Analysis of the Role of Religion in a Canadian Populist Movement: The Emergence and Dominance of the Social Credit Party in Alberta." PhD, McMaster University 1972.

Hillmer, Norman, Bohdan Kordan, and Lubomyr Luciuk, eds. *On Guard For Thee: War, Ethnicity, and the Canadian State, 1939–1945*. Ottawa: Canadian Committee for the History of the Second World War and Minister of Supply and Services Canada 1988.

History of the Federal Electoral Ridings, 1867–1980. 3 vols. Ottawa: Library of Parliament, Information and Reference Branch 1982.

Hitler, Adolf. *Mein Kampf*. Trans. Ralph Manheim. Boston: Houghton Mifflin 1943.

Hixson, William B. *Search for the American Right Wing: An Analysis of the Social Science Record, 1955–1987*. Princeton: Princeton University Press 1992.

Hlynka, Anthony. *Anthony Hlynka, Member of the Canadian House of Commons, 1940–1949*. Toronto: S. Hlynka 1982.

Hofstadter, Richard. *The Paranoid Style in American Politics, and Other Essays*. New York: Alfred A. Knopf 1966.

– *The Age of Reform: From Bryan to F.D.R.* New York: Alfred A. Knopf 1981.

Hooke, Alfred J. *30 + 5: I Know, I Was There*. Edmonton: Institute of Applied Art 1971.

Horowitz, Aron. *Striking Roots: Reflections on Five Decades of Jewish Life*. Oakville: Mosaic Press 1979.

Hughes, David R., and Evelyn Kallen. *The Anatomy of Racism: Canadian Dimensions*. Montreal: Harvest House 1976.

Huttenback, Robert. *Racism and Empire: White Settlers and Colored Immigrants in the British Self-Governing Colonies, 1830–1910*. Ithaca and London: Cornell University Press 1976.

Ionescu, Ghita, and Ernest Gellner, eds. *Populism: Its Meanings and National Characteristics*. London: Weidenfeld and Nicolson 1969.

Irving, John A. "Psychological Aspects of the Social Credit Movement in Alberta." *Canadian Journal of Psychology* 1 (1947): 17–27, 75–86, 127–40.

– "The Evolution of the Social Credit Movement." *Canadian Journal of Economics and Political Science* 14, no. 3 (Aug. 1948): 321–41.

– "The Appeal of Social Credit." *Queen's Quarterly* 60 (Summer 1953): 146–60.

– "Prairie Ideals and Realities: The Politics of Revolt." *Queen's Quarterly* 63 (Summer 1956): 188–200.

– *The Social Credit Movement in Alberta*. Toronto: University of Toronto Press 1959.

Israeli, Naheed. "Ethnic Minority Representation in the Political Party Structure of Alberta." MA, University of Calgary 1989.

Jaher, Frederic Cople. *A Scapegoat in the New Wilderness: The Origins and Rise of Anti-Semitism in America*. Cambridge: Harvard University Press 1994.

James, Norman B. *The Autobiography of a Nobody*. Toronto: J.M. Dent & Sons 1947.

Jeansonne, Glen. *Gerald L.K. Smith: Minister of Hate*. New Haven: Yale University Press 1988.

Jenkins, Philip. *Hoods and Shirts: The Extreme Right in Pennsylvania, 1925–1950*. Chapel Hill: University of North Carolina Press 1997.

Jensen, B. *The "Palestine" Plot*. Aberfeldy, Scotland: W.L. Richardson 1948.

Jews after the War: An Atlas. Montreal: Canadian Jewish Congress 1946.

Johnson, L.P.V., and Ola J. MacNutt. *Aberhart of Alberta*. Edmonton: Institute of Applied Art 1970.

Kage, Joseph. *With Faith and Thanksgiving: The Story of Two Hundred Years of Jewish Immigration and Immigrant Aid Effort in Canada, 1760–1960*. Montreal: Eagle Publishing 1962.

Kallen, Evelyn. *Spanning the Generations: A Study in Jewish Identity*. Don Mills: Longman Canada 1977.

– *Label Me Human: Minority Rights of Stigmatized Canadians*. Toronto: University of Toronto Press 1989.

Katz, Jacob. *From Prejudice to Destruction: Anti-Semitism, 1700–1933*. Cambridge: Harvard University Press 1980.

Kay, Zachariah. *Canada and Palestine: The Politics of Non-Commitment*. Jerusalem: Israel Universities Press 1978.

Kinsella, Warren. *Web of Hate: Inside Canada's Far Right Network*. Toronto: HarperCollins Publishers 1994.

Klassen, Henry C., ed. *The Canadian West: Social Change and Economic Development*. Calgary: University of Calgary 1977.

Kurelek, William, and Abraham J. Arnold. *Jewish Life in Canada*. Edmonton: Hurtig Publishers 1976.

Lappin, Ben W. *The Redeemed Children: The Story of the Rescue of War Orphans by the Jewish Community of Canada*. Toronto: University of Toronto Press 1963.

Larsson, Goran. *Fact or Fraud? The Protocols of the Elders of Zion*. Jerusalem and San Diego: AMI-Jerusalem Center for Biblical Studies and Research 1994.

Laycock, David. *Populism and Democratic Thought in the Canadian Prairies, 1910 to 1945*. Toronto: University of Toronto Press 1990.

League for Social Reconstruction. Research Committee. *Social Planning for Canada*. Toronto: Thomas Nelson & Sons 1935; Toronto and Buffalo: University of Toronto Press 1975.

- *Democracy Needs Socialism*. Toronto: Thomas Nelson & Sons 1938.

Leonoff, Cyril. *Pioneers, Pedlars and Prayer Shawls*. Victoria: Sono Nis Press 1978.

- *Pioneers, Ploughs and Prayers: The Jewish Farmers of Western Canada*. Vancouver: Jewish Historical Society of British Columbia and Jewish Western Bulletin 1982.

- *The Jewish Farmers of Western Canada*. Vancouver: Jewish Historical Society of British Columbia 1984.

Levine, Martin. "Compassion when Convenient: Canadian Attitudes towards Immigration in 1946 and 1947." MA, Carleton University 1975.

Levitt, Cyril H., and William Shaffir. *The Riot at Christie Pits*. Toronto: Lester & Orpen Dennys 1987.

Li, Peter S., ed. *Race and Ethnic Relations in Canada*. Toronto: Oxford University Press 1990.

Linder, Alice Dorothy. "Ethnic Strategies of Three Minority Groups in the City of Calgary." MA, University of Calgary 1976.

Lipset, Seymour Martin. *Agrarian Socialism: The Cooperative Commonwealth Federation in Saskatchewan*. Berkeley: University of California Press 1971.

McCollum, Watt Hugh. *Who Owns Canada*. Regina: Saskatchewan CCF Research Bureau 1935.

MacGregor, James G. *A History of Alberta*. Edmonton: Hurtig Publishers 1981.

McLaren, Angus. *Our Own Master Race: Eugenics in Canada, 1885–1945*. Toronto: McClelland and Stewart 1990.

McMann, Evelyn de R. *Canadian Who's Who Index, 1898–1984*. Toronto: University of Toronto Press 1986.

Macpherson, C.B. "The Political Theory of Social Credit." *Canadian Journal of Economics and Political Science* 14, no. 3 (Aug. 1949): 378–93.

- *Democracy in Alberta: Social Credit and the Party System*. 1953. 2nd ed. Toronto: University of Toronto Press 1962.

Malliah, H.L. "A Socio-Historical Study of the Legislators of Alberta, 1905–1967." PhD, University of Alberta 1970.

Mallory, J.R. *Social Credit and the Federal Power in Canada.* Toronto: University of Toronto Press 1954.

Mann, W.E. *Sect, Cult, and Church in Alberta.* Toronto: University of Toronto Press 1955.

Marcus, Sheldon. *Father Coughlin: The Tumultuous Life of the Priest of the Little Flower.* Boston: Little, Brown 1973.

Mardon, Ernest G., and Austin A. Mardon. *Alberta Mormon Politicians.* Edmonton: Fisher House Publishers 1992.

Marsh, Leonard. *Report on Social Security for Canada.* Ottawa: King's Printer 1943; Toronto and Buffalo: University of Toronto Press 1975.

Moore, Carl H. *The Federal Reserve System: A History of the First 75 Years.* Jefferson, NC: McFarland 1990.

Morgan, Sir Frederick. *Overture to Overlord.* London: Hodder & Stoughton 1950.

Morton, W.L. *The Progressive Party in Canada.* Toronto: University of Toronto Press 1950.

Neatby, H. Blair. *The Politics of Chaos: Canada in the Thirties.* Toronto: Macmillan of Canada 1972.

Newman, Peter C. *Renegade in Power: The Diefenbaker Years.* Toronto: McClelland and Stewart 1963.

Niranjana, Tejaswini. *Siting Translation: History, Post-Structuralism, and the Colonial Context.* Berkeley and Los Angeles: University of California Press 1992.

Owram, Doug. *Promise of Eden: The Canadian Expansionist Movement and the Idea of the West, 1856–1900.* Toronto: University of Toronto Press 1980.

Osborne, Stephen. *Social Credit for Beginners: An Armchair Guide.* Vancouver: Pulp Press 1986.

Palmer, Bruce. *Man Over Money: The Southern Populist Critique of American Capitalism.* Chapel Hill: University of North Carolina Press 1980.

Palmer, Howard. *Land of the Second Chance: A History of Ethnic Groups in Southern Alberta.* Lethbridge: Lethbridge Herald Press 1972.

– "Ethnic Relations in Wartime: Nationalism and European Minorities in Alberta during the Second World War." *Canadian Ethnic Studies* 14, no. 3 (1982): 1–23.

– *Patterns of Prejudice: A History of Nativism in Alberta.* Toronto: McClelland and Stewart 1982.

– "Ethnic Relations and the Paranoid Style: Nativism, Nationalism & Populism in Alberta, 1945–50." *Canadian Ethnic Studies* 23, no. 3 (1991): 7–31.

Palmer, Howard, and Tamara Palmer, eds. *Peoples of Alberta: Portraits of Cultural Diversity.* Saskatoon: Western Producer Prairie Books 1985.

Palmer, Howard, with Tamara Palmer. *Alberta: A New History*. Edmonton: Hurtig Publishers 1990.

Palmer, Howard, and Donald Smith, eds. *The New Provinces: Alberta and Saskatchewan, 1905–1980*. Vancouver: Tantalus Research 1980.

Parkes, James. *Anti-Semitism*. Chicago: Quadrangle 1963.

– *The Emergence of the Jewish Problem, 1879–1939*. Westport, Conn.: Greenwood Press Publishers 1970.

Paris, Erna. *Jews: An Account of Their Experience in Canada*. Toronto: Macmillan of Canada 1980.

Parsons, Stanley B. *The Populist Context: Rural Versus Urban Power on a Great Plains Frontier*. Westport, Conn.: Greenwood Press 1973.

Pashak, Leonard B. "The Populist Characteristics of the Early Social Credit Movement in Alberta." MA, University of Calgary 1971.

Pinard, Maurice. "One-Party Dominance and Third Parties." *Canadian Journal of Economics and Political Science* 33, no. 3 (Aug. 1967): 358–73.

– *The Rise of a Third Party: A Study in Crisis Politics*. Montreal and London: McGill-Queen's University Press 1975.

Pinder, John, ed. *Fifty Years of Political and Economic Planning: Looking Forward, 1931–1981*. London: Heinemann Educational Books 1981.

Pinson, Koppel, ed. *Essays on Antisemitism*. New York: Conference on Jewish Relations 1946.

Pollack, Irwin E. "Civil Rights and the Anglo-Jewish Press in Canada, 1930–1970." MA, Wilfrid Laurier University 1979.

Porter, John. *The Vertical Mosaic: An Analysis of Social Class and Power in Canada*. Toronto: University of Toronto Press 1965.

The Protocols and World Revolution, Including a Translation and Analysis of the "Protocols of the Meetings of the Zionist Men of Wisdom." Boston: Small, Maynard 1920.

Ramcharan, Subhas. *Racism: Nonwhites in Canada*. Toronto: Butterworths 1982.

Rasporich, Anthony W. *Western Canada: Past and Present*. Calgary: University of Calgary and McClelland and Stewart West 1975.

– ed. *The Making of the Modern West: Western Canada since 1945*. Calgary: University of Calgary Press 1984.

– "Early Twentieth-Century Jewish Farm Settlements in Saskatchewan: A Utopian Perspective." *Saskatchewan History* 42, no. 1 (Winter 1989): 28–40.

Reeves, John. *The Rothschilds: The Financial Rulers of Nations*. London: Sampson, Low, Marston, Searle and Rivingston 1887.

Rhinewine, Abraham. *Looking Back a Century: On the Centennial of Jewish Political Equality in Canada*. Toronto: Kraft Press 1932.

Ribuffo, Leo P. *The Old Christian Right: The Protestant Far Right from the Depression to the Cold War*. Philadelphia: Temple University Press 1983.

Richards, John, and Larry Pratt. *Prairie Capitalism: Power and Influence in the New West*. Toronto: McClelland and Stewart 1979.

Robin, Martin. *Shades of Right: Nativist and Fascist Politics in Canada, 1920–1940*. Toronto: University of Toronto Press 1992.

Robinson, Stanley. "A Logic of Conspiracy: The Apocalyptic Worldview of American Antisemitic Propagandists, 1917–1947." MA, Simon Fraser University 1989.

Rolph, W.K. *Henry Wise Wood of Alberta*. Toronto: University of Toronto Press 1950.

Rome, David. *The First Two Years*. Montreal: H.M. Caiserman 1942.

– *Canadian Jews in World War II*. 2 vols. Montreal: Canadian Jewish Congress 1947–48.

– *The Congress Archival Record of 1934*. Montreal: Canadian Jewish Congress 1976.

– *Jewish Archival Record of 1935*. Montreal: Canadian Jewish Congress 1976.

– *Our Archival Record of 1933, Hitler's Year*. Montreal: Canadian Jewish Congress 1976.

– *Clouds in the Thirties*. 13 vols. Montreal: Canadian Jewish Congress 1977–84.

– *The Jewish Congress Archival Record of 1936*. Montreal: Canadian Jewish Congress 1978.

– *Canadian Jewish Archives*. Vols. 15–25, 36–43. Montreal: Canadian Jewish Congress, 1980–82, 1986–88.

– *Samuel Becancour Hart and 1832*. Montreal: Canadian Jewish Congress 1982.

Rosenberg, Louis. *Canada's Jewish Community*. Montreal: Canadian Jewish Congress, n.d.

– *The Jewish Population of Canada*. Montreal: Canadian Jewish Congress 1947.

– *Jewish Communities in Canada*. Montreal: Canadian Jewish Congress 1957.

– *Chronology of Canadian Jewish History*. Montreal: Canadian Jewish Congress 1959.

– *Two Centuries of Jewish Life in Canada, 1760–1960*. Montreal: Canadian Jewish Congress 1961.

– *Canada's Jews: A Social and Economic Study of the Jews in Canada*. Ed. Morton Weinfeld. Montreal and Kingston: McGill-Queen's University Press 1993.

Rosenberg, Stuart E. *The Jewish Community in Canada*. 2 vols. Toronto: McClelland and Stewart 1970–71.

Roy, Patricia E. *A White Man's Province: British Columbia Politicians and Chinese and Japanese Immigrants, 1858–1914*. Vancouver: University of British Columbia Press 1989.

Roy, Ralph. *Apostles of Discord*. Boston: Beacon Press 1953.

Rycroft, Charles. *A Critical Dictionary of Psychoanalysis*. New York: Basic Books 1968.

Sachar, M., ed. *The Rise of Israel: A Documentary Record from the Nineteenth Century to 1948*. 39 vols. New York: Garland Series 1987.

Sack, B.G. *History of the Jews in Canada*. Montreal: Harvest House 1965.

– *Canadian Jews, Early in This Century*. Montreal: Canadian Jewish Congress 1975.

Sargent, Lyman Tower, ed. *Extremism in America*. New York: New York University Press 1995.

Sartre, Jean-Paul. *Anti-Semite and Jew*. Trans. George J. Becker. New York: Schocken Books 1948.

Sawatsky, John. *Gouzenko: The Untold Story*. Toronto: Macmillan of Canada 1984.

Schild, George. *Bretton Woods and Dumbarton Oaks: American Economic and Political Postwar Planning in the Summer of 1944*. New York: St. Martin's Press 1995.

Schneiderman, Harry, ed. *The American Jewish Year Book*. Vol. 36, 1934–35; vol. 40, 1938–1939. Philadelphia: Jewish Publication Society of America, 1935, 1939.

Schultz, H.J. "Portrait of a Premier: William Aberhart." *Canadian Historical Review* 45, no. 3 (Sept. 1964): 185–211.

Selick, Abel, ed. *History of B'nai B'rith in Eastern Canada*. Toronto: B'nai B'rith District Grand Lodge No. 22, 1964.

Serfaty, Meir. "Structure and Organization of Political Parties in Alberta, 1935–1971." PhD, Carleton University 1976.

Shakespeare, William. *The Merchant of Venice*. Ed. W.G. Clark. Oxford: Clarendon Press 1905.

Sharp, Paul. *The Agrarian Revolt in Western Canada: A Survey Showing American Parallels*. New York: Octagon Books 1971.

Sharpe, Sydney, and Don Braid. *Storming Babylon: Preston Manning and the Rise of the Reform Party*. Toronto: Key Porter Books 1992.

Shupe, Anson. *Wealth and Power in American Zion*. Queenston, Ont.: Edwin Mellen Press 1992.

Sinclair, Peter R. "Social Credit and Social Class: A Comment on 'The Petite Bourgeoisie and Social Credit: A Reconsideration.'" Reply to Edward Bell. *Canadian Journal of Sociology* 14, no. 3 (Summer 1989): 390–2.

Singerman, Robert. "The American Career of the *Protocols of the Elders of Zion*." *American Jewish History* 71, no. 1 (Sept. 1981): 48–78.

Smith, Denis. *Diplomacy of Fear: Canada and the Cold War, 1941–1948*. Toronto: University of Toronto Press 1988.

Spargo, John. *The Jew and American Ideals*. New York: Harper & Brothers 1921.

Speisman, Stephen A. *The Jews of Toronto: A History to 1937*. Toronto: McClelland and Stewart 1979.

Stein, Michael B. *The Dynamics of Right-Wing Protest: A Political Analysis of Social Credit in Quebec.* Toronto and Buffalo: University of Toronto Press 1973.

Stember, Charles Herbert, et al. *Jews in the Mind of America.* New York: Basic Books 1966.

Stingel, Janine. "In the Presence of Mine Enemies: Anti-Semitism in the Alberta Social Credit Party." MA, McGill University 1993.

– "Social Credit and the Jews: Anti-Semitism in the Alberta Social Credit Movement and the Response of the Canadian Jewish Congress, 1939–1949." PhD, McGill University 1997.

– "Beyond the Purge: Reviewing the Social Credit Movement's Legacy of Intolerance." Forthcoming in *Canadian Ethnic Studies.*

– "Revising the Historiography of the Social Credit Movement in Alberta: The Untold Story of Canadian Jewry." *Prairie Forum* 24, no. 1 (Spring 1999): 91–107.

Streit, Clarence K. *Union Now.* London: Jonathan Cape 1939.

– *Union Now With Britain.* New York: Harper & Brothers 1941.

Sunahara, Ann. *The Politics of Racism.* Toronto: Lorimer 1981.

Tarnopolsky, Walter. *Discrimination and the Law in Canada.* Toronto: R. De Boo 1982.

Thomas, L.G. *The Liberal Party in Alberta: A History of Politics in the Province of Alberta, 1905–1921.* Toronto: University of Toronto Press 1959.

Thomas, Lewis H., ed. *Essays on Western History.* Edmonton: University of Alberta Press 1976.

– *William Aberhart and Social Credit in Alberta.* Toronto: Copp Clark 1977.

Thompson, John Herd. *Ethnic Minorities during Two World Wars.* Ottawa: Canadian Historical Association 1991.

Thompson, John Herd, with Allen Seager. *Canada, 1922–1939: Decades of Discord.* Toronto: McClelland and Stewart 1988.

The Times (London). *The Truth About "The Protocols": A Literary Forgery.* London: Printing House Square 1921.

Topolski, Jerzy, ed. *Historiography between Modernism and Postmodernism: Contributions to the Methodology of the Historical Research.* Atlanta: Amsterdam 1994.

Trachtenberg, Joshua: *The Devil and the Jew: The Medieval Conception of the Jew and its Relation to Modern Anti-Semitism.* Cleveland and New York: Meridian Books and Jewish Publication Society of America 1963.

Troper, Harold. *Only Farmers Need Apply.* Toronto: Griffin House 1972.

Troper, Harold, and Morton Weinfeld. *Old Wounds: Jews, Ukrainians and the Hunt for Nazi War Criminals in Canada.* Chapel Hill and London: University of North Carolina Press 1989.

Tulchinsky, Gerald. "Recent Developments in Canadian Jewish Historiography." *Canadian Ethnic Studies* 14, no. 2 (1982): 114–25.

– *Taking Root: The Origins of the Canadian Jewish Community.* Toronto: Lester Publishing 1992.
– *Branching Out: The Transformation of the Canadian Jewish Community.* Toronto: General Publishing 1998.
Tzuk, Yogev. "A Jewish Communal Welfare Institution in a Changing Society, Montreal: 1920–1980." PhD, Concordia University 1981.
Ukrainian Pioneers Association. *The Ukrainian Pioneers in Alberta, Canada.* Edmonton: Ukrainian Pioneers Association in Edmonton 1970.
Valentin, Hugo. *Antisemitism Historically and Critically Examined.* Freeport: Books for Libraries Press 1936.
Vigod, Bernard L. *The Jews in Canada.* Ottawa: Canadian Historical Association 1984.
Walker, James W. St. G. *Racial Discrimination in Canada: The Black Experience.* Ottawa: Canadian Historical Association 1985.
Waller, Harold. *The Canadian Jewish Community: A National Perspective.* Philadelphia: Temple University and Centre for Jewish Community Studies 1977.
Warburg, James P. *Peace in Our Time?* New York: Harper & Brothers 1940.
Ward, Peter. *White Canada Forever: Popular Attitudes and Public Policy toward Orientals in British Columbia.* Montreal: McGill-Queen's University Press 1978.
Webster, Nesta H. *The French Revolution: A Study in Democracy.* 2nd ed. London: Constable and Company 1919.
– *The Chevalier de Boufflers: A Romance of the French Revolution.* London: John Murray 1920.
– *World Revolution: The Plot against Civilization.* Boston: Small, Maynard 1921.
– *The Socialist Network.* London: Boswell Printing & Publishing 1926.
– *The Surrender of an Empire.* London: Boswell Printing & Publishing 1931.
– *Secret Societies and Subversive Movements.* 5th ed. London: Boswell Publishing 1936.
Weinfeld, Morton, William Shaffir, and Irwin Cotler, eds. *The Canadian Jewish Mosaic.* Toronto: John Wiley & Sons 1981.
Weintraub, William. *City Unique: Montreal Days and Nights in the 1940s and '50s.* Toronto: McClelland and Stewart 1996.
Weisbord, Merrily. *The Strangest Dream: Canadian Communists, the Spy Trials, and the Cold War.* 1983. 2nd ed. Montreal: Véhicule Press 1994.
Weston, Warren. *Father of Lies.* London: M.C.P. Publication, c. 1938.
Who's Who in Canada. Toronto: International Press 1934–76.
Wistrich, Robert S. *Antisemitism: The Longest Hatred.* London: Methuen London 1991.
Wolff, Martin. *The Jews of Canada.* New York: American Jewish Committee 1926.

Woodbridge, George. *UNRRA: The History of the United Nations Relief and Rehabilitation Administration.* 3 vols. New York: Columbia University Press 1950.

Young, Walter D. *Democracy and Discontent: Progressivism, Socialism and Social Credit in the Canadian West.* Toronto: McGraw-Hill Ryerson 1969.

Zucchi, John E. *Italians in Toronto: Development of a National Identity, 1875–1935.* Montreal: McGill-Queen's University Press 1988.

Index

Abella, Irving, 184–5
Aberhart, William: career sketch,
193; conspiracy theories of, 19–
23, 46; as creator of Alberta
Social Credit, 13–14, 19–20;
death, 50, 165; on Great Depression, 9; on Holocaust, 21; on
Jewish refugees, 20; on Jews, 20–
1; meeting with Rabbi Frank,
45–6; and 1935 Alberta election,
3, 14–15; as premier, 15–16; on
Protocols, 20; religious beliefs of,
20–1; on Social Credit's anti-
Semitism, 4, 45–6
Alberta, province of, 3; economic
alienation of, 9–10, 14; economic culture of, 182–3, 189;
during Great Depression, 8–9,
14, 19; political alienation of, 9–
10, 14; political culture of, 3,
181–3
Alberta Social Credit Board: anti-
Semitism of, 48–9; creation, 47;
dissemination of anti-Semitic literature, 48–9; dissolution, 145–6;
mandate, 48; 1946 annual report
of, 128–30; *see also* Bourcier,
Byrne, *Calgary Albertan*, *Calgary Herald*, *Canadian Jewish
Weekly*, Douglas Social Credit
Council, *Edmonton Journal*,
Manning, Roper
Alberta Social Credit League, 39;
dissemination of anti-Semitic lit-
erature, 161; and Manning's
purge of anti-Semitism, 146–7;
1948 convention, 172–3
American Jewish Committee, 39,
93, 118–20
American Jewish Congress, 77,
117–20
Ansley, R.E.: career sketch, 193–4;
and Douglas Social Credit
Council, 157; firing of, 157; on
Jaques's death, 178–9
Anti-communism: *see* Jaques, Low,
Manning
Anti-Defamation League of B'nai
Brith, 117–20, 137, 168–9; as
"conspirator," 91, 132–3; on
Jaques and Smith, 141–2; on
Voice of the Electors, 168–9

Anti-Semitism:
– comments on Social Credit's: *see*
Aberhart, Bercuson, *Calgary
Albertan*, Canadian Jewish Congress, *Canadian Tribune*, Dower,
Green, Hayes, Joseph, Lieberman, MacPherson, *Montreal Star*,
Rosenberg, *Saskatoon Star-
Phoenix*, Social Credit support-
ers, *Today*
– examples within Social Credit:
see Alberta Social Credit Board,
Byrne, *Canadian Social Crediter*,
Caouette, Douglas Social Credit
Council, Gillese, Jaques, Low,
Today and Tomorrow, Union des
Electeurs, *Vers Demain*, *Voice of
the Electors*
– as philosophy of Social Credit, 3–
4, 8, 11, 180, 187, 189
– *see also* Canada, anti-Semitism
in, Conspiracy theory, Holocaust
denial, Nazism
Anti-Zionism: *see* Byrne, Canadian
Jewish Congress, Low, Manning,
Rosenberg
Arcand, Adrien, 26, 32, 33n5
Ashby, Patrick, 138; career sketch,
194; and Douglas Social Credit
Council, 157
Ashby, Roy, 138, 156; *see also*
Basic Book Club
Australian Social Crediter, 11, 91

Baker, Floyd, career sketch, 194
Bank of Canada, as "conspirator,"
4
Bank of England, 37; as "conspirator," 4, 18–19, 41
Baptist Church, on Social Credit
movement, 141
Barr, John, 14, 157
Baruch, Bernard, as "conspirator," 43–4, 49, 74, 87–8, 128–
30, 155
Basic Book Club: dissemination of
anti-Semitic literature, 138–40,

156n15; distribution of *Proto-
cols*, 139–40; and Douglas Social
Credit Council, 156
Bercuson, David, 96, 181
Bercuson, Leonard: on Congress's
public relations approach, 123–4;
on Manning's purge of anti-
Semitism, 149–50, 160–1; and
public relations approach of
Alberta branch, 126–8; on *Social
Crediter* (England), 166; on
Social Credit's anti-Semitism,
142; *see also* Canadian Jewish
Congress
Beveridge, William, as "conspirator," 41–2
Beveridge Report, as "conspirator," 48–9
Blackmore, John, 53; career sketch,
194–5; discussion with Moscov-
ich, 103; excommunication of,
141; meeting with Congress lead-
ers, 114–17; as Mormon, 116,
140–1
B'nai Brith, 29n90; as "conspira-
tor," 18, 99
Bourcier, A.V., 68, 155–6; career
sketch, 195; and Douglas Social
Credit Council, 173; on Jaques's
death, 178; and Social Credit
Board's 1946 annual report, 129–
30
Bretton Woods Conference, as
"conspirator," 62, 75
Bronfman, Samuel, 29; career
sketch, 203; on Low's anti-
Semitism, 107–8
Burnet, Jean, 9
Burton, Kenneth: and *Canadian
Social Crediter*, 156; and Douglas Social Credit Council, 173
Byrne, L.D.: as adviser to Social
Credit Board, 47–9; anti-Semitism
of, 48–9, 156; anti-Zionism of,
156–7; firing of, 156–7; promo-
tion of *Protocols*, 156; report to
Social Credit Board, 156–7, 176;

on Social Credit Board's 1946
annual report, 145

Caiserman, H.M.: on anti-Semitism
in Canada, 27, 64; on anti-
Semitism in Quebec, 27; on anti-
Semitism in *Today and Tomor-
row*, 57–8; career sketch, 204; on
Congress's public relations
approach, 34, 58–9, 62, 64, 72,
120–1, 185–6; on Jaques's anti-
Semitism, 51–2
Calgary Albertan: on Jaques and
Smith, 136–7; on Manning's
repudiation of anti-Semitism,
131–2; on Social Credit Board's
1946 annual report, 132; on
Social Credit's anti-Semitism,
131–2
Calgary Herald: on anti-Semitism in
Today and Tomorrow, 44; on
Manning's purge of anti-
Semitism, 146; on Social Credit
Board's 1946 annual report, 130
Canada: anti-Semitism in, 4–5, 7,
26–7, 30–1, 33–5, 86, 181, 186;
as tolerant nation, 86, 190
Canada, Bill of Rights (1960), 190
Canada, federal government: on
Jewish refugees, 4, 28–30, 54,
85, 186, 189
Canadian Broadcasting Corpora-
tion (CBC), 106–8; *see also*
Bronfman
Canadian Conference of Christians
and Jews, 30; as "conspirator,"
65; and Jaques, 65–7
Canadian Jewish Chronicle: on
Jaques's anti-Semitism, 176–7; on
Jaques's death, 176–7
Canadian Jewish Congress: on anti-
Semitism in Canada, 5–6n2, 29,
76–7, 184; as "conspirator,"
153–4; on Jaques's anti-Semitism,
38, 47; on Jaques's death, 176–7;
and Jewish refugees, 25, 27–9,
85; and letter to *Vancouver*

News-Herald, 162–3; on Low's
anti-Zionism, 174; mandate, 28–
30; on Manning's purge of anti-
Semitism, 151, 159, 161–2, 175–
6; and Montreal newspapers,
137–8; organization and reorganization of, 4, 6, 25–30; on
Protocols, 29; public relations
approach of, 5–6, 30, 32–6, 54,
64–5, 76–7, 86–7, 110–11, 120–
2, 161–3, 174–6, 183–91; on
public relations approach of
Alberta branch, 126–8; on Social
Credit's anti-Semitism, 4–5, 24,
30–1, 76; on Social Credit splinter groups, 159; on *Voice of the
Electors*, 168–9
– Alberta branch: on Congress's
public relations approach, 5–6,
124–5; on Low's anti-Zionism,
173–4; on Manning's purge of
anti-Semitism, 149–50; meeting
with Low, 56–7, 68–9; and
national headquarters, 36; public
relations approach of, 5–6, 47,
50–1, 56–7, 68, 103–4, 123–6,
151, 166, 173; on *Social Crediter*
(England), 166; on Social Credit's
anti-Semitism, 47, 50–1, 124–5
– *Bulletin*, 115–16
– Joint Public Relations Committee: anti-defamation work of,
33n5, 76; on anti-Semitism in
Canada, 159; on approaching
Social Credit leaders, 113–14;
creation, 29; on Jaques's anti-
Semitism, 67; on Low's anti-
Semitism, 106–7; mandate, 30;
on Ontario Social Credit League
convention, 171; public relations
approach of, 34, 58, 76, 102,
106–8, 113–14, 117, 140–2, 159,
184–5; on public relations
approach of Alberta branch,
127–8, 140; on Social Credit's
anti-Semitism, 72, 93–4, 159; on
Union des Electeurs, 159

– Western Division: on Congress's public relations approach, 35, 59; creation, 28n84; on Low's anti-Semitism, 71, 108–9; public relations approach of, 33–4, 39, 55, 71–2, 122–4, 127–8; public relations work of, 55; on Social Credit's anti-Semitism, 55, 122–3

Canadian Jewish Weekly: on anti-Semitism in *Vers Demain*, 99; on Jaques and Smith, 93; on Jaques's anti-Semitism, 176; on Jaques's death, 176; on Manning's purge of anti-Semitism, 150; on Social Credit Board's 1946 annual report, 130–1

Canadian Social Crediter, 11, 40, 154; anti-Semitism in, 68, 74, 87–91, 99–100, 104n69, 109, 132, 142–3, 146, 150, 159–60, 163, 189; on Gouzenko affair, 97–9; on Jaques and Smith, 92; on Jaques's death, 179–80; and Manning's purge of anti-Semitism, 145–6; and Mosley, 100; and *Protocols*, 68, 99–100, 150; and Social Credit supporters, 67; *see also* Burton, Gillese, Manning, Rosenberg

Canadian Tribune, on Social Credit's anti-Semitism, 49–50, 68

Caouette, Réal: anti-Semitism of, 153; career sketch, 195–6; meeting with Congress leaders, 114–17; and Union des Electeurs, 167–8

Carr, Sam, 96, 98

Cassel, Ernest, as "conspirator," 41, 74, 128–9

Christian Nationalist Crusade (United States): *see* Smith

Cohen, Meyer, as "conspirator," 89

Cohn, Norman, 17

Coldwell, M.J., 52; on Jaques's death, 177

Conspiracy theory, those accused: *see* Anti-Defamation League,

Bank of Canada, Bank of England, Baruch, Beveridge, Beveridge Report, B'nai Brith, Bretton Woods Conference, Canadian Conference of Christians and Jews, Canadian Jewish Congress, Cassel, Cohen, Depression, Dumbarton Oaks Conference, Federal Reserve Board, First World War, Freemasonry, Gold standard, Hitler, Holocaust, Israel, James, Laski, Lehman, London School of Economics, Marsh, Marsh Report, Meyer, Morgenthau Plan, Norman, Political and Economic Planning, Rothschilds, Rowell-Sirois Commission, Second World War, Sieff, Streit, Union Now Movement, United Nations Organization, United Nations Relief and Rehabilitation Administration, Warburgs

Co-operative Commonwealth Federation (CCF), 182; and anti–Social Credit campaign, 123–6; on Manning's repudiation of anti-Semitism, 132; *see also* Roper

Depression, Great, 8–9; as "conspirator," 40–1, 43, 48–9, 105

Douglas, C.H.: and A + B theorem, 12; anti-Semitic writings of, 17–19, 35, 48, 100; career sketch, 196; conspiracy theories of, 12–13, 16, 21, 24, 130; as creator of Social Credit, 11–13; on Manning, 158; paranoia of, 16; promotion of *Protocols*, 18; on Union of Electors concept, 12–13

Douglas Social Credit Council (Alberta): anti-Semitism of, 156–9; creation, 152, 155; on Manning, 164; publication of Byrne's report to Social Credit Board, 176; and *Social Crediter* (England), 158

Dower, John, 59; career sketch, 204; meeting with Low, 68–9; on Social Credit's anti-Semitism, 102

Dumbarton Oaks Conference, as "conspirator," 62, 75

Edmonton Bulletin, on *Social Crediter* (England), 166

Edmonton Journal: on Social Credit Board's dissolution, 145; on Social Credit Board's 1946 annual report, 129–30

Eisendrath, Rabbi Maurice, 33

Elections: Alberta (1935), 14–15; (1940), 15–16; (1944), 22; (1948), 126–7, 157; federal (1945), 94–5; Quebec (1948), 167–8

Elliott, David, 20–1

Even, Louis: career sketch, 196–7; and Union des Electeurs, 99, 152–3; and Union of Electors, 155; *see also* Union des Electeurs

Federal Reserve Board (United States), as "conspirator," 4, 18–19, 42, 61

Feinberg, Rabbi Abraham: address at Holy Blossom Temple, 65–6; career sketch, 204–5; on Congress's public relations approach, 86, 111; meeting with American Jewish organizations, 117–20

Fine, Joseph: career sketch, 205; meeting with American Jewish organizations, 117–20; meeting with Social Credit leaders, 114–17

Finkel, Alvin, 183

First World War, as "conspirator," 61, 105

Fitzgerald, John J.: on Gostick, 155; and Ontario Social Credit League, 154; repudiation of anti-Semitism, 171; *see also* Ontario Social Credit League

Ford, Henry, 17, 92, 99, 140

Fradkin, L.M.: on anti-Semitism in *Today and Tomorrow*, 44–5; career sketch, 205; and proposed meeting with Manning, 50; on Western Division's public relations approach, 71

Frank, Rabbi Solomon, 112; career sketch, 205–6; meeting with Aberhart, 45–6; meeting with Low, 108–9

Freemasonry, as "conspirator," 18, 48n68, 99, 139, 153, 167–8

Friedman, H.A.: on anti-Semitism in *Today and Tomorrow*, 44–5; career sketch, 206; meeting with Low, 68–9

Gallup Polls (1946, 1948), 181–2

Gillese, John Patrick: anti-Semitism of, 142, 144; career sketch, 197; and Douglas Social Credit Council, 155–6, 173; as editor of *Canadian Social Crediter*, 144; firing of, 143; *see also* Douglas Social Credit Council

Godfrey, Sam, 102

Gold standard, as "conspirator," 44, 74

Gordon, R.S., on Low's anti-Semitism, 75; *see also Today*

Gostick, Ronald, 154–5; career sketch, 197–8; *see also* Union of Electors

Gouzenko affair, 95–9, 104–5

Green, S. Hart: career sketch, 206; on Low's anti-Semitism, 71; on Social Credit's anti-Semitism, 122–3

Gregoire, J. Ernest: career sketch, 198; and Union des Electeurs, 153, 167–8

Haldeman, J.N.: career sketch, 198–9; conspiracy theories of, 101; promotion of *Protocols*, 101; repudiation of anti-Semitism, 101; on Social Credit splinter groups, 170

Hayes, Saul: career sketch, 207; as Congress officer, 29; on Congress's public relations approach, 102–3, 114, 141; on Jaques's anti-Semitism, 46–7, 137–8; on Low's anti-Semitism, 105–6; meeting with American Jewish organizations, 117–20; meeting with Low, 111–13; meeting with Social Credit leaders, 114–17; on Protocols, 102–3; on Social Credit's anti-Semitism, 62, 116–17

Hesketh, Bob, 16, 23–4

Hitler, Adolf, 26–7; as "conspirator," 18–19, 42, 54, 68, 75, 105

Hlynka, Anthony, career sketch, 199

Hofstadter, Richard, 11

Holocaust, 5, 85–7, 89–90, 114, 181–3, 189–91; as "conspirator," 4, 18–19, 63–4, 66, 89–90, 169

Holocaust denial, 54, 63–4, 89–90, 169, 190

Hooke, Alf, career sketch, 199

Irving, John, 12

Israel, state of: as "conspirator," 4, 91, 138–9, 163; creation, 165, 190

Jacobs, Samuel, 28; career sketch, 207

James, Cyril, as "conspirator," 41–2

James, Norman B.: career sketch, 199–200; conspiracy theories of, 63, 75, 88; and Douglas Social Credit Council, 157

Jaques, Norman: anti-communism of, 54, 64, 66–7, 75; on Anti-Defamation League, 133; anti-Semitism of, 36–7, 46–7, 51–2, 54, 65–6, 113, 162; career sketch, 200; conspiracy theories of, 54, 66, 91–2, 133, 135–6; daughter of, 180n97; death, 176–80; and Douglas Social Credit Council, 157; on Jewish refugees, 54, 64; paranoia of, 135–6; promotion of Protocols, 36–7, 51–2, 74–5, 135; and Rabbi Feinberg, 65–7; and Silcox, 65–7; and Smith, 92–3, 113, 133–5, 141–2; see also Caiserman, Canadian Jewish Chronicle, Canadian Jewish Congress, Canadian Jewish Weekly, Hayes, Lethbridge Herald, Livinson, Low, Reidell, Rosenberg, Steiner, Vancouver News-Herald, Wetaskiwin Times

Jewry: Alberta, 20, 24–5, 35, 123; Canadian, 4, 6–7, 24–7, 35, 188–9; and Gouzenko affair, 97–8

Joint Public Relations Committee: see Canadian Jewish Congress

Joseph, Edward, on Social Credit's anti-Semitism, 74–5

Kayfetz, Ben, 154; career sketch, 208

Keegstra, James, 180n98

Kellock-Taschereau Commission, 95–8; see also Gouzenko affair

Keynes, John Maynard, 12

King, William Lyon Mackenzie, 95, 190

Kirshenblatt, David: career sketch, 208; on Jaques's death, 176; on Manning's purge of anti-Semitism, 169; on Union des Electeurs, 167–8

La Frontière: see Morissette, Julien

Laski, Harold, as "conspirator," 129

Leduc, 1947 oil strike, 182–3, 189

Lehman, Herbert, as "conspirator," 87–8, 128

Lethbridge Herald: on Jaques's anti-Semitism, 132; on Manning's repudiation of anti-Semitism, 132

Lieberman, Moe: career sketch, 208; on Low's anti-Semitism, 71; on Social Credit's anti-Semitism, 50

Livinson, A. Jacob, on Jaques's anti-Semitism, 162–3

London School of Economics, as "conspirator," 18–19, 41–2, 46, 63, 129

Low, Solon, 51, 56; anti-communism of, 75, 104–5, 108, 112; anti-Semitism of, 56–7, 69–70, 75–6, 142; anti-Zionism of, 104–6, 108, 111–12, 169–70, 172–5; career sketch, 200–1; denial of anti-Semitism, 75, 103, 175; discussion with Moscovich, 103; on Gouzenko affair, 104; on Jaques and Smith, 135; on Jaques's anti-Semitism, 56–7, 103, 113; on Jaques's death, 179; on Jews, 71; manifesto for Social Credit movement, 172–5; on Manning, 169–70; meeting with Congress leaders, 68–9, 114–17; meeting with Hayes, 111–13; meeting with Rabbi Frank, 108; as Mormon, 71, 112, 116, 140–1; on *Protocols*, 75, 112–13, 115; on *Today*, 75; *see also* Bronfman, Canadian Jewish Congress, Gordon, Green, Hayes, Lieberman, Manning, Rosenberg

Macpherson, C.B., 48, 182–3

MacPherson, James, on Social Credit's anti-Semitism, 49–50

Major, Edmond, 168; *see also* Union des Electeurs

Manning, Ernest: anti-communism of, 182, 189; on anti-Semitism in *Canadian Social Crediter*, 144–5; career sketch, 201; conspiracy theories of, 22–4, 42–3, 59–60, 63, 131, 146, 164–5, 182, 189; on Douglas Social Credit Council, 164; firing of Ansley and

Byrne, 157; on Jews, 22; on Low's anti-Zionism, 172; as premier, 3, 23–4; purge of anti-Semitism, 4–5, 24, 143, 145–6, 156–60, 165, 171, 173, 175, 180–3, 189; religious beliefs of, 22–3, 63, 181–3; repudiations of anti-Semitism, 59–60, 131, 146, 164, 167; on Social Credit Board, 130, 145; *see also* Alberta Social Credit League, Bercuson, *Calgary Albertan*, *Calgary Herald*, Canadian Jewish Congress, *Canadian Jewish Weekly*, *Canadian Social Crediter*, Co-operative Commonwealth Federation, Douglas, Douglas Social Credit Council, Fradkin, Kirshenblatt, *Lethbridge Herald*, Low, Roper, Rosenberg, Social Credit Association of Canada, *Social Crediter*, Social Credit Secretariat, Social Credit supporters, *Today*, Union des Electeurs, Union of Electors, *Vers Demain*

Margolus, Wolfe: career sketch, 209; and public relations approach of Western Division, 123–4

Marsh, Leonard, as "conspirator," 41–2

Marsh Report, as "conspirator," 49

Maynard, Lucien, 39; career sketch, 201

Medicine Hat Daily News, on Low, 173–4

Meyer, Eugene, as "conspirator," 128–9

Montreal Gazette: on Jaques and Smith, 133–5; on Jaques's paranoia, 136; on Ontario Social Credit League, 171

Montreal Herald: on Jaques and Smith, 134

Montreal Star: on Jaques and Smith, 134; on Jaques's paranoia, 136; on Social Credit's anti-Semitism, 134

Morgan, Frederick, 89–90
Morgenthau Plan, as "conspirator," 90
Morissette, Julien, on Union des Electeurs, 167–8
Mormon Church, 140; and excommunication of Blackmore, 141
Morosnick, L.D.: on anti-Semitism in *Today and Tomorrow*, 57–9; on Congress's public relations approach, 58–9
Moscovich, Max: career sketch, 209; discussion with Social Credit leaders, 103–6
Mosley, Oswald, 100, 109, 178

National Joint Public Relations Committee: *see* Canadian Jewish Congress
Nazism, compared with Social Credit, 37–8, 44, 52, 59, 72–3, 93, 100, 102, 105–8n80, 115, 126, 134, 140, 174
Norman, Montagu, as "conspirator," 41

Olyan, Harry: career sketch, 209; meeting with Low, 56–7
Ontario Social Credit League: convention, 171; and Union of Electors, 153–5
Ottawa Journal, on Jaques's paranoia, 136
Ovens, William, 154; *see also* Ontario Social Credit League

Palestine crisis, 85, 91–2
Palmer, Howard, 21, 180–1
Paris, Erna, 98
Pinard, Maurice, 12
Political and Economic Planning (Britain), as "conspirator," 19, 43, 61
Populism, American, 10–11
Powell, G.F., 47
Protocols of the Learned Elders of Zion, description of, 16–17; *see*

also Aberhart, Basic Book Club, Byrne, Canadian Jewish Congress, *Canadian Social Crediter*, Douglas, Haldeman, Hayes, Jaques, Low, *Saskatoon Star-Phoenix*, *Vers Demain*, *Voice of the Electors*

Quebec, anti-Semitism in, 26–7, 100

Reidell, O., on Jaques's anti-Semitism, 51–2
Rome, David: career sketch, 209–10; and Congress's public relations approach, 162–3
Roper, Elmer, 59; and anti–Social Credit campaign, 123, 126; on Manning's repudiation of anti-Semitism, 132; on Social Credit Board's 1946 annual report, 130; *see also* Co-operative Commonwealth Federation
Rose, Fred, 95–6, 98, 178
Rosenberg, Louis: on Aberhart, 38–9, 46–7, 51, 53; on Alberta Social Credit League, 147; on anti-Semitism in Canada, 33–4; on anti-Semitism in *Canadian Social Crediter*, 104, 109–10, 133, 140, 148, 163–4; on anti-Semitism in *Today and Tomorrow*, 61–2; as author of *Canada's Jews*, 34; on Basic Book Club's anti-Semitism, 138–40; career sketch, 210; as Congress officer, 7, 33, 35, 55, 133; on Congress's public relations approach, 34, 38–9, 53, 109–11; on Douglas's anti-Semitism, 35–6; on Gouzenko affair, 98–9; on Jaques's anti-Semitism, 36–9, 46–7, 52–3; on Jaques's death, 177–9; on Joint Public Relations Committee, 51, 53; on Low's anti-Semitism and anti-Zionism, 72, 173, 175; on Manning's

purge of anti-Semitism, 146–9, 160–1, 163–5, 170–1, 173; on Manning's repudiations of anti-Semitism, 60–1, 133, 164–5; on 1945 federal election, 94–5; on Shnitka, 162; on Social Credit Association of Canada, 147; on Social Credit's anti-Semitism, 36, 47, 53, 57, 60–1, 72, 148–9; on Webster's anti-Semitic writings, 48

Rosenzweig, E.M., 184

Rothschilds, as "conspirators," 18, 41, 68, 74, 88, 128–9, 142, 155

Rowell-Sirois Commission, as "conspirator," 43–4

St Laurent, Louis, on Jaques's death, 177

Saskatoon Star-Phoenix, on Social Credit's anti-Semitism, 100–1

Second World War, as "conspirator," 18, 40, 105

Shnitka, Abe, 162n35

Sieff, Israel, as "conspirator," 43, 61

Silcox, Rev. C.E., and Jaques, 65–7; *see also* Canadian Conference of Christians and Jews

Six-Day War (1967), 190

Smith, Gerald L.K., 17, 92–3, 109, 113; and Jaques, 133–5, 141–2

Social Credit Association of Canada, 23–4, 147; and Manning's purge of anti-Semitism, 145–6; 1948 convention, 174–5; on Union des Electeurs, 153

Social Credit Board: *see* Alberta Social Credit Board

Social Crediter (England), 11; on Alberta Social Credit, 165–6; on Manning, 158; as publisher of Douglas's anti-Semitic writings, 18–19

Social Credit League: *see* Alberta Social Credit League, Ontario Social Credit League

Social Credit party, national, organization of, 23–4

Social Credit Secretariat (England), 11, 147, 156; on Manning, 165

Social Credit supporters: on Manning's purge of anti-Semitism, 166–7; in 1945 federal election, 94–5; on Social Credit's anti-Semitism, 4, 67, 143

Steiner, William, on Jaques's anti-Semitism, 54

Stern, Rabbi Harry, 33

Streit, Clarence, 36; as "conspirator," 37, 42–3; *see also* Union Now Movement

Strong, Anna Louise, 64

Taylor, Gordon: anti-Semitism of, 150; career sketch, 201–2; as editor of *Canadian Social Crediter*, 145, 150, 163–4

Today: on Manning's repudiation of anti-Semitism, 73; on Social Credit's anti-Semitism, 73–5, 116

Today and Tomorrow: advertisement of anti-Semitic literature, 48; anti-Semitism in, 23, 40–4, 49–50, 61–4; creation, 39–40; on Jewish refugees, 63–4; *see also* Caiserman, *Calgary Herald*, Fradkin, Friedman, Morosnick, Rosenberg

Tomyn, William, career sketch, 202

Troper, Harold, 185

Union des Electeurs (Quebec): and Alberta Social Credit League, 147; anti-Semitism of, 153–4, 167–8; creation, 152; on Manning's purge of anti-Semitism, 153–4, 158–9; and 1948 Quebec election, 167–8; and Union of Electors, 153–5; *see also* Even

Union Now Movement (United States): as "conspirator," 36–7, 39, 42–4, 46, 48, 55, 61; description, 36; on Streit, 39; *see also* Streit

Union of Electors (Ontario): and
  Manning's purge of anti-Semitism,
  152, 158–9; and Ontario Social
  Credit League, 153–5, 168; and
  Union des Electeurs, 153–5; see
  also Gostick, Voice of the Electors
United Farmers of Alberta, 10–11,
  13–14
United Nations Organization, 28;
  as "conspirator," 19, 49, 63, 87–
  8, 99, 104, 128, 155
United Nations Relief and Rehabilitation Administration, 28; as
  "conspirator," 75, 87, 89–90, 99,
  128, 138; and Morgan, 89

Vancouver News-Herald, on
  Jaques's anti-Semitism, 162–3
Vers Demain: anti-Semitism in, 99–
  100, 153–4; on Canadian Jewish

Congress, 153–4; description, 99;
  and Manning's purge of anti-
  Semitism, 152–3; publication of
  Protocols, 99–101, 112, 115–16;
  see also Canadian Jewish Weekly,
  Union des Electeurs
Voice of the Electors: creation, 154;
  anti-Semitism in, 155, 168–9;
  promotion of Protocols, 155

Warburgs, as "conspirators," 42–3,
  61, 74
Webster, Nesta, 48n68
Weinfeld, Morton, 185
Western Producer, as publisher of
  Jaques's anti-Semitism, 37–9
Wetaskiwin Times, on Jaques's anti-
  Semitism, 137

Young, Walter, 183